space

Best wishes
Cheryl Karsten

A Guide to Real Estate Development for Artists

Creating space

CHERYL KARTES

This publication is a collaborative project of
Artspace Projects, Inc., The Bay Area Partnership
and the American Council for the Arts

aca BOOKS

AMERICAN COUNCIL FOR THE ARTS

New York, New York
Copublished with Allworth Press

**CREATING SPACE: A GUIDE TO
REAL ESTATE DEVELOPMENT FOR ARTISTS**
By Cheryl Kartes

This publication is a collaborative project of
Artspace Projects, Inc., The Bay Area Partnership
and the American Council for the Arts.

Director of Publishing: Robert Porter.
Assistant Director of Publishing: Jill MacKenzie.
Cover and Interior Design by Celine A. Brandes, Photo Plus Art
Typesetting by The Desktop Shop.
Printed by Capital City Press.

Library of Congress Cataloging-in-Publication data

Kartes, Cheryl.
Creating space : a real estate development guide for artists / by Cheryl Kartes.
p. cm.
ISBN 0-915400-92-8 1.
1. Artists' studios—United States. 2. Artists—Housing—United States.
3. Real property—United States. 4. Space (Architecture)—United States.
5. Zoning—United States. I. Title.
N8520.K37 1993   93-20129
700'.68'2—dc20   CIP

Credits

The publication of **Creating Space** was made possible through a grant from the National Endowment for the Arts Visual Arts Program.

Funding for the writing of this book was made possible through Artspace Projects, Inc., from grants made by the Bush Foundation, Dayton's and Target Stores, the General Mills Foundation, the Metropolitan Council-Regional Arts Council with funds appropriated by the Minnesota Legislature, the National Endowment for the Arts, George and Francis Reid, the Standard Products Foundation, and through the Bay Area Partnership with funds from Citicorp.

Photo Credits:
Page 3, 7, 13, 20, 23, 25, 30, 39, 46, 48, 50, 52, 70, 73, 105, 108, 125, 126, 133, 157, 160, 170, 171, 195, 201, 224, 228: Cheryl Kartes.
Pages 5, 15, 143: Kim Harrington.
Pages 8, 10, 30, 59, 74, 78, 114, 124: Carmi Bee.
Pages 9, 21, 27, 65, 172, 196, 205, 208, 209, 216: Jim Crnkovich.
Page 12: Karla Faith Ness.
Page 17: Melissa Martina.
Pages 24, 147: Project Artaud, San Francisco.
Page 31: The Institute for Contemporary Art.
Page 31: Martin Cox.
Page 51, 200: Judy Ollausen.
Pages 94, 95: Dick Huss.
Pages 100, 101: Brickbottom Condominium Trust.
Pages 104, 176, 177: Gerald Gustavson.
Page 13: Ann Marsden.
Pages 111, 112: Artspace, Kansas City, MO.
Page 113: Artspace Projects, Inc., Minneapolis, MN.
Pages 134, 135: Artspace, Salt Lake City, UT.
Pages 58, 145, 153, 198, 212: Simo Neri.
Pages 152, 222: M. O'Driscoll.
Pages 153, 161, 163, 302: Thomas Dolan.
Page 156: Roy Shigley.
Page 163: Laurence Harrel.
Pages 164, 165, 166, 167: *Minneapolis Warehouse Project: Living/Working Space,* © 1979 by the Minneapolis Arts Commission.
Drawings by Richard Morrill. Reprinted by permission.
Page 187: Santa Fe Art Colony, Los Angeles, CA.

Contents

1 Personal Values: A Driving Force for Space 1

2 The Artist Project Team 14

3 Building Location and Assessments 26

4 Zoning and Building Codes 38

5 The City as a Resource and a Partner 63

6 Financing 84

8 Long-Term Control: Ownership 136

9   Design Needs 154

10 Planning and Implementation 185

11 Operations: A Self-Managed Community 206

Appendices

List of Boxes

List of Figures

Acknowledgments

Numerous individuals gave generously of their time to assist with this publication. Mention must go first to the artists who pioneered the redevelopment of historic buildings and the revitalization of commercial neighborhoods, spurring others on to renewed creativity.

Acknowledgment goes to Melisande Charles, Kris Nelson and the members of the Minneapolis Arts Commission, who early on sought a better way to secure artists' live/work spaces. The commission later founded Artspace Projects, Inc. as the first nonprofit organization in the country dedicated to developing live/work space for low- and moderate-income artists. All past and current Artspace board members are to be thanked for their vision, commitment and contributions to identifying solutions for the live/work space issues that formerly had no "answers." David Grant, Don Knutson, Gwen Lerner, Steve Thompson, Steven Schummeister, Chuck Riesenberg, Cherie Doyle, Mary Abbe Hintz, Stuart Neilsen, Patricia Fuller, David Welle, Ron Adalbert, Warren Hanson, Tom Hodne, Winston Close, John Maliga, Mary Walker and Garth Rockcastle all made significant contributions. Heartfelt thanks also to the many staff members of Artspace, who worked and continue to work with dedication and unflagging energy.

The National Artspace Development Network, founded by Artspace Projects, Inc., Bay Area Partnership, Foundation for Community of Artists, Innovative Housing, and National Artist Equity provided a base for the collaboration among organizations supporting publication of this work. Special thanks for visionary leadership and support go to Joshua Simon, Steve Costa and Robin Orden. I am especially grateful to Bob Porter of the American Council for the Arts, for his guidance and commitment to the publication of this book.

Many artists at the Lowertown Lofts and Studios at 700 are to be thanked for their insights. Special thanks go to Marla Gamble, Eric Oie, Judith Morem, TaCoumba Aiken, Seitu Jones, David Evans, Laura Stone, Mary Walker and Jill Waterhouse. Members of National Artists Equity also shared their insights; appreciation goes to Olive Mosier, Richard Mayer, Jim Minden and George Koch.

The generous efforts of editor Barbara Ryan, contributing writer Shannon King and editor Cathi McCann Murphy were essential to the birth of this publication. Thanks also to Laura Weber, Shannon King, Tom Dolan, Margie O'Driscoll, Jero Nesson, Lynn Wadsworth and Sara Trapnell for their assistance in the preparation of case studies. Additional thanks for the review of chapters goes especially to Joshua Simon and Charlie Wilson, along with Steve Costa, Rhonda Lundquist, Enid Rieser, Earthlyn Manuel, David Welle, Garth Rockcastle, Bruce Wright, Sandy Oakes, Louise Segretto, Charlie Warner, Steve Parliament, Jack Becker, Tom Rosch, Rob Buntz and Bill Betzler. Dan Gleason provided the cover design of the draft publication and some of the computer graphics in the draft. Mariann Johnson, Jane Barrash Monsein and Lonnie Helgeson provided other forms of support which are greatly appreciated.

There will always be a special place in my heart for my parents, Tony and Eddie Baron, and uncles Frank Baron, John Chura and Don Ness, who provided a hands-on introduction to collaboration, construction skills, teamwork and management of the development process. With gratitude, I especially acknowledge the support and encouragement of Patrick Kartes.

Many others who may not be mentioned above contributed in various ways to this publication. Their contributions are also valued.

Cheryl Kartes

Introduction

For more than 30 years, artists have been creatively pioneering real estate development in American cities to meet their needs for affordable space in which to create and present their work. For artists, the primary concern has long been that they have enough security to work on and invest in their spaces. For cities, the primary concern over artist spaces has been the desire to see vacant or underused buildings occupied, attracting other people and economic activities. Ever since the revitalization of New York City by artists from the 1950s through the 1960s, the value of the arts as an economic development tool has been recognized. As a result, live/work space conversions have become a topic of public policy as well as the goal of individual artists.

Typically, artists have needed to seek many sources of information to succeed in developing working and living space. *Creating Space* brings together some of that information, as well as tips on where and how to find out more. Based upon many people's perspectives and years of experience in developing and managing spaces for the arts, this book emphasizes cooperative efforts, because of the many successful artists' collaborations across the country. However, *Creating Space* will also be useful to the individual artist who wants to go it alone in developing space. Every development project is as unique as the people who are creating it—not every project will need all of the information provided in this book, and most will need more that is not provided here.

Starting with personal values as the driving force behind the desire for space, this book outlines the major steps in organizing and carrying the dream to reality, providing examples, exercises and strategies to stimulate and inform those who are about to launch the search for space.

The many facets of real estate development are treated to help artists understand the context and tackle the obstacles with knowledge and confidence—in short, to empower artists in becoming informed and active participants in the process of developing property.

"It is as if tens of millions of people had decided simultaneously to conduct risky experiments in living, using the only materials that lay at hand—their own lives."
Daniel Yankelovich
New Rules: A Society Searching for Self-Fulfillment in a World Turned Upside Down

1

Personal Values: A Driving Force for Space

The goal for many American families was once to own their own homes. Today, an increasing number of families and professional households are adopting new forms of housing—including the combinations of working and living space that artists have pioneered. Long at the forefront of defining how a city's building stock might be used for their own needs, artists have found exciting solutions that have increased the variety of housing options open to other people.

There are no precise steps to be followed in developing space. An artist on an errand may suddenly notice that an intriguing building is up for sale, an idea is born, and the process starts. Or artists at a gallery opening, lamenting their unsuitable space, may decide to join one another in the search for appropriate quarters. Or a nonprofit developer, having found potential live/work space for artists, may want artists to participate in project planning. Sometimes building owners or city agencies, seeking artists to locate in a building or area, conduct market surveys to determine artists' interests and needs, and they use artists' participation as a way of clarifying the development plans.

1.1   VALUES

Location

- A living space close to your job or shared with your work space
- Easy access to public transportation
- Proximity to galleries, restaurants, shopping, or support services
- Proximity to other artists, cultural activities
- Neighbors related through ethnicity or religion

Lifestyle

- Space in which you can both live and work
- Artists in live/work situations nearby
- Attractiveness or status implied by the space
- Access to recreational facilities or open spaces

Comfort

- Space that does not need major renovation
- Space with modern kitchen and bathroom facilities
- Large spaces to meet all your working or living needs

Positive Environment for Raising Children

- A location that allows you to raise a family if you desire to
- Proximity to schools and playgrounds for children
- Availability of playmates for your children

Ownership/Control

- Space that may be too small or in poor condition, but is privately owned
- Building that is collectively owned and managed
- Leased space that provides flexibility to move
- Space that is collectively leased and managed

Affordability

- Low monthly payments
- Energy efficiency of building and its utilities
- Quality of building's construction, roofing and insulation
- Ability to move in without making expensive repairs or renovations

Investment Potential

- Potential for your equity to grow quickly or for you to make a large profit on the resale of your space
- Investment in a neighborhood that is "on the way up"

Privacy

- Private home or space, where your activities are self-determined
- Privacy respected by neighbors
- Ability to engage in loud activities
- Potential for peace and quiet, not subject to another's loud activities

Safety

- Well-lit streets
- Security system for building
- Neighborhood association seeking to reduce crime in the area

Artists neighborhood, St. Paul. Warehouses converted to live/work and studio spaces.

tion of their work. That need may be the driving force for their decision to develop a space or building. Hundreds of artist-initiated efforts have resulted in alternative galleries, dance studios and theater spaces across the country. Most of the principles of developing space explored in this book are relevant for projects that incorporate rehearsal and presentation spaces.

STUDIO OR LIVE/ WORK SPACE?

Deciding whether you want to live and work in the same space or have a studio at a different location is the first question to answer.

Many artists prefer to work at a separate location, away from distractions of daily living and interruptions. Separate studio space is usually easy to find, and it is less costly and less problematic to develop than space for living and working. Renovating space for living and working so that it complies with codes can be prohibitively expensive, even if you do some of the work yourself. Still, many artists have found that the high initial costs of renovating live/work space are balanced by lower monthly costs. Moreover, live/work space has advantages that are hard to overlook, such as convenience, more effective time use and a single monthly payment.

If you decide to live and work in the same space, you have several options. You can rent a large apartment and use an extra room for a studio. Or you can set up a studio in the attic or basement of an apartment or house. Many artists have found small commercial buildings or storefronts with apartment space above.

Warehouses often provide the ideal solution for artists' unique spatial problems. They have large, uncluttered floor space, and good natural lighting with long windows or skylights. Also, making noise or creating fumes in a warehouse is less likely to annoy neighbors: most warehouses are far from residential areas. However, develop-

You may not feel that a market study is needed, either for yourself or other artists. Yet your values will often come into the decision-making process as negotiations and compromises inevitably arise. Awareness of those values will serve to ground your decisions. To the extent that those decisions are in keeping with your passions and beliefs, you will be sustained throughout the development process.

SPACE OPTIONS AND VALUES

No single solution meets everyone's needs at all stages of life. It is rare to find living and working spaces that meet all needs and satisfy all values. Your values may conflict with one another or with the reality of limited space or resources. Just as there may be good economic reasons to unite your home and work spaces, there may be psychological reasons to separate them. Knowing your preferences will help you evaluate options and consider the trade-offs (see the variety of housing values listed in box 1.1).

REHEARSAL OR PRESENTATION SPACE

Some artists need a venue for the presenta-

4

ing a multiunit building for live/work space by recycling an older structure requires a commitment of money, labor and time. It may not be the best choice for anyone planning to move within a short time.

Evaluate all aspects of the move you are considering, including the negative ones. Some artists have found several drawbacks to live/work space in a nonresidential neighborhood, among them:

LACK OF AMENITIES. It is 11:30 p.m. You have just hit your stride on a new piece of work. It is time for a short break. You go to the cupboard—and find it is bare. What do you do? You may have to walk down a dark street to your car, if you have one, then drive around to find an open store. Has this changed your mood or broken your flow of ideas?

Industrial or commercial buildings are often located in out-of-the-way areas, far from laundromats, drugstores, supermarkets, etc. This may pose no problem for you, but if you are accustomed to a short walk or drive down the street, adjusting to the change may be a concern.

WORKING AND LIVING, LIVING AND WORKING. Which comes first, living or working? Which is which? If you live and work in the same space, your activities will tend to run together. You will not be able to "get away" from your work. Your latest unfinished project will always be just a brushstroke away. Will you be able to relax and attend to the ordinary business of living, loving and socializing when your newest creation is crying for attention in the next room? Can you discipline yourself to work when others are taking time off?

Minneapolis Warehouse District.

**Emeryville Artists'
Cooperative, Emeryville, CA.
Live/work space: stairs lead
to office and sleeping area,
kitchen is to right.**

STRAIN ON RELATIONSHIPS. An imbalance between your work and other commitments may strain relationships with those who live with you as well as with friends and colleagues. Chances are your partners have already learned to accept your commitment to your work. But if you are always preoccupied, sooner or later this will have a detrimental effect. If you have not lived and worked in the same space before, the change could cause a major upheaval for your living companion and family members.

HEAT. Large, old buildings are often difficult to heat, and some buildings are heated only during the normal daytime workweek. In Atlanta, this probably will not be as much of an issue as in Minneapolis/St. Paul, where a lack of sufficient heat can be a real inconvenience to your creation of art, if not hazardous to your health.

NOISE. If you are located in an industrial or manufacturing district, there may be noise or vibrations from adjacent buildings and the streets. Heavy truck traffic and machinery noises would be common.

CRIME AND VANDALISM. Being off the beaten track can be unnerving, especially during late evening hours in poorly lit areas. You might want to check with local police to find out the type and frequency of crimes in the area, and what kind of patrol patterns the police use in the neighborhood.

LIVING WITH ARTISTS. An opportunity to live in a building with other artists engaged in similar activities is an opportunity for professional networking and friendships. However, it may also give rise to the feeling that you are in competition with your neighbors as artists.

AN EXERCISE IN DETERMINING SPACE NEEDS

The following exercises are designed to help you gather information about your values and needs. The first exercise is aimed at uncovering your intuitive sense of values. The second presents a series of questions that will help you identify and analyze your basic values in seeking space.

AN INTUITIVE APPROACH

Use words or doodle images for your answers. Once the answers are on paper, rather than just in your head, project planning can begin.

1. Where are you on your career path? (Imagine a road, a spiral, a ladder, a carousel—or other image—and see where you are on it.) Where you find yourself may affect your decisions about space and will probably fall into one of the following cycles or stages:

    BEGINNING. You are in an exploratory stage. Regardless of your age, you are just starting out in your artistic career. You have been a student and have acquired some materials, but have little capital. You are willing to put up with some inconveniences for the sake of economy. You have an abundance of energy and enthusiasm.

MODERATELY ESTABLISHED. You are in a territorial phase. You have been around for a while, and your work is selling. You have a good idea of what directions you need to grow in, whether you need a larger space for working, and what you need for achieving peace of mind and deepening your creative energy.

ESTABLISHED. You are in an expansive stage. By your own standards, you are feeling confident and successful. Your work is known and probably provides a good portion of your income. The space you are in has been adequate for your needs, but now you want something more than adequate. You may want more amenities than you have had. You are ready to reward yourself for your accomplishments, and you can afford to do it.

BEGINNING AGAIN. Perhaps other lifestyle changes are allowing you to return to your art. Or you may be feeling the impulse to explore new media or new kinds of messages. Your values may or may not have changed, but your needs have because you want to move in new directions. You are back in phase one, exploratory, but with valuable experience to guide you.

2. Think about the last three spaces you have lived or worked in. List—or draw—two or three of the most positive elements of those locations, and indicate how they contributed to your creative energy and productivity.

3. Now list or draw two or three of the most negative elements of those locations, and indicate how they were obstacles to the development of your work.

4. Describe or draw your *ideal* living and working environment.

An Analytical Approach

The primary factors your should consider in your move will include the following: (a) location, (b) working requirements, (c) size and (d) resources. Listed below are some of the basic questions you will want to ask yourself. Later chapters deal with many of these issues in greater detail.

Location

What type of environment is best for you? The location you choose—urban downtown, suburban, residential, commercial, etc.—will determine the type of buildings you will find. For example, you will rarely find warehouse buildings in residential neighborhoods, but former schools, churches, firehouses and storefront space are good possibilities for meeting your space needs.

In addition to the building itself (discussed in chapter 3), you will want to consider the following:

1. **PARKING.**   Is parking available in the area? What is the monthly cost?

2. **PUBLIC TRANSPORTATION.**   What bus/train/subway service is available?

3. **SERVICES.**   How far away is the building from a grocery store, drugstore, hardware store, laundromat, art supply store, galleries or other needed services? Is proximity to schools or religious institutions important to you?

4. **SOCIAL NETWORK.**   How far will you be from friends, family or associates?

5. **NOISE.**   Will noise be a problem? Especially in warm weather months you may hear or feel vibrations from

Sculptor's studio, Seattle. Large windows and high ceilings.

8

Piano Craft Guild, Boston. High ceilings in former piano factory.

commuter traffic, fire trucks, or the corner bar discharging its patrons. Does the nature of your own noise—equipment, tools or rehearsal activities—suggest looking for building types where you will be a welcome neighbor?

Working Requirements

1. **WINDOWS.** Do you need much natural light? Will a large window area also cause excessive heat build-up in the summer? Is enough of the window area operable to provide good ventilation? Will you be working in the studio at night when artificial light will have to be provided? How important is window direction? Streets in some cities are on a diagonal axis, affecting how the sunlight hits the building.

2. **DOORS.** Does your work require large or double door openings to move things in or out?

3. **FLOORS.** How critical is the type of floor for your work? Does your work require load-bearing capability or prevent you from considering non-fireproof floor surfaces?

4. **CEILING HEIGHT.** Does the scale of your work necessitate a high ceiling? Height is a particular concern for rehearsal and presentation spaces. For example, visual artists may benefit from the ability to create their work in a space comparable to the space in which the work may later be presented.

5. **WATER AND PLUMBING.** Is water access within your studio important? Do you need wide drains? Cold and hot water? Special fixtures?

6. **ACCESS.** Will you need twenty-four-hours-a-day, seven-days-a-week access? Do you need a loading dock and freight elevator to move materials and equipment in and out? (If you need to move only one piece of large equipment, say a printing press, it may be possible to have it hoisted through a window by a crane.)

7. **ELECTRICAL.** What are the electrical requirements of your equipment? How many outlets do you need for equipment and lighting?

Equipment usage requirements _____
Number of outlets _____

8. **ENVIRONMENTAL.** Will your work be affected by vibrations caused by a manufacturing tenant on the floor above or below you or caused by passing truck traffic or trains? Is dust a concern? Other environmental concerns?

Vibration free _____

Noise _____

Ventilation _____

Other factors _____

9. **WALLS.** Do you require soundproof walls? Are there metal or wooden studs? Will you need to hang heavy artwork or storage shelving?

10. **OTHER REQUIREMENTS.** What other requirements do you have for your work area?

Space Needs

Warehouse and commercial space is typically priced by the number of square feet. Therefore, you will find it helpful to know how many square feet of space you need. Square feet (or area) is calculated by multiplying the width times the length of the space. For example, a space 30 feet wide by 40 feet long has an area of 1,200 square feet. If you are unsure about how much space you need, try to visualize your actual needs.

STUDIO. If you currently have a studio, measure it to determine the area. If it is inadequate, decide what square footage would make it usable. Should it be 10 feet wider? 20 feet longer?

If you do not have a studio, what factors are the most critical for you? How does size affect your artistic endeavors? Do you foresee working on a larger scale in the next few years, or would you like the option to explore a larger scale?

- Number of pieces you work on at any one time _____

- Distance needed to lay out or view your work _____
- Areas needed to carry out particular processes _____
- Total estimated studio area _____

LIVING AREA. Living area may vary from 300 square feet to more than 1,000 square feet depending on your living habits as well as how many people will be occupying the space.

Lowertown Lofts. Moving in.

10

Measure your current space as a guide to how much you need. (A typical two-bedroom apartment is roughly 1,000 square feet.) Living areas can be efficient or wasteful depending on how well they are laid out.

- ■ Estimated living area _____

REHEARSAL OR PRESENTATION SPACES. Your rehearsal, theater and gallery activities will have specific demands. Resources such as *Building for the Arts: A Guidebook for the Planning & Design of Cultural Facilities* by Catherine R. Brown, William B. Fleissig and William R. Morris (see bibliography) provide checklists for developing a complete building program and other information to increase your awareness of space demands. Your city's building inspections department will also have specific requirements to protect the public you invite into your space (see chapter 4).

- ■ Estimated rehearsal area _____
- ■ Estimated presentation area _____

STORAGE. Storage space can be important. Determine the materials, props or completed artwork that you need to store and calculate the floor area required for this purpose. Remember that high ceiling spaces allow more storage in a smaller area.

- ■ Estimated storage area _____

OFFICE/OTHER USES. If you plan to sell work from your space, you may want a separate area to show your work or to receive potential buyers. You might be able to do this in your studio

Project Artaud, San Francisco. Performance space in cooperative live/work development.

or living area, but consider the possibility of additional space. What other space needs do you have?

■ Estimated area for other uses _____

Add the above estimates for total area needed:

1. **Studio** _____
2. **Living** _____
3. **Rehearsal** _____
4. **Presentation** _____
5. **Storage** _____
6. **Office/Other** _____
   Total square feet _____

Resource Limitations

Most artists want inexpensive space. In many cities real estate appreciation, heating costs and property taxes have significantly increased rents as well as the purchasing and carrying costs of commercial property. You can expect to pay the same, or more, for a live/work space as for an apartment.

Almost everyone has heard about someone who has a live/work space that rents for an incredibly low price. Inexpensive places do exist, but often you get what you pay for. Do not expect to have all your needs satisfied if your rent is well below the market rate. Consider how much work and money will be required to improve a space in a substandard building. If you do not have the cash and plan to put in your own labor, consider how much of it you are truly willing to commit.

CALCULATING SPACE COSTS. Cost per square foot is the basis for determining your monthly cost. For a rental, multiply the annual rental rate times the number of square feet to get your annual cost for a base rent. Divide annual base rent by 12 (months) to determine your monthly cost (see example 1).

Example 1:

A: $$\frac{\$4.00 \text{ per sq. ft. per year} \times 1,000 \text{ sq. ft.}}{12 \text{ months}}$$
$$= \$333.33 \text{ per month.}$$

B: $0.33 per sq. ft. per month × 1,000 sq. ft.
$$= \$333.33 \text{ per month.}$$

Comparing the cost per square foot of one space to another is one way to assess the value of one space to another. The layout of the space or other amenities may also influence your decision to choose one space over another. In example 2, the monthly cost of "B" is higher, but you would have access to nearly twice as much space for a lower cost per square foot.

Example 2:

A: $$\frac{\$333.33/\text{month} \times 12 \text{ months}}{1,000 \text{ sq. ft.}}$$
$$= \$4.00 \text{ per sq. ft.}$$

B: $$\frac{\$500/\text{month} \times 12 \text{ months}}{1,900 \text{ sq. ft.}}$$
$$= \$3.16 \text{ per sq. ft.}$$

EVALUATING FINANCIAL RESOURCES AND NEEDS. Evaluating your financial resources will clarify which types of spaces you should investigate. One of the first steps in assessing a building or space is to prepare a preliminary budget, which should include income and expenses. The following questions should help focus your attention on present and anticipated sources and uses of funds.

1. **MONTHLY EXPENSES:**

   How much do you now pay per month for living space? Include rent, heating costs, average electrical bill and other monthly utilities.

**Studios at 700, Minneapolis.
Artist doing construction work
on warehouse studio space.**

How much do you now pay for studio space?

How much do you expect your monthly living space costs to increase by next year?

How much do you expect your average monthly studio costs to increase by next year?

How much do you expect your average monthly income to increase by next year?

Total amount you can afford to pay each month for the space you now seek?

2. **ACQUISITION AND/OR RENOVATION COSTS:**

How much money is available for a down payment?

How much money do you have available to invest in improvements?

How much money could you realistically borrow from family, friends or a lending institution?

Total amount available to invest in your space.

INVESTING SKILLS AND TIME AS DEVELOPMENT RESOURCES. Doing some or all of the work yourself is an alternative to hiring someone to make improvements for a space and an affordable approach for many artists. If you are unskilled in construction, you might be able to barter with a friend or licensed contractor who does possess these skills.

1. **SKILLS:**

Space planning
Drafting plans
Demolition
Transporting materials
Basic carpentry
Construction cleanup
Putting up Sheetrock and taping
Painting
Floor refinishing
Other skills

2. **TIME:**

How much time do you have to work or barter?

- Number of hours free per week
- Other blocks of time (vacations, weekends, etc.)

How long are you willing to work to develop a space?

- One month only _____
- Three months _____
- Six months _____
- Longer than six months _____

Be realistic about the amount of time you can commit to creating a studio or live/work space. As a rule of thumb, it almost always takes more time than you think it will. The time you spend on developing a space is time you will not have for creating art. However, the benefits of having a space that meets your needs are often great enough to justify the expense and time.

NEXT STEPS: DECIDING ON YOUR PERSONAL ROLE IN THE PROJECT

Throughout the process of locating or developing space in which to live or work, you will need to make decisions based on your values and priorities. One of the big decisions you may have to make is whether to go it alone or to join or create a group to pursue the goal of developing space. Although the notion of the artist exploring his or her unique vision in splendid isolation has held sway for a long time, a strong movement toward group housing enterprises has also emerged. Artists working together can pool their resources and ensure that the spaces they occupy will remain available and affordable despite neighborhood changes.

The more money you have, the less cooperation and assistance you will need from others to carry out your vision and achieve your space goals. If you can afford the acquisition and renovation of a small commercial building, you may decide to move ahead, carrying out the project as a personal plan.

In addition, if you are a risk-taker with enough financial resources to back you up, you may consider acting as the developer of the building, controlling the design, financing, construction and marketing of the finished units. This route, if successful, could provide you with a source of earned income to support your artistic career. That income—earned from developing, owning or leasing a building—has to be balanced against certain costs: the time you spend planning and overseeing the property's development;

the risk you take in finding tenants or covering the cost of vacant spaces; and the time, frustration and legal expenses you incur by becoming a landlord. However, if you manage your project well, you may have enough income to cover operating deficits and future repairs to the building's structural and mechanical systems while retaining your arts career.

On the other hand, if the price, location or size of your preferred space—or any combination of those three factors—necessitates including other artists or tenants in your project, your strategy must include working with others. In addition, your planning must be more thorough. The next chapter examines how a group might be organized to pursue the project as a collaborative venture.

212 North Second Street, Minneapolis. Artist working with contractor to convert warehouse to live/work space.

*"What brings people together and enables them to advance together
in these institutions is not only a vision of a better future,
but also their belief that by pooling their efforts, by working
together, rather than singly; in unity, rather than in
isolation; their accomplishments can be vastly greater."*

Boris Shiskin
former Secretary,
Housing Committee, American Federation
of Labor-Congress of Industrial Organizations (AFL-CIO)

2
The Artist
Project Team

THE PROJECT CONCEPT

At the core of every successful development project is clarity in its concept. The project concept is the driving force from which all further action flows. Once you or your group has a vision of what the project might be, you can proceed with testing the idea, reframing, reshaping and readjusting it until the idea takes final form. In real estate, the final form is influenced by a variety of forces: the proposed tenants and their activities, neighborhood and city negotiations, city code and tenant requirements, financing and construction constraints, and ongoing management plans.

Development efforts are business ventures. If artists join together to secure a building or a large space in a warehouse without recognizing the business ramifications of their venture, they risk destroying friendships and crippling the project. This chapter focuses on ways to organize the team so that it can enter the world of real estate development as a business enterprise as well as an expression of the artists' individual and collective needs.

Emeryville Artists' Cooperative, Emeryville, CA. Resident artists in main hall.

ORGANIZING A PROJECT TEAM

The project concept will clarify whether or not it will be necessary to collaborate with a building owner, developer, and/or a city agency to complete the project team. Regardless of when your collaboration begins to include other partners, it will be important for the artists in the project to use an organizational structure that provides reassurance that your group can uphold its end of the project administratively and financially.

The amount of risk other partners must assume in the project is reduced to the extent that they are assured of the amount of space that will be needed by your group, the amount of cash flow that is available to pay for that space, that the group's leadership fairly represents decisions on behalf of the group and that the group will carry out the steps that are agreed upon. The partners will also want assurance that when the project is ready for occupancy, the group will be a solid entity, ready to take possession of the premises.

PRELIMINARY AGREEMENTS

As the size or cost of a building increases, so does the need for a plan for selecting the members and organizing the efforts of your group. A project team of artists should begin with preliminary agreement on the following:

- the process for becoming a member
- responsibilities of membership
- a shared commitment to undertake the development process
- respect for each other as people, not necessarily as artists
- confidence in one another's ability to pay the agreed-upon share of monthly costs (what can members comfortably afford?)
- a schedule with assigned responsibility for carrying out tasks
- representative leadership on behalf of the group

The rapport within the group is more important than career status or specific skills. As options present themselves, group members need to be able to think through the alternatives and ultimately make decisions as one body. The development process will provide learning experiences for the entire group.

As the project evolves and more artists are needed to make commitments for spaces in the project, the group should plan a selection process for tenants. Examples of tenant selection criteria and procedures are included as appendix 2.1 (see also discussion in chapter 11).

ORGANIZATIONAL STRUCTURE

A group of people is not inherently an organization; it is more like an amoeba. It may be capable of endless divisions and subdivisions, but it will accomplish nothing. Organization provides a "head" for an amorphous body and gives direction through leadership. Organization

16

creates a structure for decision making and a division of labor, so that steps can be taken efficiently toward a goal. Unless the group is extremely small (five or less), it will likely benefit from an organizational structure. The elements for establishing successful project teams are: (a) education, (b) leadership, (c) structure, (d) communication and (e) commitment.

Education

Because there are so many things to know about the development process, the group should create opportunities for its own education during the organizing stage. The better informed a group is, the better the chances of success. Written materials can be gathered from a variety of sources—the library, government agencies and other sources of technical assistance. If you need technical assistance in organizing your group or in directing the development process, you may want to seek out an artist service organization or nonprofit developer in your area. Such organizations sometimes even act as co-developers of projects. See appendix 2.2 for a list of some nonprofit organizations providing referrals, development expertise or technical assistance to artists seeking to develop space.

The group may visit other projects to talk with artist-tenants about their experiences in developing space. The building search itself can be educational. The more buildings you see, the more you will learn about what you do and do not want.

Workshops may be useful at various stages to provide education and build commitment within the group. Workshops can be held with any, or all, of the group's collaborators—consultants, real estate brokers, attorneys, developers, architects, contractors, city inspectors, etc.

If your group wants to form a cooperative, it might sponsor a workshop inviting one or more outside authorities to speak to the group about the workings of a cooperative. Another workshop might focus on zoning issues or fire safety. Officials from city zoning or fire departments are generally willing to talk to a group about their requirements.

Some of these outside authorities may in time become part of your "development team" of technical experts, serving as an ongoing resource. A development consultant or a nonprofit developer may lead your group through a variety of informational meetings or provide overall guidance.

Leadership

It takes all personality types—the visionary, the compromiser and the devil's advocate, among them—to ensure that all issues are properly addressed. A group of individuals with varied temperaments, backgrounds, lifestyles, values and needs may have difficulties in learning how to work with one another toward a common goal. In most groups, consensus is unlikely, and attempting to achieve it can slow you down. It is best to agree at the outset to respect the diversity of opinions within the group. Much can be learned from those whose style is the most different from your own.

At the same time, resistance to group decision-making processes and ego clashes may weaken your group. Hence it is important to identify how the group wants to overcome such challenges. Leadership from one or more group members provides the potential for continually keeping the common goal before the group and demonstrating the efficiency of organized and unified action. Leadership may be shared by several parties, and responsibilities may be rotated. If the group is too large for all members to share equally in responsibility, a few members may be selected to assume greater responsibility.

The task of the group's leadership is to foster an environment of communication, trust and consensus to ensure that the group weathers difficulties in the development process. Communication is enhanced by gathering information, seeking opinions about proposed solutions, clarifying and elaborating on ideas to explore their full impact, periodically summarizing ideas and bringing closure through decisions. Trust is encouraged when there is a climate of acceptance for diverse styles, opinions and methods among the membership. Consensus is born through sensitive solutions to conflict and through compromise.

In most cases, the group will benefit if it has a leader who has no vested interest in the outcome, yet is committed to the gains of all parties. This leader—perhaps a consultant—may assist the group in solving problems and keeping priorities in focus. The ideal skills of this type of leader would include a sense of humor and an informed view of likely obstacles and challenges. The leader's role may include encouraging leadership skills within the group to emerge through committee tasks.

Beyond initiating action and monitoring results, the best leadership, whether individual or broad based, will energize and involve other people, ensure that all voices are heard, attend to the emotional life of the group and be alert to signs of leadership qualities in others.

Structure

Early on, the group should establish operating procedures or guidelines the group will use to handle its business and to define a decision-making process. It should establish a regular schedule of meetings and a policy for handling certain activities or decisions. For example, the group may wish to establish a conflict-of-interest policy so that if a perceived conflict arises, procedures for dealing with it are already in place.

Generally, committees are expected to research alternatives and propose a course of action for the group. They propose these actions through "motions," and once a motion has been adopted,

the policy is recorded in written minutes, to answer questions that arise later. Adherence to these policies will avert conflict and dissension within the group.

During early planning stages, the group should define its common mission or goal and adopt it in the form of a written resolution. This statement of mission expresses the reason for the organization's existence and will act as a unifying force. Imagination and vision should be a part of the goal-setting process. Discussions should be open and wide-ranging, and everyone should be given an opportunity to express his or her views.

Although the group may eventually decide to form a cooperative or other legal structure, it is

Studios at 700, Minneapolis. Member artists gathering during construction.

easier to begin with a less formal structure, such as an unincorporated tenants association. This will establish an organization capable of making decisions and resolving disputes, keeping the membership informed, distributing the burden of work and acting on behalf of the group. An unincorporated tenants association essentially involves a written contract providing a structure through which all parties agree on how they will operate. The parties cover the expenses of the group, but remain individually liable.

In contrast, in an incorporated tenants association such as a cooperative or nonprofit organization, the corporation is liable and not the individual members. In most projects, incorporation occurs closer to the time of project occupancy. The agreements made while the group was unincorporated provide the framework for the corporation.

Most tenants associations have borrowed the language, structure and responsibilities of members, officers, and committees from the typical nonprofit or cooperative corporation's legal structure. All these structural elements help smooth the process of working together. (See also chapter 8 and appendices, 8.1, Articles of Incorporation, and 8.2, Bylaws, for further guidance on the structure.)

OFFICERS. The group empowers officers to perform specific functions on its behalf. Even if your group chooses not to have specific "officers," it should define its expectations of the leadership. Typical expectations of officer positions are as follows:

1. **PRESIDENT OR CHAIR.** The key to productive meetings is an effective president (or chairperson). A good president shares the group's values. The main tasks of a president are to maintain orderly meetings, employing parliamentary procedure and providing all a chance to speak; keep discussion on the topic; remain neutral; summarize points of view presented after discussion; ensure clear decisions that are made democratically; follow up on decisions made, making sure things get done; plan meetings with other officers; and initiate group self-evaluation. The president also coordinates efforts of committees. In addition, the president usually acts as the primary contact with outside consultants and the membership.

2. **VICE PRESIDENT (OPTIONAL).** The vice president assumes the duties and responsibilities of the president when he or she is not available. In addition, the vice president carries out special tasks assigned by the president. Often the vice president is asked to assume responsibility for communications with the membership.

3. **SECRETARY.** The secretary may be responsible for keeping accurate records of correspondence and retaining copies of all legal documents. Important duties include taking minutes, preparing a final copy and filing them when adopted; maintaining the association's records and files; ensuring timely notices of meetings; consulting with the president or executive committee on agenda; making sure unfinished business is included; and ensuring a quorum at meetings.

4. **TREASURER.** Once your group has funds to manage, a treasurer ensures an accurate account of all receipts and disbursements. The treasurer works with the finance committee and oversees the work of a paid bookkeeper if one is available. The treasurer maintains the group's financial records and bank accounts; is responsible for dues collection and accounting; issues reports regularly, ensuring that budgets

and reports are understood; and advises the group on the implications of financial transactions before they are undertaken.

COMMITTEES. There are two types of committees—"standing" committees for ongoing responsibilities and "ad hoc" or "special" committees for specific short-term tasks. The types of committees needed are often dictated by the scope of the project. To clarify expectations, prepare a written job description outlining the committee's purpose, specific responsibilities and reporting schedule; add the names of the committee members as they are selected. The following are possible committees:

- Management and Governance Committee
- Site and Acquisition Committee
- Design Committee
- Tenant Selection Committee
- Finance (and Fund Raising, as appropriate) Committee
- Public Relations Committee

Before committees are formed, the group should sit down together and explore the kinds of resources existing within the group. Those resources include designers, graphic artists, those with access to photocopying, and experienced public relations people as well as those with construction-related skills that may translate into "sweat equity" for renovation of a building. The combined talents of a group can be considerable and will translate into great savings.

Assign people to tasks they really want to do. Professionals in one field might prefer to serve on a committee that allows them to learn something totally different.

Communications

Spoken and written communication is one of the most important organizational tools and the key to building the group's interdependence. Establish a system of communications. One method of relaying information about meetings, contacts or negotiations is to form a "calling tree." For example, five people could act as regular liaisons, each volunteering to call five others. More costly, but valuable to the committee, are written notices and documentation. Written documentation of a committee's actions will keep a broader network of interested parties informed and provide a record of your progress.

BASIC MEETING PROCEDURES. Many people like the feel of casual, informal meetings. Almost everyone, however, appreciates the benefits of speedy and efficient decision making. Several centuries of experience have shown that three invaluable tools for maximizing effectiveness and minimizing wasted time are (1) an agenda, (2) parliamentary procedures and (3) written minutes and resolutions.

1. **Agenda.** The agenda lists the topics to be discussed at a meeting. An agenda is prepared and distributed by the president and secretary, perhaps in consultation with the executive committee or other members of your development team. Distributing an agenda before the meeting keeps members' attention on those points, reducing time-consuming digressions. At the meeting, it is helpful to list the items of business on large sheets of paper or on a blackboard that can be seen by everyone, especially if an agenda has not been passed out before the meeting. If someone brings up a worthwhile subject that is not on the agenda, the subject should be called "out of order" at the time, but added under "new business."

2. **Parliamentary Procedures.** Do not assume that everyone knows the rules of parliamentary procedure. Set aside some time to explain

them and the purpose they serve. Some of the fundamentals follow:

MOTIONS. To propose an action requiring a decision by the group, you must state a motion, for example: "I move we create a gallery space in the common area of the entrance hall." Every motion must receive a "second" from someone else who agrees the motion should be discussed. If there is no second, the motion is not discussed.

VOTING. Everyone is given a chance to speak for or against the motion. The president calls for a vote, asking: "All those in favor?" then "All those opposed?" and "Any abstentions?" The simple majority rules, unless the group has chosen to commit to consensus or to some other proportion of the group. Common reasons for abstaining from a vote include a conflict of interest, insufficient information or an inability to decide. A conflict of interest should be declared and recorded after the motion and before the discussion. In some cases, the member with a conflict may choose to leave the room during the discussion and vote.

Lowertown Lofts, St. Paul. Resident artists meeting with development team.

AMENDMENTS. Amendments are used to change or add to the main motion, for example: "I move we put in a skylight over the hallway and make it a gallery area." A second is also required for the amendment. Discussion follows. The amendment is always voted on separately and before the main motion. This procedure allows people to vote against the amendment, but for the main motion, if that is their preference. Separate ideas that are related, but different from the main motion, should not be allowed as amendments to the main motion, for example: "I move we purchase some chairs for the entrance hall." A vote on the gallery space should be taken first. Then a new motion can be proposed.

CALLING THE QUESTION. When someone feels that enough discussion has taken place on a motion, he or she may call for a vote or "call the question." The president then asks for a vote on the "question." If members agree there has been enough discussion, they vote "in favor." If the "question" carries, a vote is immediately taken on the motion under discussion. If the "question" is defeated, the group continues to discuss the motion.

SPEAKER'S LIST. If there is an item on the agenda that many people want to speak about, a speaker's list is signed at the beginning of the meeting by those who want to speak to the agenda item. The president or chair then calls each speaker in order on the list, which ensures that everyone who wishes to speak will have a turn.

AD HOC COMMITTEE. When a discussion becomes too complicated for a decision to be made, an ad hoc committee may be created to study the issues in detail and report back at the next meeting. The issue could also simply be deferred, or a motion "tabled" until the next meeting.

3. Minutes and Resolutions. Minutes are the record of the time and place of a meeting, who was present and what business was conducted. The actual wording of motions, the persons who

**Lowertown Lofts. Resident
artists in common area.**

made and seconded them, and the number of votes are recorded accurately. The minutes should also reflect the person(s) responsible for following up on required decisions. Some groups require that motions be written out by the mover to assist the secretary.

Groups should make important decisions in the form of resolutions. After a vote on a motion for a resolution has been taken and passed, a resolution is prepared and signed by the secretary. This prevents challenges to actions. Resolutions are especially important in connection with signing contracts and other legal documents on behalf of the association or cooperative. The resolution provides evidence that the president was properly authorized to sign particular documents. However, before any documents (articles, bylaws, contracts with professionals, etc.) are signed, they should be reviewed by the organization's attorney.

GROUP DECISION-MAKING PROCESSES. Generating ideas and reaching consensus often depend upon techniques that differ from parliamentary procedure. Through procedures that gather all points of view within the room, individuals feel they have been heard and that they are a valued part of the team. Conflict and controversy often have a positive effect by producing creative solutions and giving rise to true collaboration, whereas suppression of conflict denies the group the opportunity to forge deeper bonds and find better solutions. (See box 2.1.)

PARTY TIME. In addition to well-run business meetings, occasional social gatherings will benefit communications. Individuals enjoy the opportunity of meeting informally to get to know one another better. Not only do social functions foster a sense of community and strengthen the

2.1   IDEA GENERATION

One frequently used strategy for gaining broad input or seeking agreement when there appear to be many conflicting ideas follows:

1. Identify and clarify the issue or problem. If the group is large, divide it into smaller groups for brainstorming.

2. Spend 5 to 15 minutes brainstorming ideas, concerns or solutions related to the topic. List ideas on paper or spend time relaxing, deep breathing and visualizing ideas that you draw on paper. In brainstorming, no one criticizes or makes comments about another person's ideas. The idea is to create as many ideas as possible.

3. Ask someone to act as a recorder, listing ideas on large sheets of newsprint. If several groups are present, each group contributes one idea or concern at a time, alternating with other groups until all are listed.

4. Spend a few minutes clarifying ideas and combining concerns that seem to be related. Refine the ideas into truly different ideas and suggestions.

5. Ask each person now to rank his or her top five concerns in priority order—with five (5) being the highest or most important of their concerns.

6. Have the recorder read each concern and then ask for a show of hands for each possible ranking—from 1 through 5—of the concern. The recorder writes the sum of the individual rankings next to each statement. As an alternative, have each person go to the newsprint sheets and record the priority he or she assigns to each statement.

7. Add up the numbers. The statement with the highest number is the highest priority of the group.

8. Recopy the statements on a clean sheet of newsprint, starting with the highest priority.

9. Use the group's priority concerns as the basis for preparing goal statements, one for each concern. Each goal should state only what the desired end condition will be. Refine these statements until all members can accept them. A committee may be assigned the task of drafting goal statements to be presented at a later meeting.

10. Once the group's goals have been prepared, they can be used in the formulation of a shared vision or purpose statement, if one has not already been created by the group. It is also an opportunity to review your vision or purpose statement to ensure its alignment with your new goals.

11. Next, use the goal statements to create an action plan. Objective statements describe how the goal will be accomplished, by whom, and by when. It may be helpful to think about what would assist the attainment of the goal. Likewise, consider how to minimize obstacles to the completion of the goal.

12. Review and confirm what has been agreed upon and how those decisions will be implemented. Each person should make note of what tasks he or she has agreed to carry out, with whom, with what available resources, and when the task must be done.

Designers' Space, Inc., Austin. Sweat equity.

group's purpose, but they can also serve to promote good relations with people in the neighborhood.

Inevitably there will be strained negotiations, delays and temporarily insoluble problems. Remember your ultimate goals, seek "win-win" solutions to your negotiations and periodically reward all the participants in the project with some fun and recognition.

Commitment

TIME, ENERGY, CASH DEPOSITS AND "SWEAT EQUITY". The project's initiators must be committed and able to devote time and energy to organizing the group. They also convene meet-

ings and deal with realtors, bankers, land owners and city officials. The membership must generally make an equal commitment of ongoing support and long-term participation. Without such a foundation, the project may flounder. A constantly changing membership will quickly become disorganized and demoralized.

Outside investors and lending institutions will seek evidence that the group is stable. By securing tenants for a live/work space project during the planning phase, you provide assurance to partners and lenders of the marketability of the project.

A cash deposit or down payment from every member entering into a long-term lease or sale provides assurance of his or her commitment. Deposits are often used to defray the cost of initial

Project Artaud, San Francisco. Sweat equity.

others. The larger your project, the more likely your group will need to be active in building support within the community to complete the project. Some artists have joined together to present open studio tours as a way of increasing support for the development of live/work space. Well-attended events have been hosted in Austin, Boston, Indianapolis, Minneapolis, Phoenix, Saint Paul, Salt Lake City, San Francisco, Seattle, Tucson and other cities.

AGREEMENTS. Agreements developed during the planning process regarding future management plans answer questions and build commitment among future tenants. Thinking through the changes that will occur over time will increase the group's ability to operate as a unified whole. Considering those possible changes is especially important in a cooperative structure, in which the group shares financial responsibilities. A member may have the opportunity to spend a year in Europe. Could he or she sublet? Who would be responsible for finding a replacement? What would happen if someone fails to meet his or her financial obligations or work responsibilities? What are the group's feelings about children, social habits or pets? How will maintenance and work responsibilities be shared?

Some of these issues may seem trivial or too far down the road to be of great concern. But issues that seem irrelevant at one time may become critical if they pop up unresolved in the middle of a highly charged, emotional situation. It is best to anticipate them.

Written agreements should be developed to cover any expected areas of conflict. Do not cast them in stone; do have them ready so that you can clear any roadblocks. Some matters, such as handling the sale of shares in a cooperative, will eventually have to be addressed in written legal

development steps. The group should establish a policy concerning the return of a deposit if a participant wishes to drop out of the project. In many artist-initiated projects, deposits are "at risk" and not refundable.

Beyond an initial deposit, the members may also be expected to provide their share of the equity needed for financing the project if other sources cannot be identified. An escrow account may be appropriate for some projects. Maintaining a waiting list of other candidates eases the disruption of having a member choose not to proceed once a lease or purchase agreement has been secured.

Another kind of commitment is shown by a member's willingness to work within the organization. "Sweat equity" tends to be a fundamental investment of an artist-initiated development project. Whether contributing carpentry skills for a renovation project or working on committees and making phone calls, you are contributing to the health of the organization and getting closer to the realization of your goal.

Another aspect of sweat equity is the role members play in seeking the involvement of

Studios at 700. Open house.

documents with the assistance of an attorney. See chapter 11 for information about issues you may wish to plan for.

Time and Process

Your group needs to borrow only the aspects of structure that seem pertinent to your situation or stage of organization. Remember, you do not need everything organized at once. As the group progresses through planning stages, the roles, responsibilities and schedules will change. The process may move too quickly or too slowly for some members of the group. Organizing your group may be taken on directly by the interested artists in the community, or with technical assistance from future partners in your project. Most importantly, remember to be flexible and retain your sense of humor!

"Three things are to be looked to in a building: that it stand on the right spot; that it be securely founded; that it be successfully executed."
Goethe

3
Building Location and Assessment

Finding the right building or site involves balancing the needs of location, size, configuration and affordability. Because affordability is dependent in part on the quality of a structure and its related renovation or construction costs, the focus in this chapter is on assessing the structure's current condition.

ESTABLISHING CRITERIA FOR THE SITE

When artists approach the development of space as a group, they need to decide first what their most important shared values are and how much space will be required to meet their needs. Once the group decides on these criteria, its representatives can look at sites to ascertain how well each site meets the group's objectives. After the best sites have been identified, the larger group will want to look at them.

In preparing to research sites, the group should include attention to five basic questions (elaborated in box 3.1):

1. What are the development trends in the area(s) under consideration?

2. What is "the highest and best use" projected in the marketplace?

3. Does the property have the required and desired amenities?

4. Does the property meet the group's building or renovation criteria?

5. What are the conditions of possible tenure—for example, public or private ownership, lease?

TYPES OF BUILDINGS TO CONSIDER

The type of building will influence the configuration of the space. Older warehouse buildings are often post and beam construction. This provides large open spaces interrupted only by support posts (columns) rising every sixteen to twenty feet. Storefronts or narrow commercial buildings generally do not have columns but will have bearing walls in the eighteen- to twenty-two-foot range. It is possible to find 1,000 square feet or more on a floor in a storefront, but it will likely be long and narrow, e.g., twenty feet wide by fifty feet long. Likewise, it is possible to have smaller studio spaces in large warehouse buildings, but

Lowertown Lofts, St. Paul. Interior before construction.

3.1   CHECKLIST OF BASIC QUESTIONS ABOUT THE SITE

1. What are the development trends in the area(s) under consideration?
   a. Has the area attracted the attention of developers?
   b. Are city efforts under way to encourage development activity?
   c. What effect will development trends have on the perceived property values in these areas?

2. What is "the highest and best use" projected in the marketplace?
   a. What is the property value as assessed by a broker, appraiser or tax assessor?
   b. What is the city's comprehensive plan for the area's preferred use—housing, retail, office, industrial or arts district?
   c. What are the zoning regulations on the proposed use?
   d. Is there potential for community or governmental support?
   e. Is the property underused and undervalued due to the previous occupancy?

3. Does the property have the required and desired amenities?
   a. Proximity to work, presentation venues, friends, professional associates?
   b. Commercial services (grocery, supplies, laundromat, bank, etc.)?
   c. Parking, public transit, handicap accessibility?
   d. Lack of noise, distractions?
   e. Audience access, neighboring uses, effect on image for organizations?
   f. Access to schools, playgrounds, parks, churches or synagogues?

4. Does the property meet the group's building or renovation criteria?
   a. Have the space needs or art forms to be served been identified, projected for all users?
   b. What are the square footage requirements, identified by types of activities?
   c. What are the window and light direction needs?
   d. What type of floor is needed?
   e. Does the property have access to loading docks, freight elevators, large doors?
   f. Do the ceiling heights meet those required for each activity?
   g. Do plumbing, electrical, heating, ventilation, fire and sound separations meet needs and requirements?
   h. Does the property meet growth plans or program requirements for your presentations to the community, whether periodic open studios as individual artists or as an artist-run organization presenting visual or performing arts?
   i. What is the architectural quality of the building: historic status, renovation viability and condition of space?
   j. What is the character of the neighborhood, both current and potential?

5. What are the conditions of possible tenure?
   a. Public or private ownership, availability to purchase?
   b. Terms of lease, purchase, or free use?
   c. Financial feasibility of construction or renovation, ongoing affordability?

3.2 EXAMPLES OF DIFFERENT TYPES OF BUILDINGS CONVERTED FOR ARTISTS' USES

The Torpedo Factory in Alexandria, Virginia (now providing studio and retail space to over 225 artists), was a World Wars I and II torpedo factory prior to storing federal records. It was renovated in 1974 as a bicentennial project, largely through sweat equity by artists in the community. Initially, rent was $3 per square foot, although rent has risen since then. After operating and maintenance expenses are covered, a surplus of funds is returned to the city's general funds.

Project Studios One, formerly a public school, P.S. 1, in Long Island City, Queens, New York, has been low rent studio, performance and exhibition space since 1976 under the guidance of The Institute for Art and Urban Resources, Inc. The fundamental objective was to recycle abandoned or underutilized urban resources, such as buildings and surplus materials, into work spaces and materials for artists. They secured a 20-year lease at $1,000 per year. Additional funding sources now provide some artists' honoraria, material fees, and publications. A dynamic mix of artists from around the world continue to seek to work and exhibit there.

The former Chickering Piano factory, now called *The Piano Craft Guild*, in Boston's South End was developed between 1971 and 1974 by for-profit developers for $21,000 per live/work unit, including developer's fees and acquisition costs. Its 174 units meet many artists' needs with no interior bearing walls, high ceilings (ten to twenty feet) and spaces averaging 100 sq. ft. The lobby serves as a gallery, and arts-related retail space is available. Low development costs were augmented by Massachusetts Housing Finance Agency financing and a rent subsidy making the units affordable to a range of low- and moderate- income artists with approximately 25 percent market rate units.

LACE: Los Angeles Contemporary Exhibitions is a nonprofit artist-initiated project that now houses performance space, a video screening room, a bookstore, exhibition space, and four live/work lofts for low-income artists. The building was a former car dealership which has been purchased by the group.

---

a large area often must be divided into smaller spaces.

Buildings that no longer can be used efficiently for their original purposes have proven to be wonderful for conversion to live/work and other arts uses. The arts have moved into former train depots, firehouses, schools, churches, factories, military bases, car dealerships, gymnasiums, movie theaters, and bowling alleys.

Cities are constantly being rebuilt. The recycling of structures for new, viable uses is common, especially when the structure is architecturally worthy of salvaging. Many of the structures artists have renovated are not historically noteworthy, but lent themselves well to artists' needs. In nearly all cities, vacant lots are also available for new "in-fill" construction. New construction sites allow you to assess a site on its own merits, assuming an affordable new building can be designed to meet your needs. Most artists, however, will look to buildings they can renovate (See box 3.2).

Torpedo Factory, Alexandria. Overhead view of studio in converted warehouse.

SOURCES OF INFORMATION ABOUT SITES

Ads and Personal Investigations

Numerous sources of information are available to aid your search for space. Check the classified ads in newspapers and periodicals; walk or drive around the desired location to spot posted signs; and tune in to the "artists' grapevine" by asking other artists where to look. A neighborhood organization or nonprofit developer can also help you to find the right building at the right price.

County/City Tax Assessors, Planning or Development Offices

County and city agencies are sometimes excellent sources of information about low-cost

Piano Craft Guild, Boston. Facade of former piano factory.

**Project Studios One (P.S. 1),
Long Island City. Facade of
former public school.**

**LACE: Los Angeles Contemporary Exhibitions, Los
Angeles. Facade of former car dealership.**

buildings. Planning departments can provide you with maps showing current or proposed land uses. They may also suggest properties or neighborhoods where the city would welcome redevelopment.

Most cities with abandoned properties have established formal or informal procedures to (1) inventory vacant or deteriorating structures; (2) hold sales when properties are tax delinquent; (3) provide incentives to upgrade qualified properties; (4) condemn properties that pose a hazard; and (5) demolish and clear unoccupied or hazardous structures. Property disposition takes place most actively in larger northeastern cities, where surplus properties exist in large numbers.

Properties in an area of high abandonment have more difficulty in securing mortgages or improvement loans. Before investing in such a property, check into your ability to secure the funds you will need for the full job of renovation. Many artists who began to upgrade abandoned areas have been successful; many others have suffered financial distress. Consider the current social and economic conditions within the neighborhood and whether the property was abandoned because of uneconomical costs of operation or renovation.

City agencies as well as lenders can sometimes answer questions about buildings that will become available through foreclosure proceedings. (See chapter 5 for more on the city's potential role in arts-related development projects.)

Real Estate Brokers and Agents

After looking over some locations, getting an idea of what is available, clarifying what you really want, need and can afford, you may want to find a real estate agent to work with you—if one has not already found you.

The real estate broker is a licensed agent

committed by state laws to bring the "highest and best use" or highest price for a property. As such, brokers traditionally represent the owner in their negotiations with you. A broker has a vested interest in achieving the highest possible purchase or lease price for a property because the broker's commission is based on a percentage of the lease or purchase price. Keep in mind, too, that if your space needs are small, the broker may limit the time he or she will work with you, because even if you successfully secure the space the broker's commission would be small.

In some states, legislation allows the broker to represent both parties in a transaction and to be compensated by both parties. This arrangement, known as dual agency, is illegal in many states unless the broker receives the written consent of all parties to the transaction.

Be direct with your agent. Discuss specific sites you have visited and areas that seem suitable. Anticipate providing information about your group's financial situation. Share your thinking about the type of ownership and financing you will need. An arts use may be especially attractive for properties that have had difficulty attracting tenants or buyers, and you may find the broker of great assistance in negotiating on your behalf.

ASSESSING THE BUILDING

Once your search has turned up one or more sites with the kind of potential you are looking for, you are ready for the next phase of evaluation. Is the site itself in the "right" place and at the "right" price? How can you determine whether the asking price for a building is a fair market price? How much will it cost to acquire and renovate?

CHECKING ZONING, BUILDING CODES AND ORDINANCES: IS IT THE RIGHT PLACE?

Most urban zoning laws divide the city into residential, commercial and industrial zones, defining what types of activities are permitted in each area. Certain types of art activities, such as glass blowing or welding, may be restricted to special zoning districts. Will your activities produce noise, heat or dust? Will you require the use of flammable or toxic materials? Will your activities involve large, bulky objects? Welding equipment? Kilns? Do you envision using some space for commercial sales? Will there be art classes, performances or galleries open to the public? All of the above uses are affected by zoning, building codes, parking and other requirements.

If you have any doubts about whether your building is in compliance with local occupancy codes, contact the city. Some municipalities provide an inspection service covering compliance with building and zoning codes for fire safety, health hazards and housing requirements. Knowing what the city will require will help you estimate renovation costs. (See chapter 4 for information about meeting the code requirements in a renovation.)

SURVEYING THE BUILDING AND SITE: IS IT THE RIGHT STRUCTURE?

Before you begin to negotiate for a particular property, you may wish to have a professional evaluation of the structure by an architect, structural engineer or contractor. But even in the looking stages, you can find out much by yourself with some simple techniques.

Wear old clothes and be prepared to get dirty. Your inspection of the building should take you from outside to inside and top to bottom. Bring along a checklist of criteria to be met, a list of questions and a notebook to record what you find. Among the basic tools you will need when surveying a building are a tape measure, flashlight, pocket knife and plumb line (a string with a weight attached will do).

Use the Building Evaluation Checklist in appendix 3.1 to help you keep track of observations as you do the following:

- assess degree of settling: the building should be "plumb" or at right angles to its foundation
- examine all masonry for signs of cracking or opening up
- examine roof and cornices for cracks, crumbling, damage or signs of leakage; note condition of chimneys, skylights, vents, etc.
- assess ease of access for materials and equipment through entries
- turn on all faucets, flush all toilets and look for corrosion and leakage
- have all systems turned on during your visit: heat, air conditioning, ventilation
- note type and amount, age and condition of electrical power (see chapter 4)
- note condition of floors, walls, ceilings, stairs, halls, windows, elevators
- note construction type, load-bearing capacity of floors
- note efficiency of building layout and stair locations
- determine building and zoning code requirements of your new use (see chapter 4)

Environmental Risks

When evaluating a building, you should ask the agent and the owner specifically about any known geological or industrial hazards affecting the building or the neighborhood. If the site is a

**Small commercial building, Minneapolis.
Converted to live/work space.**

former commercial or industrial property, check to see whether an environmental audit has been done or will be required by the city or the lenders. The costs of removing asbestos or other hazardous elements that may contaminate a property could make your plans financially unfeasible.

Soils

What are the unique features of the site? The type and condition of the soil affects the ability of the foundation to hold the building load above it. How much of the site is usable? Are there signs of soil erosion around the foundation or signs of standing water or drainage problems? Clean sand or gravel allows good drainage, but both are poor as topsoil for growing things. Most soils are a combination of silt and clay. Clay comes in many

degrees of elasticity; all types can swell up with moisture.

Foundations

There are various types of foundations; they all share the purpose of transferring the weight of the building to the ground and anchoring it. The foundation should raise the building above the moisture in the ground and provide a level surface to build on.

Check stone, masonry or brick foundations for loose bricks and mortar, settling, spalling and cracks. Concrete footings with concrete block walls are usually found on newer buildings. Look for cracks of 1/8 inch or more, settling and gaps between the footing and soil. If wooden plates, posts, studs or joists were used, check for rot or termites.

Exterior Walls, Entrances, Docks and Windows

With wood-frame, concrete, concrete block or metal buildings, the possible problems include bulges, missing material, sagging, cracking, poor vertical alignment, corrosion, pests and rot. Doors, loading docks and windows should also be checked for rot, corrosion, attachments, closure and breakage. Some defects, such as cracks in stucco or broken or missing material, may be cosmetic rather than structural.

A masonry (brick) building should have its veneer "tied" to the interior structure and not falling away. Look for deteriorating bricks and loose mortar. Replacing mortar—repointing/ tuck-pointing—can be expensive.

Roof

Ask questions about the roof's age and condition. If access is possible and if it is safe and not too steep, ask to go up on the roof. Check gutters and downspouts for corrosion and attachment to the building.

What type of roofing does the structure have? Asphalt shingles are good for 15 to 20 years. Look for worn, brittle or missing shingles. Tar and gravel built-up roofs last 15 to 30 years. The roof should not be spongy. Look for holes, cracks and bubbles. Wood shingles usually last up to 30 years. Look for missing shingles, warped shingles and rot. Copper, terne metal or aluminum often lasts more than 50 years. Look for signs of corrosion. Tile or slate lasts indefinitely. Check for broken or missing material.

Check for "ponding" if the roof is flat and for sagging if it is sloped. Inspect all vents and chimneys. Are they missing material or clogged? Fascia, eaves and decorative details should be checked for rotting, weathering and the degree to which they are level or plumb.

Interior

Start from the top floor and work your way down to the basement. Look for the same kinds of problems in the foundation on the inside as on the outside, such as deterioration, termites and signs of leaks or dampness. Observe the alignment and conditions of floors, walls, structural columns, ceilings, stairs and corridors throughout. Determine which walls are structural and load-bearing.

Check each floor by jumping on it to see if it is spongy. Next check visually, or with a marble and the plumb line, to determine if the floors are level and the walls are plumb. At some point you will want to take the dimensions of the spaces and sketch the floor plans. These will be useful for your rough estimates and for renovation plans.

Mechanical Systems

Evaluating mechanical systems is more difficult than appraising structural conditions. You should check them visually at least. You will need to know their condition and whether the systems have the capacity to meet your needs. The cost of professional help at this point is minimal compared with the costs of unanticipated major overhauls or replacement of existing systems.

Request an inspection by your local building or health department. Utility company representatives may also be able to evaluate the systems and suggest ways of saving energy.

Heating, ventilating and air conditioning (HVAC) systems should be tested to see how well they work. Check on operational efficiency and noise level by asking current tenants about their experiences, if possible. If major changes are planned in the layout of the building, the present locations may be unsuitable. Ask the seller to let you see records of the costs of operating the systems. An old system may no longer be efficient.

Plumbing systems should be checked for overall condition, adequacy of size and materials used. Test for leakage, corrosion and functionality of plumbing fixtures.

Check electrical systems from inside and outside the building. The location, amount and type of electrical service can be important considerations. Look for fraying wires and alterations to the system.

If there is an elevator, check its record of maintenance and inspections. Ask for an inspection by the building department, especially if the elevator has not been used recently.

Emergency systems, if present, should be in working order. Ask the owner about recent testing and any special features.

ESTABLISHING VALUE: IS IT THE RIGHT PRICE?

The building you think is "right" for you may have been sitting vacant for months or even years, and the owner may give you the deal of the

36

century. The same building may be on the edge of an area slated for new development, with property values skyrocketing overnight.

In the marketplace, value is relative. The fair market value is based upon what a buyer is willing to pay and a seller is willing to accept, given reasonable promotion of the property in the marketplace, with full disclosure of information about the property, and no abnormal pressure to conclude a transaction.

Standard Valuation Techniques

When analyzing the best use of a property, a real estate broker assesses such factors as potential market demand, environmental conditions, future development potential of the area and the competition of similar properties in the area. The broker may choose one or more valuation methods to reach a decision about the property's value. Once this analysis is done, the broker recommends a sales price to the seller.

After conditions for purchase are agreed to, an appraisal is sought. An appraiser prepares a report that reconciles the information from all methods of valuation and states an estimate of the fair market value of the property. The appraisal provides lenders with an objective view of the property's value. Based on the appraiser's judgment of the fair market value or the income available for debt service, the lender will determine the amount of the loan to make for the appraised property. All loan packages include an appraisal, although appraisals may also be prepared for reasons other than financing a sale. (See chapter 6 for more on financing.)

Three primary approaches are used for real estate valuation or appraisal: the market approach, the cost approach and the income approach. Because a property's value is critical to the decisions made by the seller, the buyer, the

investor and the lender when negotiating about a property, it may help to know about the process.

MARKET APPROACH. The market approach compares prices of three to five similar properties that have sold recently as a guide to estimating the value of the property for sale. These properties are called "comps." Data compared include the date of sale, sales price, financing terms, location of the property and a description of each property's physical characteristics. Adjustments are made—that is, values are added or subtracted—to the sales price of each comp, depending on whether it lacks a feature of the subject property or has a feature that the subject property lacks. The result is the adjusted market price. This is the dollar value of each comparable sale after it has gone through an adjustment process to make it the same as the subject property. The comps' prices are then averaged or correlated to determine the fair market value of the subject property.

COST APPROACH. The cost approach starts with the cost of a similar parcel of vacant

3.3 THE COST APPROACH TO EVALUATING PROPERTY

Estimated cost of "vacant" land		$ 30,000
Estimated cost of new construction for a similar building	$250,000	
Less depreciation	- 70,000	
	$180,000	
Indicated value of building		+180,000
Appraised property value		$210,000

land, then adds the projected cost of new construction for a similar building—lumber, concrete, plumbing, wiring, fees and wages, etc.—at today's costs. A depreciation factor is then subtracted (see box 3.3).

INCOME APPROACH. The income approach takes three factors into account: (1) how much income the property will generate, (2) how long it will last and at what cost, and (3) the rate of return on the amount of investment that can be paid to investors and how that rate compares with other investment opportunities. The future income stream is "capitalized" or converted to a current value of net income that would be available to an investor.

Buyer's Valuation Process

Regardless of the valuation technique used to set a price for the building, as a buyer your task is to determine at what price the building does or does not work for you.

Annual Property Operating Data

If the property is listed on a Multiple Listing Service (MLS), the broker will provide you with a summary of the property's key features: dimensions, amenities, zoning, taxes and other valuable information.

Request a copy of the owner's Annual Operating Statement or Annual Property Operating Data (APOD) for specific information that will help you prepare an estimate of your total costs.

Preparing a Preliminary Budget

With the information you have gathered about the building's condition, annual operating data, asking price and preferred financing terms, you are ready to start putting your plans on paper.

An essential first step in your evaluation is preparing a preliminary budget of the first year's expenses for acquisition, renovation and operating costs. If you plan to lease space to others, you need to calculate the likely income from leasing the space, based on the rentable square footage and what your members can afford. After subtracting your expenses from your income, you will see whether changes are necessary to ensure that the project can succeed financially.

If you are buying a building for which you or your group can afford the rent or qualify for a standard mortgage or a contract for deed, your monthly payment can be estimated relatively quickly. Then, you need only decide whether the price is reasonable and the payment affordable.

If you are buying the building as an investment to lease to other arts uses or if other investors are needed to help you finance the project, you should employ the income approach, which will serve best as a way of evaluating the project as a business investment. The preliminary budget exercise, which can be prepared by an accountant, will include a calculation of the first year's tax benefits for investors, if applicable.

Testing project feasibility and reworking plans until the project is feasible are explored more fully in later chapters.

"Conversions such as ours are not, can not, and really should not be viewed as conventional housing. What we need is a policy which addresses the unique needs and problems of live/work space in a flexible manner, and provides a mechanism to facilitate dialogue between each live/work complex and the various city agencies involved in their fate."

Rick Parcurar
Former Executive Director
Project Artaud, San Francisco, California

4

Zoning and Building Codes

Zoning and building codes determine *what* can be built and *where* it can be located. In most cities, building codes pose the more difficult hurdle of the two for artists, because of the expense of meeting them. However, zoning is a key issue to start with, especially if you seek ownership or long-term lease control of the space. Ignoring zoning regulations risks both your time and money.

Zoning is a governmental system of land use control that (1) divides residential from professional uses (business or commercial, and manufacturing or industrial zones); (2) promotes uniformity, encourages compatible uses and protects existing land users from the effects of "undesirable" uses, giving each zone specific building restrictions and requirements; and (3) promotes a city's plans and policies for growth and development. Zoning also limits the number of districts in which nonunion labor or "sweat equity" is allowed. It is sometimes slow to respond to the changing uses of urban space.

Studios at 700, Minneapolis.
Contractor installing
Sheetrock to meet building
code specifications.

WHY IS ZONING AN ISSUE?

In many cities artists and other residents are prohibited by ordinance from living in manufacturing and commercial districts. Artists also face zoning codes that prohibit what may be considered manufacturing activity in residential districts. Because of the conflict between city regulations and the often undefined legal status of artists' uses, building owners and lenders often hesitate to participate in projects proposed for artists.

Because zoning ordinances were passed when cities were young, difficulties arise when changes in uses occur without corresponding changes in regulations. For example, since the 1950s many industries have moved from within city limits to locations providing greater operating

4.1   A VARIANCE REQUEST DENIED

In a 1980 request for a zoning variance to allow the conversion of a loft building in the SoHo area of New York City, one business and building owner wrote to the Board of Standards and Appeals:

Our creditor banks have strongly urged that we relocate our manufacturing operation in a more efficient plant . . . . our building contains no physical attributes which are beneficial to our manufacturing operation. We base this statement on 35 years of continually increasing difficulties. . . .it has been impossible to attract any manufacturing tenants because of the physical attributes of the building. . . .the building is old and obsolete. Unless a variance of the Zoning Resolution is granted, it will have to be abandoned since it is no longer viable or desirable for regular M-1 use. . . . this situation was not created by the owner but arises only when the Zoning Resolution as it is now written is applied to this building.

The zoning variance was not approved for a live/work conversion because of the zoning restriction that limited conversion of buildings with frontage on Broadway to a lot coverage not exceeding 3,600 square feet. The building was later developed for office and exhibition space.

convenience. This has left vacant warehouses, factories, storefronts and other structures. These structures, though often suitable for alternative uses, are limited by old zoning code requirements.

In the case of artists' conversions for combined living and working uses of former commercial spaces, a fundamental difficulty arises from the long-established division between residential and professional zones, and their different codes of safety and building compliance.

Early interpretations of the building code for the conversion of warehouse or factory lofts to residential use were so stringent and economically prohibitive as to deter any would-be landlord or artist from bringing loft buildings up to code. It was an even greater deterrent if the zoning would not allow a residential conversion. (See box 4.1.) Such circumstances left artists at risk for the time and money invested in making their own units livable.

THE RIGHT ZONE FOR YOUR ACTIVITY

Is the building you have located in a residential, commercial, industrial or mixed-use zone? Consider the activities that will go on in the building. Does the building seem suitable, both from your own point of view and the city inspectors'? Certain types of art activities, such as glass blowing or welding, may be restricted to special zoning districts. If your medium falls into this category, check with the city zoning office before you begin looking for a space.

Will your activities produce noise, heat or dust? Will they require the use of flammable or toxic materials? Do you have large, bulky objects, welding equipment or kilns? Do you envision using part of the space for commercial sales? Will there be art classes or galleries open to the public? The inclusion of activities open to the public, such as galleries or classes, can affect zoning, building code, parking and other requirements.

HOME OCCUPATION STATUS AND THE INTERNAL REVENUE SERVICE

Many artists have legitimately worked out of their homes without a conflict with zoning. This is especially true if the art work does not produce a profit and can be considered for income purposes a "hobby." However, if you claim being an artist as your chief occupation while working from your home, that use would be considered illegal in many cities.

In some cities, including Boston, San Francisco, Seattle, and Tucson, live/work space may be permitted in residentially zoned areas if that use meets the requirements of a "home occupation." Some key elements of a home occupation are described below. However, you should check with your city for a complete definition applicable to your situation.

Definition of Home Occupation

A home occupation is an occupation that is carried on in a dwelling by its resident and that does not involve the conduct of retail, auto repair, commercial food service or manufacturing business. The occupation is considered incidental and secondary to the use of the dwelling for dwelling purposes and does not change the character of the dwelling. Home occupations must be compatible with other residential uses and maintain the character of residential neighborhoods.

Home occupations are often defined to include professional offices, home beauty shops, home crafts and occupations that by custom are considered as a use accessory to a dwelling. Home occupations must generally be conducted entirely within the dwelling and by no more than two persons, one of whom must reside within the dwelling. Services are generally provided to no more than one customer at a time.

Requirements for meeting the home occupation status may include no allowance for structural alterations or enlargements for the purpose of conducting the home occupation. Additionally, no detriments to the residential character of the neighborhood are allowed—for example, the emission of noise, odor, smoke, dust, gas, heat, glare, vibration, electrical interference, traffic congestion or any other annoyance resulting from the home occupation. Products or materials must usually be stored indoors. Many artists cannot meet the above definition because of the nature of their work or their equipment, although for those who can, their space needs can be easily resolved.

Internal Revenue Service Office-in-the-Home Deductions

To deduct office-in-the-home expenses, you must show a net profit of income from your art/business at the end of the tax year—before you deduct the allowable percentage of your mortgage, taxes or utilities. If you are renting space, you are limited to a percentage of the utilities and rent you pay. You cannot deduct as a business expense any amount greater than what you have earned in gross income.

If you do not have a profit and you claim home-office expenses, you may have to undergo an audit. If you do show a profit, you need to assess whether you would benefit more from claiming your state's homeowner or renter's rebate on property tax than from claiming the federal government's office-in-the-home deduc-

tion. If you are in a low tax bracket, you may find that the property tax rebate is more advantageous.

If you claim office-in-the-home deductions, you must be able to define clearly the square footage of space that is used for business use only. Even if you simply walk through an area to get to another living area, the area cannot be considered "business use only." Therefore, it is not allowable.

These issues may be important to your design considerations when you plan your space. Before claiming this deduction, you should also consider the length of time you expect to live in your space, because of the complications should you sell it. Check with the IRS and your accountant for advice on whether to claim this deduction.

ZONING CHANGES AND AMENDMENTS

Codes can be changed by amendments, and the way codes are applied can be changed by variances. All these processes, however, may add months to the completion of a project. Therefore, if at all possible, you should try to work within existing codes.

Zoning laws can be amended or struck down if they can be proved—usually through legal proceedings—to be unclear; discriminatory; unreasonable; not for the protection of the public health, safety, and general welfare; or not applied to all property in a similar manner.

Variances allow an individual property to deviate somewhat from zoning code requirements. Variances do not involve a zoning change. They can be granted when compliance with a specific requirement of the zoning district would not allow the establishment of a permitted use in

CONCEPT PLAN REVIEW

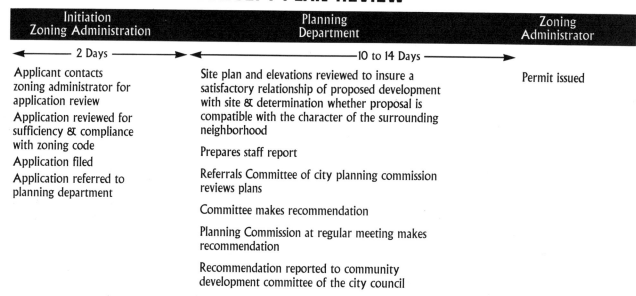

Initiation Zoning Administration	Planning Department	Zoning Administrator
◄──── 2 Days ────►	◄────────── 10 to 14 Days ──────────►	
Applicant contacts zoning administrator for application review	Site plan and elevations reviewed to insure a satisfactory relationship of proposed development with site & determination whether proposal is compatible with the character of the surrounding neighborhood	Permit issued
Application reviewed for sufficiency & compliance with zoning code	Prepares staff report	
Application filed	Referrals Committee of city planning commission reviews plans	
Application referred to planning department	Committee makes recommendation	
	Planning Commission at regular meeting makes recommendation	
	Recommendation reported to community development committee of the city council	

the district. The variance must be consistent with the general objectives of the zoning applied to the district.

Appeals for variances or special exceptions usually entail a public hearing at which owners and occupants of adjoining properties are invited to comment. If the variance is approved, a permit is issued by the Director or Superintendent of Buildings. Renewal of the permit may be required after a specified time.

Existing uses or structures located in a district in which they are not permitted are termed "nonconforming." If these uses or structures existed legally before a change in zoning, they are considered "legal nonconforming" and may be informally referred to as "grandfathered." Grandfather clauses allow continued use of current

mechanical systems only if those systems meet current minimum standards of the local maintenance code. Changes of use or alterations of nonconforming structures usually need the approval of the zoning office. In some instances they may require the approval of public review and planning commissions.

You can find out about specific applications of zoning and code regulations by working directly with your city's zoning and inspections departments. Find out first if residential and work uses are permitted in the zone. Then determine what changes can be made to the building within the existing regulations. Additional assistance, if needed, may be sought from an architect, attorney or your local office of Volunteer Lawyers for the Arts. (See figures 1, 2, 3, 4 and 5.)

REZONING PROCEDURE

Applicant	Zoning Administrator		Planning Department
◄──── No Time-Line Variable ────►	◄──────────── 15 to 20 Days ────────────►		
Applies for rezoning at office of zoning administration	Sends consent petitions to city attorney for review for compliance to city-state requirements	Transmits files to planning department	Pre-trial hearing meeting with zoning administration
Obtains certified list of owners of property within 100 ft of site of proposed rezoning	Makes map of area within 350 ft of site and prepares data	Prepares and mails notice of public hearings to property owners within 350 ft 10 days prior to hearing	Reviews application. Collects any needed support data.
	Applicant photographs area		Staff recommendation prepared
Obtains consent of two-thirds of property owners within 100 ft	After city attorney approves petition, files application with city clerk	Sends posters to applicant for posting on subject property 10 days prior to hearing	Public hearing held by city planning commission (Wednesday before first city council meeting of each month. Check on times.)
Obtains certified list of owners of property within 350 ft of site	Sends notice of hearing to city clerk for publication in finance and commerce 15 days prior to public hearing by planning commission		

ZONING OPTION FLOW CHART

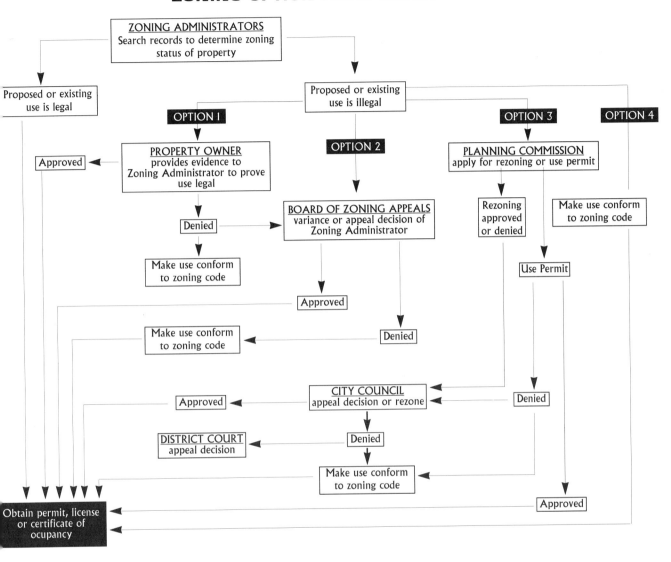

Plannning Dept (cont)	Zoning Administrator	City Council	Mayor	City Clerk	Zoning Administration
10 - 14 days usually ◀——6 Days——▶		◀—10 Days—▶	5 Days	1 + days	*recorded on zoning maps
City planning commission makes recommendation	Sends notice of zoning and planning committee meeing to property owners within 350 ft	Zoning and planning committee holds hearing	Signature	Publication in finance and commerce 8 days after council meeting	
Recommendation transmitted to city clerk		Makes recommendation to city council			
		City council acts			

*Average time from starting process to end- 10 to 12 weeks

BUILDING AND SITE PLAN REVIEW

44

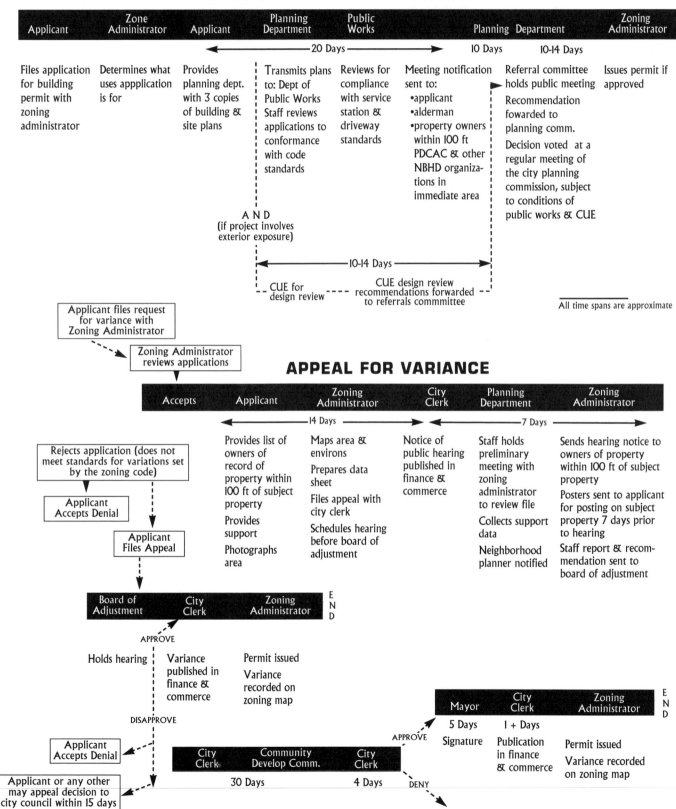

Applicant	Zone Administrator	Applicant	Planning Department	Public Works		Planning Department	Zoning Administrator
			← 20 Days →		10 Days	10-14 Days	
Files application for building permit with zoning administrator	Determines what uses appplication is for	Provides planning dept. with 3 copies of building & site plans	Transmits plans to: Dept of Public Works Staff reviews applications to conformance with code standards	Reviews for compliance with service station & driveway standards	Meeting notification sent to: •applicant •alderman •property owners within 100 ft PDCAC & other NBHD organizations in immediate area	Referral committee holds public meeting Recommendation fowarded to planning comm. Decision voted at a regular meeting of the city planning commission, subject to conditions of public works & CUE	Issues permit if approved

A N D
(if project involves exterior exposure)

← 10-14 Days →

CUE for design review   CUE design review recommendations forwarded to referrals commmittee

All time spans are approximate

Applicant files request for variance with Zoning Administrator

Zoning Administrator reviews applications

APPEAL FOR VARIANCE

Accepts	Applicant	Zoning Administrator	City Clerk	Planning Department	Zoning Administrator
	← 14 Days →			← 7 Days →	
	Provides list of owners of record of property within 100 ft of subject property Provides support Photographs area	Maps area & environs Prepares data sheet Files appeal with city clerk Schedules hearing before board of adjustment	Notice of public hearing published in finance & commerce	Staff holds preliminary meeting with zoning administrator to review file Collects support data Neighborhood planner notified	Sends hearing notice to owners of property within 100 ft of subject property Posters sent to applicant for posting on subject property 7 days prior to hearing Staff report & recommendation sent to board of adjustment

Rejects application (does not meet standards for variations set by the zoning code)

Applicant Accepts Denial

Applicant Files Appeal

Board of Adjustment	City Clerk	Zoning Administrator

E N D

APPROVE

Holds hearing | Variance published in finance & commerce | Permit issued Variance recorded on zoning map

DISAPPROVE

Applicant Accepts Denial

City Clerk	Community Develop Comm.	City Clerk
	30 Days	4 Days

Applicant or any other may appeal decision to city council within 15 days

APPROVE

	Mayor	City Clerk	Zoning Administrator
	5 Days	1 + Days	
	Signature	Publication in finance & commerce	Permit issued Variance recorded on zoning map

E N D

DENY

45

GENERAL BUILDING CODE INFORMATION

Once zoning regulations have been met, most artist-pioneers have found that meeting building and fire safety codes presents an even more challenging hurdle to creating legal live/work spaces. Building codes set forth the responsibilities of building owners and occupants; establish licensing or bonding requirements; and provide for code administration, enforcement and penalties. State and local governments across the country have enacted such codes to protect the public's health, safety and welfare against unreliable construction practices.

The building code establishes minimum standards for the following:

■ acceptable materials and construction methods

■ structural loads and stresses (earthquake code in some states)

■ size and location of rooms

■ windows and ventilation

■ lighting and other electrical installations

■ plumbing, heating, appliances and equipment

■ fire ratings, separations and protection devices

■ number, width and length of hallways, stair towers and exits, etc.

Any changes in an older building must comply with current building codes. If a building is converted into a new, more restrictive use (for example, residential), it must comply with the codes for that new use. Codes written for new construction, however, often lose whatever clarity they may have when reinterpreted for renovation. Their application often becomes difficult and subjective. In such a situation, the emphasis is generally on complying with the intent of the code.

For a live/work space conversion, confusion sometimes arises over which code—residential, commercial or manufacturing—or which combination of codes should apply. Commercial and industrial codes are usually inadequate to protect residents' health and safety; residential codes may be impossible to meet in an old warehouse—or the cost of doing so may be prohibitive. Unless your city has prepared policies that specifically address live/work space conversions, you will be working with inspectors who must interpret for renovation projects the same strict rules that apply to new construction. You may find it helpful to review the language developed by San Francisco for such conversions, summarized in chapter 5 (see box 5.5), in negotiating variances or "equivalencies" for your project.

BUILDING CODE COMPLIANCE

"If there is a law in the one code that says you must do it . . . there is a law in another code that says you can't."

Anonymous Chicago live/work space renovator;
Pioneering in the Urban Wilderness

Your ultimate objective is to obtain a Certificate of Occupancy ("C of O") or a Certificate of Code Compliance. The required certificate will be issued after the inspections department has made its final inspection and found that the work done complies with code requirements. Without this certificate, the building cannot be legally occupied. Failure to comply with code requirements may be cause for eviction, particularly in a long lease arrangement.

Typical building code requirements are summarized in the next few pages. Before you rent space or purchase a building, review these requirements to determine whether a building already complies or to assess how much work will be required to bring a building into compliance. To gain approval for a residential use of a commercial/manufacturing building, certain aspects of the whole building must be in compliance. Such requirements are the basis for developing or

Lowertown Lofts, St. Paul. Live/work space.

46

rehabilitating a number of units in a building at a time, to justify the expense of "common area" improvements, such as adding a fire-rated stair tower to meet exit requirements.

It is possible to provide only general information here. You and your architect and development consultant will need to take a close look at the specific requirements applicable to the building you have selected. Either you or your architect should ask a field inspector at your municipal building code office to visit the site of your proposed project and to inform you of the requirements. Meeting the code requirements in an affordable way may depend upon your preliminary planning and upon how the inspector interprets the code.

Working with the Inspections Department

The inspections department appreciates being approached early in the planning process.

Likewise, knowing what the city requires will help you to assess what the renovation may cost. A field inspector will look at the space before you prepare a floor plan to provide preliminary information about your design ideas. Your design solution will later be translated into detailed architectural plans and written specifications. Once you are confident that your plan meets the city's requirements, it is time to seek a plan review and apply for a construction permit.

Plan Review

Before a building permit is granted, the design of a new or renovated structure (or any part of the structure) must meet building code requirements. At least two copies of floor plans and construction drawings must be submitted to the plan review office at the inspections department.

The completed design plan should indicate how development plans will meet the intent of the building code requirements. The plan reviewer will contact your field inspector if there is a question about some aspect of your design solution. They will go over the plan with you and indicate any problems.

Once the plans have been approved by the plan reviewer, a dated stamp will be marked on the plan and a copy placed on file with the inspections department. A copy should be given to you. The inspections department staff person will fill out a permit application which refers to the plan, the work to be performed and the fees to be paid.

In many cities, you will not need an appointment to meet with a plan reviewer, although you may wait indefinitely until one is available to meet with you. If your project is large or requires an equivalence approval, you should plan to set up a formal meeting with the plan reviewer. In some cases, you may ask to have other key officials present in anticipation of negotiating an equivalence request.

Get It in Writing

It is important to document all discussions and agreements reached with building officials. Sometimes staff change. Also, people remember agreements differently. If there are to be changes from what you thought was agreed upon, it will save you time and trouble in the long run to uncover these differences early on.

The approved plan will provide the best documentation for agreements. Still, it is advisable to send a letter restating any other agreements made. Note the date of the meeting or phone call, what was discussed and who was present. Begin the letter with something like: "It is my understanding, from our meeting of (date), that the following is acceptable. . . ." Conclude the letter with a statement like the following: "I will presume that this is a fair and accurate statement of our conversation unless I hear from you otherwise." Include your address and a telephone

number where you can be reached during the day. Keep a copy of the letter for your files.

Call the official you met with within a couple of days to confirm that your letter was received and that the changes and agreements reached as outlined in your letter were indeed acceptable.

Fees and Time Limits

The fees to be paid once your plan is approved include a Building Permit Fee, Plan Checking Fee and possible other local fees, such as a Sewer Access Charge (SAC). The building permit fee is based on the value of the work to be completed. Value includes the cost of labor that may be a "sweat equity" contribution to the project. The fees are so much per hundred or thousand dollar interval. Plan checking fees, which are assessed by local formulas, cover the time spent by the inspections office reviewing plans.

The fees must be paid before the building permit is issued. If no permit is issued, the application for a permit typically expires 120 days after the date of the application. If no work is started, the permit may expire 180 days after the date of issuance. The applicant may request an extension by a written request to the building inspections office showing that circumstances beyond the control of the applicant prevented work from starting. Again, check your local policies.

Your Continuing Relationship with the Inspections Department

Your relationship with the inspections department continues after your building permit has been approved and paid for. If you are the permit holder, during construction you must notify appropriate field inspectors when each stage of work is ready for their approval. Required

48

inspections include (1) footings in new building construction; (2) exterior and interior framing of walls; (3) frame inspection after framing, fire blocking, vents and pipes are complete; (4) wallboard inspection before the joints and fasteners are taped and finished; and (5) energy requirements for insulation. A rule of thumb is to have the work inspected before you cover it up.

The inspectors may, at their discretion, withhold approval and require that certain tasks be redone.

Your permit has to be posted in a conspicuous place so that the inspector can examine it and make entries regarding the inspection of work. If no permit is posted, an inspector who discovers the renovation project may issue a Cease Work Order, which may result in a fine and the requirement to get an approved plan and permit. Inspectors tend to be less cooperative at this stage than if approached at the outset of the project.

Contractors

In some cases general construction may be done by anyone. However, building officials are likely to require that any electric, plumbing, heating or ventilation contractor you hire is licensed. If a contractor is to be hired, the contractor may take out the permit as defined in the contract. During the course of construction, the contractor will call out inspectors to check and verify that the work meets the code as it is completed.

As part of your preliminary planning, you should check with the building inspections department in your area or ask your field inspector what requirements exist. (See chapter 10 for more on the construction process.)

Final Inspection

A final inspection is made after the work is completed and the building is ready for occupan-

Coldside Building, Minneapolis. Enclosing steel posts with Sheetrock to meet code requirements in former warehouse.

4.2 COMPLYING WITH BUILDING CODES

1. Review general building code requirements. Consult your city inspector, an architect or your contractor for information if necessary.

2. Conceptualize improvements to be made.

3. Request a preliminary site visit from the field inspector (usually done by the one who will prepare the plans).

4. Prepare or have prepared a scale floor plan and construction documents to indicate proposed improvements. Detailed specifications show the location and types of changes; a narrative describes the materials and assemblies.

5. Submit plans for approval to inspections department plan reviewer.

IF YOUR PLAN IS *NOT* APPROVED—

Revise and resubmit it.

IF YOUR PLAN *IS* APPROVED—

1. Make application for a building permit.

2. Pay permit fees.

3. Start construction.

4. Request preliminary inspections (framing, wallboard, etc.).

5. Complete work.

6. Request final inspection.

7. Post the Certificate of Occupancy.

cy. If the final inspection determines that your project complies with the building code, the building official will issue a Certificate of Occupancy, which must be posted in a conspicuous place and removed only by the building official. (See box 4.2.)

UNDERSTANDING THE "SYSTEM"

With all the jokes and stories about payoffs and corruption in inspections departments of major cities, one might assume that payoffs are more common than they are. Most payoff stories are related to developers and architects trying to push a project through quickly or attempting to avoid costly delays from revisions to the plans. Although some sweat-equity renovators have used payoffs to avoid confrontation on their renovation plans, it is generally unnecessary and certainly illegal.

Sweat-equity renovators found working without a permit have been pressured by both construction unions and the inspections department. If your project is large or involves public funds, following the straight and narrow path will protect you from unnecessary repercussions. If the expense of your renovation plans is a problem, you can file permits for portions of the required work, a little at a time. Paying for several permits may ease your cash flow problem, although the overall cost of permit fees will tend to be higher, because there are higher priced fee scales on the lower cost projects.

Some artists have expressed concern that zoning and building codes so unclear as to foster interpretations are unfair and warrant rewriting. They place a burden on those attempting to follow the letter of the law. Renovators of live/work space sometimes reframe the terminology, indulging in "creative semantics" to demonstrate to officials that the intent of the code was being met.

However, using such language to disguise the truth seldom works, and inspectors may or may not have a sense of humor about it.

Generally, all that is required for establishing a cooperative working relationship is for you to discuss your project and any proposed solutions to problems with the inspections department voluntarily.

GENERAL RESIDENTIAL REQUIREMENTS

Because building codes were designed for residential or commercial uses, but not for multiple uses within one unit, the codes are typically

Designers' Space, Inc., Austin. Studio, gallery, rehearsal and performance spaces.

not explicit. Codes are often applied in anticipation of the "highest use" a unit will receive. Therefore, residential use requirements may be required of the entire unit. Complying with these fully may be costly.

The following is a general guide to some residential code requirements. Always seek specific information for your own community before obtaining a building.

1. There must be fire separation between occupancies. Hourly fire-resistive ratings of materials/assemblies are used. One acceptable combination is 5/8-inch Sheetrock and metal studs.

2. There must be 2 enclosed fire-rated exits from occupied space above the ground floor to the exterior of the building. (New York City has accepted the presence of a sprinkler system as an alternative to a second exit.)

3. Maximum travel distance, the spacing of exits, and dead-end corridors are all carefully regulated. For fire code, stairways and corridors must have exit signs and be maintained free of storage or trash after occupancy.

4. Public corridors must be at least 44 inches wide; and all unit entry doors serving such corridors must be at least 36 inches wide. Corridor doors must be at least 20-minute fire-rated and have self-closing devices. In your layout of spaces on the floor, remember to plan for the movement of large materials, equipment and artwork. Wider halls and double doors are valuable amenities.

5. Stair width is regulated by occupant load, which is determined by the size of the building. In buildings with an occupant load of more than 50 people, stairways must generally be at least 44 inches wide.

Studios at 700. Studio with excellent natural light source.

6. There must be sound control as well as fire separation (see item 1 above) between all dwelling units. Equivalencies have been allowed in some conversions in which the depth of the floorboards has been determined to meet the requirements. Leveling cement over wood floors is frequently recommended to meet both requirements.

7. All dwelling units must have a separate bathroom with a toilet, lavatory and a bath: either a tub or shower. Each living space must also have a kitchen with a kitchen sink. Exceptions may be made for rooming or boarding house type living. Toilet facilities must be located in a clear space not less than 30 inches wide and not less than 24 inches in front of toilet stools.

8. The ceiling must be at least 7 feet 6 inches high in habitable rooms, and 7 feet high in other areas. (San Francisco accepts 6 feet 6 inches under a mezzanine up to one-third of the size of the studio.)

9. All habitable rooms must have ventilation. Habitable rooms are defined as enclosed floor space intended for living, sleeping, cooking or eating purposes, excluding storage and stairways, etc. Bathrooms and laundry rooms, although not considered habitable rooms for purposes of requiring natural light, do require mechanical ventilation.

10. All habitable rooms must have a natural light source, either windows or skylights. The light source must equal at least 8-10 percent of the floor area of the room (the percentage varying from city to

52

117 North Washington, Minneapolis. Live/work space with skylights.

city)—one-half of which must be operable for ventilation. Live/work units of large square footage may find this requirement excessive. One solution is to designate part of the unit as windowless storage space.

11. There must be an electrical outlet every 10-12 feet (the distance varying from city to city). There must be an outlet no more than 6 feet from any passageway to limit the use of extension cords. Each bathroom must have a wall receptacle (ground fault circuit) adjacent to the washbasin. There must be one switch-controlled lighting outlet in each habitable room, including the bathroom and the kitchen.

12. Each dwelling unit requires its own electric meter and service (generally, 100-amp, single-phase service, although other solutions have been successfully negotiated).

13. All habitable rooms must have heating plant facilities capable of heating them to 68°F at a distance of 36 inches above the floor and 3 feet from the outside wall at all times. (This is a requirement in northern cities only.)

14. Smoke detectors are generally required, particularly in or adjacent to sleeping areas. Sprinkler systems, if required, must be operative and well maintained to meet fire code.

53

ELECTRICAL AND PLUMBING REQUIREMENTS

Most cities require licensed contractors to be responsible for electrical, plumbing, heating or other mechanical work in both residential and commercial buildings. Homeowner permits are allowed only on owner-occupied, single-family detached dwellings. For improvements in a warehouse conversion or most other live/work space projects, a licensed contractor must usually obtain the permit and perform the installation or repair.

Electrical and plumbing work is usually needed in all live/work space renovations as part of code-required improvements. Planning is always the first step. You can save time, money and annoyance by first taking a careful look at what needs have to be met, what materials have to be used and what obstacles might arise. Such planning will prepare you for working effectively with your plumber and electrician. Think through the design requirements of your activities. An architect helping to plan your overall unit(s) can specify requirements and fixtures to the contractor on your behalf. Your specifications for the design can influence the cost and effectiveness of the result. As in working with all contractors, you should be as clear as possible about your priorities and expectations. The more you are aware of, the less likely the contractor is to create unnecessary expense in solving your problem.

MEETING ELECTRICAL NEEDS

Minor electrical improvements can sometimes be handled by knowledgeable artists, driven by economic necessity. The basic concepts are easily managed, and most artists already possess adequate tools for the job. Mistakes, however, may cause anything from minor shocks to unexpected electrical fires and to untimely deaths. Clearly, doing even minor electrical work

is not a task to take on casually. To speed the work of an electrician and save money in a single-unit project, artists have sometimes undertaken preparatory work, such as predrilling holes. At a minimum, the areas to be worked on should be cleared for easy access. In a multiunit project, concern for safety should override concern for cost savings.

You may find the information in box 4.3 useful for identifying the amount of electrical service that is available and for evaluating the improvements needed to the building or house you may renovate. Many states use the National Electrical Code and may add or delete portions by amendment from time to time. The Federal Housing Administration (FHA) and the Veterans Administration (VA) use the same code for mortgage commitment inspections.

MEETING PLUMBING NEEDS

Because plumbing skills and tools are so specialized, it is the task least likely to be taken on, even by committed do-it-yourselfers. Again, plumbing codes require that a licensed plumbing contractor be responsible for plumbing work in both residential and commercial buildings.

Most warehouse spaces are unlikely to have much plumbing to alter. What is there may need to be replaced to meet the new uses. The primary source of cost savings is the grouping of fixtures closest to the plumbing waste stack, including "back-to-back" repeated design arrangements in multiunit projects.

It can be financially prohibitive to plan for gas appliances if the building does not already have gas lines to the building. Again, inform your architect, if you are working with one, of the features you or your group desire and the cost limitations. Evaluate the design before plans are submitted for city plan review or to the plumber.

If you are able to get a homeowner's permit, get a book about plumbing and plan the design

4.3 ELECTRICAL REQUIREMENTS

Basic electrical requirements and information include the following:

Electrical Service

1. **30 Amp Service (115 volts)**
   a. Has two wires from the service pole to house.
   b. Was installed from approximately 1914 through the late 1930s.
   c. Was used to replace gas lights with electric lights.
   d. Can handle only a limited amount of lighting and minor appliances safely.
   e. Usually overfused and illegally altered.
   f. Usually (originally) only one or two circuits.
   g. 30 amp existing service—single family or duplex structure: alterations and additions are not permitted.

2. **60 Amp Service (115/230 volts—3 wire drop)**
   a. Service panel with main pull-out disconnect and cartridge fuses, and pull-out disconnect with cartridges for electric range, etc.
   b. Usually with four fuses below for house circuits.
   c. Usually grounded to water pipes.
   d. Usually have branch panels with extra fuses.
   e. 60 amp service: if the existing service is not overloaded by extensive alterations and if not more than one of four major electrical appliances is included, minor additions can be allowed. Major appliances are 220V electrical range, 220V electric clothes dryer, electric water heater, central-type air conditioner.

3. **100 Amp Service (115/230 volts—3 wire drop)**
   a. Usually installed with circuit breaker panel (now).
   b. Will be more than adequate for most electrical loads.
   c. If a new service is to be installed, it must be a minimum of 100 amps for a single dwelling. Each dwelling unit within a building being constructed or renovated for residential uses must have its own 100 amp service.

4. **Commercial and Warehouse Building Electrical Service**
   a. The amount of service is determined by the sizes and gauges of the wires entering the building in the service entrance pipe. The wires are carried by conduit into a meter service panel. The main disconnect, if properly installed, will have a notification label describing the amount of service to the building (for example, 100 amp, 200 amp). Old storage buildings, especially those with direct current (DC), will require new service brought from the source of power in the basement.
   b. Additionally, commercial buildings are allowed to "tap off" the main service for up to six additional service panels by what is called the "6 Disconnect Rule." Therefore, you cannot simply add up the amperage of each service panel you locate to arrive at the total amperage.
   c. Allow your field inspector and/or your electrician to determine what further service must be brought to the building before you buy or lease if you plan to renovate for code-compliant living/ working use.

Electric Wire

1. **Knob and Tube** (early 1900s to 1930)
   a. Glass knobs for surface attachment of wires to framing members.
   b. Glass tubes through which wires pass through the joist or stud.
   c. May still be adequate if not illegally altered or overloaded. Old knob and tubing wiring in basement or attic that has not been illegally altered, cannot be ordered removed. Alterations or additions cannot be made, however; the system must be upgraded.

2. **BX Cable** (1930 to present)
   a. Also known as armored cable.
   b. Used mostly for concealed wiring in walls and ceilings.

3. **E.M.T. Conduit** (1932 to present)
    a. Electric metallic tubing—used as raceways to carry conductors (wires) with proper connectors and metal boxes.
    b. An excellent grounded system.

4. **Nonmetallic Cable** (1943 to 1947) (During metal shortage)
    Woven cloth or rubber outer protection without ground wire. Used in some cities. Not legally used in others.

5. **Greenfield** (1947 to present)
    a. Also known as flexible metal conduit.
    b. Used to carry conductors (wires).
    c. With proper metal connector and boxes—an excellent grounded system.

6. **Romex** (1972 to present)
    a. Also known as nonmetallic sheathed cable.
    b. Has grounding wire within.

Fixtures and Receptacles

1. **Hanging Light Fixtures**
    a. All hanging fixtures with frayed wires must be rewired or replaced.
    b. Hanging light fixtures in closets must be replaced with an approved fixture mounted on ceiling or wall.
    c. Hanging lights in basement or cellar must be replaced with porcelain type mounted on an approved box and properly grounded.

2. **Floor-Mounted Receptacles**
    a. Old Edison-style, single-receptacle and new duplex type must have approved cover plates.
    b. The cover plate must be a waterproof type if located in area where floors are washed and must be metal type in carpeted areas.

3. **Receptacle Minimums**
    a. All habitable rooms up to 120 square feet, excluding closet areas, require two points of use. Either one ceiling- or wall-light fixture and one duplex receptacle or, if no direct-wired light fixture, two duplex receptacles. Habitable rooms are living rooms, dining rooms, bedrooms, kitchens and family rooms.
    b. Add one additional duplex receptacle for each additional 80 square feet of floor area or fraction thereof. New receptacles must be evenly spaced.
    c. Kitchen: In addition to the above floor area requirement add one 20 amp appliance circuit and receptacle to be located in the countertop work area. If more than one receptacle is required, each duplex receptacle must be of the 20 amp type.
    d. Dining Room: All receptacles installed to comply with the square footage requirement must be of the 20 amp type.
    e. Laundry: Separate 20 amp circuit and receptacle.
    f. Furnace: Separate 15 amp circuit recommended.
    g. Bathroom:
    (1) If wall-hung or medicine cabinet light fixture is metal, it must be grounded.
    (2) Existing receptacles must be grounded.
    (3) New receptacles must be Ground Fault Interrupter (GFI) type.

4. **Exterior Receptacles**
    a. Existing receptacles must be grounded.
    b. New receptacles must be GFI type.

5. **Garage**
    a. Existing wiring must be grounded.
    b. New or rewired receptacles must be GFI type.

6. **Miscellaneous**
    a. All junction boxes must have covers.
    b. Loose junction, receptacle and switch boxes must be secured.
    c. Cracked, broken and missing receptacle and switch plates must be replaced.
    d. Extension cords used as a permanent source of supply must be removed and additional receptacles installed to service needs of occupant.
    e. Nonrigid wiring must be installed through joists in basement or cellar and not on surface of joists.

requirements of your activities. Each fixture usually has four pipes running to it, including a waste pipe, hot and cold water lines and a vent. Codes are based on scientific calculations of the activity of water or gas within the pipes. Requirements are to protect you, in part, from water reversing its movement and polluting the clean water supply or to keep you from breathing sewer gas and catching diseases. You may realize cost savings from using existing fixtures, as long as they are in good working condition. However, if you will be the owner of the final project, both you and the lender may prefer that new fixtures are installed.

The information in box 4.4 may help you to identify the type of plumbing system in your building. Your state or city may use one of several national plumbing codes and may add or delete portions by amendment from time to time.

FIRE AND HEALTH HAZARDS IN ARTISTS' LIVE/WORK SPACES*

Dealing with building codes, inspectors and red tape may make you forget that building codes serve an important purpose—your safety and that of others. The two primary health hazards related to artists and construction of live/work spaces are the dangers of fire and toxic vapors.

HAZARDOUS PROCESSES

Many artists use processes employing flammable materials near other processes involving heat, flame or electricity. It is not uncommon to find artists who weld; solder; cast metal; fire ceramic and enamel kilns; use aerosol sprays, turpentine and other solvent-containing products near kitchen stoves or other appliances that have pilot lights; use propane torches on encaustics; heat wax for batik, etc. Any of these processes can cause a fire, endangering you, your family, other artists and the community—and possibly incurring large property losses. It is your responsibility to take proper precautions against this kind of tragedy.

Minimal fire safety regulations are the basis for many of the standard building code requirements already listed. "Fire-rated" refers to fire-retardant material. For corridor walls this is usually two to three layers of 5/8-inch sheetrock (a fire-retardant type).

STORAGE OF FLAMMABLES AND COMBUSTIBLES

Most artists store varying amounts of flammable and combustible liquids such as solvents (turpentine, lacquer and paint thinners, denatured alcohol, etc.), paints, inks, plastics, resins and other materials. Poor storage conditions and a source of ignition can easily combine to cause disastrous fires. Flammable liquids ignite at temperatures under 100°F and combustible liquids ignite at temperatures over 100°F.

Solvents with flash points—a measure of a liquid's "ease of ignition"—at or near room temperature are particularly hazardous. Substitution of high flash-point solvents for low ones is always recommended. For example, mineral spirits, with a flash point of 100°-140°F, are much safer than the similar VM&P naphtha, which has a flash point of 20°-40°F. Heating a liquid with a high flash point can also be dangerous. Turpentine, with a flash point of 95°F must be used with care at high ambient temperatures or in direct sunlight. It must also be stored in an area that will not overheat.

* Much of the information in this section on Fire and Health Hazards in Artists' Live/Work Spaces was adapted from materials of the Center for Safety in the Arts, New York, NY.

The items below are typically covered by the plumbing code.

1. Cast Iron Pipe

a. Primarily used for waste and soil stacks. The size used depends on how many fixtures empty into it and how long the run is between the first and last fixtures.
b. Joined together end to end with lap fittings using either oakum or hemp packed into the joint and filled with liquid lead, melted in a crucible.
c. The "No-Hub" joint uses a gasket and a metal sleeve around the joint.

2. Galvanized Pipe

a. Historically used for water delivery systems, although they rust quickly.
b. Best used for draining a sink or used for venting with no water running through.
c. Usually connected by threaded fittings.

3. Black Pipe

a. Used for gas and heating systems.
b. Uses threaded joints caulked with "pipe dope" or "Teflon tape."

4. Copper and Brass Pipe

a. Preferred for water delivery systems, pipes do not rust.
b. Joined together by brazed, soldered or threaded fittings.

5. PVC, CPVC and ABS Pipe

a. Heavy plastic pipe which cements together by the application of a solvent.
b. Restricted use or illegal in most commercial districts; most used in suburban or rural areas. Not usually recommended for water delivery systems.
c. Less heat resistant and less strong than other types; must be supported by more hangers and clamps.

6. Fittings and Joints

a. Fittings are used to connect sections of pipe to one another to direct the flow of water or gas.
b. Fitting types include the following: the "tee" (T), which splits the system into two lines at right angles; the "wye" (Y), which is similar to the T, splitting the system but at a shallow angle; the "ninety" (90 degrees), which turns the line at right angles; the "forty-five" (45 degrees), which turns the line half of the 90 degree turn; an "elbow" or a "bend," which has rounded right-angle turns. A "union" tightens simultaneously both ends of the pipes it is connecting. A "coupling" connects one pipe to another end to end with a sleeve. A "reducer" connects a small pipe to a larger pipe.
c. Unused openings of fittings are closed with a "cap," "plug" or "clean-out" of various styles.
d. Threaded joints attach one pipe to another by a twist-on method.
e. Sweated joints are fittings and pipes joined by brazing, sweat soldering or silver soldering.

7. Fixtures

Fixtures are anything connected to the piping system which consume fresh water or gas. Fixtures include a sink, toilet (water closet), bathtub, washer or gas heater.

8. Floor Drains

a. Clean-out plugs must be installed.
b. Backwater valves are required for all plumbing fixtures in "dwelling areas" located below grade.
c. Floor drains require a backwater valve assembly and clean-out plug.

9. Water Heater

a. Must have temperature and pressure relief valve.
b. Must have 3/4-inch overflow tube to within 18 inches of the floor.
c. Must have full-flow (gate) valve on cold water supply.
d. Unions are required on the hot and cold water supplies.
e. Must have gas shut-off valve on supply side of union on gas line.
f. Use fixed connectors or approved stainless flexible connectors on gas line.
g. Type "L" or soft copper tube may be used for gas piping.
h. Through-wall direct-vent water heaters do not have a draft hood.
i. Vent pipes must be secured and not back-pitched.
j. A dirt tee must be installed at the base of the gas supply pipe that drops down to an appliance controlled by a thermostat.

10. Lavatory and Bathtub

The bathroom sink and tub must have anti-syphon faucets.

11. Water Closet (Toilet)

a. Must have anti-syphon ball-cock.
b. Must provide water shut-off valve.

12. Code Traps, Waste Lines and Vent Lines

Must be installed on the following fixtures: (1) Laundry Trays; (2) Kitchen Sinks; (3) Lavatory(s) (Bath, Sinks); and (4) Bathtubs or Showers.

13. Waste Stack/Clean-out Plugs

a. Must have a minimum of one clean-out plug in main stack or secondary stacks.
b. Size of the waste stack is determined by the number of fixtures that feed into it; renovation plans may require an addition to, or replacement of, entire stack.

14. Gas Range, Gas Space Heater and Gas Clothes Dryer

a. Locate access point for gas lines to the building; evaluate price of providing gas line, if not already available.
b. Must have approved gas shut-off valve on supply side of union.
c. Must not use flexible corrugated-type connectors.

58

Pigments, dyes, and many other substances used by artists are toxic.

The following seven rules will help to reduce fire hazards in artists' studios:

1. Design a work space that is as far as possible from ambient heat sources and sleeping areas.

2. Use fire-retardant materials.

3. Choose the least flammable liquids.

4. Reduce the amounts of flammable and combustible liquids to a minimum. Keep only amounts needed for use over a short time in the studio. Check requirements for "use" permits that are required by your city, for example, for five gallons or more. Some fire departments want to know where your flammable liquids are stored.

5. Use safety-approved storage containers, including double-walled cabinets which protect the contents from heating up and exploding from a nearby fire, allowing more time to evacuate the premises.

6. Label hazardous materials as to contents and safe handling procedures. For example: "DANGER— FLAMMABLE— KEEP AWAY FROM HEAT, SPARKS AND OPEN FLAMES." "KEEP CLOSED WHEN NOT IN USE."

7. Keep an "A:B:C"-type fire extinguisher on hand to reduce the spread of small electrical, solvent or ordinary combustion fire.

TOXIC SUBSTANCES AND VAPORS

Artists use many of the same toxic substances used in industry—solvents, pigments, dyes, wood, stone, metals, etc.—and, like industrial workers, they develop occupational illnesses. Studies show that artists are at greater risk than industrial workers because they work longer hours and often live and work in the same

contaminated atmosphere. Therefore, artists' families or others sharing the live/work space are also at risk. Unseen vapors can find their way through windows, air shafts, hallways, etc. into other living quarters, so anyone living near or adjacent to artists' live/work spaces may be exposed to significant amounts of toxic substances.

Many people think that companies are playing it safe by overstating the hazards in the warning labels they place on their products. Actually, just the opposite is true. Many products are inadequately labeled, and few tell you about the cumulative effects of exposure.

Using products in live/work spaces increases the danger of ingestion with foods and contact with skin. A number of paint pigments contain heavy metals which are known to be dangerous, and the toxicity of some modern synthetic pigments is not known. Aerosol sprays, such as those used for fixatives, retouching paint sprays, varnishes, and adhesives are extremely dangerous unless used in such a way that the vapors will not be breathed.

SOME COMMON AIRBORNE DANGERS

CERAMICS. Inhalation of silica dust from handling clay in dry form can cause "potter's rot." Symptoms, which develop over years, include shortness of breath and loss of chest expansion. Inhaling large quantities of kaolin dust can also cause clogging of the lungs. The most hazardous operations are the mixing of clay dust and breaking up dry grog. Contamination of the studio with lead-based glazes and clay dust is a major hazard. Toxic fumes and gasses are also produced during firing. It is essential that kilns be ventilated to the outside, either by chimneys or by overhead hood ventilation systems.

WOODWORKING. Frequent inhalation of sawdust can cause chronic respiratory problems including asthma and sinus problems and an acute illness resembling pneumonia. Different woods cause varying types of health hazards; for example, hardwoods can be a cause of nasal/sinus cancer.

METAL CASTING. Metal fumes may cause an acute disease called metal fume fever. This is especially true of zinc oxide fumes, but includes other oxides as well. Symptoms are similar to the flu. In the lost wax process, the plaster or clay used as a negative mold contains many hazardous additives, including silica flour, which can cause silicosis. Polyurethane foam or Styrofoam

Pilsen East, Chicago. Outdoor courtyard and ceramics studio at converted commercial building.

4.5   HEALTH HAZARDS RESOURCE INFORMATION

For in-depth information on health hazards, consult the Center for Safety in the Arts (CSA) at:

Center for Safety in the Arts
5 Beekman Street, Suite 1030
New York, NY 10038
Telephone: (212) 227-6220

Dr. Michael McCann is executive director of CSA, which has a variety of programs to assist you in dealing with hazards in the arts, including the following:

1. **Art Hazards Information Center:** The Information Center answers phone calls and letters on a daily basis from anyone seeking information about art related health hazards. The Center's other services include research on potential hazards of materials and processes used in the arts; publishing and distributing books, articles and data sheets; and making referrals to physicians in occupational medicine, suppliers of personal protective equipment, ventilation experts, etc.

2. *Art Hazards News:* CSA publishes a four-page newsletter 10 times a year covering new hazards, precautions, legislation and government regulations, lawsuits and a calendar of related events.

3. **Educational Programs:** CSA has a number of educational programs to inform artists, teachers, conservators and others interested in health hazards in the arts.

4. **Consultation Programs:** CSA offers two types of consultation programs for universities, schools, theaters, museums and other nonprofit arts institutions. "On Site Consultation" consists of a one-day inspection of facilities with a report on hazards found and recommendations for their correction. "Planning Consultation" helps planners ensure that adequate safety features are included at the planning stage of a new or renovated structure. There is a charge for consultation services.

5. **Health Hazards Computer Bulletin Board:** Using a computer modem to contact (212) 385-2034, you can get information on the use or storage of flammable or toxic materials and other arts hazards through numerous data sheets and bulletins that may be downloaded on a 24-hour basis.

The Center also carries a variety of publications on health hazards for artists. Contact the Center for a full listing.

A useful and up-to-date book that covers practical and legal aspects of health and safety for artists is *The Artists Complete Health and Safety Guide* by Monona Rossol. Published by Allworth Press, the 320-page paperback book is available for $16.95 plus $4.00 shipping and handling from the American Council for the Arts, 1 E. 53rd St., New York, NY 10022.

Additional sources of information about arts health hazards include the following:

Joy Turner Luke
Chair, Materials Research Committee
National Artists Equity Association
P.O. Box 28065, Central Station
Washington, DC 20038
(202) 628-9633

Communication Directorate
Canadian Department of National Health and Welfare
Health Protection Branch
Brooke Claxton Building, 5th Floor
Holland Avenue, Tunney's Pasture
Ottawa, Ontario, Canada K1A OK9
(613) 957-2991, for information and publications
(613) 957-1852, for product safety information

as an adaptation of lost wax through the vaporization process releases cyanide and toxic gasses during decomposition. Good ventilation or approved respirators should be used in these processes.

These are only a few examples of dangers associated with various art materials. Harmful vapors also arise from materials such as turpentine and silk-screen inks, solvents, and metallic fumes from welding, etching metals, photo baths. (See box 4.5 for sources of information about health hazards.)

RENOVATION

The process of renovation can entail many health hazards, especially to pregnant women and children, so it is best to have those family members stay away from the area being renovated.

PAINT AND PAINT STRIPPERS. Paint strippers, enamel paints, and even latex paints, epoxies and varnishes contain chemicals that can cause headaches, dizziness, nausea and other adverse health effects in adults or children. They are especially dangerous for pregnant women and can cause miscarriages or birth defects. Because many older paints are lead-based, exposure to dust from sanding or to fumes from torches or heat guns can cause lead poisoning.

ASBESTOS. Another hazard connected with renovation is contact with asbestos used in older buildings. Asbestos was often wrapped lengthwise around pipes and looks like gray, corrugated cardboard. Asbestos presents a health hazard when its fibers are released into the air, inhaled and trapped in the lungs. Releases can occur when asbestos pipe insulation tears or decays. One of the visual clues to the presence of decaying asbestos is the appearance of small piles of fluffy fibers on floors underneath pipes. Such fibers should be removed with a wet mop—not swept, dusted or vacuumed.

Cities have legal restrictions for asbestos removal and disposal. Inspectors may require the professional removal of asbestos as part of your renovation project, which can be costly. Specialists can encapsulate the asbestos with special chemicals that soak all the way through the asbestos. Repair done with special tapes or paints, available from hardware stores or heating contractors, may be an adequate cure, but be certain to label what has been wrapped. If you are determined to remove it yourself, take every precaution, including finding out more about it and using a tight-fitting heavy-duty mask with a wetted down and changeable filter. Do the work before you move in, so that you can clean the area thoroughly.

VENTILATION SYSTEMS. There are basically two types of ventilation systems: (1) general ventilation, which dilutes toxic vapors and dust with fresh air, so that the concentrations are at lower, safer levels; and (2) local or exhaust ventilation, which removes toxic fumes at their source before they enter the breathing environment. The latter type is essential if highly toxic materials are being used. Local or exhaust ventilation requires installation of an exhaust hood to trap the fumes or dust, a duct to carry the contaminant to the outside and an exhaust fan.

Local or exhaust ventilation should be used with any of the following processes: welding, carbon arc, acid baths for etching (particularly with nitric acid), silk-screen drying and wash-up, spraying operations, grinding and sanding, and processes producing asbestos-containing dusts.

Ventilating systems, though often overlooked, are extremely important to your health. Before installing a system, make sure it is adequate for the proposed use. When exhausting solvents, you need to have a fan that is "explosion proof." Most heating, ventilating and air conditioning (HVAC) engineers lack experience and training in venting industrial toxins, so you may need to contact an industrial ventilation engineer. (See box 4.6.)

4.6   STEPS TO MINIMIZE HEALTH HAZARDS

■ Exercise responsibility when choosing the work you will do in your live/work space. Some processes should never be done in or close to living spaces. These include cyanide bath gold plating, urethane resin casting, lead melting and casting, or any processes involving large amounts of solvents or solvent-containing products, such as silk-screen printing with solvent-based inks. Choose less hazardous processes and materials that can be used safely within the limits of your particular space.

■ Separate living and working areas. Design interior walls and spaces so that kitchens, bedrooms and other living areas are divided from work areas. Even relatively safe materials can be dangerous with constant exposure. Take special care in areas where children or pregnant women are likely to spend time.

■ Install adequate ventilation systems, which will protect you, during the time you work, and others from traveling air pollutants. Make sure the air exhausted by your system does not contaminate your neighbor's space.

■ Keep a personal "exposure log" listing the materials you use and any significant reactions you have to materials or processes. This will be extremely helpful to your physician in case of an emergency or as a part of regular examinations. Keep the log updated. Note any flulike symptoms. Many toxic reactions begin with headaches, dizziness, fatigue, nausea, blurred vision or coughing and breathing difficulties.

■ Inform your insurance agent. Your insurance agent needs to have a good understanding of what you do in your live/work space or studio. Withholding information can work against you in the long run. For example, having more than a few gallons of solvent may result in the cancellation of coverage under a normal homeowner's fire policy unless you add a rider to cover that risk. Coverage may also be cancelled if you are working as an artist professionally, because homeowner's policies cover only typical home risks. Some large insurance companies have safety experts you can consult free of charge.

5

The City as a Resource and a Partner

Public bodies control two scarce resources of a city, its land and its capital, and public officials are stewards of the "public purpose" for which government resources are made available. You may find that you need to involve the city as a resource for helping you realize your space goals. Today, as the value of the arts in the economic development of cities has become more widely recognized, artists and arts organizations in a wide range of cities are finding tangible support from their local governments. (See boxes 5.1 and 5.2.)

Your reasons for involving city government in your development project may include any one or a combination of the following needs:

- zoning and building code changes or variances
- coordination with other development activities in the area
- information and trouble-shooting assistance
- assistance in removing development obstacles
- city services or infrastructure changes
- public financial support or development incentives (more about this in chapter 6)

64

5.1 CITIES THAT HAVE REVISED CODE INTERPRETATIONS

Cities that have reviewed the interpretation of codes governing combined live/work space include the following:

Austin, Texas
Boston, Massachusetts
Chicago, Illinois
Emeryville, Laguna Beach, Los Angeles, Oakland, San Diego, and San Francisco, California
Minneapolis and St. Paul, Minnesota
New York City, New York
Salt Lake City, Utah
Seattle, Washington
Washington, D.C.

5.2 CITIES WITH CULTURAL DISTRICTS

Cities that have planned formal or informal cultural districts as a means of ensuring the vitality of their downtowns include the following:

Atlanta, Georgia
Austin, Dallas and San Antonio, Texas
Boston, Massachusetts
Cleveland, Ohio
Costa Mesa, Los Angeles and San Francisco, California
Minneapolis and St. Paul, Minnesota
New Haven, Connecticut
New Orleans, Louisiana
New York City, New York
Philadelphia, Pennsylvania
Phoenix and Tucson, Arizona
Pittsburgh, Pennsylvania
Washington, D.C.
Winston-Salem, North Carolina

In some projects the city's role may be limited to approving permits. In other development efforts the city may take a more active role. Typically, it is not the role of the city to step in and act as a developer. Rather, the public sector generally creates the framework for private investment and development. Most public agencies limit their economic development strategies to doing those things that the private sector is unwilling or unable to do on behalf of the public good. These may include the following:

■ identifying comprehensive or long-range plans for development priorities within the community (for example, housing, economic development)

■ identifying specific development opportunities and constraints

■ preparing development guidelines to signal to developers the city's interest in negotiating on desirable projects

■ removing development obstacles

■ enhancing existing development opportunities

■ providing physical improvements (for example, streets, infrastructure)

■ providing public financing support or other incentives

■ addressing legal issues or actions

PUBLIC/PRIVATE PARTNERSHIPS FOR THE ARTS

Nearly every economic and programmatic aspect of city life is now a potential forum for cooperative action to maximize available community resources. As in any collaborative effort, a partnership of both public and private parties is most effective when all parties share a common stated goal and have a clear understanding of one another's needs, expectations, skills and resources.

Lowertown Lofts, St. Paul; groundbreaking ceremony. From right: finance partner, mayor, artist, for-profit partner, artist.

Involving other partners in the development does not necessarily mean all participants will be equal partners, nor legally organized as a partnership or joint venture. However, the combined skills and resources from the arts, the public sector, and private owners or developers may be needed to bring a live/work space project to fruition.

Any one of these sectors may provide the initial impetus and vision for the project, since multiple benefits from such projects are available to each. Other parties are brought in to help refine the vision, shape the planning and share the risks. Tasks and responsibilities are allocated to the sector with the greatest capacity to tap needed expertise or resources. The final project plans incorporate responses to each sector's goals.

Experience suggests that the city can best use its influence to initiate and build community partnerships to effect the financing required for projects. In some cities, you may find a responsive city staff person to assist your group in making connections and building support. In other cities, the city council representatives are the people to approach. (See box 5.3.)

How to Approach the City

City programs are structured to respond to the needs of developers. Artists wishing to involve their city will be more successful if they can speak the language of a developer. Do your homework first. Review the city's master plan, investigate the city's history of financing development projects and find out what zoning and building codes you

5.3   ST. PAUL, MINNESOTA: PARTNERSHIP WITH THE ARTS

Cities maintain a wide spectrum of involvement with artists and arts programming. St. Paul, Minnesota, identified its strength as an entrepreneurial agent and chose to use its real estate tools and policies on behalf of the arts, initiating policies to support arts organizations and artists through its Arts Development Program. The program considers requests for comprehensive services in the areas of resource development, technical assistance for space development, financing, programming, communications, public art and urban design advocacy, and project services.

The program's strength is its ability to draw upon internal expertise and services provided to businesses on behalf of the "arts industry." Real estate and business development services provide facility infrastructures that encourage opportunities for job creation and retention in the arts. The city uses its influence and financial resources to initiate and support projects that will have a long-term impact on city growth and vitality.

St. Paul uses public financing as a tool to attract private investment in relatively unconventional projects. Success with early projects has shown that artists, arts businesses and arts organizations can perform as cooperative and financially responsible partners in the community. Public financing in some projects was the first money committed to a project, which then gained the interest of private developers who joined as partners.

Subsequent to a successful partnership with Artspace Projects, Inc., the St. Paul Art Collective, and Asset Development Services, Inc., on the Lowertown Lofts, the city project managers affirmed their commitment to future artist live/work space projects. They defined the requirements for such projects requesting financial assistance. To meet the needs of artists, the city recognized key elements of preplanning that led to success and are now required of all developers of artist spaces—for-profit and nonprofit—before the commitment of city financing. The required elements are as follows:

- criteria for selecting artists
- preleasing or ownership commitments and waiting list
- development of a cooperative tenant management structure
- operational structure to maintain ongoing commitment to artists
- artist involvement in planning design of building's interior
- definition of post-construction artist improvements
- feasible financing plan, maintaining long-term costs affordable to artists
- other usual requirements of city financing programs, such as meeting low to moderate income qualifications by tenants; financing restrictions and ceiling for per project participation; and written terms of other lender loans
- future right of leasehold cooperatives to purchase property at restricted level
- opportunity for Artspace to act as co-general partner in any projects proposed by profit-motivated developers
- other conditions as required by a specific project or financing program

The city recognized that well-conceived and structured live/work space projects were still likely to experience a financial gap that must be closed in creative ways to be affordable for low- and moderate-income artists. To help close the affordability gap, the city has used public financing, loan guarantees and assistance in negotiating for Program Related Investments or grant funds from philanthropic sources.

will need to meet. Your ideas will gain support if they are presented clearly, provide a rationale and purpose for your project and delineate how you hope to put the project together. In addition, your willingness to take the advice of government agency staff members will help the project progress.

If you encounter difficulties in securing support, you may have to shop around for other sources of private or governmental assistance to use as leverage. It is not uncommon to get commitments from one public agency that are dependent on the action of another. The willingness of one public agency to support you may be used in a second approach to the other.

The fund-raising principle "people give to people, not causes" applies here. People tend to be helpful when they can see their own interests reflected in a cause or when they can respond as individuals to others in need. In the case of a city, you need to think about where the power affecting your project resides and how to access that power. If your council has influence, begin building your base of support by meeting with each city council member separately. Spend time gaining an understanding of their concerns. Be prepared to present your project concept, illustrate its value to the community, provide evidence of community support and describe the type of city assistance that is needed. Present your needs in terms that reflect the interests of council members and be open to their ideas for practical and realistic solutions. Once informed about your project, they will direct you to other offices for appropriate assistance.

The Role of Artists as Community Leaders

Life as an artist may be hard—especially if you are working alone and getting by on a poverty level income. From this viewpoint, it may be difficult to see yourself as having something valuable to contribute to the community, especially in

the public policy arena. However, for a great city to develop, it must have the investment of vision and energy from those who live within it. Cities are constantly in a state of being rebuilt and redefined, and the great cities are much more than a collection of buildings. Artists must make their voices heard alongside the other movers and shakers who shape our cities.

Assist the politician in doing his or her job by demonstrating the value of your proposal or idea. If you have difficulty, reassess your goals and revamp your approach. Assess what power you have assembled and use that to apply some political pressure if appropriate.

Competition for Public Resources and Assistance

When public resource allocations are being made, the arts have commonly been dismissed or devalued. It can be difficult to to ask for assistance from the city, given the extent of other urban problems. Yet, it is possible to frame the discussion of your project in light of the city's priorities. While being compassionate and sensitive to the competing needs within your community—such as housing for the homeless—it is also important to remember that artists' space is primarily a work-space issue, not a housing issue. Artists are seldom competing for residential space. They are most often seeking vacant commercial space, which may not have a more economically valid use.

One useful argument is that, by moving into an abandoned commercial or manufacturing property, artists often make available low-cost housing units elsewhere for the benefit of other low-income people.

The problems for artists are several:

■ their use of space for both working and living is often incompatible with residential neighborhoods

- code and financing restrictions often inhibit artists' renovation of vacant commercial space
- competition for space typically increases after artists have made a commitment to an area. The property value increases once improvements are made, often forcing artists to move again due to increased rental value

The underlying problem faced by artists is the need for access to funds enabling them to control their spaces permanently. Creative thinking may help you to form a new "currency" of exchange with your city. The arts, including artist housing projects, have the ability to give back more than they receive in public assistance. For example, the trade of community arts programming in exchange for needed financing, loan guarantees, zoning variances or other assistance from the city is a proven successful solution. Your collateral becomes a commitment to serve a broader public need in partnership with the city's goals.

Artists and advocates working with them must use their creative skills in framing requests to public bodies. They need to remind themselves and others that artists are also small business people. They need to find a manner of communicating with the city that does not pit the arts against other low-income people or minority businesses. By translating your activities into the language of public policy, you will help city officials to identify ways of assisting your project.

ZONING AND BUILDING CODES AS TOOLS OF PUBLIC POLICY

Most communities have created comprehensive plans, reflected in their zoning policies, which seek to direct future growth. The value of a given property is created by the number of people who want to use a particular parcel of land for a specific purpose. To the extent that zoning channels that demand toward certain properties

and away from others, it may affect the value of a property.

In some cities, the public-sector attitude toward the combined live/work spaces that artists have developed, often in violation of codes, has been benign neglect or indifference. In other cities, growing numbers of artists—tired of being pressured to move from their spaces—have been calling upon their city governments with increasing frequency to acknowledge their presence and needs. Such actions have sometimes led to a thorough look at changes in lifestyles and industries. As a result, some states have amended zoning ordinances or instituted policies related specifically to artists' live/work spaces.

The need for new uses for buildings and districts in urban centers is evident, and the phenomena of salvaged and recycled urban properties are now common. Because zoning and building code officials have increasing experience and familiarity with live/work space renovations, conflicts between artist space projects and the city's public policies have decreased.

Community-Wide Zoning Changes

Real estate development is a local issue, requiring a local solution. Each city must determine for itself the best way to integrate artists' live/work spaces into the community. Experiences in several cities, discussed later in this chapter, show the value of artists' participation in the public discussions that led to revisions of zoning and building codes.

Some approaches to zoning changes that have been tried in relation to artists' live/work space include allowing live/work space in:

- a limited geographical area, artists only—a districting approach
- commercial and manufacturing districts throughout the city—a dispersing approach

- the downtown area, as one option for diversified housing for all incomes, not restricted to artists
- a variety of zoning districts under special conditions or requiring special approvals

Research and preparation will aid a community of artists and their supporters who are attempting to remove zoning obstacles or to bring about significant zoning changes. Appropriate zoning and building code policies may be evaluated by taking into account the existing patterns of suitable buildings; the size of the arts community; current and desired occupancy preferences; and municipal development goals.

A carefully planned strategy involves gaining input from all the city departments and the people who will be affected by the proposed changes. A variance may only take a few months, whereas a major zoning change will probably take one or more years to complete. Public relations and education are tools in gaining the community support necessary to approve a zoning change.

CULTURAL PLANNING, ARTS DISTRICTS AND ARTS-INCLUSIVE MIXED-USE DEVELOPMENTS. During the past 10 years, research and planning for the arts have been occurring in nearly every major U.S. city, each addressing the needs and opportunities appropriate to its own community. Some cities have incorporated the arts as part of the city's master plan; others have prepared specific cultural plans.

CULTURAL PLANS. The Chicago Cultural Plan (1985-1986), a comprehensive strategy for nurturing Chicago's artists and arts organizations, emphasized neighborhood involvement in planning and enlisted both political and grassroots support. Recommendations from neighborhood meetings were refined at citywide conferences, resulting in a planning document. Recommendations included the revision of Chicago's zoning and building codes, the creation of a "space registry" and the provision of city-owned buildings for redevelopment by the arts.

Other cities' plans that have included artists' live/work space are Oakland's "Cultural Plan," Philadelphia's "Plan for Center City," San Francisco's "Master Plan," Los Angeles' "Task Force on the Arts," Minneapolis' "Metro Plan 2000," St. Paul's "Arts Development Plan," and Washington, D.C.'s "Art Space: Report of the Mayor's Blue Ribbon Committee for Promotion of the Arts and Economic Development."

ARTS DISTRICTS. Some cities have used zoning and other cultural planning activities as tools to encourage the concentration of artists in certain districts. The planning of cultural districts enables the city to provide special policy protection to encourage retention or enhancement of arts activities in the designated area. Beyond a desire to meet the needs of the arts community, a city typically seeks the benefits of creating a place where citizens and tourists can gather for entertainment and of enhancing business.

Tucson began planning an arts district in 1987, incorporating artists' live/work space into the city's redevelopment plan for the downtown. In the same year, the city approved regulations to allow artists to live and work in the historic district. Artists, intent on securing an equity position in exchange for their role in attracting new business and tourists downtown, took part in the planning activities.

The Tucson master plan includes implementation and management strategies for the Arts District to guide public and private investment in public spaces, amenities and new land uses. The city also coordinated efforts within its divisions and local development corporations to make available all potential sources of financing to ensure the plans would be effective. At a conference on

70

space for the arts in Tucson, a supportive city council member told the artists to keep the dialogue going with the city "to remind us of what the original goal was here." With enthusiasm and commitment, all parties seem to be ensuring that the desired goal is being met. Moreover, the numbers of resident artists and arts organizations have grown substantially since the district was founded.

In Boston, artists and arts organizations are working with city agencies to develop the city's Midtown Cultural District Plan (1987-present) to revive an ailing theater district. The concentration of cultural activities will include affordable performing and exhibition spaces for emerging artists.

New Orleans also fostered a participatory process with artists, residents and commercial interests in creating the "Arts in the Cultural Sector" plan for downtown (1988-present). The plan includes a live/work space element. Although low-cost space is also available for artists to work elsewhere in the city, the planning participants recognized that the energy of artists living and creating within an arts district is important to the vitality of that district.

ARTS-INCLUSIVE MIXED-USE DEVELOP-MENTS. Some developers have proposed a mixed-use development to a city, using the arts as a draw for any combination of retail, restaurant, office and hotel uses. Mixed-use projects have had success using mid-sized or major arts organizations as anchor tenants, while meeting city goals for revitalizing an area.

Although individual artists have found performing, demonstrating or exhibiting opportunities in mixed-use projects, the costs of the space developed in such projects have exceeded what most artists can afford for studio, rehearsal

Mixed-media sculpture studio, Tucson. The city is working to designate a cultural district.

or living space. For further information about these projects, see Harold Snedcof, *Cultural Facilities in Mixed-Use Development*, published by the Urban Land Institute, 1985.

Arts Economic Impact and Marketing Studies

Projects that show their ability to stimulate other economic growth are the most likely to be assisted. The findings of economic impact studies, even when they are less than comprehensive, and other research have helped to validate public investments in the arts and have shown that the arts profoundly influence the economies of our cities. (Many studies focus on the major cultural institutions within an area, but do not include the for-profit sector of the arts community, individual artists or groups of artists without tax-exempt status.) Studies have found that people drawn to arts programming—studio open houses or performances, for example—are often customers of nearby restaurants, bars and businesses.

The findings from these studies provide useful information for public officials. Similarly, comprehensive marketing studies commissioned by the arts community also help to build support in the public arena by educating lenders and public officials. State arts agencies or local arts commissions should have information about arts economic impact or other studies on your community.

Typically, an economic impact study for the arts measures arts-related spending in three ways:

- direct—all annual expenditures for conducting an arts program

- indirect—spending that is recirculated through the economy

- audience-related or -induced spending —expenses incurred by audience members to participate in the arts

Consider balancing your statements about the impact of the arts on the economy with a reminder of the arts' intrinsic value. Many people warn that the arts should not be reduced to statistics nor touted as an economic development tool. As the highest form of human expression, the arts, it is feared, will be harmed if manipulated for other purposes. Also, be prepared to deliver the value-added features your project proposes.

Artist Certification and Licensing

Several cities have used certification or licensing programs to ensure that special provisions are protected for artists' use. For example, zoning ordinances may include a definition of "artist." Certification is usually a prerequisite to an artist's acceptance into a live/work district or project that has received district designation, public funding or financing.

Typically, certification criteria will include an assessment of the artist's (1) education, (2) slides of current artwork, (3) stated needs for space, (4) income qualifications (depending on the project), (5) commitment to an arts career, (6) references from other artists, (7) personality (especially in a cooperative project). The actual selection criteria may be weighted or altered by a specific project's objectives. The assessment may be carried out by an artist peer review committee or a project staff person or team.

ZONING, BUILDING CODE AND DISTRICTING POLICIES IN SELECTED CITIES

To provide an overview of the issues and solutions for artist spaces in a variety of regions of the United States, the following section

72

profiles the responses of cities toward zoning, building code and districting concerns of living/working space. The cities are New York, Seattle, Boston, Chicago, Minneapolis/St. Paul, Los Angeles and San Francisco. These summaries provide a historical view of key policy issues facing cities. The new zoning ordinance for San Francisco—City Wide Live/Work Controls—is summarized in part to assist you in identifying definitions and language that may be useful for your city to adopt.

For a more thorough look at the histories of public policy and zoning issues in various communities, see *Artists Live/Work Space: Changing Public Policy,* a project and publication of Artists Equity Association, Inc., Northern California Chapter, 1981.

NEW YORK CITY

New York City has been faced with enormous demands for affordable residential space. The city has also sought to maintain as many buildings as possible for manufacturing uses to keep jobs available within the city. The desire to legitimize loft living in the area south of Houston Street—SoHo—led to zoning changes that provided for special artist live/work districts, with strict limitations including an Artist Certification procedure. Such a response represents a "districting" approach. SoHo is best known for having discovered the synergistic benefits—and problems—of concentrating artists and arts activities.

Having once had the highest concentration of industrial activity in the nation, Manhattan lost 50 percent of its manufacturing tenants between 1947 and 1976. As manufacturing tenants left, artists in search of low-cost space in which to live and work began to move into the vacated quarters. Artists began to organize in 1961, establishing the Artists Tenants Association (ATA).

Artists later worked to save the SoHo district from being cleared for construction of a major arterial highway.

Artists, city planners, property owners, city and state legislators, and community groups succeeded in achieving legislative reforms as well as zoning and building code changes while the conversion of numerous manufacturing buildings to meet artists' space needs continued. Recognizing the value of artists to the economy and cultural life of the city and seeing the need for public intervention, the state legislature amended the Multiple Dwelling Law (MDL) in 1963 to permit the conversion of vacant commercial buildings for artists' live/work spaces. The Artist-in-Residence (AIR) concept was also put into place at this time. In 1965 and again in 1971, the requirements for health and safety standards were relaxed. The MDL amendment in 1971 also permitted live/work space conversions in SoHo buildings that retained some manufacturing or commercial uses. At the same time the city established an aesthetically neutral Artist Certification procedure to prevent nonartists from taking advantage of these relaxed provisions. In 1976, artist occupancy of the NoHo and TriBeCa areas was legalized.

As another amendment to the MDL, the Loft Legalization Bill-MDL was passed in 1982. As a result, the legal status of most lofts was reviewed. Lofts that met residential requirements received rent control and other benefits. The right to sell fixtures and improvements (once only) to either the next tenant or the landlord was also approved. A revision of the co-op and condo conversion law was also passed in 1982.

In 1983, New York City announced the "Artist Home Ownership Program" (AHOP), under which it offered eight vacant or abandoned city-owned buildings for conversion and ownership by artists. The plan met with friction from other low-income residents in the neighborhood, who pointed out the tremendous need for housing

73

Apex Belltown Co-op, Seattle. Shared kitchen area.

The magnitude of New York and its problems continues to impede artists' efforts to secure low-cost space. However, the New York Department of Cultural Affairs and several nonprofit arts organizations help artist-initiated live/work space projects to gain access to technical assistance and financing resources to secure long-term control and ownership opportunities. A revolving loan pool for capital improvements is available for organizations, although not for individual artists.

Overall, New York City has benefited from artists' development activity through the preservation of historic commercial districts, increased rental income and tax revenues, and ancillary economic growth. These benefits have been so significant that other cities and developers have sought to duplicate the New York experience in their own communities.

SEATTLE

Seattle's arts planners, after having researched the live/work space models created by New York, studied the perceptions and needs of the Seattle community to develop a policy that fit the city's needs. Their efforts to involve the building, fire and zoning offices of the city in their research and their process for gaining community participation have served as a model for other cities.

In 1976, the Seattle Arts Commission recognized that the live/work needs of the city's artists were in conflict with city zoning policies. Through its Independent Creative Artists Project, the Arts Commission initially involved artists, the Washington Volunteer Lawyers for the Arts and AIA Building and Codes Committee architects in responding to issues raised by the Department of Community Development.

nonartists. They also feared the arrival of artists as the first step toward their own eventual displacement from gentrification. The failure of the AHOP program was attributed to lack of minority involvement and the failure of artists to build support with their potential neighbors.

In 1985, the city proposed a new program offering 28 vacant city-owned buildings. Greater effort was given to minority outreach and communication with neighborhood representatives; the buildings were scattered among four boroughs; and other restrictions were placed on them. No city financing was made available, although tax abatements were possible. However, few projects were initiated. Those completed provide renovated live/work units offered for sale (co-op) or rental to income-qualifying artists certified by the Department of Cultural Affairs.

86 South Street, Boston. Condominium unit.

The zoning legislation was changed to allow artists to be integrated throughout the community, representing a "dispersing" approach. Because artists were already living illegally throughout the community, this approach best met the arts community's needs.

In the midst of their lobbying to change the zoning laws, the artists gained public support through a model "watchperson's project," whereby artists not only lived and worked in buildings, but also served as guards. Artists also participated in providing studio tours for the public to demystify perceptions of artists and to educate the public about their space needs.

The Department of Construction and Land Use published a bulletin defining zoning and building code requirements and procedures applicable to an artist's live/work space. The Seattle Arts Commission published the *Seattle Artists' Housing Handbook* in 1980 as an overview of how to find and develop space that meets artists' needs.

The Seattle Arts Commission and Allied Arts of Seattle continue to meet with artists to assess space needs. Because of the lack of available building stock for artists' studios, the agencies are now considering new construction projects and a staff position to deal with real estate development.

BOSTON

As early as the late 1950s, artists inhabited obsolete warehouse buildings in inner-city Boston areas, most of them in violation of Boston's zoning and building code requirements. As one result of the Plante Shoe Factory fire in Boston's Jamaica Plain on February 1, 1976, the public became more aware of the difficulties artists faced in seeking to live and work in Boston. The factory's owner had been taken to court for fire safety and building code violations in 1973. However, both the owner and the 70 or so artists ignored the ruling prohibiting residential use of the building. No lives were lost when the 750,000-square-foot building burned to the ground, but the artists were left with nothing. Artists rallied to seek a resolution of artist housing issues with the city.

Subsequently, a code enforcement crackdown began throughout Boston on buildings providing studio space to artists. Requests for residential zoning variances of some properties were submitted and denied. Presentations were made to the Zoning Board of Appeals, augmented by letters from other supporting groups defending the concept of live/work space. Three-year conditional use permits were approved, enabling artists to reside in manufacturing buildings if they used no more than 25 percent of the floor space for residential purposes and complied with building and health codes. The impact of residential uses in commercial and light industrial buildings was evaluated by the Boston Redevelopment Authority.

During this same period, The Artists Foundation, Inc., of Boston developed its Art Space Project in cooperation with the Massachusetts Institute of Technology and others. The Art Space Project included extensive research on zoning options, research on artists' live/work space projects, a model survey of artists' space needs, and pilot development efforts aimed at converting vacant public-sector buildings by using private-sector financing with no public subsidies. The project also evaluated a "dollar-leveraging" approach of mixed uses to enable artists to purchase their units.

Special-use permits allowing conditional residential uses in manufacturing areas have restricted residential conversions to artists, slowing but not stopping gentrification. While artists were concentrated in manufacturing districts, the special-use permits were intended to avoid New York City's experience of creating defined districts and artist certification procedures.

Within residential neighborhoods, the zoning code permits office use by "professional" residents as an accessory use. A traditional "home occupation" is permitted as long as residential use is dominant, equipment is only incidental, no outside help is employed, and no classes or sales of merchandise are held on the premises. Artists were not specifically identified as "professional" residents, although they could argue the point if necessary. For many artists, residential spaces are both inadequate and illegal for their intended uses.

Within the framework of growing community awareness of both artists' needs for space and new solutions for meeting those needs, the artists occupying the Fort Point area of South Boston (since 1976) organized as a nonprofit group in 1980.

The Fort Point Arts Community (FPAC) sought to have a voice in the future of its neighborhood as redevelopment activities threatened its displacement. FPAC hired Jero Nesson as its first executive director in 1982 and began its first project, the development of 35 cooperatively owned live/work units. FPAC continues to work toward improving zoning and building code regulations for live/work space along with continuing efforts to secure and develop permanent, affordable spaces; assisting artists in their interactions with landlords and city officials; and increasing public awareness through monthly exhibitions, annual open studios tours, a newsletter and classes. In 1986 Nesson, with funding from the Massachusetts Council on the Arts and Humanities, established ArtistSpace to provide development expertise to groups of artists seeking to create live/work space throughout Massachusetts.

Although more explicit live/work space legislation has not yet been developed in Boston or elsewhere in Massachusetts, successful development efforts have nonetheless secured workable interpretations of the codes. FPAC has begun to research code amendments from other cities and to plan a new strategy for clarifying Boston's codes for the future.

CHICAGO

Chicago has a large population of artists, who tend to be dispersed throughout the city. Like most cities, Chicago has yet to establish clear policies or ordinances for live/work space occupancies. Artist live/work space is permitted in commercial buildings above the first floor, but not in industrial buildings or in residences. Strong opposition to amending the restrictions on home/work space, which grew out of the unions' fight against cottage industries, remains. The Chicago building codes are the most restrictive in the country, and renovation costs are extremely high. Artists live illegally in some industrial buildings, at the whim of landlords and for the most part ignored by the city.

Within the last 10 years, artists have been attracted to the River North area, west of Michigan Avenue. Galleries and supportive shops have moved in, other renovation has occurred and artists are already being forced out by increased rents. City agencies have expressed the same concern as those in New York City—that manufacturing and industrial buildings must be retained for prospective manufacturers. Therefore, renovations for new uses are limited.

In *The Chicago ArtSpace Study*, completed in March 1986 (see box 5.4), Enid Rieser noted that the industrial areas immediately surrounding Chicago's loop had already become too expensive for artists or galleries. Rieser noted that there was

no specific category for live/work occupancy, although the "Class J" occupancy was closest. Class J/miscellaneous structures provides a classification for dormitories and work spaces for firehouses, which may be located in commercial, business or industrial areas. Rieser recommended that two options in Chicago's Enterprise Zone programs be made available to artists. One is the "urban homestead" program, which had not been advertised as available to artists. The second is the "shopstead" program, which had not formerly been applicable to artists.

As a result of *The ArtsSpace Study* and Chicago's Cultural Plan, the Departments of Cultural Affairs and Economic Development, through funding from the National Endowment for the Arts (NEA), made grants of up to $20,000 to fund design fees and other planning costs of development projects. Nonprofit groups wanting to develop artist live/work space or arts organizations with space projects can apply for the funds. A loan pool has also been established for capital improvements for mid-sized arts organizations at 1.5 percent with long-term payment schedules.

For the past few years, a city council committee has been working with the Departments of Cultural Affairs and Economic Development and the Zoning Commissioner to develop an amendment to the zoning code to permit live/work space in certain types of industrial areas. Research has been undertaken to evaluate the need for restricted artist districts, artist certification, artists' space and alternative policies to make artist live/work space an option available to building owners.

Temporarily, at least, the issue of artist live/work space has lost momentum. The reasons include the large amount of vacant space, the city's hope that manufacturing uses will return, the recent changes of three mayoral administrations, a lack of passionate need rising from the artist community and the lack of a nonprofit or other developer to initiate affordable live/work

5.4   TWENTY CITY PROGRAMS TO HELP MEET ARTISTS' SPACE NEEDS

The following excerpt is from Enid Rieser's 1986 report, *The Chicago Artspace Study,* to the Chicago Department of Cultural Affairs summarizing programs and policies from seven cities. These program descriptions may provide guidance for planning or evaluating programs and services for your own community.

In surveying art space support throughout North America, the study focused on seven cities in the United States and Canada which had initiated or actively encouraged the most effective and innovative programs. The cities were Evanston, Illinois; Los Angeles, California; Minneapolis/St. Paul, Minnesota; New York, New York; San Francisco, California; Seattle, Washington; and Winnipeg, Manitoba. A listing of these programs, either currently in operation or nearing implementation, follows:

1. Subsidized rent in public buildings in exchange for community service projects such as free or reduced price tickets for performances, public lectures, workshops for community participation, and programs taken to schools, hospitals, senior citizen centers and the like.

2. Amendments to the municipal code to provide alternative building standards to assist and make feasible both the reuse of existing buildings and the construction of new buildings as joint living and work quarters for the artists.

3. Creation of new zoning categories to permit mixed residential and industrial or commercial use for artists and artisans.

4. Provision for active involvement by artists and arts organizations in planning of publicly assisted mixed-use developments.

5. Percent for art programs that require that a percentage of development costs, less land, for private as well as public buildings, be used for permanent, on-site works of art and other visual and performing arts projects.

6. City supported mixed-use development with commercial users paying market value rents on the first floor to help subsidize upper floor artist rentals.

7. Support for "sweat equity" projects in which artist/tenants do post-construction clean-up, paint walls, finish floors and build any special features into their units such as lofts or storage in exchange for ownership rights.

8. Technical services to artists and arts organizations in establishing tenants' associations, and understanding building codes, leasing, realty law and procedures.

9. Creation of "arts enterprise zones" in targeted areas in which profit and nonprofit arts organizations have clustered office spaces, rehearsal spaces, retail shop spaces and galleries, along with studio and living spaces for individual artists.

10. City supported and subsidized artists housing projects.

11. Tax incentives for the rehabilitation and conversion of nonresidential buildings in targeted areas for artists live/work space.

12. Revolving loan funds to give artists seed money to purchase space.

13. Computerized listings of spaces available for artists.

14. Reimbursement of moving expenses for relocation to targeted areas.

15. Provision of warehouse space for Materials for the Arts programs in which business and other groups donate unused materials needed by artists.

16. Use of revenue-sharing funds for the creation of cultural centers such as costume banks, technology banks, graphic service centers, and mural resource centers.

17. Licensing and space assignments for the selling of handcrafted works exclusively by the artist.

18. Grants and low-cost loans to bring artist spaces up to city housing and building codes.

19. Provision for administrative service centers for artists to provide use of office equipment, telephone answering and mailbox services.

20. City-operated or subsidized artist housing projects.

The above represents programs operated by both city agencies and nonprofit organizations in the above named cities. At the time of Rieser's study, none of these programs were available in Chicago.

Reprinted with permission of Enid Rieser.

78

space development. For artists who can afford market-rate rents, several developers have renovated former warehouse buildings for studio, office and residential uses, albeit, not usually within one unit.

MINNEAPOLIS AND ST. PAUL

Minneapolis and St. Paul each have cumulative zoning regulations, with residential land use possible in nearly any area of the city, except heavy manufacturing districts (called "industrial" in St. Paul). Residential conversions are allowable on the upper floors of warehouse, manufacturing and commercial buildings. This zoning method does not restrict residential uses to artists.

St. Paul's zoning ordinance was amended specifically to permit, in commercial and industrial zoning districts, the use of artist studios as both dwelling places and places of work by artists, artisans or craftspersons engaged in the application, teaching or performance of the arts.

The *Minneapolis Warehouse: Artist Living Space/Working Space Project*, conducted between 1977 and 1978, examined 80 buildings to assess their conversion potential for affordable, code-compliant artists' live/work uses. Another goal was to develop ways of protecting low- and moderate-income artists from displacement caused by their inability to compete with middle- and high-income people for space.

To implement the findings and recommendations of the study, the Minneapolis Arts Commission formed Artspace Projects, Inc., in 1978 as a nonprofit developer. Initial funding came from Minneapolis Community Development

212 North Center Street, Los Angeles. Live/work space.

Block Grants. Artspace has since developed more than 250 units of studio and studio/living spaces in Minneapolis and provided technical assistance to artists who developed many more.

Artspace also began to build a partnership with the city of St. Paul through the New Works/ St. Paul Space Study, New Works/St. Paul Exhibition and Performance Series, the Arts Development Plan and several artist live/work development projects. The Lowertown Lofts Artist Cooperative, an example of a public/private partnership in St. Paul, is described in chapter 6.

Most Artspace development projects have followed a "districting" model by concentrating development of a number of units within an area. In addition, through the provision of technical services to artists capable of developing their own spaces, Artspace has also fostered a "dispersing" model to integrate artists within the broader community. One of Artspace's roles has been as a liaison between artists and the departments of planning, zoning and building codes. Artspace has cooperated with the city in preparing handouts and organizing workshops on building code requirements and procedures for live/work space conversions as well as negotiating and advising on variance requests.

Artspace maintains a database of spaces available for studio, studio/living, rehearsal and performance uses throughout the seven-county area. Some buildings are later researched for their development potential; others are referred to artists in space listings mailed biweekly. Artspace requires artists seeking space listings to fill out an application form that allows basic market information to be gathered for development projects. Questions on the artist registration form help certify artists for Artspace development projects. Early on, rehabilitation grants and, later, revolving loan funds have provided financing for code-required improvements in Artspace development projects and in artists' private development efforts. A comprehensive program, born from

planning within each city, serves the diversity of artists' space needs in the Twin Cities.

LOS ANGELES

Live/work space is dispersed in Los Angeles because of the range of housing and buildings that accommodate live/work space needs. The concentration of artists has increased in the downtown since the city instituted an overlaying of zones and, beginning in 1974, a petitioning process to encourage living/ working space conversions.

Los Angeles created the Commercial and Artcraft district (C.A.) "for artcraft activities combined with commercial and residential uses." A C.A. district may be proposed in any part of the city, in areas of three acres or more, with signatures from 75 percent of the property owners and lessees providing support for the petition. As a result, there is no concentration of artists that would threaten to lead to displacement.

Wherever a C.A. zone overlays a residential zone, the residential building codes apply. Residential uses are permitted if limited to an accessory use in commercial and manufacturing zones with a C.A. overlay. Los Angeles maintains a goal of expanding the downtown residential base, which includes the presence of artists. Los Angeles also established a series of zoning and building code changes in the early 1980s called the Artists-In-Residence ordinance (A-I-R). This ordinance allows an artist to apply for a conditional-use permit, with the landlord's permission. The approval process includes a public hearing and the meeting of three requirements, as follows:

1. The artist must be engaged in business as an artist, with a business tax registration certificate verifying his/her profession.

2. Neighboring uses and those of the artist must be able to coexist.

5.5   PRIORITY POLICIES IN THE SAN FRANCISCO CITY PLANNING CODE

The following are priority policies affecting live/work space in San Francisco, California*:

Policy 1:

- Neighborhood-serving retail activities are generally located at ground level in commercial or industrial structures, and live/work units are generally located in upper-level spaces in such structures.
- Retail businesses and live/work tenants do not share the same kinds of spaces as a rule and therefore are not expected to compete for similar spaces.
- Retail uses generally pay higher rents, and it is not expected that live/work tenants would displace retail activities.
- The addition of live/work units in upper-level spaces of commercial or industrial structures is not expected to adversely affect neighborhood-serving retail businesses.

Policy 2:

The proposed legislation includes provisions for conserving and protecting existing neighborhood character and housing by:

- requiring conditional-use authorization for conversion of nonresidential, nonconforming-use structures in RH or RM Districts to live/work use (to insure participation by neighbors and neighborhood groups in the process to develop specific conditions for approval of individual live/work projects);
- requiring residential densities and residential parking standards for conversion of non-conforming-use structures in RH or RM Districts to live/work units;
- prohibiting the conversion of dwelling units to live/work units in RH or RM Districts;
- requiring conditional-use authorization for conversion of dwelling units to live/work units in C or M Districts; and
- recognizing the need to facilitate preservation of artists, craftspersons, and similarly situated individuals as vital and important components of the city's cultural and economic diversity.

Policy 3:

- The city's supply of affordable housing will be preserved and enhanced by the legalization of affordable housing for artists, craftspersons, and similarly situated small business-persons who share specific and extraordinary space needs by tailoring land use categories, parking, and open space standards to the particular needs of these groups.
- The conversion of underutilized upper-level spaces and providing very flexible density, open space, parking and freight loading standards for live/work units make live/work occupancy an attractive and affordable use.

- Legislation and building code standards will make live/work units one of the highest and best uses for these upper-level loft spaces as low-cost housing.
- Legalization of several hundred existing live/work units throughout the city's C and M Districts will preserve existing affordable housing for these tenants.
- Encouraging additional conversions will enhance the supply of affordable housing for households with specific and unique space needs.
- To the extent that specialized housing needs are met, the legislation would likely result in an increase in the supply of traditional dwelling units for other community residents with the effect of stabilizing rental rates for housing throughout the city.

Policy 4:

- Combining live and work activities within one space will reduce travel and congestion on transit services and city streets.
- Neighborhood parking is not expected to be adversely affected due to parking standards established for live/work use.

Policy 5:

- Industrial and service establishments are not expected to be displaced because they do not generally use the upper-level loft spaces that live/work units are expected to use.
- Artist live/work tenants pay similar rents as service and industrial activities and are not expected to "out-bid" them in a competition for space.
- Facilitating the development of small or "start-up" arts-related services, by allowing them to combine their living and working space, is expected to encourage and strengthen the service sector.

Policy 6:

- The building code standards for live/work quarters establish adequate life safety standards for live/work occupancy permits.

Policy 7:

- The preservation of landmark and historic buildings is expected to be facilitated by affordable conversion to live/work use.

Policy 8:

- The proposed legislation for live/work conversions is not expected to have an effect on parks, open space, public vistas, or sunlight access to these resources.

---

*Paraphrased with permission of the City of San Francisco.

82

3. The health, safety and welfare of the artist must be shown not to be endangered by the proposed use in a plan to meet all relevant building and safety codes (amended for this use).

The A-I-R ordinance designates that such a unit must be a minimum of 750 square feet, a maximum 33 percent of which is for living uses. Bath, shower and toilet requirements are the same as guest-room requirements, and heating is not required. Both living and working areas require smoke detectors. A serious difficulty is interpreting and meeting the earthquake code, applied to buildings constructed or renovated after 1930.

In late 1990, Los Angeles Artspace was formed as a nonprofit developer of live/work space for low- and moderate- income artists. An outgrowth of California Lawyers for the Arts (CLA), it is being modeled after Artspace in the Twin Cities as well as groups in Seattle and New York City. Another program of CLA, Arthouse/LA opened its doors in January 1991.

SAN FRANCISCO

Artists are dispersed throughout San Francisco, although there is a concentration in the South of Market (SOMA) district. Over the past decade, the SOMA district became too expensive for many artists, as businesses and offices expanded into the area. As part of the city's rezoning plan to preserve small businesses in SOMA, the area was identified as an arts and entertainment district, and planning codes sensitive to artists' live/work uses were drafted. But since the SOMA area was already too expensive for "not-yet-commercial" artists, artists, arts advocates and numerous representatives of the city began to create citywide live/work space zoning regulations.

Community concern about the city's cultural future has increased. Diverse cultural offerings for tourists and citizens have been threatened by pressures on artists' access to space, which increased as a result of the 1989 earthquake. Since the mid-1970s, the Bay Area has undertaken an extensive assessment of public policy issues, researched the needs and preferences of artists, evaluated models and resources, and taken action to resolve some of the space problems faced by artists. San Francisco has also reinterpreted local zoning ordinances and building codes, adopting amendments that would reduce the expense of meeting the code for artists.

In 1979, the Northern California Chapter of National Artists Equity published a report entitled *Live/Work Space—Changing Public Policy* to explore nuances of zoning issues and new responses to them. Their project, which included public meetings and a conference, encouraged the reassessment of public policy issues concerned with live/work space, including gentrification, employment and economic revitalization, technologies, energy conservation, ecology and lifestyles. Through that effort, artists in California were the first to recognize in a formal way that the issue of combined living and working space goes far beyond the arts community, including small business owners, inventors, farmers, service providers and people with handicaps or other special needs. In 1984, the Bay Area Partnership hosted a regional conference on space for artists which enhanced collaborations among California Lawyers for the Arts, the San Francisco Arts Commission, State-Locals Partnership Program, Innovative Housing and the Bay Area Partnership. Through this collaboration, ArtHouse was initiated first in San Francisco and later in Oakland.

By the end of 1988, artists, arts advocates, community representatives and city officials had completed a four-year community planning process to amend the City Planning Code, the city's zoning ordinance. They created new categories of uses called live/work units and arts activities and spaces. Some of the language in their ordinance is used here to clarify key policy issues for other cities considering a similar effort.

The 1988 zoning ordinance includes the following provisions:

- permits artist live/work units and arts activities as a principal use in residential/commercial, commercial and manufacturing districts
- establishes conditions for allowing live/ work units limited to arts activities as a conditional use in existing nonresidential structures in RH and RM residential districts
- restricts the conversion of dwelling units to live/work units
- modifies nonconforming use provisions with respect to live/work units
- establishes parking, density, and open space standards, with exceptions, for live/work units and arts activities

As part of its creation of a zoning ordinance that limits live/work units to arts activities, the city defined the terminology in the ordinance, rather than leaving it open to interpretation:

Arts Activities shall include: Performance; exhibition (except the exhibition of films); rehearsal; production; post-production; schools of any of the following: dance, music, dramatic art, film, video, graphic art, painting, draw-

ing, sculpture, small scale glass works, ceramics, textiles, woodworking, photography, custom made jewelry or apparel, and other visual, performance, sound arts and crafts.

Commercial arts and art-related business service uses include, but are not limited to: recording and editing services; small scale film and video developing and printing; titling; video and film libraries; special effects production; fashion and photo stylists; production, sale and rental of theatrical wardrobes; and studio property production and rental companies.

Art Spaces shall include: studios, workshops, galleries, museums, archives, theaters, and other similar spaces customarily used principally for arts activities, exclusive of movie theaters, dance halls, adult entertainment, and any other establishment where liquor is customarily served during performances.

Architecture and literature are not considered arts activities, because neither one can be distinguished from other office activities. Welding is not allowed within a live/work unit as a building code requirement.

The proposed legislation is consistent with eight priority policies of the City Planning Code (see box 5.5).

"If you would know the value of money, go and try to borrow some."
Benjamin Franklin, Poor Richard's Almanac

6
Financing

Financing sources are like rocks in a stream, some above and others below the surface, and always changing their position in the flow. Just as you may select different rocks each time you step across the stream, so must you select from financing sources which are currently at the surface when you package your project's financing.

This chapter outlines the possibilities for financing by providing a political and economic context, an overview of the lending process, and descriptions of possible sources. The chapter then offers information for packaging several financing sources to achieve affordability, including general information about preparing a prospectus and the pro forma. Worksheets for planning your financial strategy conclude the chapter.

The Political and Economic Context for Affordable Financing

Throughout the 1960s, real estate financing was relatively easy to secure. Someone seeking a loan would prepare a loan application or development prospectus. The lender would have the property appraised, check the credit references and estimate the size of loan that could be provided. The project was usually on its way.

By the 1970s, however, as a result of changing patterns of private investment, lenders could no longer originate loans for their own investment portfolios. People had shifted investments from their bank savings accounts to stocks, bonds, money market funds, gold etc. for higher yields. High unemployment and inflation also reduced the funds available for mortgages. Therefore, a secondary market was created as a money pipeline between lenders and borrowers. Lenders now sell loans they originate to the Federal National Mortgage Association (FNMA), the Federal Home Loan Mortgage Corporation (FHLMC), the Government National Mortgage Association (GNMA), or the Mortgage Guaranty Insurance Corporation (MGIC). These organizations receive their funds from investors who participate in the secondary market through securities dealers.

One significant effect of the increased use and expansion of the secondary mortgage market in the 1970s was standardization of loan applications, appraisal methods, promissory notes and mortgage formats. With standardization, lenders adopted conservative and fairly inflexible underwriting criteria, which have hindered artists' ability to qualify for loans for live/work projects. Another hindrance to financing for live/work space projects is the dependence of most lenders upon Federal Housing Administration (FHA) insurance programs, which define building standards in terms of traditional housing.

The interest rate a borrower must pay to obtain a loan is dependent upon the cost of money to the lender and the amount of perceived risk. During the 1970s, rates of 8 to 11 percent were charged to home loan borrowers. By the early 1980s, national economic conditions created great uncertainty among lenders. Lenders were no longer willing to provide long-term, fixed-rate mortgages. They instituted variable-rate mortgages, with interest rates that rise and fall during the life of the loan to reflect current conditions. By 1982, the rate for conventional loans had risen to as high as 19 to 21 percent for "conservative deals."

Although interest rates on loans rose with inflation rates, the interest paid to depositors by banks and savings and loans was fixed. Shifting patterns of private investment put pressure on Congress to deregulate the banking industry. The 1982 savings and loan (S&L) deregulation allowed thrifts to abandon low-paying home loans in favor of higher paying junk bonds, speculative loans on office buildings, shopping centers, high-rise apartments and other commercial real estate. By the mid-1980s, some cities were overbuilt, properties stood vacant, developers went bankrupt, and foreclosures could not pay off the debts based on inflated values. Additionally, home foreclosures skyrocketed, in part because many mortgages with variable interest rates became unaffordable. At present, a lack of funds for mortgages continues to prevent many S&Ls from making real estate loans. As a result of renewed economic prosperity in some sectors, however, interest rates have come down and the availability of loan funds have increased somewhat. Fixed-rate, long-term mortgages have returned, benefitting buyers of mortgageable properties, such as homes and condominiums.

Federal government housing, financing and tax laws all affect affordable live/work development. Federal financing programs are channelled through cities, housing finance agencies, redevelopment authorities or lenders—with restrictions intended to target specific housing and economic development priorities of national concern. In order to be used for arts development projects, the broad goals of federal programs must be interpreted at the local level. Congress continues to propose tax, budget and legislative proposals that may eventually affect the sources and amounts of funds available to assist the housing and economic development activities in our communities. After years of cutting funding for affordable housing programs, Congress adopted the Cranston-Gonzalez Affordable Housing Act in late 1990. As financing sources, governmental programs are discussed later in greater detail.

BASICS OF REAL ESTATE FINANCING

Surveys of buildings and potential tenant markets can provide you with the basic information needed for developing a preliminary budget. Refer to the information you gathered with the buyer's valuation process concluding Chapter Three to aid your preparation of a budget. Your planning continues with the evaluation of financing sources and creation of a five year cash flow projection that "tests" the feasibility of a project. Rework these plans and numbers until you arrive at a budget that provides the lender with the confidence needed to provide financing to allow you to acquire and renovate the building. To assist you, sample forms are provided in the appendix.

Uses and Sources of Funds

The major budget components of financing a real estate property or development project are the "sources" and "uses" of funds. Uses are expenditures required to get the project built. Sources are the type and amount of funding required to cover those expenditures. Different uses, or costs, are associated with each of the four phases of the development process: predevelopment, acquisition, development and operations. Uses are often referred to as either "soft costs" or "hard costs." Soft costs include appraisals, permits and consultant fees, while hard costs are the "bricks and mortar" expenses which include acquisitions, materials and labor. These uses of funds are summarized on the project pro forma. See the sample preliminary project pro forma in appendix 6.1 for an example of how sources and uses are represented to form a project budget.

Predevelopment costs are those incurred in planning and structuring the renovation of the property and are generally considered soft costs. They may include an option on property, architecture and engineering design fees, legal fees (entity documents, filing, tax opinion, etc.), accounting/financial planning fees, printing (prospectus, marketing materials, etc.), lender's commitment feed (points, etc.), syndication sales fees, and permit fees.

Acquisition costs include all costs associated with acquiring the property, which will be affected by the manner in which the property is acquired, such as outright ownership (mortgages, contract for deed, etc.), partial ownership (equity-sharing, syndication, etc.) or a long-term lease (legal fees, leasing co-op). Costs may be incurred for an appraisal, title insurance, environmental impact or toxicity studies, closing costs, escrow taxes, liability insurance, and the broker's commission.

Development costs are those expended in renovating the property and are considered hard costs. They will include materials and labor, taxes and insurance during construction, interest on money borrowed, the investor's profit and/or developer's profit, and contingency fees.

Operations are expenses for maintaining the

property after occupancy and include taxes, insurance, utilities, repair, maintenance, vacancy, bad debts, management costs, and capital improvements. Monthly payments by residents of the completed project must be enough to cover the debt payments, interest on the debt, and the monthly costs of maintaining the property (management and operating costs, or M&Os). With a single unit, the lender will use a percentage of your annual income as a factor in determining your capacity to cover these costs. In a multi-unit project, financial projections are made based on a pro forma and a cash flow projection for 5 to 10 years. (See appendices 6.1, pro forma; 6.2, estimate of equity and financing source; and 6.3, cash flow projection.) The income of the entire project must be shown to be adequate to meet all monthly expenses. The monthly costs of maintaining the property are otherwise independent of the financing costs and will require payment regardless of the financing devices used to proceed with the project.

Once you have projected the uses of funds, you then identify the potential sources of financing. Two primary types of financing are available: equity and debt. Equity typically is the investment made by buyers of a property. Debt is borrowed capital. Unless the funds needed come entirely from your personal savings, financing requires some use of other people's money. Whether that financing is in the form of an investment by others or borrowed funds, there is generally a cost associated with using someone else's money. This cost is calculated as interest in the case of debt and profit or return on investment in the case of equity. The return a lender or investor requires for an investment in a project with a specific level of risk is the "market rate" for that investment.

In some circumstances, a lender or an investor may be willing to accept a below market return. This is the case with subsidized funds. Subsidies are below market interest rate (BMIR)

funds provided to encourage activities that benefit the public. These funds are often available in the form of both debt and equity to subsidize creation of affordable housing or economic development in depressed neighborhoods. There are a number of options within each financing source, some of which are shown in box 6.1. These sources are discussed in greater detail, beginning on page 97.

There are many nuances within this basic framework of equity and debt sources. The funds available for a project will change as the financial climate and the public policy agenda change. This chapter provides an introduction to the sources that have evolved and gives some insight into how your project might be viewed by those you approach for financing.

One of the first sources considered is a private loan. A local lender, through the analysis conducted during the lending process, can tell you whether a single mortgage will suffice or if additional sources of financing are needed. Not every source is available to every project in every city. Your project may require packaging a number of sources in order to find a financing scheme compatible with the chosen market.

Obtaining expert advice from professionals will help you to realize benefits from new programs, changed tax laws and alternative solutions. Needed expertise may come from a development consultant, a nonprofit development partner, an accountant, an attorney, or other professionals.

THE LENDING PROCESS

The lending process for a loan for a home or small building may be as direct as completing a loan application which provides the lender with information about the property and the borrower. Some of the information requested on that application will be the same as required for a larger development project. You can indicate the type of loan, interest rate, and payment schedule you

6.1 FINANCING OPTIONS

Equity Sources:

Private (only):

- artist/resident savings or investments, as in a down payment
- investments by the developer or development partners
- investments by passive investors through limited partnership (attracted by indirect economic incentives achieved through legal structure, project finance structure, historic tax credits or other tax benefits advantageous to investors)

Debt Sources:

Private:

- commercial banks
- mutual savings banks
- savings & loan associations
- savings & loan service corporations
- mortgage bankers and brokers
- insurance companies and pension funds (large projects)
- credit unions
- owner financing: contract for deed
- private loan agreements with patrons, friends or relatives
- public financing channelled through private lenders

Public:

- housing rental rehab loans through city or state programs
- proceeds of tax exempt bonds sold by the city to investors
- CDBG, HODAG, UDAG or HUD federal programs through the city
- energy conservation programs through the city or state
- property acquisition or write-down through the city
- program-related investment or loan guarantees through the city

Subsidy Sources:

Private:

- "bargain sale"/property write-down by the owner
- reduced professional fees as a consultant's in-kind contribution
- reduced material costs from suppliers, as an in-kind contribution
- program-related investments with BMIR or interest-only payments from foundations (most channeled through a nonprofit or city agency)
- tax-deductible gifts or grants (from foundations, corporations or individuals) contributed through a nonprofit development sponsor or city agency
- LISC interest rate write-down, loan guarantee or BMIR loan
- market rate loans from commercial lenders with interest only payments

Public:

- tax increment financing (interest rate reduction subsidy)
- local/state/federal government grant programs
- homestead property tax treatment, affecting private homes, condos, cooperatives or leased limited equity cooperatives
- interest-only payments on low-interest loans from the city
- deferment of principal and interest on city loans
- forgiving of interest by the city if project purpose maintained for X years

prefer as part of your loan request. Your project may require a more formal presentation of a prospectus, which is described in greater detail later.

The decision to lend funds to a project encompasses an assessment of the planning, the quality of the presentation by the development team, and the ability of the project to meet standard underwriting criteria used by most lenders.

Loan Documents

Real estate debt financing is most commonly accomplished with the use of mortgages. The mortgage is the contract that secures a specific property as collateral for a debt, evidenced by a promissory note. The borrower is called the mortgagor and the lender is called the mortgagee.

A promissory note of a mortgage loan is a separate contract that specifies the amount of money borrowed and the conditions under which it will be repaid. If the terms of the loan are not met, the lender may seek legal recourse through the promissory note or through the mortgage. Typically, the lender seeks recourse first through the mortgage, which allows foreclosure on the property if the terms of the promissory note are not met.

In some states, a trust deed is used rather than a mortgage. Under a deed of trust, the borrower is called the trustor, the lender is called the beneficiary, and a neutral party, who holds the title "in trust" until the debt is paid, is called the trustee. If the borrower fails to meet the conditions of the loan, the trustee can sell the property to repay the loan.

When more capital is needed than the first mortgage can provide, additional "junior" mortgages, subordinate to the first mortgage, can be issued. The seniority of the mortgage or trust deed is indicated by its designation as "first," "second," "third" or "fourth." Second or lower positioned mortgages are usually written for shorter terms and higher interest rates because they carry more risk of not being paid back. The same property is typically the collateral for all of the mortgages.

LOAN PAYMENT SCHEDULES

Mortgages or trust deeds may be structured with any combination of repayment schedule agreeable to all parties to the loan. The "fixed-rate fully amortized mortgage" is the most frequently used payment schedule. It has constant periodic payments of principal and interest. In the early years of the mortgage, interest is the major portion of the payments, whereas in later years principal is the major component.

A "partially amortized mortgage" requires periodic payments of principal with the balance due at the end of the term. The final lump-sum payment is called a "balloon" payment. An "interest-only" or "straight-term mortgage" requires no principal payments during the term of the mortgage.

Inflationary pressures caused the creation of "variable rate" or "adjustable rate mortgages" (ARMs), in which the interest rate may vary over the term of the mortgage either by a predetermined index or changes in the cost of capital. One benefit of ARMs is that they have lower initial interest rates. Thus they allow access to ownership for those whose income is too low to qualify for fixed-rate loans. Another benefit of ARMs, for those people planning to sell within two to five years, is their lower payments for the short term. A variation is "graduated-payment mortgages," where the interest rate stays the same but the monthly payments start out low, then rise over time above the level of a conventional mortgage with the same terms to cover unpaid principal.

A new loan that equals or exceeds the balance of any existing loans may be called a "wraparound," "blanket," or "extended first mortgage." Such a loan is used to facilitate the sale of a property by releasing new funds. In a cooperative, one mortgage is taken for the entire project, with members purchasing a "share" in the cooperative corporation equal to their share of the mortgage and other costs. Cooperatives are therefore said to have a blanket mortgage covering all of the units.

Construction Loans

If your project entails major renovation or new construction, you may go through a two-step process of financing. The equity and "permanent" mortgage are sources of long-term funds. An "interim," "swing" or "construction loan" would be obtained first to cover acquisition and renovation costs. The interim period is usually for 18 months or less, depending on the length of construction time.

Construction lenders include all types of financial institutions from commercial banks to S&Ls and insurance companies. The construction lending department is usually staffed by specialists who are experts in lien law, construction practices and progress payments.

The loan will be based on a percentage of the anticipated value of the property after construction or renovation is completed. Also, with construction financing, the developer normally draws on the loan funds as the work proceeds instead of receiving the entire amount at one time. Often, to begin, the developer requires a minimum of 25 percent of the value after renovation.

Because of the risk, construction financing is higher priced than permanent or "take-out" financing. Risks include delays, materials price increases and liens placed on the property by subcontractors who have not been promptly paid. On average, construction loans are priced at 1 to 3 percent more than permanent financing costs.

The construction lender usually specializes in this type of loan and expects to be "taken out"—paid off—by the permanent lender when

the project is completed. The same lender will sometimes make a commitment to permanent financing, available after the work is completed. If not, the group must go shopping for another loan. Refinancing can be advantageous because the interest rate is usually lower on permanent financing.

THE COSTS OF BORROWING

Because of the amount of funds borrowed and the duration of a mortgage, even small variations in interest rates can translate into tens of thousands of dollars over the life of the mortgage. Interest is the compensation paid for the use of money. Interest rates are lower when the supply of money is expanded and lenders are under pressure to "get the money out" rapidly. Expectations for whether rates will be rising or falling will influence the desire of the lender to make a loan, the type of loan offered, and the rate charged. The business sections of many newspapers regularly publish the current interest rates being charged by various lenders.

A point is a charge for making a loan, representing 1 percent of the loan. Points are usually deducted from the loan proceeds. The interest rate is often supplemented by one or more points to increase the yield to the lender. Points are not considered as interest if charged to offset lender expense incurred in making the loan.

If you are likely to sell or refinance in ten years or less, you may find a lower overall cost by paying a higher loan interest rate with no points ("point-free"), than you would by paying a lower interest rate with points. Typically, the effect of the true cost of points will be less the longer you plan to stay with the property.

Commitment fees and loan brokerage fees may also need to be paid to the lender. Commitment fees are charged for the promise of securing loan funds for a future date. Brokerage fees are paid to a mortgage broker for "placing" a loan with a lender. A mortgage company or S&L may act as a mortgage broker, charging 1 to 5 points for placing the loan with another lender. Some banks now charge for legal fees and other costs of completing the loan as additional fees to the borrower, so be sure to check the small print of the loan documents.

CALCULATING AFFORDABLE DEBT

To calculate the maximum monthly mortgage payment you can qualify for, a quick rule of thumb is the following: (1) your monthly payment cannot exceed approximately 28 percent of your annual income divided by 12 months; and (2) your total monthly debt payments include the mortgage plus all other recurring debt expenses. The total of these can not exceed 36 percent of your annual income divided by 12 months. Recurring debt expenses include credit card payments, child support, student loans, car payments, etc. Lenders recognize that insurance, taxes, food, clothing, health care, transportation and entertainment expenses must also come from the borrower's income.

To ascertain the combined income capacity of your group for securing a mortgage, make the calculations in box 6.2 for each member and total the results. Whatever the group cannot afford as debt must be allocated to an equity contribution when calculating the project budget and financing needs.

The maximum loan (principal and interest) that a lender will make to your project depends in part on the capacity of the project to cover amortized payments to repay the loan. The terms of the loan, including the size of downpayment, interest rate, points and fees payable, and the number of years over which the loan will be repaid all affect the size of the loan the lender will make. A quick comparison of the effect of different interest rates over different payback periods is shown in box 6.3. For more complete comparative information, use a financial calculator with a variety of alternatives for estimated interest rates, number of payments (terms) and the anticipated size of mortgage to explore financing scenarios for your project.

MEETING WITH THE LENDER

To make the best use of your time when meeting with a lender, be prepared to discuss: (1) the purpose of the loan, (2) how much capital you need, (3) when you will need the funds, (4) how

---

6.2   CALCULATING AFFORDABLE DEBT

Total annual income $ _____ × 28% = $ _____ Annual Debt Service, 12 months = $ _____ /M

Total annual income $ _____ × 8% = $ _____ Max. Allowable recurring debt/yr. or $ _____ /M

Total annual income $ _____ × 36% = $ _____ Maximum Total Debt Capacity: $ _____ /M

6.3   AMORTIZATION SCHEDULE

Equal Monthly Payments to Amortize a Loan of $1,000

Rate (percent)	Terms (years) 20	25	30	35
8	$ 8.37	$ 7.72	$ 7.34	$ 7.11
8 1/4	8.53	7.89	7.52	7.29
8 1/2	8.68	8.06	7.69	7.47
8 3/4	8.84	8.23	7.87	7.66
9	9.00	8.40	8.05	7.84
9 1/4	9.16	8.57	8.23	8.03
9 1/2	8.33	8.74	8.41	8.22
9 3/4	9.49	8.92	8.60	8.41
10	9.66	9.09	8.78	8.60
10 1/4	9.82	9.27	8.97	8.79
10 1/2	9.99	9.45	9.15	8.99
10 3/4	10.15	9.62	9.33	9.18
11	10.32	9.80	9.52	9.37
11 1/4	10.49	9.98	9.71	9.56
11 1/2	10.66	10.16	9.90	9.76
11 3/4	10.84	10.35	10.09	9.96
12	11.01	10.53	10.29	10.16
12 1/4	11.19	10.72	10.48	10.35
12 1/2	11.36	10.90	10.67	10.55
12 3/4	11.54	11.09	10.87	10.75

Source: Reprinted by permission from *The Thorndike Encyclopedia of Banking and Financial Tables: Revised Edition* by David Thorndike, copyright © 1980, Warren, Gorham and Lamont Inc., 210 South Street, Boston, Massachusetts. All rights reserved.

the project needs. It may be appropriate for you to ask what additional information is needed or to suggest a visit to your current space(s). Ask the lender whether any problems are anticipated with your loan application. If so, have the lender outline each possible difficulty and potential solutions. Obtain a list of commitment requirements and a timeline by which you may receive preliminary approval.

Translate your resources and expenses into the language understood by the lender. Describe your activities in terms of the combined needs of low/moderate income housing, small business, commercial and economic development lending. Lenders may be unfamiliar with the need to combine working and living activity. Most lenders have guidelines that prevent a loan for residential use to be applied towards the cost of upgrading studio (business/commercial) space.

What the Lender Looks For

The analysis and approval of a loan application are said to reflect the "seven Cs of credit": (1) character (trustworthy applicant); (2) capacity (repayment ability); (3) capital (equity); (4) collateral (recourse for unpaid debt); (5) conditions (terms); (6) communication (honesty between lender and applicant); and (7) commitment (signing note/commitment to borrower).

Lenders are "risk evaluators." When a lender reviews a real estate loan application, she or he assesses the probability of being repaid on time and in full. In deciding which loans to approve, the lender uses underwriting guidelines typically to reflect the following:

APPRAISAL AND TITLE SEARCH. An appraisal of the property and a title search determine the fair market value of the property and condition of the title. If the appraised value is lower than the purchase price, the lender will require the buyer to make a larger cash down

long you will need the funds, (5) when the funds can be repaid, (6) a market study or committed resident list, (7) project feasibility and (8) cashflow projections with a narrative explanation of assumptions.

In your meeting with the lender, you will present the prospectus materials and describe payment to protect the lender from over-lending on the value of the property. If the title search reveals problems with claiming clear ownership of the property, the lender would ask to have those cleared before approving a loan. These aspects of the property are important to the lender because, if the buyer defaults, the lender will use the property to recover the loan.

ECONOMIC LIFE OF THE STRUCTURE.

The age, quality of proposed construction or renovation, and current state of repair of the structure will be assessed to ensure that the term of the loan will not outlast the economic life of the structure serving as collateral.

LOAN-TO-VALUE RATIO.

Loans are often offered at 70 percent of the value of the property, protecting the lender from a drop in property value that could exceed the amount of the outstanding loan. The proposed down payment (equity), the size of loan requested, and the amount of other financing needed are combined and converted into a "loan-to-value" ratio. Loan-to-value ratios from 70 percent to 90 percent are within an acceptable range, but the higher ratios represent higher risk to the lender. The lender may require the borrower to seek FHA or private mortgage insurance, or pay a higher interest rate. The effect of the loan-to-value criteria may require other sources of subordinated debt rather than a higher equity contribution from low- to moderate-income artists.

FUNDS FOR CLOSING.

The lender assesses the source and amount of the borrower's funds for the closing—that is, the time when all documents are signed and title to the property is transferred to the buyer. Lenders tend to expect a higher probability of default and foreclosure if the borrower must borrow the down payment or the closing settlement funds.

USES OF THE PROPERTY.

The lender assesses the proposed use of the property and the borrower's attitude to determine the likelihood of repayment during periods of poor economic conditions. Lenders consider that monthly payments are more likely to be made on owner-occupied projects, which are also more likely to be well maintained. Projects dependent on rental income to repay the debt are considered to be riskier.

COMPARATIVE COSTS.

The lender compares costs on what the borrower will pay if the loan is approved. Artists that have been paying for separate work space and housing may be able to show a cost savings if seeking financing for a combined live/work space.

RECORD OF DEBT REPAYMENT.

The borrower's past record of debt repayments is seen by the lender as an indicator of the borrower's future commitment to repay the requested loan. Borrowers with a history of credit collections, adverse judgments, bankruptcies or pending lawsuits will have a difficult time proving their intentions to repay the requested loan.

PROJECT PRO FORMA.

The lender examines the project pro forma for a multi-unit project to determine whether the projected monthly income is sufficient, given the estimated costs to run the project. The project pro forma is a detailed financial analysis showing total project costs and containing a cash-flow projection (5 to 10 years) of annual income and expenses. The lender will look at the debt coverage ratio which equals the net operating income (NOI) divided by the debt service (DS). The debt coverage ratio (DCR) tells the number of times the income will "cover" the debt service, with ratios of 1.2 to 1.4 preferred by lenders. More information about the pro forma is available later in the chapter.

SITE AND STRUCTURE

In 1984, glass artist Dick Huss had the opportunity to purchase a two-story, commercial building. The building had 5,780 square feet of space for living, working, and exhibiting, plus a stone-walled courtyard that could be converted to outside exhibition space.

Built in the early 1900s, the triangular brick building was structurally sound. Its last commercial use had been a headquarters for a transfer company, and a cement block addition had been built to house the company trucks. In the 1940s, tenants occupied a second-floor apartment, which since that time had never been remodeled. The floors were oak, but they were in very poor condition.

FINANCING

Huss used his own savings and sold several major pieces of art to raise a $20,000 down payment on the purchase price of $65,000. Huss met with the mayor and received letters of recommendation from his councilmember and from three galleries to support his loan request from the bank. A $45,000 mortgage at 14 percent interest was financed by First Bank East and guaranteed by one of Huss's patrons. Money still had to be found, however, to convert the building into live/work space.

The Dayton-Bluff Neighborhood Housing Service (NHS) was delighted to have Huss move into the neighborhood and, after a year, committed to finance the residential portion of the project of $72,000 at 9 percent interest. Huss spent $65,000 on the upstairs living quarters; with the rest, he stabilized the basement with new footings and beams and replaced the roof. Because Huss would be living on the premises, he could also take advantage of favorable homestead tax breaks. Huss moved into the space in October 1985.

At the same time that Huss applied to the NHS, he also applied for a commercial loan to rehabilitate the building's first floor, which would house his studio and a retail gallery. He planned to take advantage of a low-interest loan program offered by the city of St. Paul. Through the program, the city will fund up to half of a requested loan if the applicant can procure equivalent financing from a commercial bank. An applicant must undergo the bank's typical underwriting approval process for the full amount, which the city relies on for its commercial evaluation.

In May 1985, with the help of a friend who had a background in construction management and commercial lending, Huss prepared a loan package complete with financial statements and an outline for a business plan to support the project and presented it to the bank. Although the project was approved by the city, the bank denied the loan because the financial statements weren't strong enough.

Huss did not give up. In January 1986, Huss applied to Artspace Projects, Inc. for revolving loan program funds to install new doors and windows in the studio's hot glass manufacturing area, which currently serves as a main entrance for clients as well as a work entry way. The request was granted, and the old garage doors were replaced with attractive, anodized aluminum bronze doors (double-paned and insulated) with coordinated, vented windows. Total cost for the renovations was $7,500, including materials, installation, and hardware.

Studio exterior before conversion.

Exterior after conversion.

94

Interior before conversion.

Interior after conversion.

Huss continued to explore government programs and worked to strengthen his financial base. In 1989, he reapplied to the city and to Norwest Bank St. Paul and was approved by both, each for 50 percent of his projected project costs. The city approved a loan of $49,000 at 4 percent interest for a 15-year term, and the bank approved a standard commercial loan of $49,000 at 12 percent interest over 15 years. By combining the two loans, the effective interest rate for Huss's project was 9.12 percent, a savings in interest costs of approximately $275 per month from what he would have had to pay if a bank had financed the full amount of his project.

The project was completed in 1990. Although it took some work, Dick Huss's experience shows that city and neighborhood agencies can be a valuable resource for project financing.

WHAT BANKS WANT

"Everyone I have talked to has stressed, 'what is your business plan?'" says Huss. "Ninety percent of new businesses fail because they don't have a strong business plan. This is why banks don't want to talk to you if you don't have a business history." Huss structures his business plan according to four types of art works: limited edition; mold- blown pieces; one-of-a-kind pieces; and marble making. He makes business projections by showing how much income he would produce in each category if he worked for 60 days.

Huss finds that running his own gallery has many advantages: he has reduced his commission costs, and he can deal with clients directly on a retail basis. These two advantages have improved his cash flow and have strengthened the business plan that he presents to banks.

Advises Huss, "When you go into a bank to meet with a loan officer, you should bring the following:

- taxes for three years
- projections on what it costs to run your studio
- expenses before and after income
- yearly interest payments, plus principal, if you own property
- cash flow projections for a year into the future

"The banks break this down and make spreadsheets in to evaluate your project and make their decision. They want to know if you are 'bankable.' You need to prove this with a history, recordkeeping, reputation, and growth."

FINAL ADVICE

Dick Huss offers some general words of advice for others about to embark on similar live/work conversion enterprises:

- Talk to as many people who have done it as you can.
- Establish goals and get help from other professionals.
- Find out what your market is and whether you can afford it.
- Get a list of reputable contractors.
- Find out what programs offer low interest loans.
- Learn to be very patient.
- Make a commitment and have the tenacity to stick to it.
- Create as many win/win situations as you can.
- Learn to be frustrated, but not angry.
- Have a plan, direction, and goals— then go for it.

ABILITY TO PAY. Gross monthly income is compared to total housing expense, with lenders requiring 28 percent or less of annual income going towards the borrower's mortgage debt payments. Total monthly payments on the mortgage and other debts should not exceed 36 percent of one's income. Existing debts and liabilities are compared to total assets to determine the net worth of the borrower. Inadequate net worth or monthly cash flow may reduce the amount of the loan approved or result in loan denial. The borrower's liquid assets are noted to determine the borrower's ability to recover from significant unexpected expenses or income loss. For a sole ownership project or condominium, the lender assesses the reliability of the person's job or income source, income adequacy, net worth and credit rating. In a multi-unit project, the lender will tend to look first at the ability of the real estate to repay the debt through projected rental income, then at the developer's net worth. If the project is being syndicated, the development team and the syndicator's reputation will be assessed for their credibility to carry the project through. If the project is perceived as risky, the lender may require the deposit by the borrower of a cash loan guarantee with the lender, separate from the downpayment and refundable at a later date.

RELATIONSHIP TO ARTISTS. Artists frequently exceed the "percent of income criteria" due to low incomes and the extra cost of space for their work, even though their work in that space may not be a significant source of income. Grants, awards, and residencies are seldom considered dependable sources of income for artists or artist-run organizations. Artists with irregular income or cash flow often have a difficult time qualifying for a loan independently. Cooperatives, allowing artists to qualify as a group, have been the most successful vehicle for providing long-term ownership benefits to artists. A resident selection policy in a cooperative has flexibility for a more lenient view of these underwriting criteria because of the group's ability to qualify under a blanket mortgage.

Reassuring the Lender

Creating a "new use" in an underdeveloped or distressed area may be considered risky by lenders. Lenders hesitate to find themselves the owners of a special-use residential project that is far from other residential properties or lacking in other residential amenities. The lack of investment in an area is considered "proof" by some lenders that investment would be unwise. Lenders are reluctant to provide loans to stimulate such activity, unless there are preexisting buyers or tenants who want the space. Offset lenders' fears and reluctance by involving other public sources of support and by organizing your group to confirm 100 percent occupancy.

Rather than a full-fledged lease, a "commitment to lease" contract can be drawn up which lays out the conditions under which a prospective tenant agrees to take space in the project. A less formal variation is to use letters from prospective buyers/tenants expressing their interest, rather than signed agreements.

Conventional loans are those which are not insured or guaranteed by FHA or VA insurance programs, protection for lenders against losses due to nonrepayment. Private mortgage insurance may be requested by your lender if the project or the residents cannot qualify for FHA or VA mortgage insurance.

The Lender's Response

The lending institution will analyze, and possibly adjust, the submitted plans and documents. If the project is approved at this stage, the lender will make a mortgage commitment subject to certain terms and conditions, which may include: (1) completion of the project in accordance with the plans and specifications; (2) completion within a certain time period and within a certain budget; and (3) firm leases for a portion of the spaces at specified rents to provide further evidence that the project is financially feasible. Depending on the type of loan and perceived risk, loan amortization schedules typically extend up to thirty years.

Loan Denials

Most loans are denied on the basis of the economic risk of the proposal or the inability to repay the loan. Refusal of a loan is also acceptable if the property is in violation of zoning laws, significant health, safety or building codes, deed covenants, conditions or restrictions, or other factors such as known geological hazards, environmental hazards or demolition plans. Lenders are increasingly concerned about lending on former commercial or industrial sites (for example, gasoline stations, dry cleaners) proposed for redevelopment without some kind of environmental audit disclosing any anticipated costs of removing asbestos or other hazardous elements that contaminate a property.

The federal Equal Credit Opportunity Act (ECOA) prohibits discrimination based on age, sex, marital status, race, color, religion, country of national origin, receipt of public assistance or the exercising of rights under the Consumer Credit Protection Act. A lender cannot deny a loan based on the racial composition or the income level of the neighborhood.

If your loan has been turned down, ask for recommendations on improving your proposal and finding other sources of financing. Perhaps another lender would be receptive. Consider repackaging your project with other sources of equity or subsidy to lower the amount of debt required, to include BMIR funds for a lower blended interest rate, or to extend the amortized payback schedule. You could also consider lower-

ing the project cost through revised architectural plans. Using financing tools in a creative way can make most projects financeable.

Loan Foreclosure

Foreclosure is the legal process begun by a mortgagee or lien creditor to gain title to property owned by the mortgagor. Conditions for a default of the mortgage are described in the mortgage. Since providing legal notice to foreclose takes some time, a mortgagee will prefer for the default to be cured through payment of the debt or a "work-out" plan to revise the loan terms. Private lenders tend to act more quickly in foreclosing to protect against increased losses when debts continue to go unpaid.

There are standard procedures for each of the four foreclosure periods: (1) the collection period; (2) the preforeclosure period; (3) the foreclosure; and (4) the postforeclosure period. What happens during each period varies from lender to lender. States with statutory redemption legislation permit foreclosed-property owners to pay the debt with interest and reclaim title even for a stated period of time after the foreclosure sale of the property.

NOTES ON SOURCES OF FINANCING

Financing sources must include equity and usually require some form of debt, although either equity or debt may come from more than one source. To provide you with a broader understanding of the options available to you, this section summarizes debt sources first, because they tend to be more familiar, then describes equity sources, and then some sources which may be either equity or debt.

Discovering what sources of financing will be available for your project may require interview-

98

ing a number of lenders or mortgage brokers. Seek recommendations from others with similar types of projects to locate a lender who will understand and support your project. Lenders who indicate that they are not currently interested in lending on projects such as yours may simply not be capable of making a loan of the size you need.

DEBT SOURCES

Private

COMMERCIAL BANKS AND MUTUAL SAVINGS BANKS. Commercial banks have ranked second in residential lending and emphasize construction loans because of their shorter maturities. Because of their lending role on commercial properties, commercial banks may be the best source for mortgages on live/work projects. Located primarily in the northeastern United States, mutual savings banks also place a high percentage of their loans into real estate.

SAVINGS AND LOAN ASSOCIATIONS. Before the current thrift industry crisis, which began in 1989, savings and loan associations (also called homestead associations in Louisiana or cooperative banks in Massachusetts) were the largest source of loan money for long-term mortgages on residential real estate. They are owned by their depositors and usually specialize in loans in limited local geographic areas. They may or may not be a ready source of funds for a project in your area.

MORTGAGE BANKER, BROKER OR MORTGAGE COMPANY. A mortgage banker or mortgage company makes mortgage loans and sells them to long-term investors. Life insurance companies, pension funds, trust funds, savings institutions or government agencies generally in-

vest in blocks of mortgages. Mortgage brokers can be a good place to start looking for a loan. They do not lend their own money, but specialize in bringing borrowers and lenders together.

INSURANCE COMPANIES AND PENSION FUNDS. Only very experienced developers are able to attract insurance companies or pension funds for their projects. These lenders tend to be interested in very safe institutional real estate and traditional investment opportunities. Since live/work space is not fully accepted as a traditional investment vehicle, this is not a likely source for your project.

CREDIT UNIONS. Credit unions are primarily sources of consumer loans, although some have begun to lend first and second mortgages. As nonprofit cooperatives owned by those who save and borrow with them, credit unions are governed by their member owners. The Artists Community Federal Credit Union is national in scope, although you must become a member of one of its member organizations. Contact (212) 385-0595 for more information.

CONTRACT FOR DEED OR OWNER (SELLER) FINANCING. Sometimes a property is sold with the seller providing the mortgage directly, especially where institutional financing is unavailable or the property is difficult to sell. Alternatives include a "purchase money mortgage," the "installment land contract" and "contract for deed."

Owner financing can be used when the seller prefers to receive payments over time to spread out the taxes that they would pay on their gain from the sale. Owner financing may be used in a subordinate position with a construction or permanent loan received from a lending institution, reducing the amount the institution would lend.

The owner financing may take a subordinated loan position as a junior lien behind a construction or permanent loan. When the buyer is allowed to substitute a promissory note for cash, the seller is said to be "taking back paper."

Owner financing can be used for additional debt beyond the buyer's assumption of the seller's mortgage. When the seller lends a portion of the debt, usually subordinate to the first mortgage and for a shorter term, it is called "carry-back financing." The Brickbottom project in Sommerville, MA, used $1 million in seller financing as one of four sources that totalled $21.8 million to buy and renovate the building. See box 6.5 as an example of incorporating seller financing as part of a complete financing structure.

With a contract, the title does not immediately pass to the new owner. Hence it is important to have the title examined before entering a contract to purchase the property. The buyer should also record the contract to establish the buyer's interest in the property. One risk in owner financing is that a default on the contract payments may lead to a more sudden loss of the property than would occur following the mortgage foreclosure provisions of a lending institution (the notice requirements and redemption rights vary from state to state).

Owner financing can also be used in a leasehold situation in which the owner is willing to secure funds to finance renovation in return for agreements with the tenant. Typically, the rent will reflect payments to the owner to cover the financing debt in addition to other rental costs.

PRIVATE LOAN AGREEMENTS WITH PATRONS, FRIENDS OR RELATIVES. Loans can be made between private parties by mutual agreement. In most cases, it is best to secure legal advice and prepare a written contract, such as a promissory note, to clarify the terms of the agreement.

DEBT SOURCES

Private Subsidies

Debt sources that tend to function as private subsidies generally are available to nonprofit and other developers who agree to provide public benefits in exchange for lower interest rates or other favorable terms.

COMMUNITY REINVESTMENT ACT LOANS. The Community Reinvestment Act of 1977 (CRA) encourages commercial banks and savings and loans to meet the credit needs of all groups in their communities, including those of older or low- and moderate-income neighborhoods. Many banks have established CRA departments to administer loans for affordable housing and other community needs. In some cities, the nonprofit development community has used this legislation to negotiate greater financing participation by the lenders in their communities.

LOCAL INITIATIVES SUPPORT CORPORATION (LISC) AND THE NATIONAL EQUITY FUND. The Local Initiatives Support Corporation (LISC), with offices in more than 28 cities, raises funds from local and national sources. It provides grants, loans and technical assistance to support low-income housing and economic development projects by local nonprofit community-based developers. The syndication affiliate of LISC is the National Equity Fund (NEF), which seeks investments by corporations, which use the Investment Tax Credit to increase the return on their investments.

A LISC local advisory committee reviews projects to advise NEF investments. LISC and NEF seek to ensure that projects will meet the development goals of the community to support housing and commercial and small business projects in distressed neighborhoods where private invest-

6.5   BRICKBOTTOM ARTIST COOPERATIVE
Somerville, Massachusetts

The Fort Point (MA) Arts Community, Inc., of South Boston, organized the Brickbottom Artist Cooperative as its second project with the development guidance of ArtistSpace, Inc. and Ercolini & Associates. Bruner/Cott & Associates served as the primary architects for the project, a five-story, 250,000 square foot warehouse complex.

The project concept began with 90 limited-equity, cooperatively owned artists' live/work studios and 62 market-rate condominium units (with no resale restrictions). The income generated from the initial sale of the condos would be used to underwrite the cost of the artist coop units.

Artists involved in planning the project each committed $1,000 initially, providing $100,000 in cash for predevelopment costs. The city's board of aldermen had to amend the city's zoning ordinance to allow residential use in industrial zones by special permit. The Somerville Arts Council provided $10,000 toward the cost of developing a community gallery space in the project, which is now run by a subsidiary nonprofit artists association. The Community Economic Development Assistance Corporation, a state agency, provided a $125,000 predevelopment loan. The First Mutual Bank of Boston provided $12.8 million in construction financing. When construction was completed and the condo units were sold, the construction loan was reduced by approximately $5.6 million. The artists provided about $764,000 in equity. The project construction was completed in April 1988.

During the year in which refinancing the construction loan was being negotiated, the condo market experienced a downturn, and nonartist purchasers backed out on approximately 35 of the 62 presold condos. To cover costs while these units were being resold, the artists secured an agreement from the construction lender to use the reserve fund. The artists also learned that the nonprofit cooperative would incur liability for significant capital gains taxes on the sale of the condo units. During negotiations with lenders, the artists decided to simplify the project and convert all of the units to condos, with residential mortgages at interest rates of approximately 10 percent.

Building facade.

Artists gathering in courtyard.

Because the artists came to the lenders as a large group, because the coop blanket mortgage would have been at higher commercial rates, and because the original artist units were developed for a lower price, many artists qualified for separate mortgages under the refinancing plan that would not otherwise have met standard underwriting criteria elsewhere. The project was refinanced, and the 90-studio coop was converted to separate condominiums in 1989.

The sale prices of the original 62 condos were about $110 per square foot, which included premium design elements, better views, and better parking. The artists, as developers, paid about $70 per square foot for the 90 less-developed spaces. Due to the large need for live/work space, artists who had not participated in planning the original project purchased 70 percent of the 62 "premium" condos at the higher rates.

Financing Structure of Brickbottom Artists Project

Sources of Funds

Mutual Bank Loan	$12,000,000
Seller Financing	1,000,000
Condo Proceeds	8,038,000
Borrower (Artists) Equity	764,000
Total Sources	$21,802,000

Uses of Funds

Acquisition	5,300,000
Construction Cost	6,367,900
Soft Costs	2,096,100
Fees & Taxes	761,816
Pay Down Mutual Bank	6,276,184
Pay Down Seller Financing	1,000,000
Total Uses	$21,802,000

ment must be encouraged to re-enter. LISC provided approximately $80,000 in pre-development funds and interim financing on the Northern Warehouse Project by Artspace Projects, Inc. in St. Paul.

PROGRAM-RELATED INVESTMENTS (PRIS)—PRIVATE FOUNDATION BMIR LOANS.

Program-Related Investments (PRIs) are loans, loan guarantees and equity investments made by foundations at below-market interest rates. Investments are funded either by a foundation's principal assets or by a grant budget from the interest earned on endowment funds. PRIs may be approved for construction loans, bridge loans, mortgages or other loan needs that will earn a return on the foundation's investment on the basis of both financial and charitable purposes.

Although PRIs can be a method of extending a foundation's investment within a community, they are not well known and represent some additional work to both a foundation and the borrowing organization. The nonprofit must provide evidence of financial stability and its ability to repay the loan. The foundation must have the expertise to review and service the loan request, considering risk factors for both parties so that community need can be met without jeopardizing funding resources for other projects. PRIs benefit all parties when they successfully recycle limited foundation assets, meet increased community needs, expand the reach of the funder's grant-making, leverage other community resources or strengthen the capacity of the nonprofit to meet their program goals. The Ford Foundation is known for its PRI program leadership and may be a source of additional information about this investment tool.

Artspace Projects, Inc. of Minneapolis established its Revolving Loan Fund in 1981, making loans directly to artists for renovating 41 studio and live/work units. Recently, Artspace has rein-

vigorated the fund with a $100,000 program-related investment from the Jerome Foundation of St. Paul, matched by the city of St. Paul. Loans are slated for leasehold improvements by artists of the Northern Warehouse project in St. Paul. In the Lowertown Lofts project, a program-related investment of the McKnight Foundation was channelled into the project through a BMIR loan from the Lowertown Redevelopment Corporation.

DEBT SOURCES

Public Subsidies

LOCAL/STATE/FEDERAL GOVERNMENT LOAN PROGRAMS. Local/State/Federal Government Loan Programs can be either debt or equity, depending on the terms the government agency requires for their use. In some cases, the financing may begin as a loan and the debt is later forgiven if certain terms are met. In these cases, the debt would essentially convert to equity when those terms are met. Bond sales and legislative appropriations have subsidized below-market interest rate (BMIR) financing programs. These funds are then recirculated as loans through city, county or state housing redevelopment authorities. A description of Local/State/Federal Government Financing Programs is listed below under the category of "Equity Sources: Public Subsidies."

EQUITY SOURCES

Private

PERSONAL EQUITY FROM SAVINGS OR INVESTMENTS FOR DOWNPAYMENT. All projects require some equity, primarily to provide assurance to other lenders or investors that the borrower has personal funds at risk and is therefore committed to the success of the project. Personal savings are usually a part of every equity package.

INVESTMENTS BY DEVELOPMENT PARTNERS. In a development project where a number of people have joined together as the development team—for example, artists working with a nonprofit developer—the equity will be the combined invested resources of that team rather than a down payment from a single party.

MULTIPLE INVESTORS/SYNDICATION. Syndication is the process of raising equity capital from more than one investor. Syndicated investors can provide all the funds for a project or can be combined with other mortgaged or subsidy sources.

In the United States, most of the money raised through syndication has been raised for housing projects in the United States. Syndications are usually organized by a developer, real estate broker, securities dealer, attorney or others using either the general partnership, limited partnership or tenants-in-common organizational structures. Subchapter "S" Corporations, Real Estate Investment Trusts (REITs), joint ventures and master limited partnerships are other ownership forms that can be used. Since the 1986 Tax Law Reform, the general partnership has some advantages over the others.

PUBLIC OFFERINGS. Syndications may be of any size. However, those with more than 35 investors must be registered as "public offering funds." Many public funds are established as "blind pools," attracting many small investors. Public funds are limited in the amount of "front-end" expenses and fees that can be charged by the syndicator. Public syndications must be sold through a prospectus and filed with a registration statement under the 1933 Securities Act. Public fund units are often sold by investment bankers, stock brokers and others licensed to sell securities.

PRIVATE PLACEMENTS. Syndications with 35 or fewer investors are organized according to "Regulation D" requirements for "private placements." The amount of equity funds needed for a project would be shared by up to 35 investors. Private placements have no restrictions on "front-end" costs, but costs are regulated in effect by what the project or market will bear. Restrictions are placed on the manner in which the placement is offered to private investors, which may include all of the project development team and/or others.

SYNDICATION FEES. A syndication can be costly to organize and sell, so the proposed project requires enough cash flow or yield for investors to make the investment proposal worthy of offering to investors. The syndicator may receive an "organization fee," a "management fee," a "promoted interest" and/or a share in residual proceeds as compensation for packaging and selling the financing plan to investors. The syndicator is often an active principal and may serve as the managing partner in a general partnership.

There are many ways to structure a nonprofit's role in a syndicated project, each having implications for the operational control and affordability of the project. To start, an inexperienced nonprofit can become a partner with an experienced syndicator to learn the process, dividing up responsibilities and decision-making authority based on respective areas of expertise.

The Lowertown Lofts (box 6.6) and the Northern Warehouse in St. Paul are both examples of live/work space projects by Artspace Projects, Inc. done in partnership with for-profit partners as syndicated projects.

6.6 LOWERTOWN LOFTS ARTIST COOPERATIVE
St. Paul, Minnesota

Building facade.

Organizational and Financial Structure
DEVELOPED BY A PUBLIC/PRIVATE
PARTNERSHIP OF:

- Artspace Projects, Inc. (nonprofit developer/project consultant)
- Asset Development Corporation (for-profit developer)
- City of St. Paul, Department of Planning and Economic Development
- St. Paul Art Collective (nonprofit artists group)
- Lowertown Redevelopment Corporation (gap financing, project review)
- Other development team members included: architects Hammel, Green & Abrahamson, attorneys Briggs & Morgan, and Acton Construction

ORGANIZATIONAL STRUCTURE
Owner: Lowertown Lofts Limited Partnership composed of:

- nonprofit co-general partner/subsidiary corporation (SPACHC)
- for-profit co-general partner/subsidiary corporation (AA, Inc.)
- limited partner investors

Lessor: Lowertown Lofts Artists Cooperative

- created by Artspace Projects and the St. Paul Art Collective, with management training provided by Common Space, Inc.
- holds a 20-year master lease from the Lowertown Lofts Limited Partnership, with the option to purchase after the 10th year.

KEY FEATURES

- Artists were encouraged to participate in planning committees that provided direction for the design of the units, the organizational structure, the membership criteria and selection process, and refinement of the financing structure.
- The leasehold limited equity cooperative was used to ensure affordability for low-moderate income artists, to make formal self-management by the residents, and to prepare the tenants for their future role as property owners.
- Artists paid $100 for their membership share in the cooperative, which would be increased in value by $1,000 for the value of sweat equity improvements made by the initial members. Additional improvements made to their individual units are monitored by a design committee and compensated through a "transfer-value" policy.
- The organizational and financing structure combined to make use of favorable homestead tax rates, ITCs for rehabilitating historic properties, and other tax benefits to create

affordable financing when commercial interest rates were 19-20 percent.

- The city structured its NPP/CDBG loan to help the coop purchase the property from the partnership in the 11th year, after the significant tax benefits had been expended. The master lease provides an option to purchase at a fixed price of $1,500,000. As an interest payment on the NPP loan, the city will receive a participation of 50 percent in the net equity reversion of the partnership on sale. This loan, including the city's participation interest, may be assumed by the coop on a subordinated basis to the new financing it must obtain when it exercises its option to purchase the property. The equity participation interest must be repaid only if the property is later sold by the cooperative. If the coop does not exercise its option to purchase, the NPP loan must be repaid to the city by the partnership. The city would then redirect the grant funds portion of the repayment to support the development of space for more low-moderate income artists through Artspace Projects, Inc. or another nonprofit artist service organization in the Twin Cities.

Live/work space.

FINANCING STRUCTURE

**HRA Tax-Exempt Revenue Bond
Authorization** $540,000

1st mortgage: American National Bank purchased bond and provided loan at 12% interest.

Program Related Investment (PRI) $177,000

2nd mortgage: Lowertown Redevelopment
Corporation, with PRI funds provided by the
McKnight Foundation.

Multi-Family Rental Rehab Program $ 77,500

3rd mortgage: Loan from UDAG and CDBG
sources with 10-year term at an average rate of 7%.

Atrium.

Neighborhood Partnership Program $250,000

4th mortgage: CDBG loan at 0% interest for 10
years, with a substantial penalty if the Lowertown Lofts Limited Partnership does not sell to
the Lowertown Lofts Cooperative in the 11th year.

Limited Partnership Equity $300,000

Private investors receive tax benefits of accelerated depreciation, ITCs for rehabilitating historic
property, cash flow from homestead tax treatment of leased limited-equity cooperative, etc.

Grant Funds $70,000

The Bush Foundation and Dayton Hudson
Foundation provided funds for the project
which were assigned to the city and aggre-
gated with the NPP loan, subject to its terms. If
the coop does not purchase the building from
the partnership in the 11th year, the granted
portion of the loan would be used to support
the development of other spaces for low and
moderate income artists. Additionally, several
other foundations provided general operating
grants to Artspace Projects, Inc. and the St.
Paul Art Collective during the development
period.

**Non-Cash Contributions to the Financing Package
(estimated value)** $380,500

Includes property value write-down from for-
profit developer and in-kind contributions of
partially donated services by:

■ Hammel, Green & Abrahamson, architects
■ Briggs & Morgan, attorneys
■ Asset Development, for-profit developer
■ Artspace Projects, Inc., nonprofit developer
■ Project Management Associates, construction
   management
■ Lowertown Lofts Cooperative
■ International Design Center)

Total Project: $1,795.500

EQUITY SOURCES: PRIVATE SUBSIDIES

EQUITY SHARING. All multiple-owner legal structures represent a form of shared-equity investments. A special equity-sharing model was developed in the early 1980s to assist renters who wanted to be home buyers. Equity-sharing, as it is called, is a custom-designed form of co-purchasing residential real estate and sharing the benefits. Developers may set up equity-sharing relationships to sell condominium units in a project, using an attorney to prepare the necessary contracts.

To become an equity partner, an investor typically provides the down-payment capital for a buyer who is short of cash. Buyers select a property for which their income is sufficient to meet at least 90 percent of the monthly operating costs, including principal, interest, taxes and insurance. The equity partner provides the full down payment and may share in monthly costs in exchange for a percentage of interest in the property. The buyer pays the closing costs. The equity partner does not share in the use of the property. After five years, the occupants can either buy out the ownership interest of the equity partner or sell the house. Proceeds from the sale are first used to pay back the equity partner's down payment: the remainder is split evenly between the occupants and the equity partner.

Many people have found this a successful means of acquiring down-payment capital. It is most effective, however, in "hot" property markets in which the appreciated value of the property is assured. Once the proceeds are split and the remainder of the mortgage paid off, the former resident can use the profits for a down payment on another property.

PHILANTHROPIC SUPPORT. If you are applying for philanthropic support from founda-

tions or corporate giving programs, you need to have the required tax-exempt status, defined by section 501(c)3 of the tax code. Examine the potential funder's grant-making policies. Many funders will not fund real estate construction or renovation projects. Other funding sources may give low-interest loans (program-related investments) rather than outright grants. There may be significant competition for available funds.

NONPROFIT/TAX-EXEMPT STATUS. A nonprofit partner provides the stewardship of the "public purpose" for a project receiving funds from government or philanthropic sources. Grants or other support from the city or funders may be channeled into the project as a grant or a loan from the nonprofit. Grants may also be received as equity contributions to the project, reducing the amount of debt service and increasing affordability.

When a nonprofit syndicates a project, it may be necessary and possible to seek "bridge financing" from public and foundation sources. These funds are to cover project costs over the period of time that syndication proceeds are being received from other investors.

Grant funds supported planning activity and "soft costs" for the Lowertown Lofts by Artspace Projects, Inc. The St. Paul Art Collective was reorganized to act on behalf of the artists in Lowertown and became the recipient of funds granted by the Dayton Hudson Foundation, The Bush Foundation and the City of St. Paul.

Artists often organize to carry out their creative ideas, the result being a new nonprofit organization that provides a vehicle for the creation, exhibition or performance of the artists' work. The desire to provide educational programming or other forms of public outreach that serve a public purpose may be good reasons to seek 501(c)(3) status. Some states require that a cooperative also be established as a 501(c)(3). A 501(c)(3) is not intended, however, to be established solely as a means of passing through contributed dollars for the private benefit of members of a group. Additional guidance for establishing a 501(c)(3) can be found in chapter 8 on Ownership and through an attorney familiar with establishing nonprofits.

TAX MOTIVATED CONTRIBUTION: BARGAIN SALE OR PROPERTY WRITE DOWN, INCLUDING SURPLUS PROPERTIES. One way to reduce the total project cost and the amount you need to finance is to obtain the property through a bargain sale, property write-down or gift of the property to a nonprofit organization. The building's owner or investors may receive an income tax deduction equal to the fair market value of their contribution, for all or a portion of a property's value. For an owner, the tax consequences of a gift have been affected by the 1986 tax laws for capital gains treatment of the gain received over basis in the property. The property may be subject to a recapture of accelerated depreciation, creating the potential for taxable income even though the owner received no income for the property.

A "property write down" from the forprofit partner and owner of the property, Asset Development, Inc. (a contribution of $195,000 worth of the property's value) was used with the Lowertown Lofts as part of the overall financing plan to reduce financeable costs.

A common form of city participation in a development project is the "write down" of land costs. The city redevelopment agency may already own a parcel of land or acquire it through voluntary sale or condemnation. The developer may buy or lease the property from the agency at a reduced price, often with restrictions related to city development goals, such as the development of low-income housing. The costs incurred by the city for this type of transaction are then credited as an expenditure from the appropriate funding source, for example, a housing program.

IN-KIND CONTRIBUTIONS—THROUGH REDUCED PROFESSIONAL FEES OR MATERIAL COSTS. "In-kind contributions" are a familiar tool to the arts community, whether through volunteered professional services, reduced fees or material costs, or contributed materials from suppliers. The Lowertown Lofts overall financing plan benefitted significantly from the contributions of services from project consultants, the artists involved in the planning, and both the nonprofit and the forprofit developers as co-general partners. In-kind contributions of materials were also made to many other projects developed by Artspace Projects, Inc. in the Twin Cities area.

SWEAT EQUITY. Like in-kind contributions, sweat equity is not a direct source of financing. However, because the cost of the labor performed by licensed contractors accounts for approximately half of the total construction cost in a renovation project, any labor that artist-owners or residents can perform efficiently and skillfully can reduce the amount of financing needed. In a group of artists, it is likely that skills in painting and other construction tasks are available. Historically, most artist spaces have been developed primarily with sweat equity and by using personal savings and credit accounts in lieu of standard financing.

Even in multi-unit projects with one or more sources of financing, an artist's sweat equity can be a valuable contribution to lowering overall project costs. Although financing sources will want licensed contractors to ensure that the work done meets code, some noncode required tasks, including cleaning up construction debris, painting taped Sheetrock and providing miscellaneous fixtures or storage features, may be legitimately provided by the artist-residents after all code-required work is completed.

In the Lowertown Lofts project, artists' contribution of time toward project planning was

Lowertown Lofts.
Artist refinishing floor.

counted as contributed hours to match a portion of the public funding. Project costs were also reduced by postconstruction labor that artists provided within their own units.

EQUITY SOURCES: PUBLIC SUBSIDIES

Local / State / Federal Government Financing Programs

As mentioned earlier, government programs can be either debt or equity, depending on the terms the government agency requires for their use. These programs most often are a form of public subsidy, including a wide variety of government financing programs for low- and moderate-income groups, small business, and economic development enhancements. Funding cutbacks on both the national and local level forced many programs to dissolve or radically revise their guidelines. Because of their relevance, Invest-

ment Tax Credits (ITCs) for renovation of historic properties, the Low-Income Housing Tax Credit, the Cranston-Gonzalez National Affordable Housing Act of 1990, and local property tax incentives are highlighted below. For more information on government programs—federal, state or local level—available in your area, it is best to contact the appropriate government agency, which may include the following:

- Department of Housing and Urban Development (HUD)
- State Housing Finance Agency or Housing Authority
- National Consumer Cooperative Bank
- Small Business Administration
- National Trust for Historic Preservation
- City Department of Planning and Economic Development
- Community Development Agencies

INVESTMENT TAX CREDITS FOR HISTORIC PROPERTIES. Historic buildings offer the kind of space artists are often looking for, so this can be a path worth pursuing. Some Investment Tax Credits (ITCs) remain for the rehabilitation of certified historic buildings, which may aid in attracting investors. The ITC was used for the Lowertown Lofts and the Northern Warehouse projects in St. Paul, by Artspace Projects, Inc.

A certified historic structure is any building that is listed individually in the National Register of Historic Places, or located in a registered historic district and certified as being of historic significance to the district. Information about the ITC, rehabilitation credits, preservation grants, the process of certification or available buildings may be obtained from your State Historic Preservation Office or local Historical Society. Your legal counsel or accountant should be consulted to find out how ITCs apply to any particular project.

LOW-INCOME HOUSING TAX CREDIT. Since 1986, the Low-Income Housing Tax Credit has been available on a per capita basis to states, which then parcel out the credit to nonprofit or forprofit developers based on proposals submitted. The program is evaluated and refunded annually. Each state has used 100 percent of the credits available to them, often early in their annual availability. In 1990, the Low-Income Housing Tax Credit aided the development of 125,000 affordable housing units. California and Connecticut have provided state enhancements of the credit, while some other states have programs linked with the Low-Income Housing Tax Credit. See box 6.7 for resource information about the credit.

The Low-Income Housing Tax Credit has become popular with corporations as a vehicle for socially responsible investment and is also most beneficial to corporate limited partnership investors. Restrictions make the credit difficult to use: (1) the amount of the credit is too low to attract some investors and (2) fewer investors can qualify to take advantage of the credit. In response, consortiums of investors who do qualify have been organized specifically for investment in low- and moderate-income housing projects. The Northern Warehouse Artists Cooperative in St. Paul, MN, includes the investment of the Metropolitan Housing Partnership, an equity investment pool of 13 corporations, in return for low-income housing and historic tax credits.

CRANSTON-GONZALEZ NATIONAL AFFORDABLE HOUSING ACT OF 1990. The Cranston-Gonzalez Affordable Housing Act of 1990 provides a variety of new programs available to local governments and gives them power to establish and administer their own housing programs. Access to these programs will depend upon the "Comprehensive Housing Affordability Strategy" (CHAS) prepared by your local community. The strategy must describe projected housing needs, the extent of homelessness, and outline the plans to meet the purposes of the act. The programs that may be useful for live/work projects will depend upon the existing community priorities and whether artists wanting access to these programs work with their local government to ensure the adoption of public policies that recognize the arts industry and live/work needs in local CHAS plans.

An example of one of the programs available through the CHAS plans is the HOME Investment Partnership Act. The purpose of the HOME program is to expand the supply of affordable very-low- and low-income housing, to increase the amount of rental housing, to enhance the capacity of nonprofit developers and to leverage federal funds with state, local and private sources.

LOCAL PROPERTY TAX INCENTIVES AND SURPLUS PROPERTIES. Many cities contain districts with vacant or rundown buildings. Although these buildings may be structurally sound, their age, condition and the changing needs of industrial and commercial tenants make it unlikely that they will be occupied or renovated

110

6.7 RESOURCE INFORMATION FOR THE LOW-INCOME HOUSING TAX CREDIT, CRANSTON-GONZALEZ AFFORDABLE HOUSING ACT, AND OTHER FEDERAL PROGRAMS AND POLICIES

The National Low Income Housing Coalition (NLIHC) is a membership organization dedicated to advocacy, organizing and education programs to encourage decent housing for all low-income people.

The National Low Income Housing Information Service (LIHIS) is affiliated with NLIHC and is dedicated to research, education, and technical assistance to those who seek solutions to low-income housing issues. LIHIS provides extensive information on federal policy and programs through publications and electronic mail.

Two publications provide policy information about the Low-Income Housing Tax Credit. They are: *State Administration of the Low-Income Housing Tax Credit,* © 1988, and *Honoring the Promise: State and Local Initiatives to Preserve Subsidized Rental Housing,* © 1990. For more information about the Cranston-Gonzalez Affordable Housing Act, see the publication *Briefing Materials on the National Affordable Housing Act of 1990,* © 1991, or the *CHAS Monitor,* published periodically. These publications and other sources of federal policy information are available from:

The National Low Income Housing Coalition and National Low Income Housing Information Service
1012 14th Street, N.W., #1500
Washington, DC 20005
(202) 662-1530

for their original uses. Cities often have programs to encourage reusing these buildings in new ways, to prevent the erosion of the city's tax base. Major cities have increasingly adopted varying forms of tax deferment and tax abatement legislation as tools for encouraging redevelopment. The following strategies may be available in your area:

- deferred or phased assessment
- current use taxation (as opposed to highest use)
- tax exemption and abatement legislation (for example, New York's J-51)
- tax increment districts

Since 1976, New York's J-51 tax exemption and abatement legislation has permitted an exemption from increased assessments resulting from improvements for a period of 12 years. The law also permits an abatement against the tax that would be due on the building without the improvements. Although not restricted to the arts, this legislation has benefitted the renovation of some artist live/work buildings in New York City through the encouragement of rehabilitation and conversion of nonresidential buildings to residential uses.

To the building's owner, the principal benefit of property tax incentives is to decrease annual operating expenses and consequently increase cash flow. Additional cash flow can aid in applying for a larger loan from a lending institution. In New York, for example, in addition to the basic mortgage loan, a second incremental loan is available based on the value of the estimated tax savings discounted as an annuity for the abatement period. Tax incentives can make a marginal project feasible and lower the initial cash outlay of the investor.

HOMESTEAD PROPERTY TAX TREATMENT. Condominiums, cooperatives and leased limited equity cooperatives benefit from being treated as home ownership options for property tax purposes in several states. The assessment value reduction is often a significant savings in property taxes compared to commercial properties and households that rent. Other states have passed tax limitation measures which may aid in keeping property taxes from rising unreasonably.

OTHER SOURCES

Debt or Equity

PUBLIC/PRIVATE PARTNERSHIPS AND FINANCING POOLS. In learning to take charge of low-income housing projects, many nonprofit developers have become sophisticated, putting virtually every available subsidy and financing source to work. Through "partnerships" with bankers, foundations, businesses and government agencies. Some communities, seeking economies of scale, have created a centralized financing source with public and private commitments of loans and grant support for projects developed by nonprofit neighborhood organizations. Other communities have created equity pools to channel corporate and other investments into financing for low-income housing.

A revolving loan pool may be established as a public/private partnership between funders and a city agency, with the city handling the loan review and servicing if an appropriate nonprofit is unavailable. Community leadership could provide direction and oversight to the lending decisions. The National Development Council of New York City and the National Trust for Historic Preservation in Washington, D.C. are excellent sources for information about the establishment and administration of revolving loan funds.

ARTS PATRONAGE. An arts patron can play a key role in the development of artists' spaces, with direct and indirect support. The

201 Wyandote, Kansas City, MO. Building owner has donated 4,000 sq. ft. on first and second floors as gallery space for artists in the building.

patron may be a sympathetic developer/landlord, such as Mel Mallin in Kansas City; a limited partner in syndication; or a source of the seed money for a risky but worthwhile project. The patron may be willing to purchase a desired building for the project in exchange for a commitment to a master lease by the artist-tenants. A patron can also help by providing free professional services such as legal, architectural or financial expertise. The involvement of a patron in an artists' space project can enhance the project's financial stability and credibility.

Some of the same people who support the arts in your community may also own vacant or underutilized buildings in the locale in which you are interested. Meeting with them can help you determine their interest in taking part in a project. One generous scenario might be an owner's willingness to grant the building's ownership to the project team, with the provision that the project team secure all other funds and cause all other needed improvements to be made.

Clues for gaining a patron's participation and active support come from the capital drive fund-raising process used by major arts institutions, hospitals and other large nonprofit organizations. Key factors include building a sense of involvement and commitment to the vision, finding a way to meet the personal needs or desires of the patron, and translating the vision into rational, logical arguments that make sense on paper.

COMPARING AND PACKAGING SEVERAL OPTIONS

Don't fall in love with a building unless you can secure financing at a price that provides a workable solution for your needs. Sometimes a new building can be built for less than you could renovate the old building with which you have fallen in love. A governmental lender, in particular, will assess whether your proposed project can equitably compete against other solutions. Compare your project with other options to determine if it is the best choice available.

As mentioned earlier, a single mortgage may be adequate or additional sources of financing may be needed. Your project may require packag-

Delaware Lofts, Kansas City. Owned by the same arts patron as the Wyandote building, who allows artists full design freedom to alter the spaces they rent.

Northern Artists' Cooperative, St. Paul. 52 live/work spaces financed with ITC historic tax credits, low income housing tax credits, investment by an equity partner (Metropolitan Housing Partnership, a consortium of 13 corporations), and other local and state financing assistance, including the Local Initiative Support Corporation (LISC).

ing a number of sources in order to blend the overall financing rate, to find a financing scenario that is affordable or to share the risk between two or more sources. The process of combining financing tools requires the use of a pro forma to evaluate the financial impact of each source. A prospectus will be needed to disclose information as you attract other investors for equity participation. This chapter concludes with sample forms to aid your financial planning for a project.

AFFORDABLE FINANCING

Developers, especially those committed to providing affordable housing to low- and moderate-income people have become extraordinarily resourceful and creative in the ways they package the financing for their projects.

Dick Huss, Brickbottom, and the Lowertown Lofts illustrate the way financial tools can be combined to achieve success (see boxes 6.4-6.6). The financing tools summarized below all have been used to achieve affordable projects.

Several projects have sold or rented condominiums, office or retail space at market rates to offset the cost of artist live/work spaces within a project. This strategy has worked with varying degrees of success. These projects include Westbeth in New York City, the Piano Craft Guild and the Brickbottom projects in Boston, and the Lowertown Lofts and the Northern Warehouse in St. Paul.

One way to achieve affordable monthly costs for low to moderate income residents has been to include some sources of funds that either do not need to be paid back—grants—or do not require a high return to the investor—program-related investments from foundations. By including these sources in the financing mix, interest rates can be blended to lower the overall interest rate and enhance the project feasibility. The Lower-

114

town Lofts and the Northern Warehouse in St. Paul are examples.

Tax benefits and tax credits have been another successful mechanism to achieve affordable project finances. Benefits from the Investment Tax Credit (ITC) on historic properties continue to be available. Tax benefits to investors through limited partnerships still represent a viable option for projects that provide an adequate rate of return through cash flow to the investor. The Piano Craft Guild in Boston used enhanced tax benefits for limited partner investors. The Lowertown Lofts in St. Paul used both ITC/historic properties and enhanced tax benefits for limited partner investors. The Northern Warehouse in St. Paul used low-income housing credits and ITC/historic properties.

Adding governmental sources of funds or loan guarantees has been another way to lower the overall cost of financing a project. Bond sales and state legislative appropriations have also subsidized through city, county or state housing redevelopment authorities.

Federal government mortgage insurance or federal and state below-market interest rate (BMIR) subsidy programs have been used by some artist live/work projects, such as Westbeth in New York City, the Piano Craft Guild in Boston, and Artists' Housing in Baltimore. Such programs have been available for cooperatives, low-moderate-income rental developments, and condominiums, although availability has been limited. Some states have programs which replicate federal programs, but most BMIR programs

Westbeth, New York City. The J.M. Kaplan Fund, a private foundation, developed these 383 live/work spaces, with assistance from public and private grants, and an FHA guaranteed mortgage.

6.8 GENERALIZED FORMULA FOR ESTIMATING COSTS OF OWNING LIVE/WORK STUDIOS

Acquisition (per sq. ft.)	$10	$14	$18	$22	$26	$30
Construction Costs (per sq. ft.)	25	25	25	25	25	25
Other Costs (per sq. ft.)[1]	5	5	5	5	5	5
Total Costs (Gross) (per sq. ft.)	40	44	48	52	56	60
Total Cost (net useable sq. ft. of studio space)[2]	46	51	55	59	64	69
Cost per 1,000 sq. ft. of studio space	$46,000	$51,000	$55,000	$59,000	$64,000	$69,000

DOWNPAYMENT (10%)	4,600	5,100	5,500	5,900	6,400	6,900
Mortgage (90%)	41,400	45,900	50,500	54,100	58,600	62,100
Monthly Mortgage Payment[3]	363	403	443	474	514	545
Annual Mortgage Payment	4,356	4,836	5,316	5,688	6,618	6,540
Annual Mortgage Payment (per sq. ft.)	4.35	4.83	5.31	5.68	6.16	6.53
Monthly Operating Costs	172	172	172	172	172	172
Annual Operating Costs	2,070	2,070	2,070	2,070	2,070	2,070
Annual Operating Costs (per sq. ft.)	2.07	2.07	2.07	2.07	2.07	2.07
Total Annual Costs (per sq. ft.)	6.42	6.42	6.42	6.42	6.42	6.42
Total Monthly Costs ("rent")[4]	535	575	615	646	686	717

DOWNPAYMENT (20%)	9,200	10,200	11,000	11,800	12,800	13,800
Mortgage (80%)	36,800	40,800	44,000	47,200	51,200	55,200
Monthly Mortgage Payment[3]	323	358	386	414	449	484
Annual Mortgage Payment	3,875	4,296	4,632	4,968	5,392	5,813
Annual Mortgage Payment (per sq. ft.)	3.87	4.29	4.63	4.96	5.39	5.81
Monthly Operating Costs	172	172	172	172	172	172
Annual Operating Costs	2,070	2,070	2,070	2,070	2,070	2,070
Annual Operating Costs (per sq. ft.)	2.07	2.07	2.07	2.07	2.07	2.07
Total Annual Costs (per sq. ft.)	5.94	6.36	6.70	7.03	7.46	7.88
Total Monthly Costs ("rent")[4]	495	530	558	585	622	657

1 Architectural, engineering, legal, financing costs, etc.
2 Assumes 15% for common space.
3 Assumes interest rate at 10%, 30-year term.
4 These figures will be lower if you take standard deductions
  for home ownership and business-related expenses on federal tax.

NOTE: Construction, "other costs" and operating costs are based
upon our experience with other artist projects.

Source: Reprinted by permission from *Artists in Space,* by Jero Nesson,
courtesy The Fort Point Artists' Community of South Boston.

have been federal funds granted to cities. Some of these programs are being renamed and others are being terminated as part of the adoption of the Cranston-Gonzalez National Affordable Housing Act.

Competition with other low-income groups makes it difficult for artist groups to obtain government subsidies. However, if the project is viewed in terms that meet public policy objectives, cities may choose to participate as financing partners for large projects. Public policy objec-

tives may be to provide job creation or job retention for the city's arts industry, to meet the housing needs of artists as low-moderate-income residents or to spur economic development in a designated area. Cities are most likely to draw upon more renewable sources, such as bond sales and recycling loan programs. Nonprofit developers that have succeeded in attracting public subsidy sources include Artspace Projects, Inc., in Minneapolis and St. Paul; Artspace, Inc., in Salt Lake City, UT; and Art Housing, Inc., in Baltimore, MD.

6.9 CALCULATING PROJECT COSTS BASED ON ARTISTS/ MARKET LIMITATIONS

Suppose you want to build or renovate a live/work building to rent out. The following example illustrates the basic process to determine whether a rental project will pay for itself. If you calculate the potential income the building will produce and then subtract nonconstruction costs, you will know how much money per square foot is available for construction. Lower rents would require lower interest rates, land costs or construction costs. In this way, you can "work backwards" into the pro forma calculations.

EXAMPLE: Land (or a building) has been found in an attractive location for a price of $150,000. Artists would be willing to pay seven dollars a square foot on an annual basis ($7 per square foot, per year) for developed buildings in the same neighborhood. You want to build 18-20 units within 25,000 square feet, so the maximum yearly income would be roughly $175,000 ($7 x 25,000 sq. ft. = $175,000).

Next, subtract a vacancy allowance from that number. In this case, because artists will be involved in planning the project and it will be preleased, a vacancy allowance of 5 percent, or $8,750, has been used. (Projects built upon speculation should plan for a 10-15 percent vacancy.) Yearly operating expenses, such as management costs, are also roughly calculated to be 5 percent of yearly income, so another $8,750 must be subtracted. To find the yearly income available (known as Net Operating Income or NOI), you would subtract $17,500 ($8,750 + $8,750) from the maximum yearly income of $175,000, leaving $157,500 NOI.

Annual interest and principal costs must be paid on the money borrowed for the project. Most lending institutions determine how much annual interest and principal a developer can pay (affordable debt service) by dividing projected yearly income by a debt coverage factor (called the Debt Coverage Ratio or DCR, which can range from 1.1 to 1.4). The affordable debt service for this project, then, is $152,174 (maximum yearly income of $175,000 / 1.15 DCR = $152,174 annual debt service or D/S).

PROJECTING PROJECT COSTS

Cost estimates can be difficult, especially for renovation, because there are often problems that come up only when the work is under way. Factors affecting cost estimates for renovation projects include project delays, inflation, unexpected asbestos removal or major structural problems, all of which can bring havoc to a project budget. Do not underestimate construction costs in the pro forma.

For a smaller project, get a rough estimate of costs by noting what needs to be done and then doing some research on prices of materials and labor. Cost-estimating manuals are available from the business section of a library. For a larger project, costs can be estimated for you by the architect or contractors with whom you are working. If you plan to use union contractors for construction, consider using a negotiated contract to secure cost estimates. Request a project agreement that provides for an increased use of

The portion of a loan which is paid each year in debt service (principal and interest) is called the mortgage constant (represented in calculations by the letter "c"). Using mortgage tables (see box 6.3), the constant can be calculated by multiplying the debt service by 12 and dividing that number by the loan amount. For our purposes here, the mortgage constant for a 10 percent loan amortized over 30 years would be 10.53 percent ($8.78 x 12 / $1,000 = .1053 or 10.53 percent). The maximum loan amount, then, would be determined by dividing the affordable debt service of $152,174 by the mortgage constant of 10.53 percent (.1053). The bank, then, would lend the project $1,445,147 ($152,174 D/S / 10.53 c = $1,445,147 maximum loan available).

Cash flow (CF) is now determined by subtracting the annual debt service from yearly income ($175,000 maximum yearly income - $152,174 annual debt service = $22,826 CF). The equity contribution for the project is then determined by capitalizing the cash flow, that is, dividing the cash flow by the expected rate of return. If $22,826 represents an expected return of 12 percent, the equity contribution would be $190,216 ($22,826 CF / 12% rate of return = $190,216 equity contribution).

Now calculate the maximum total project budget by adding together the two sources of income—the equity contribution of $190,216 and the loan amount of $1,445,147. The result ($1,635,363) should be the maximum figure used in estimating a total project budget.

The money available for construction is the amount remaining in the project budget after land has been purchased and "soft costs" have been subtracted. Soft costs include architectural and engineering fees, legal fees, financing costs, and all expenses that are not "bricks and mortar." With soft costs estimated at $210,000 and land/building costs of $150,000, you would subtract $360,000 ($210,000 + $150,000 = $360,000) from the project budget of $1,635,363, which would leave $1,275,363 available to build or renovate the building ($1,635,363 - $360,000 = $1,275,363).

The construction budget ($1,275,363) divided by the total square footage (25,000) yields the cost per square foot ($51.01). If a project of sufficient quality to generate the projected rents can be built for $51.00 per square foot, it is a winner.

apprentices and helpers to aid in lowering construction costs, with a "not to exceed" estimate on the total project cost.

For a preliminary assessment of project costs, you can use an average square foot cost for your community multiplied by the number of square feet in the building. As an example of this method, the chart in box 6.8 shows the effect on monthly costs if the amount of acquisition cost changes. The chart also shows the difference in the resulting monthly costs between providing ten percent (10%) and twenty percent (20%) in downpayment funds.

Another way to calculate project costs and financing solutions is to begin with what the artists can afford. Once you know how much rental income the artists can provide for the building, you can subtract non-construction costs to find how much money per square foot is available for construction costs. If the amount of funds available are inadequate to meet the projected costs, you can reevaluate the project using additional sources of equity and debt subsidies to determine a feasible financing scenario. As an example of beginning with what the artists can afford, see box 6.9.

THE PROSPECTUS: AN INVESTOR PRESENTATION PACKAGE

State and federal laws require project organizers to disclose the pertinent facts about a partnership offering when seeking investors. As the number of investors increases, disclosure requirements increase dramatically. The organizers prepare a disclosure statement or "prospectus". A similar package may be prepared for lenders when requesting a loan, especially if you are packaging several equity and debt sources for your financing strategy.

A prospectus is often 8 1/2" x 11," velo or plastic spiral bound, with reduced scale drawings of the proposed project. The information is organized by a table of contents and may be in any order that makes sense for your project. Photos, reprinted news articles, or other supplementary material may be included at your discretion. The prospectus typically includes the following information:

- **PROJECT DOCUMENTATION.** A project description should be summarized, with an appraisal, legal description, and title or evidence of site control. The building, site, zoning, building code compliance and analysis of its structural condition are described. Summarize the timeline for development of the project. State the loan request amount, terms, and conditions.
- **NEED, "CASE" OR MARKET STATEMENT.** A market analysis confirms the need for the project and the assumptions used for income and expense projections. Firm commitments from building users are the best evidence of economic feasibility. A description of the area, its economy, competing projects, and future demand expectations can enhance feasibility projections.
- **MANAGEMENT.** Provide governance or management plan, as appropriate. If applicable, include an outline of partnership and/or co-op structure and summary of lease provisions related to income projections.
- **ARCHITECTURAL SCHEMATIC PLANS.** Reduced-scale schematic drawings of the proposed development are bound with the prospectus. Construction drawings may be requested as supplemental information.
- **QUALIFICATIONS OF THE DEVELOPMENT TEAM.** Provide the background and experience of the principals, partners, or leadership behind the plan, and describe successes in areas compatible with present endeavors. These may include

the developer/sponsor, arts representatives, architect/engineers, contractor, accountant/financial analyst, and property manager. An arts group should include a copy of its 501(c)(3) verification, a list of its board of directors and a summary of its history and programs.

■ **COST ANALYSIS.** Include a statement of the cost for the construction or rehabilitation work, provided by the architect, project engineer and/or contractor.

■ **PRO FORMA.** Include a detailed financial analysis showing total project costs and a cash flow projection (5 to 10 years) of annual income and expenses, justifying the economic feasibility of the project. See appendices 6.1, 6.2 and 6.3.

■ **FINANCIAL CAPACITY OF DEVELOPMENT TEAM.** Provide documentation of the financial capacity of owner or developer (other than annual property income) through past and current financial statements.

■ **COMMITMENTS.** Notice of committed third-party resources (permanent loan commitment, junior mortgages, public loan guarantee, etc.) are optional, depending on the project. A prospectus also requires a copy of the partnership agreement.

WHAT THE INVESTOR LOOKS FOR

Unmoved by the factors that may cause someone to buy a personal residence, equity investors evaluate the prospectus and pro forma in an unemotional way, not unlike lenders. The key concerns are a return on their investment (interest) and a return of the investment (principal).

The willingness of an investor or lender to participate in your project will depend on their perception of your chances for success. In business terms, your chances for success are referred to as the degree of risk. Lenders or investors compare the level of risk in your development proposal to the risk level of other investments available. Their starting point is a zero-risk investment such as interest received from a two-year Unites States treasury bond or "T-bill." From there, an investor would look at investments with increasingly higher levels of risk and would require correspondingly higher rates of return. If an investor believes that the chances of completing a project and returning their funds are slim, the investment will be viewed as too risky and no promise of future profit will convince anyone to risk their funds on it. The return a lender or investor requires for an investment in a project with a specific level of risk is the "market rate" for that investment.

The investment return is available through several key benefits of investing in real estate, which include: (1) cash flow from rent money returned to investors after debt and operating costs are paid; (2) mortgage principle reduction/equity build-up rental income used to pay off debt for the owner or investors; (3) tax benefits, including depreciation applied to reduce other taxable income, low-income housing credit and historic properties investment tax credits, where applicable; and (4) appreciation of the property's value over the time the investors share its ownership. Real estate is the only investment mechanism that offers all four opportunities for increasing an investor's income. See appendix 6.4 to calculate the benefits of a real estate investment for equity investors.

Some of the same underwriting criteria used by mortgage lenders will be considered by investors when evaluating a prospectus for a syndicated project, but will now be the only factors considered by them. The benefits of investing in real estate take different forms and are received at different times, making it necessary for several calculations to determine an investment's cumulative effect, including its tax consequences. The calculations they are most interested in are the Cash Flow Rate After Tax (CFRATx) and the Internal Rate of Return (IRR).

The CFRATx incorporates applicable tax shelters and tax credits as part of a cash-flow analysis. It does not take into account the appreciation of the property, however. The IRR provides a more complete measure of the return on investment, incorporating all benefits into a single composite number.

Other factors that may concern the investor's evaluation of a prospectus include: (1) the degree of risk, the possible loss of capital or earnings on the investment; (2) liquidity of the investment, the time it takes to convert an asset to cash; (3) management qualifications of the development team or the need for investor involvement in monitoring the investment; and (4) the overall yield resulting from the investment compared to alternative investments.

TESTING FEASIBILITY THROUGH THE PRO FORMA

The Pro Forma Income and Expense Schedule is an operating cash flow statement. It represents the cash flow that is available to repay debt and to provide the owners with a return on their equity investment. A sample pro forma is included as appendix 6.1.

To prepare a pro forma, estimate rent levels as though the project was fully occupied. Subtract 5 to 15 percent of your potential rent as a vacancy factor to find the effective gross rent or gross operating income (GOI). Identify and list the amounts of all expected operating costs. The difference between the effective gross rent that is collected and the operating expenses is called net operating income (NOI). NOI is the cash flow available to pay the lenders and owner or investors. After the debt service (DS) is subtracted from NOI, the resulting number is the cash flow before tax (CFBTx), or the income available to the owner or investors. Investors will want to know the impact of the four real estate tax benefits on the CFBTx, which results in the cash flow after tax (CFATx) equation.

A cash flow projection takes the same equations into consideration and compares them with any changes in the projections from year to year, including increased rental income, taxes or operating expenses, such as an adjustable rate mortgage, which entails changes in the debt service. A sample cash flow projection is provided as appendix 6.3.

Just as changes in income and expenses change the bottom line from year to year, the pro forma is a reality test. It allows you to explore a combination of feasibility factors or financing ideas. If a lender does not provide the full amount you requested, return to the pro forma as a road map for testing mid-course corrections and additions.

"Every time I try to take out a new lease on life,
the landlord raises the rent."
Ashleigh Brilliant

7
Long-Term Control:
Leasing

TYPES OF LONG-TERM CONTROL

One issue that "hits us where we live" is control of our environment, our basic need for security and for a sense of well-being. For artists, the security of owning a home or of having a long lease on a property may enhance the sense of creative well-being.

There are many ways to have control over one's environment besides the outright purchase of an apartment or building. Each option usually entails a different type of control and responsibility. Ownership builds equity, but leasing or shared ownership may offer more immediate and possibly future financial benefits or opportunities to realize other personal goals.

BENEFITS OF LEASING

In some locations and for some people, ownership is not an option. Leasing space has its own benefits, including the following:

MOBILITY. You are committed to the space only for the duration of your lease agreement. Once your lease terminates, you are free to experiment in other buildings.

IMMEDIATE ACCESS TO SPACE. Separate studio space or traditional forms of housing are the most available options, and they may meet your needs and financial ability adequately. Or you may be lucky enough to assume the lease for a live/work space that has already been developed by an owner or previous tenant, although these spaces are rarely available.

REDUCED RISK. Leasing, unlike ownership, has few risks if you understand your lease and invest accordingly. In contrast, if you own property, the greater your percentage of individual ownership, the more responsibility you assume and the more you risk of both time and financial assets on your investment in space.

REDUCED RESPONSIBILITY. If you lease, you will generally be free from having to maintain or repair the property, thus allowing you more time for meeting your primary goals. Responsibility for paying taxes and utilities can be negotiated.

BEST USE OF LIMITED FUNDS. If you lack funds for down payments or have insufficient cash flow to cover monthly carrying costs, leasing may solve your immediate needs for space. Leasing gives you stability when you prepare for future opportunities.

BENEFITS OF OWNERSHIP

Ownership also has many benefits and may be preferred over leasing for the following reasons:

INCREASED CONTROL. Ownership provides greater rights over how to use property. You have control over the length of time you choose to remain in the space and over the types of improvements to make.

ABILITY TO BUILD EQUITY. Owning property increases your net worth, allowing you to leverage further purchases or to expand your financial base. Any investments you make for improvements often increase the financial benefits that accrue as a result.

FINANCIAL GROWTH POTENTIAL. As an owner, you realize benefits that come from appreciation of the property and from tax benefits that lower your actual or comparative costs.

LOWER LONG-TERM COSTS. Unlike the person who leases, you as an owner have stable expenses over the long term. You are protected from the inflationary and market pressures that represent increased expenses for the nonowner. Eventually, too, owners can pay the cost of the property in full, which limits their ongoing expenses to taxes, utilities, insurance, and maintenance.

PROTECTED INVESTMENT OF TIME AND MONEY. If you are committed to a community and to the space you have renovated, ownership provides the means to make full use of the improvement and to focus time on your other priorities. Owning the property may be especially important if moving your equipment is costly.

CONSIDERING LONG-TERM CONTROL OPTIONS

Box 7.1 lists the different types of long-term tenant control and/or ownership. Each has its own rights and responsibilities, advantages and disadvantages. Only you can decide which option best meets your needs.

The information in this book will acquaint you with the fundamental aspects of the most commonly used forms of control, comparing the principles of each. Shared forms of leasing or ownership can reduce the costs, the risks, and the responsibilities. The financing may dictate the type of control available. In any project you plan, seek competent legal advice regarding your state's interpretation of these principles.

Drafting a document is less time-consuming once the project terms and relationship of the parties are fully understood. Although you can save some costs by being fairly clear about what you need in the document before contacting an attorney, remember that lawyers may help you to understand your options much more quickly. If you are working through a nonprofit developer or service program, an attorney may be willing to donate time as a pro-bono contribution to your project.

Seek recommendations from others as to

which law firm will be familiar with real estate law or have experience with a similar project. A lawyer usually will meet with you for one hour free of charge to determine the job that needs to be done and the probable cost. Lawyers generally work

---

7.1   OPTIONS FOR LONG-TERM CONTROL

■ *Leasing*
    Individual
    Unincorporated Association
    Nonprofit Corporation
    Leasehold Cooperative

■ *Sole Ownership*

■ *Multiple Owners*
    Tenants in Common
    Joint Tenancy
    Tenancy by the Entirety
    Community Property
    General Partnership
    Limited Partnership
    Joint Venture
    Syndication
    For-profit Corporations
    Nonprofit Corporations
    Real Estate Investment Trusts

■ *Condominiums*
    Townhomes
    Planned Unit Developments

■ *Cooperatives*
    Limited Equity Cooperative
    Full Equity, No Appreciation Cooperative
    Combination Appreciation Formula Cooperative
    Leasehold Cooperative

124

out estimates and bill at an hourly rate. You can also ask for a "not to exceed" fee arrangement.

The balance of this chapter focuses on various types of leases, and chapter 8 describes the different ownership structures, including cooperative ownership.

LEASING: THE RIGHT TO USE A SPACE

Leasing may be a simple, contractual agreement between an individual tenant and a landlord. Or, it may take more complicated shared forms, involving unincorporated associations, cooperatives, corporations or partnerships.

THE LEASE DOCUMENT

Think of a building as raw material and the lease as your most basic tool. It is a dull-looking tool, and the sound it makes is a drone that can put you to sleep. Pinch yourself—and *read* the lease. Carefully.

A lease is a communication tool for agreements that can be written to either party's advantage. Unlike oral agreements that can quickly be forgotten or interpreted differently, the lease, once signed, is a legal contract binding you and the other party to its contents. Because the lease binds you legally to certain obligations, it is important to ask for what you want and to understand clearly what you and the landlord have agreed upon.

Because most leases are prepared by the building owner, they tend to be more beneficial to the landlord. You may negotiate rental rates, taxes, utilities, insurance and maintenance, as well as improvement or fixtures added to the property. You may also negotiate the rate of rental increases, structuring them for a long-term

Pilsen East, Chicago. Storefront studio with floor removed. Rental units in this development were renovated creatively to provide light and space.

tenancy instead of letting yourself be subject to arbitrary increases with little advance notice. You may also ask for changes in the definition of the landlord's responsibilities. An artist should confirm that there are no restrictions on the time of day artistic endeavors may be pursued or that the generation of noise, dust or fumes will not be determined to be a "nuisance" and cause a default under the terms of the lease agreement.

Also, if the owner agrees to make improvements or to finance improvements, it is best to clarify the details before disagreements arise. Negotiate the broad features of your lease before you make any major investments of money or time. Planning your renovation needs may be a necessary part of the negotiation process. (See chapter 10 for more points on your negotiations.)

125

You do not have to sign a lease immediately. You have the right to scrutinize its contents, have an attorney review it, and negotiate changes if you feel they are needed. Some leases take months of work before they adequately reflect the agreements of both parties and can be signed.

To test the validity of seemingly onerous provisions, the lease must be litigated in a court of law. Much of the contents of a lease will never be an issue unless it reaches a legal battle. With this in mind, you should proceed on the safe side and *get everything—both additions and deletions—in writing.*

Various organizations may be available to help you with negotiations or with finding an attorney. These include Volunteer Lawyers for the Arts in numerous cities, as well as Artspace Projects, Inc. in the Twin Cities, Artspace in Salt Lake City, ArtistSpace, Inc. in Boston, ArtHouse in Los Angeles, Oakland or San Francisco, or National Artist's Equity.

TYPES OF LEASES

The standard residential lease is call a "gross" lease. It states that the tenant pays a predetermined amount of rent, plus some utilities; the landlord handles all other expenses.

Studios and live/work space leases are often connected with income-producing properties. These usually require a commercial "net" or "net-net" lease, in which the tenant agrees to pay property charges such as taxes, insurance and maintenance. A variation is the "absolute," "net, net, net" or "triple net" leases, in which the tenant is typically responsible for all expenses and maintenance as well as structural repairs. Regardless of what the lease is called, read it carefully to see what expenses you will be responsible for.

A long-term (10 to 25 years, or more) absolute net lease can be used as the basis for obtaining rehabilitation financing. A group rent-ing space under this type of arrangement may be able to rent portions of the property to others at a slightly higher rate, reflecting the improvement the group has made to the building.

Long-term leases often include an escalator clause to allow the rent to be raised during the tenancy to reflect changing market values, inflation and so forth.

212 North Washington, Minneapolis. Kitchen in live/work space.

117 North Washington, Minneapolis. Studio in live/work space.

IMPORTANT LEASE CLAUSES

Following are examples of typical subjects that lease clauses cover:

MAINTENANCE AND USE OF THE PREM- ISES BY TENANT. This clause should be written to define clearly how you will use the space, so that you will be protected against any default because of your use of the studio. If you plan to live in the space, the lease *must* include that use. If the lease does not indicate that use, and if the space were to be cited as not complying with the residential code, the owner would not be required to renovate the building to meet that code. So be sure—regardless of your oral agreement with the building's owner—that your lease specifies that you are going to live in the space. If you violate the terms of your lease and if the building's owner is under pressure, the owner may simply declare a default under the lease terms and require you to move, regardless of work you have personally completed in the space.

INSURANCE. Nearly every lease makes reference to liability areas that the tenants will be responsible for. Read carefully what kind of insurance, whether personal injury or property insurance, you will be expected to carry. Most likely, you will have to carry one or more policies.

You should seek a reasonable range of liability and, if possible, only for your actual "space," property or visitors. Even if your lease does not require you to carry insurance, you may want to carry some. Consider the risks of having to pay for a potential loss from your own pocket before deciding against insurance coverage.

The cost of insurance is dependent on a variety of factors, including the following:

1. **THE PERILS COVERED.** The range of coverage includes loss or damage from fire, lightning, windstorm, explosion, riot, vandalism, robbery and theft. Other perils can be added by endorsements to the policy, at extra charge.

2. **TYPE AND LOCATION OF THE BUILDING.** The fire rating of a building greatly influences policy costs. Rates may be higher for a building in poor condition. It can be difficult to get insurance to cover warehouse space.

3. **SPECIAL COVERAGE.** Insurance companies generally require that works of art, musical instruments, camera equipment and the like have their value validated before a loss occurs. Completed art work should be documented and a value—selling price—should be established, with documentation kept in a safe-deposit box. Work in progress can be valued by ascertaining the cost of the materials plus an hourly rate at the time of the loss. The Homeowner's Fine Art Form provides good coverage for artists who are not yet professionally established or have made few sales.

Another consideration is "subrogation" and the "waiver of subrogation." Under the laws of negligence, a property owner can sue those persons who cause damage to his or her property. If the suit is successful, the owner is entitled to reimbursement by the negligent party. If a tenant was shown to have damaged the landlord's property through negligence—for example, by fire—the landlord's insurance company could sue the tenant by way of subrogation for repayment of damages. Although the tenant's liability coverage will cover costs up to the total amount of coverage paid for, the tenant would be better protected by asking the landlord to add a waiver of subrogation clause to the lease.

The following guidelines will help you to make the best decisions in purchasing insurance:

■ Insure your major risks first

■ Do not insure small losses—the higher your deductible, the lower your policy cost

■ Shop before buying—rates may differ greatly

■ Get help from a good agent, one who takes the time to understand your needs

■ Contact other artists for referrals—not all companies insure works of art, but most have adaptable policies

DEFAULT BY TENANT. Check the lease carefully to see whether there are any areas in which you could be found in default just by signing the lease. If you plan to live in the space without that use being legally agreed to, in writing, by the owner or lessor, you will be in default of the lease. You may also be in default by being a "nuisance," so if you plan to make loud sounds—music, equipment noise, etc.—have that acknowledged in the lease. Leases have standard clauses for these issues, but you should have the clauses rewritten to meet your needs.

Also, check what will happen if you do default. In some cases the leases can be terminated immediately without notice. In others, you may have an opportunity to cure the default. If the sections of the lease dealing with these provisions seem inappropriate or unwarranted, question the lessor and try to change them. Do not sign the lease if you cannot reach an agreement with the lessor.

CONDITION OF PREMISES. If you are planning any major renovation of the space at your expense, or if the landlord has agreed to renovate at his or her expense or compensate you for yours, the details of the agreement and the current condition of the space should be written as an addendum to the lease. Or you and the landlord may agree upon the space "as is" along with certain repairs that need to be done. For example, if the landlord is to replace broken windows before your occupancy, state the date of expected completion and the consequence should that date be missed.

By law, at the end of a lease, any fixtures or "attached" improvements become the property of the landlord. At the very least, you will want to ensure the length of your tenancy to make optimal use of the improvements. You may also be able to negotiate the removal of certain improvements when you leave. Artists have sometimes negotiated for a reimbursement of their leasehold improvements at the termination of the lease. Typically, artists keep attached improvements to a minimum, for example, by building movable storage units that may be moved to the next space.

LANDLORD AND TENANT LAWS

Most states have laws to protect tenants of residential properties. However, these protections do not extend to residential use of commercial buildings unless, at a minimum, both the certificate of occupancy and the lease acknowledge that the space meets residential requirements. As each state has its own laws governing

landlord-tenant relationships, you need to check your own state's laws for more specific information on your situation. If problems arise, you should be familiar with the state laws that define your rights and those of your landlord. (Some cities have services that can assist you in this research, such as Legal Aid or Volunteer Lawyers for the Arts.)

Disputes between landlords and tenants commonly arise over (1) the landlord's cancellation of lease due to the tenant's failure to pay rent on time; (2) the tenant's failure to give written notice within stipulated time frames for vacating a property; (3) security deposits, interest, rights of withholding, damages; (4) property abandonment; (5) unlawful ouster from property and penalties; and (6) unlawful termination of utilities. Your lease often reflects aspects of these responsibilities and provisions.

PROTECTIVE FEATURES

Among the more common features of protective residential legislation are the following:

CANCELLATION OF LEASES IN CERTAIN CASES. If a landlord brings action against a tenant for failure to pay rent, the action is the equivalent of a demand for the rent. If the tenant brings to court the rent that is owed, plus interest, court costs and attorney's fees, the tenant may be restored to the property and the original lease. If not, the lease is canceled and the landlord recovers possession of the property.

In some states, if the lease is for a term of more than 20 years, the landlord must notify the tenant, along with all creditors who might have a lien on the property, in writing, that the lease will be canceled unless payment is made. Payment must be made within 30 days, or within a time specified in the original lease, after the written notice is given. If payment is not made, the landlord may repossess the property.

In some states, the tenant can be restored to possession at any time within six months of a repossession, he or she pays the landlord or brings to court the back rent, accumulated interest and legal fees.

RENT LIABILITY: DESTROYED OR UNTENANTABLE SPACE. In many states, if a building is damaged through no fault or negligence of the tenant and is afterwards determined to be unfit for occupancy, the tenant may leave the premises and will not be liable for the rent, unless some other agreement was made in writing previously, such as a provision in the lease.

NOTICE OF VACATING THE BUILDING. A tenant in northern climates may be guilty of a misdemeanor if, between November 15 and April 15, he or she abandons or vacates a building that has plumbing, water, steam or other pipes that may freeze, without giving three days' notice to the landlord, owner or agent.

COVENANTS OF LESSOR. The lessor (landlord) is responsible for the following:

1. That the premises are fit for the residential use intended. *Note:* The minimum standards for the residential use of a commercial building should have been met by the landlord if she or he is offering a residential lease.

   A tenant may choose to assume responsibility for meeting the residential code through an agreement to renovate the space, with residential use clearly stated in the lease. In some cities, the building inspections department and other governmental bodies may not require the landlord to be responsible for meeting minimum residential standards in a commercial building if such an agreement was made with the tenant.

2. That the premises are kept in compliance with health and safety codes and in reasonable repair—except when disrepair has been caused by the willful, malicious, or irresponsible conduct of the tenant (lessee).

3. That repairs and maintenance are carried out. The landlord and tenant may agree that the tenant is to perform specified repairs or maintenance normally the responsibility of the landlord, but this agreement must be made in writing.

WITHHOLDING OF, AND INTEREST ON, SECURITY DEPOSITS; DAMAGES. Any deposit that functions to secure the rental agreement and is not an advance payment of rent is subject to the following:

1. The deposit may be required to be retained by the landlord during the tenancy, with simple interest, at a specified rate, computed from the first day of the next month following the payment of the deposit to the last day of the month of legal tenancy.

2. The landlord shall return the deposit plus interest, as described above, within a specified period after termination of the tenancy *and* after receipt of the tenant's mailing address or delivery instruction. The landlord may withhold from the amount payable only what is necessary to remedy a default in payment of rent (or other funds due to the landlord by agreement); or to restore the premises to their original condition, with the exception of ordinary wear and tear.

3. If a landlord fails to provide a written statement of damages within a specified period after termination of tenancy and the receipt of tenant's mailing address, she or he is liable for damages in the

amount equal to the deposit withheld, plus interest.

4. If the property is sold or transferred, the landlord or, if the landlord dies, the landlord's agent must either transfer the deposit plus interest to the landlord's successor and notify the tenant of the transfer along with the address of the transferee or return the deposit plus interest to the tenant.

5. The landlord is subject to punitive damages if she or he has not complied with notification procedures or is otherwise shown to have retained the deposit in bad faith.

6. A tenant may not withhold payment of all or any portion of rent for the last payment period of a rental agreement on the grounds that the deposit should serve as a payment for the rent. Rent and the deposit are legally two different things. A tenant withholding payment on these grounds is liable for damages of the amount in default, plus interest.

7. A tenant may take action for the recovery of a deposit in the county where the rental property is located or, at the option of the tenant, in the county of the landlord's resident.

CODE VIOLATIONS, DISCLOSURE. All code violation records pertaining to a particular parcel of real property and the buildings on it are available to persons having a reasonable need to examine them. Reasonable notice should be given to the custodians of the records. Any copy of the records is at the expense of the person obtaining the information.

Persons to whom the records are available include, but are not limited to: (1) any person having a legal or beneficial interest in the premises, including a tenant; (2) any person considering in good faith the lease or purchase of the premises; or (3) a party to any action related to the premises.

PROPERTY ABANDONMENT. If a tenant abandons rented premises, the landlord may take possession of the tenant's personal property left on the premises. The tenant is liable for reasonable costs incurred by the landlord in removing, storing and caring for the property. After a specified period, the landlord may sell the property and may apply a reasonable amount of the proceeds to his costs. Any remaining proceeds shall go to the tenant.

Before the sale, a landlord must make efforts to notify the tenant by personally serving notice in writing or sending a certified letter to the last known address with a return receipt, and by posting notice of the sale in a conspicuous place on the premises for at least two weeks. Other rulings may provide for a tenant to retake possession of the property and for the damages the landlord is subject to if the landlord has unlawfully taken possession of a tenant's personal property.

UNLAWFUL OUSTER OR EXCLUSION PENALTY. A landlord who unlawfully removes or excludes a tenant, or intentionally interrupts the services of utilities (electric, heat, gas or water) with the intent to remove or exclude the tenant is guilty of a misdemeanor.

UNLAWFUL TERMINATION OF UTILITIES. If a landlord's agent causes the interruption of electricity, heat, gas or water services to the tenant, the tenant may recover damages and reasonable attorney's fees. The tenant may not recover damages if (1) the tenant was given notice of the interruption or (2) the landlord made a good faith effort to restore the service or (3) the interruption was for the purpose of correcting defective equip-

7.2   MULTIPLE TENANT LEASES

Building owners often want the confidence of knowing whom they can contact if payments are not being made by a tenant. Hence they may ask for only one signature on the legal documents signed to lease a space. Confident that all artists in one's group are committed to "their fair share," one member may sign on behalf of the group. For a leaseholder with adequate personal financial resources, that solution may serve everyone's interests well.

If there is no contract other than the oral agreements of the members, memories may falter, dissension may occur, and perhaps someone may move out on short notice without paying his or her rent. Only the member whose signature is on the lease has any legal responsibility to cover that portion of the payment until a new group member is found.

Variations of the above scenario occurred in several artist-organized projects in the Twin Cities before Artspace Projects, Inc. created a development strategy to assist studio-only projects—an "unincorporated affiliation" agreement.

Artspace involved the artists in project planning and negotiated a long-term lease on their behalf. A tenant agreement, with the basic structure of a leasehold cooperative, was developed with artist input on how they would like to make decisions as a group and manage their operations. All members of the group signed the lease agreement and the tenant agreement. A lease addendum provided each member's name, address and phone number for the building owner's information. The tenant's "unincorporated affiliation" agreement was used in lieu of an occupancy or sublease agreement.

The key benefit of this model is the ease with which it can be established. Little or no legal assistance is needed. Yet the model provides a framework for the group to interact effectively. It is an informal structure that has few of the requirements of other legal structures.

The master lease includes an agreement that, should any member of the group change during the lease period, the owner will be sent a letter noting the tenant's name and address to be removed and the new tenant's name and address to be added. Tenants whose names have been removed from the lease are no longer liable for their share of the rent.

More than half of the eight groups that have used this process through Artspace elected to pay a small fee to the group treasurer for the collection of rents and other accounting tasks. In some cases, an additional stipend was approved for other officers, who were kept active in continuing discussions with the building owner on behalf of the rest of the tenants.

Artspace negotiated a period of rent-free time to construct walls and other amenities on behalf of the group. In two cases, the groups took primary responsibility for the construction of their space, with technical assistance from Artspace. All artists were responsible for any refinements they needed built into their spaces and for the finish painting of walls or floors.

The groups using this organizational form, ranging in size from 6 to 27 units, have found they need to meet rarely. They have a process in place for changing or removing members; and new tenants need to be accepted only by the group rather than having to negotiate lease terms with the building owner. The group adds operating policies, as needed, that ensure smooth operations. The benefit to the landlord is a long-term tenant, only one rent check to collect, and a large space user—comparable to former warehousing or commercial tenants.

Studios at 700, Minneapolis. Printmaking studio.

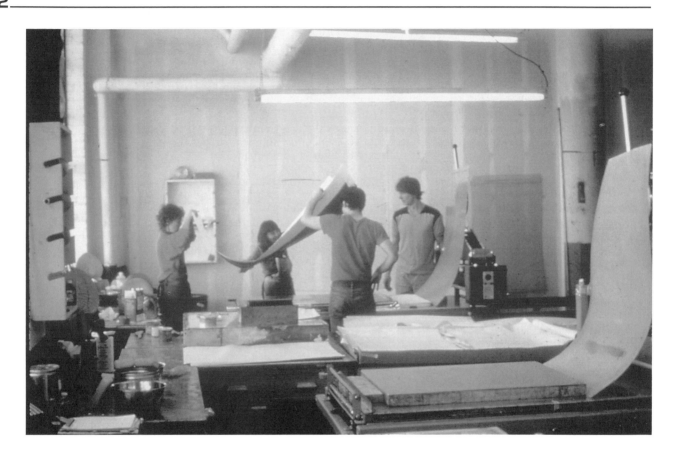

ment, and a good faith effort was made to reinstate the service within a reasonable length of time.

CAUTION CONCERNING COMMERCIAL LEASES

The protections of a residential lease can be achieved only by meeting requirements for a residential certificate of occupancy. If you are provided with a commercial lease, those protective measures generally do not apply. The caveat emptor principle in real estate reminds you to beware of promises, especially those that are not in writing. You should read any commercial lease thoroughly so that you are certain of your obliga-

tions and the results if you should default on any of the agreements in the lease.

It is entirely appropriate to enlist the aid of others to help you understand your lease or to negotiate changes in the lease for you. The cost of having a real estate attorney act on your behalf may be insignificant compared with the costs you may incur by not having understood the conditions of your lease.

MULTIPLE-TENANT LEASE STRUCTURES

Several artists wishing to lease together may form (1) an unincorporated affiliation or association, (2) a nonprofit corporation or (3) a leasehold cooperative. The lease agreement will note the organizational structure of the legal entity that signs the lease.

UNINCORPORATED AFFILIATION. The unincorporated tenant affiliation is formed by a contractual agreement between tenants in relationship to a jointly signed lease. The Studios at 700, developed by Artspace Projects, Inc. in Minneapolis, is a successful example of this lease form (see box 10.1).

NONPROFIT CORPORATION AND LEASE-HOLD COOPERATIVE. Both the nonprofit corporation and the leasehold cooperative may be organized for either leasing or ownership purposes. A. Salon, Ltd. of Washington, D.C. is a nonprofit cooperative that provides services to its members, including organizing exhibits, teaching opportunities, discount purchases of art supplies and studio space. A. Salon, Ltd. has acquired space with long-term leases for studios for its members in two projects, the Jackson School Art Center and the Takoma Metro Art Center. Artspace, Inc. in Salt Lake City is an example of a nonprofit corporation with a 25-year master lease. (See box 7.3.) The Emeryville Artists Cooperative in Emeryville, California began as a leasehold cooperative and later became a nonprofit housing cooperative (see box 8.4). These structures are described more fully in chapter 8 because of their adaptability for ownership projects.

Studios at 700. Textile artists' studio.

134

Annual fundraising event in the community garden.

7.3 PIERPONT PROJECT
Salt Lake City, Utah

Artspace, Inc. of Salt Lake City is a non-profit organization committed to providing low-cost housing and studio space to artists and their families as a means of advancing the arts. Artspace, Inc. was successful in securing $383,000 in city CDBG funds (in stages) and other grants to pay for the development costs of live/work units and studios in a project secured by a long-term lease.

In 1983, Artspace, Inc. secured a 25-year lease and negotiated the change of M-1 zoning regulations to allow conditional use permits for artists to live and work in their studios. The development of live/work spaces necessitated a requirement to meet earthquake code provisions, increasing their renovation costs. Artists in the project provided significant amounts of sweat equity to bring their units into compliance with codes. The project was completed in phases. Rental revenues cover all operating and administrative costs to ensure self-sufficiency.

The project includes 21 live/work spaces and 32 studios. A nonprofit performing arts company is in residence, including its rehearsal and small performing space. There are also four other arts organizations housed within the project, including Very Special Arts Utah, whose exhibition space serves handicapped and disabled artists throughout Utah.

Construction in progress.

Finished live/work space.

Unfinished studio in use.

The artists have reached into the community with several projects, taking seriously a commitment to revitalize the blighted neighborhood in which their building is located. Exterior improvements provided handicap accessibility and handsome railings and landscaping were designed to enhance the neighborhood as a whole. In partnership with the neighborhood family shelter, the artists led an effort to turn a former public dumping ground into an urban garden that is shared with their neighbors.

In addition to hosting an annual neighborhood celebration that includes children's art activities, the artists have built an outdoor studio facility which allows the public to become more aware of their activities. The artists in Pierpont Project are committed to continuing their outreach efforts by being a resource to the city in seeking creative solutions to urban problems and by enhancing the cultural character of the community.

"... when I ask you to earn money and have a room of your own, I am asking you to live in the presence of reality, an invigorating life, it would appear, whether one can impart it or not."

Virginia Woolf
A Room of One's Own

8
Long-Term Control: Ownership

Ownership provides the greatest number of rights to the use of a property. It is the highest degree of long-term control you can have. With that control come both benefits and drawbacks. In addition, when comparing the forms of ownership and control available for your project, you will find that each has its strengths and weaknesses. As you plan the overall structure of your project, you will need to assess the trade-offs that must be made and modify or mix features to meet your specific project needs. Most of all, you will need to take responsibility for understanding the choice that is best for your needs. A brief comparison of the different forms of ownership structures follows.

SOLE OWNERSHIP

Sole ownership or fee simple ownership is the most common form of outright ownership of buildings and land. Under this type, the individual receives a deed to a building and the land on which it is built.

He or she pays taxes on both, and the title is usually subject to a mortgage.

Fee simple ownership features the greatest degree of control and the greatest opportunity to build up equity. The major advantage of sole ownership is the flexibility of making decisions without conferring with co-owners. Sole owners decide how the property will be used, how much to charge if it is rented, how it will be managed, and when to sell and at what price or terms. Moreover, transfers of ownership are the least restrictive with this form of ownership.

ADVANTAGES

The economic benefits of this form of ownership accrue only to the property owner and not to the tenants. An on-site owner receives important tax benefits, including homestead treatment of property taxes and deductible local property tax and mortgage-interest payments.

DISADVANTAGES

Fee simple ownership usually requires a substantial down payment that may be beyond the means of the average artist. Almost all warehouses and older commercial buildings are much larger than the typical single family home. Therefore, it is unlikely that any one individual with a low or moderate income could afford to purchase and rehabilitate such a building. Some storefronts or other small commercial buildings are in the same range as houses and, for some artists, are within the range of affordability.

Perhaps you can afford the down payment, you can raise sufficient funds for rehab, and you decide you would like to help your fellow artists while making a worthwhile personal investment. You know artists, you are aware of their needs, you want the arts to flourish, and you believe you could help create a "community of artists"—an ideal for many artists.

But what are you really letting yourself in for? Remember, as a landlord, you must determine the prevailing rents, find and negotiate with tenants, prepare contracts, collect the rent, keep the property in repair, and manage your finances. Or, at least, you need to hire someone to handle these tasks for you.

MULTIPLE OWNER AND MULTIPLE TENANT STRUCTURES

Many forces are responsible for creating the need for condominiums and cooperatives—multiple-owner and multiple-tenant structures. Among the most important are land scarcity in desirable areas, disenchantment with responsibilities for maintenance, a strong desire for ownership rather than renting, increased costs of financing, and the continuing escalation of construction costs.

When two or more persons wish to share the ownership of a single property, they may do so in one of the following ways, each of which is described below.

- Tenants in Common
- Joint Tenancy
- Tenancy by the Entirety
- Community Property
- General Partnership
- Limited Partnership
- Joint Venture
- Syndication
- Corporations
- Real Estate Investment Trusts
- Condominiums
- Cooperatives

138

TENANTS IN COMMON

Tenancy in common, though it is not a legal partnership, is a legal form of ownership related to the joint venture and partnership forms of ownership. As tenants in common, each tenant owns an undivided interest in the whole property. The ownership interest of each partner is proportionate to his or her cash investment, which need not be the same size. Each owner may independently sell, mortgage, give away or devise their individual interest. Each tenant in common has a separate legal title to his undivided interest, with the legal right to sell or dispose of that interest without the permission of the others. If a co-owner dies, interest passes to the heirs, not to the other co-owners. The tenants in common form of ownership is most appropriate for small groups of tenants—six or fewer—among whom a less formal structure can still ensure accountability.

Partners may hold tenancy through a lease with the partnership. The partnership document should specify rents and other economic relationships between the tenants and the partnership. There should be reference to the preferred arrangements to remove tenants and to remove partners, especially buy-out arrangements.

The tenants provide the partnership with proportionate shares of payments that cover mortgage and operational expenses. The partnership files an informational tax return and the partners receive a K-1 statement as to their proportionate share of income over expenses on the property. The partnership itself does not pay taxes. Instead, the partners pay their proportionate share of taxes due.

A tenancy in common gives tenant-partners an actual and direct financial interest in the property. However, because it is not a legal partnership, parties are not held personally liable for actions of other parties.

The advantages of such an arrangement are that property tax and interest tax deductions are available to partners, as are homestead property tax benefits (similar to co-ops and condos). Tenancy in common avoids the hassles of filing corporate income tax returns and paying corporate taxes (as a co-op or condo association is required to do).

Among the financial disadvantages are that tenants in common will have a more difficult time mortgaging or selling their interest than will condo owners. The purchase of a party's interest in a tenants-in-common arrangement requires title checks, the filing of deeds, and payment of the mortgage registration tax—a more expensive and cumbersome transfer than that of co-ops.

JOINT TENANCY

The most distinguishing characteristic of the joint tenancy form of ownership is the right of survivorship. The legal philosophy is that the joint tenants represent a singular ownership unit. The death of one joint tenant reduces the number of persons owning the unit, but the unit remains intact. It is a form frequently used by married or "committed" couples to avoid probate and legal expenses. A joint tenancy can be terminated by one tenant's conveyance of his or her interest.

TENANCY BY THE ENTIRETY

Some states use tenancy by the entirety specifically as a form of joint tenancy for married persons. The two key characteristics are that (1) the surviving spouse becomes the sole owner of the property at the death of the other, and (2) during the lifetime of both spouses, neither has a disposable interest in the property.

COMMUNITY PROPERTY

Community property law treats a husband and wife as equal partners, with, in theory, each owning one-half interest in a property. This form of co-ownership requires the signature of both spouses before it can be conveyed or mortgaged. Each spouse may determine the recipient of their one-half interest in the property at their time of death, if declared in a will. Arizona, California, Idaho, Louisiana, Nevada, New Mexico, Texas, Washington and Wisconsin have community property laws.

PARTNERSHIP

In a partnership, two or more people share in ownership of an enterprise or business. A partnership is a common method of carrying on business because it offers certain tax advantages. The partnership itself is not taxed; the partners are taxed through individual income tax. This "conduit" tax treatment prevents the partners from having to pay taxes twice, at the organizational level and the individual level. For low-income artists, however, there are no particular tax advantages. They are not operating real estate as a business, but simply want to own the place where they live and work.

One attraction of the partnership form of ownership is that partnerships are much easier to form than cooperatives or condominium associations. It is not legally necessary to incorporate or write bylaws or file many legal documents as it is in co-op or condominium associations. The management structure is also more flexible. Partnership documents are easier for most lawyers to understand because they do more of them.

General Partnership

Unlike the cooperative, in which members purchase shares in the corporation, in a general partnership each partner is equal and holds an undivided interest in the property of the partnership. Each partner shares control of all phases of the operation. Profits and liabilities are shared equally.

Unfortunately, because management issues do not have to be spelled out in partnership legal documents, partners seldom address the issue of management. In any multi-unit building with live/work studios, no matter what legal structure is used, tenants will inevitably face management issues. When responsibilities and procedures are not spelled out, discord is likely to occur within the partnership. In developing policies that address the relationships of the tenant/partners to each other, you may find it helpful to examine the treatment that co-op documents give to these issues.

PARTNERSHIP FORMATION. Before visiting an attorney to draft a partnership agreement, the partners should discuss the terms of management and economic issues. They may wish to contact lending institutions about their underwriting standards for the partnership form of ownership to see what they would require.

The partners should prepare a written description of the terms of agreement for the attorney to review. The terms should include the purchase details, how the square footage is to be divided among the partners, a projection of the equitable division of costs and investments, how economic relationships and the responsibilities to each other are to be handled, what happens if a partner wants to leave the partnership, etc. The lender's requirements also need to be provided in the document.

LIABILITY. In a general partnership, each partner is personally liable for the full debts of the partnership, even if those debts have been incurred by another partner. You may wish to weigh the benefits of partnership ownership with the tenants-in-common form, in which the parties are not held personally liable for actions of other parties.

WITHDRAWAL FROM THE PARTNERSHIP.
Interest in the partnership is not as freely transferrable as it is in some other forms of ownership. When the partnership is formed, the legal documents should include provisions on the handling of disputes and discord among the partners.

Limited Partnership

As in a general partnership, two or more partners are involved in a limited partnership. In the latter form, however, there are general partners who exercise full management control and retain full liability for all debts. The general partners may be individuals or corporations. The limited partners have financial investments in the partnership, but their liability is limited to the amount of their investments. They have no management role in the project. Essentially, the limited partners exchange direct control over their investment for conduit tax treatment and limited liability.

The limited partnership form has been used to attract private investors for live/work space development by passing through or "selling off" the tax benefits to those who can use them. However, changes in the tax law—specifically "passive activity rules"—have diminished the tax advantages of pass-through losses from real estate for most "noncorporate" investors. Limited partners can no longer deduct their real estate "losses" from their employment, business, or portfolio income sources.

LIMITED PARTNERSHIP FORMATION.
The general partner is typically responsible for organizing the proposed project. Although the general partner may be your cooperative corporation, most investors and potential lenders will require a general partner with some development experience and substantial assets.

Artists without assets will find it difficult to secure investors or potential lenders. This problem may be solved by finding a second or networth general partner who will share the risks and responsibility. The second partner could be a for-profit or a nonprofit corporation, a funding source for artists' support, a revolving fund or a private party, including the building owner or the project's general contractor. Roles for the co-general partners should be defined for the periods before and after construction.

The limited partnership form provides ways to structure relationships for projects that have the potential to attract public or private subsidies, special mortgage terms and favorable financing or tax arrangements. Partnership fees may be an extra resource for expenses or other project needs. With a decision-making role in the development, artists could affect decisions to return profits to the project.

JOINT VENTURE

A joint venture is treated as a partnership for tax purposes. The difference is that a joint venture is formed to develop a single project. Each member of a venture makes a contribution to a real estate project by contributing either concept, talent or capital. Typically, all parties need one another for the project to succeed. The filing requirements of the state where the venture is formed must be followed.

SYNDICATION

Syndication (discussed in chapter 6) is the joining of individuals or corporations to pursue investment in a project that is too large for any of the parties to undertake individually. Syndication refers to a limited partnership in which the general partner contributes organizational talent and management services, and the limited partner provides investment capital. General partners receive compensation for their role in directing the project.

The Ark, San Francisco. This new construction has been proposed by Artspace Development Corporation to provide affordable live/work spaces. The project will have 29 units, a performance space and a variety of common areas.

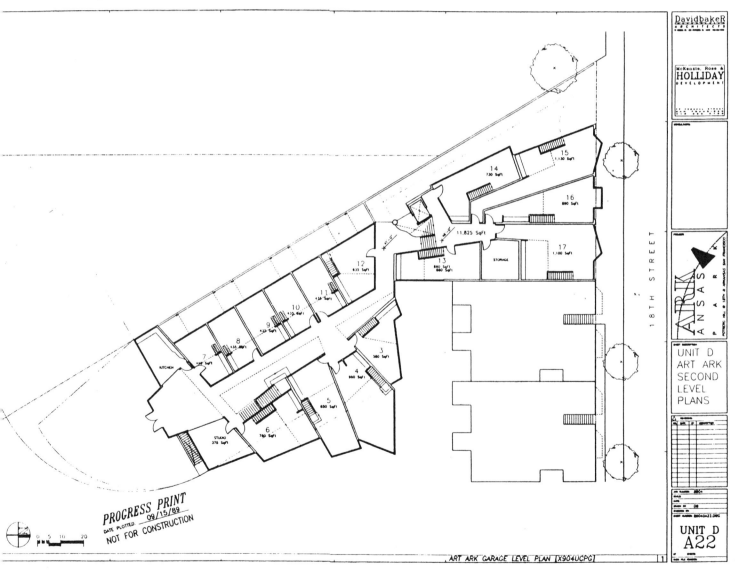

CORPORATION

Corporations are legal entities that can buy, sell, own, and operate property in the name of the corporation. Corporations are characterized by the following:

1. A number of individuals join as associates, owners or members.

2. There is an intention to earn a profit while carrying out business in a for-profit corporation. In a nonprofit corporation, the intention is to serve a public or not-for-profit purpose, often for the benefit of its members.

3. Management is centralized, with decision-making authority in the hands of a small group.

4. Associates, owners or members have limited liability for the debts of the organization.

5. Associates, owners or members in a for-profit corporation have the right to transfer their interests without the consent of other members. A nonprofit corporation can reserve the right to select a replacement for the transfer of a member's share.

6. The organization has continuity of life, regardless of the transfer of an interest by an associate, owner or member.

For-Profit Corporation

For-profit corporations are legal entities that buy, sell, own, and operate property in the name of the corporation, with profit as the motivation for their business activities. Stockholders purchase shares of stock as evidence of ownership. The corporation pays income taxes on its profits. After taxes, profits are used to pay dividends to the stockholders, who must again pay personal taxes on that income.

A variation called the Subchapter "S" corporation avoids double taxation if organized with less than 35 stockholders. Subchapter "S" corporations receive tax treatment as a partnership, passing income and losses to its shareholders directly without prior taxation. This form may be used to advantage by a general partner in a limited partnership, making it possible to limit liability while receiving tax benefits. While the corporation form of ownership provides protection from unlimited liability, the double taxation feature would not benefit a project of more than 35 units.

Nonprofit Corporation

Nonprofit corporations established to buy, sell, own, and operate property do so for a public benefit, not for the private gain of any person associated with the corporation.

For a nonprofit to qualify as tax exempt and receive tax-deductible contributions on behalf of the group, it must be organized for a qualifying public purpose—for example, educational programs. (See box 8.1 for an example of the articles of incorporation for nonprofit corporations.) Typically, artists seeking a tax-exempt status solely for the leasing of space have been unsuccessful in meeting the public-benefit requirements of the IRS.

To avoid certain taxation problems, cooperatives may take the form of a nonprofit corporation, as discussed more fully later in this chapter. In some states, such as California, lenders prefer to finance cooperatives that are organized as 501(c)(3) tax-exempt nonprofit corporations. Artist live/work space projects with 501(c)(3) status include the following:

■ Project Artaud, San Francisco, California

■ Emeryville Cooperative, Emeryville, California (see box 8.4)

■ The Ark—Artspace Development Corporation, San Francisco, California

8.1 SAMPLE LANGUAGE FROM ARTICLES OF INCORPORATION FOR A NONPROFIT CORPORATION

The articles of incorporation should reflect the goals and purposes the group wishes to achieve. Typical language in articles of incorporation for 501(c)(3) applications may contain the following elements. The final preparation of the articles, bylaws and 501(c)(3) application should be reviewed with an attorney. Key elements are:

1. This corporation is a nonprofit public benefit corporation organized for the purpose of education and social welfare purposes within the meaning of Section 501(c)(3), including but not limited to:
   a. promotion, support and encouragement of all arts media;
   b. provision of housing and work space to low- and moderate-income artists;
   c. provision of studio and gallery space for the use of artists;
   d. provision of theater space for use by performing arts organizations;
   e. provision of classroom and studio space for public educational programs in the arts;
   f. leasing, subleasing, purchasing, or otherwise acquiring improved or unimproved real property for rehabilitation, conversion or construction of low-cost space to be managed, leased, subleased, or resold to artists or arts organizations for any of the above defined uses;
   g. education of the public to the role of the arts in personal life, community life and economic development through presentations, conferences, and other educational workshops;
   h. provision of services and training to artists and arts organizations to improve their capabilities in the rehabilitation and utilization of space and facilities;
   i. solicit funds, accept gifts, grants, and contributions to put to productive use all funds and property this corporation may own and distribute income and property exclusively for the purposes set forth;

2. The corporation's activities and earnings shall in no way, directly or indirectly, afford pecuniary gain nor private benefit to any member, director, nor officer.

3. No part of the activities, funds, or property of this corporation shall be used in propaganda or attempting to influence legislation.

4. Upon dissolution of this corporation after providing for the debts and obligations, the remaining assets shall be distributed to a nonprofit established under Section 501(c)(3).

Project Artaud, San Francisco.
Performance space.

Nonprofit status has also been established for a broader role as nonprofit developer, typically for more than one project within a community. Examples include the following:

■ Artspace Projects, Inc., Minneapolis, Minnesota

■ Artspace, Inc., Salt Lake City, Utah

■ L.A. Artspace, Los Angeles, California

■ ArtistSpace, Inc., Boston, Massachusetts

■ Fort Point Arts Community of South Boston, Boston, Massachusetts

■ Artspace Inc., Austin, Texas

144

REAL ESTATE INVESTMENT TRUST

The real estate investment trust (REIT) combines the advantages of the corporate form of ownership with single taxation treatment. The trust pays advisers to manage investments on behalf of beneficiaries to the trust, which acts as a mutual fund type of investment. Money is pooled—the minimum is 100 investors—from the sale of low-cost "beneficial interests," which are freely transferable. REIT income received by a tax-exempt organization is not taxed as unrelated business income and may offer a way for a non-profit developer to organize an investment pool. Although a REIT may be a source of financing, it is not a viable form of tenant-controlled ownership for a live/work space project because of complex governmental rules for operating a REIT.

CONDOMINIUM

The condominium is one of several forms of ownership to combine community living with community ownership. In the United States, the 1961 National Housing Act defined condominium ownership standards, permitting dwelling units to exist and to be individually owned within a larger property. The remainder of the property and its facilities are held jointly with other owners. Variations of the condominium form include town houses and planned unit developments.

The exact locations of the building structure on the property and the dwelling unit within the structure are described in the "plat" (location map) and architectural plans. Each is also described in legal language in a "master deed." When the master deed is recorded, the property becomes subject to the condominium laws of the state in which the condominium is located.

The jointly held common property (common estate) is maintained and operated by an associa-

tion with a board of directors elected from among the owners of the individual dwelling units. The internal government is controlled by the condominium declaration bylaws recorded with the master deed.

The structure and activities of the condominium association as the governing body of the common areas resemble those of the cooperative corporation. The major difference is that a cooperative corporation owns everything, whereas the condominium association owns nothing.

For many people, the condominium approach provides a desirable balance because it permits sole ownership of a dwelling unit but joint control of common areas so that individual owners do not have to assume direct responsibility for maintenance. The financial advantages of the condominium are that individual owners can sublet, sell or refinance their units at any time without restriction. They may also deduct property taxes and mortgage interest paid from their taxable income if they itemize deductions. Residents are individually and personally liable for any debts or damages associated with unit ownership. They are not liable for any default of their neighbors, except that they may need to carry the common area expenses associated with abandoned or vacated units.

Financing Condominiums

Individual owners are responsible for their own financing, including obtaining a mortgage, paying property taxes and paying for repairs to their dwelling units. In addition, residents pay dues to the association for their share of expenses for common elements.

Condominium owners own their individual estates and a common interest, defined by a percentage of a total area, in the common estate. The owner's share in the common estate would be roughly proportional to the value of his or her unit. Roofs occasionally need repair, the common

Project Artaud. Ceramics studio.

hallways periodically need repainting, the exterior of the building must be kept up, mechanical equipment has to be serviced and the insurance policies covering the condominium project have to be paid. These and other common expenses are paid by the unit owners in proportion to their shares in the ownership of common elements. Condo association assessments exceeding expenditures are either returned to members or applied to the following year's expenses.

Dwelling units in condominiums approved by HUD before construction have been financed under both subsidized and unsubsidized financing programs. Check with your local HUD office to find out current requirements.

Transferring Ownership

Owners are responsible for their own financing. They may choose to refinance, and they are not restricted by the condominium association in the means used to sell their units. Residents risk loss of equity in case of foreclosure or in a declining housing market. Gains from resale of the unit are subject to taxation.

Taxes

Taxes, based on the established value of the unit, are paid directly by each condominium owner as part of the monthly mortgage payment and are held in escrow by the lender. Condominiums and cooperatives may be treated differently for property tax and usury law purposes in some states. Variant benefits may determine which form of community-owned housing—condominiums or cooperatives—may prevail in your state. (See box 8.2.)

COOPERATIVE

A cooperative is formed by a group of people to obtain services or housing for themselves more effectively or more economically than could be obtained individually. The primary purpose of a cooperative is to serve its members, not to provide profit to others. Cooperative housing provides to its members the financial benefits of home ownership and increased control over their immediate environment.

The following principles, noted by the National Association of Housing Cooperatives, underlie cooperative businesses and provide their distinguishing features:

- control is democratic, with each member having one vote

- there is a limited return on membership shares and investments

- membership is open and voluntary, with no discrimination on an illegal basis, such as age, race, sex, but with discrimination on any other basis, such as artist members

- continual education is provided to members

- excess profits are returned and losses are shared; and

- there is cooperation with other cooperatives

Corporate Structure

Cooperative ownership requires tenants to form a nonprofit corporation for the purpose of owning and operating the project. The corporation holds title to the dwelling units and directly assumes the mortgage, tax, and other obligations necessary to finance and operate the project, thereby relieving the members from direct liability for those items. Rather than directly owning their units, tenant/shareholders own stock or a membership share certificate in the corporation and lease a dwelling unit through an occupancy agreement.

Members support the corporation through their proportionate share of the budget, as reflected in their occupancy agreement.

8.2   TECHNICAL ASSISTANCE ON CONDOMINIUMS

The National Community Association Institute and its 40 regional chapters provide training and educational programs for all types of condominium and cooperative housing. Information is available on organization, management of common areas, house rules, insurance, reserves etc. Assistance is available through:

The National Community Association Institute
1423 Powhatin Street, Suite 7
Alexandria, Virginia 22314
(703) 548-8600

The board of directors estimates the annual cost to operate the corporation and to pay the debt on the property. If the budget is overestimated, the cooperative may vote to increase its operating or replacement reserves, to expand its services to members, or to provide a "patronage refund."

Control by Tenant/Members

Membership also gives the right to participate in the operation of the corporation, either directly as a member of the board or indirectly as a voter. In effect, members become in part their own landlord, sharing rights and responsibilities with other members of the corporation.

The law permits only the elected board to act for the corporation. The purpose of a board is to eliminate one-person decisions. The board is often kept small in number, usually five or seven. However, co-ops with less than 15 units may choose to have all members also serve on the board to share responsibilities fully.

**Project Artaud.
Artist in live/work space.**

The success of a cooperative depends on the ability of individual members to cooperate. Wise decisions must be made collectively, and potential problems need to be dealt with effectively in the corporation's bylaws. The stake of control and equity promotes pride and self-help activity. Dedicated leadership is also necessary to maintain the group's goals and sense of unity and to encourage continued participation by members.

Although tenant/shareholders may be able to manage and maintain the cooperative's premises effectively themselves, many cooperatives contract for a professional management and maintenance service.

The individual tenant/shareholder's rights to use, and responsibilities to maintain and improve, the dwelling unit are set forth in the corporation's bylaws and declarations.

Financial Advantages

The one characteristic of cooperative housing that separates it from other forms of ownership is the way it is financed. In most states, cooperative housing is financed by a single loan or "blanket mortgage" made to the corporation, rather than directly to individual owners. Advantages usually include lower overall financing costs to the members and the ability to mix credit-worthy cooperative members with those who may not qualify independently. In cooperatives that restrict the amount of equity to be earned on the transfer value or sale of its shares (discussed below), the entry cost for low- and moderate-income people provides an affordable ownership option. Eventually, the cooperative pays the mortgage in full, reducing expenses only to ongoing operating and maintenance costs.

The financial advantages of cooperative housing over some other forms of housing include savings in development costs, construction, maintenance, operations, insurance, and taxes. Also, because cooperatives have historically been used for other types of shared purchasing of supplies and marketing of products, the members of a cooperative housing project may choose to expand the services that the co-op provides to its members.

Financial Disadvantages

A blanket mortgage may present difficulties when tenants wish to sell their shares. In addition, because the single blanket mortgage is made to the corporation rather than individuals, most financial institutions will not accept an individual's equity in cooperative stock as security for a loan.

In some parts of the country, financing may be more difficult to arrange because lenders are relatively unfamiliar with cooperatives. Lenders typically seek the real estate as collateral in the event of a default.

Another disadvantage is the shared liability if tenants default on payments. If one tenant defaults on payment and if the cooperative is unprepared to cover the cost of that unit's monthly expenses, the lender can foreclose on the entire property, affecting all tenants. Shared liability is resolved by maintaining an operating reserve and by setting policies for handling the cash flow problems of tenants/members.

Loans for new tenants to purchase an outgoing member's share are available from the National Cooperative Bank or other private lenders. It may be difficult for a low-income artist to qualify for a share loan if a sizable equity has been accrued.

Liability

Although the corporation holds title and directly assumes liability for the mortgage, tax, and other obligations necessary to finance and operate the cooperative, each tenant/shareholder in a cooperative is jointly liable through a proprietary lease. Therefore, if another shareholder defaults on his or her pro rata share of the ongoing costs of the cooperative, these costs may be distributed among the remaining stockholders.

Transferring Membership

When tenant/shareholders move out, they may sell their proportionate share in the cooperative (rather than give a deed). Generally, many people who could not qualify for a mortgage large enough to buy a condo can afford to meet payments for share loans. Some cooperatives reserve the right to purchase the share from the outgoing member, and most request the right to select and/or approve the incoming member.

Taxes

Generally, a housing cooperative member receives the same basic tax advantages of the homeowner, including state homestead property tax rates and deductible mortgage interest and property taxes for federal tax purposes. The member is allowed to deduct his or her share in proportion to the share he or she owns.

Forming a Cooperative Corporation

All cooperatives establish the members as the primary structural unit. The members then elect a board of directors. Other units of organization may vary, but all basically follow the pattern in the organizational chart in figure 8.1.

DOCUMENTS NEEDED. A cooperative is both an organized community and a business. It has to perform well as a business to succeed. Establishing a corporation to manage a live/work space development requires the preparation of a number of business-related documents, including the following:

- articles of incorporation
- bylaws
- lease or occupancy agreement
- tenant/membership admission policies
- house rules and operating policies
- financing documents, as required
- contracts for services (for the development and the management periods)

Three key documents need be prepared when creating a cooperative: (1) articles of incorporation, (2) bylaws and (3) the occupancy agreement.

The articles of incorporation (see appendix 8.1) tend to be broadly written, focusing on the most important legal functions of the organization. The articles are registered with the Secretary

ORGANIZATIONAL CHART, COOPERATIVES

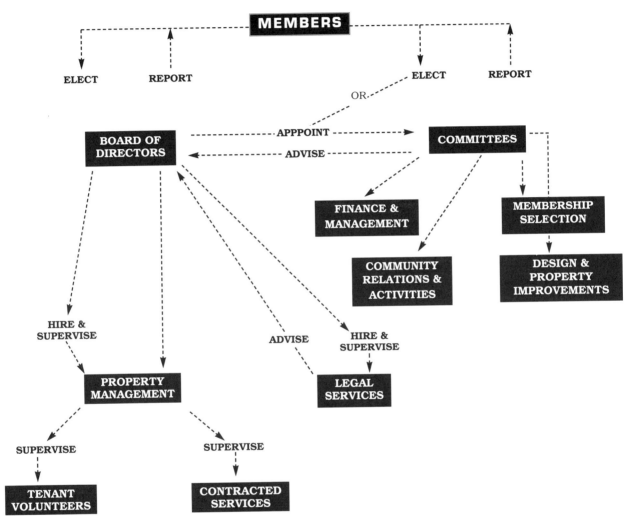

of State and require the approval of the state for any changes made later. The articles refer to bylaws, which contain a detailed description of the manner in which the cooperative will manage itself.

The bylaws (see appendix 8.2) govern operations of the cooperative and guarantee democratic control by its members. The bylaws define the rights and obligations of members and stipulate the processes for selecting or terminating members, the method for electing a board of directors, and the extent of the board's powers and duties. The bylaws are not filed with any local or state authority and may be changed by the cooperative membership through voting procedures detailed in the bylaws.

An occupancy agreement is the lease from the cooperative to the tenant/shareholder. It defines the rights and responsibilities of the members and refers to the cooperative's articles of incorporation, the bylaws, and the house rules and operating policies. In a leasing cooperative, the occupancy agreement also refers to the master lease.

Planning the Documents

The development team and/or the prospective tenants should work together to create these documents. This is the appropriate time to clarify the shared values of the tenants by using standard planning techniques.

If you have primary responsibility for this aspect of planning for the group, do not simply present "finished" documents to the group. At least part of the group should take part in identifying issues and setting priorities, in discussing ways to handle various situations, and in preparing written statements that reflect the group's agreements on each topic.

Use the sample documents provided in the appendix or those from other cooperatives to create your documents. A copy of your state's legislation on forming cooperatives will clarify what constitutes a legally structured cooperative. Other aspects of how you organize or choose to operate are left to your discretion. Establishing an advisory group with skills in political or community processes and legal or financial expertise will assist your planning.

Building Community

A sense of community within a cooperative (or other structure borrowing from cooperative principles) may be fostered by sharing in tasks or by creating social activities to celebrate the milestones of the group. In a socially successful cooperative, members do the following:

- participate in creating or refining the governing structure
- think of themselves as "owners"
- take and share responsibility through committee assignments
- emerge as leaders within areas of personal interests or expertise
- expand knowledge and skills through interaction with the group
- meet common needs through expressed shared values
- develop loyalty, which builds a stable "neighborhood" environment

Limiting Equity

Most cooperatives restrict the rate at which equity can accrue on membership shares. Increases in equity are determined according to formulas that are decided when the cooperative is first established. The type of equity formula chosen often reflects the requirements of insured loan programs or public financing. Some formulas reflect the shared social values of the members.

Members of a cooperative must balance the equity needs of the member who is leaving with the cooperative's need to attract the type of members it is established to serve. An artist's cooperative is intended to serve its members by providing live/work space. Therefore, its equity policies should focus on the "use value" rather than the profit potential for the sale of a share. The savings accrued by lower overall housing costs may be invested in one's art career rather than in a mortgage as a form of "forced savings." If an artist

---

8.3 TECHNICAL ASSISTANCE FOR CREATING A COOPERATIVE

A number of nonprofit groups offer technical assistance for the creation of cooperatives. You may wish to check initially within your own community for the group(s) available to you. The National Association of Housing Cooperatives and its ten Regional Cooperative Housing Associations provide access to a wide range of technical information and services. Service options include publications, direct training, conferences, newsletters and legislative lobbying on behalf of cooperatives. Assistance is available from:

National Association of Housing Cooperatives
1614 King Street
Alexandria, Virginia 22314
(703) 549-5201

is seeking primarily to profit from the resale of his or her unit, other forms of ownership may be more appropriate choices.

Methods to establish members' equity include the following:

1. **NO EQUITY.** Upon departure, the member receives the cost of the original membership share, plus the depreciated value of improvements made, less debt owed to the cooperative.

2. **CONSTANT DOLLAR EQUITY.** The value of a membership share is increased by a standard inflation index.

3. **PERCENTAGE FORMULA.** There are a variety of formulas, for example, 1 percent annually may be applied to the value of the unit defined at time of construction.

4. **FULL EQUITY WITHOUT APPRECIATION.** The original cost of the share plus the amount of the principal paid on the mortgage to date is paid for the share.

5. **COMBINATION FORMULAS.** The transfer value of a share may be the sum of several factors, sometimes with a "not to exceed" stipulation. The factors may include (a) the original price paid for the share, (b) pro rata share of the mortgage payments, (c) the depreciated value of depreciable improvements, (d) the fair market value of nondepreciable improvements, (e) real property capital contributions to the corporate reserve account and (f) an inflation factor, such as accumulated interest.

6. **SPECULATIVE EQUITY.** Shares may be sold for "whatever the market will bear," or full market value of the property. Because of the large demand for housing in New York, most cooperatives have been established as "market rate,"

although they may be unaffordable to future artists. (See box 8.3.)

A Leasing Cooperative

A cooperative corporation that leases the property occupied by its members is called a "leasing cooperative." A leasing co-op may be a group of artists seeking a long-term lease and self-management control for a floor of a building for studio use. Leasing co-ops are also used to raise project development capital, providing the tax benefits of a rental project as an exchange to investors. The master lease provided to the leasing cooperative may define the right to purchase the property at a later date.

The St. Paul Lowertown Lofts Artists Cooperative has a 20-year lease with an option to buy after 10 years, defined in its master lease. (See box 6.6.) This choice of control was made because of financing requirements.

Resident members of leasing cooperatives can enjoy most of the benefits of ownership cooperatives without the financial responsibilities of ownership. Publicly and privately owned properties which are not for sale under present laws or tax regulations may be available under the leasing approach.

Members of leasing cooperatives have a voice and a vote in the management of their spaces. They may participate in the same kinds of committees and activities as ownership cooperatives. Members may have the same forms of occupancy agreements, reserves and equity accumulation from the growth of the corporate assets. The significant difference is that the cooperative acquires the use of the premises through a long-term lease rather than through a mortgage.

Advantages to both tenants and owners can be safeguarded by the lease. Provisions may define and ensure sound maintenance and operations, determine initial and continuing occupancy, establish budgets and adequate rent schedules,

152

8.4 EMERYVILLE (AND 45TH STREET) ARTISTS COOPERATIVE
Emeryville, California

Since its establishment in 1974, the Emeryville Artists Cooperative has grown to 60 studios in three warehouses with approximately 90 residents. In 1980, the artists incorporated and took master leases on the buildings, managing them as a low-moderate income leased housing cooperative.

In 1985, the 45th Street Artists Cooperative was incorporated under the aegis of the Cooperative Corporations Code of California as a public-benefit, nonprofit corporation to purchase one of the buildings as a limited-equity housing cooperative, also serving artists in low-moderate income households. Through its limited equity structure, the coop was eligible for public funds. Artists can buy shares of the property and own their spaces, but can never sell at a profit. Only the value of improvements will be paid back. This sale/purchase closed in January 1987 as a joint venture with the City of Emeryville Redevelopment Agency. The cooperative purchased the building with $70,000 from the artists, a $453,100 loan from SAMCO, a nonprofit low-income housing agency, and a $721,900 55-year loan from the city.

Studio.

and guarantee information and reports will be provided as required. The articles and bylaws of the leased cooperative corporation would be closely patterned after the usual ownership cooperative.

Ideally, the master lease should be for a term of at least 10 years, with rights of renewal, to ensure the effectiveness of member participation. In a leasing cooperative, the master lease forms the most critical element of organization and structure. A qualified attorney should be engaged to negotiate or review the contract on behalf of all of the members before a lease is signed.

Artists in common area.

In 1988, they purchased the other property, comprising two continuous buildings. The $1.6 million purchase price was financed with a $900,000 loan from First Nationwide Bank, a $348,800 five-year loan from the city, $75,000 from the artists, and a $400,000 loan from the building seller.

Artists from the Emeryville Cooperative have reached into the community with studio tours, and programs which include: Youth Art Program, Artist in the Community, Artist in Residence program, and the Emeryville Annual Art Exhibition.

Artist in her studio.

*"Architecture is the making of spaces which evoke
a feeling of appropriateness of use."*
Louis I. Kahn, architect

9
Design Needs

How can you develop your space so that it will positively influence
your mood, thoughts, creativity and productivity and save your
pocketbook?

DO YOU NEED
TO HIRE AN ARCHITECT?

Your first thoughts about hiring an architect may be that an
architect provides a "luxury" service, one you will not even
consider if you are on a bare-bones budget. This assumption may be
correct. Often, however, architects can save you money. The more complex the project, the more likely you are to need an architect.

DO IT YOURSELF

For simple projects you do not need to hire an architect. For example, in a storefront or small commercial building in which the design work is straightforward, you can prepare the information needed by the inspections department. However, the more you do yourself, the more legal and technical responsibility you accept.

To get a permit for your project, your local building department will require you to submit scale drawings and specifications showing locations of exits, halls, walls, windows, cabinets, plumbing fixtures and electrical outlets, switches and fixtures. Drawings should show dimensions; note how the sprinkler, plumbing and electrical systems will meet codes; and detail the building materials you plan to use, including the appropriate rating of sheetrock and doors. The larger or more complex the project, the more important it is to lay out plumbing, heating and electrical systems efficiently.

The drawings required should include at least a floor plan with dimensions—a view from above, as in a map. Depending on your alteration plans, you may also be required to submit elevations, which are side views from outside or inside the building, and sections—a cutaway view showing what the building is made of. The purpose of the drawings is to make clear what building materials are being used, how they will fit together and how the building is structurally supported.

Before purchasing or leasing, you should invite a city building inspector to go over the building layout. The inspector will compare your plans for the intended new use with existing systems and structures. If changes are required in the heating plant, drains, ventilation, exits, etc., the inspector can give you an idea about what needs to be done. The inspector will also tell you whether any of your proposed new uses will entail further requirements for improving or upgrading the building. By incorporating this information into your plans, you will be better able to estimate the total costs of your proposed project.

If you intend to seek bids from contractors, provide detailed specifications to each bidding contractor to ensure that contractors are bidding on the same tasks, layout and materials (see discussion in chapter 10). Otherwise, it will be impossible to evaluate their bids fairly or to ensure quality control during construction. For some projects, knowledgeable contractors can provide you with plans for the layout of their work to comply with code requirements. However, it is the person who takes out the permit who is responsible for ensuring that the work actually meets code.

AN ARCHITECT'S PERSPECTIVE

Today's architects are not only artists but also engineers and problem solvers. The right architect for the job will design a building that addresses both practical and aesthetic needs, resulting in a well-built, integrated, functional and visually pleasing structure. Architects keep abreast of the latest innovations in their field, for example, energy-efficient design, building technology and new materials. They also understand the legal and jurisdictional implications of a construction project. Architects work closely with tradespeople like builders, plumbers and electricians to ensure that clients receive quality workmanship at a reasonable price.

Before contacting a design professional, you should know as much as possible about what you want. If you do not know, the architect can take you through a needs assessment and programming exercise. You may need only a consultation or a set of working drawings. Or you may want the architect to oversee construction and handle all details. Such decisions should be made with

South Prescott Village, Oakland. Architect's plans for artists' live/work development.

your total budget in mind. Architects can help to assess special needs and to plan the efficient use of your space. For altering the structure of the building, such as taking out walls or enlarging windows, an architect or a structural engineer can recommend appropriate construction materials or workmanship. If more than one person is making design decisions, an architect can aid the group in setting priorities for multiple design goals, helping to bring opposing points of view together, and more efficiently organizing space requirements. Typically, an architect will do the following:

- present design alternatives using new materials and spatial concepts you might not be aware of

- work with full understanding of existing code requirements

- provide professional design and construction problem-solving skills

- provide preliminary cost estimates to help with feasibility decisions before you get contractors' bids

- prepare construction documents, drawings and specifications for bids on construction labor and materials, inspections approval and permits, and for historic building investment tax credits, if applicable

- oversee the construction process, perhaps in cooperation with a project manager, and

- interact with contractors, answer contractors' questions and review change-order requests

**25 North Fourth, Minneapolis. Two views of
live/work space.**

WORKING WITH AN ARCHITECT

Work with the architect begins by clarifying the building program—translating the specific space needs you have for various activities and the relationship of those activities to one another. Rough sketches of space functions and building elements are prepared. After sketching, refining and revising design ideas, the architect presents several design alternatives. As a client, you should feel free to ask questions, critique plans and ask for explanations of anything you do not understand. Once you have selected a specific concept, the design is developed in detail. You should review these documents carefully to ensure that they fully meet your building program and budget expectations.

Once the design has been developed, the architect will prepare a set of specifications—a written description of what materials are being used and how they are to be installed. This document, often called the Project Manual or the "spec," in conjunction with the required drawings, constitutes the construction documents. Construction documents are the legal basis of the construction contract.

The specs should provide all the information a contractor needs to build the project, and the contractor can legally deviate from them—and be paid for that deviation—only if he or she first receives a change order signed by both owner and architect. This system ensures firm control over the cost overruns that often plague projects. From the beginning, it is clear exactly what the owner is getting and for how much (the negotiated contract price).

LOCATING A GOOD ARCHITECT

Architects rarely advertise, so to find the right firm or individual, it may be necessary to make inquiries and do some investigating on your own. The following steps are a way to start:

- obtain referrals from friends or other professionals for architects who specialize in the type of services you need
- visit the site of a project that you like and ask who was responsible
- review local architectural and construction magazines; make notes on buildings you like and who did them
- call your state or local headquarters of the American Institute of Architects (AIA), which will make referrals or send you a directory
- review the Request for Proposal and Design Competition sections of this chapter

Before hiring an architect, you should have a personal interview to make sure you are comfortable with him or her. Does the architect share an interest in the type of project you want to undertake? Does he or she have an understanding of your art form and space needs? Look at the architect's portfolio to see whether you like the work.

Volunteer Resources

If you are organized as a nonprofit group, you might invite an architect to sit on your board of directors. As a sponsor, he or she might volunteer advice during the early stages and provide planning help without expense to you. Some firms provide nonprofit organizations with a discounted rate, ranging from one-quarter to one-third of their regular fees, if they are credited as sponsors or donors.

Another route is to obtain preliminary design alternatives as part of an architectural student thesis project. This approach is especially useful if you are trying to develop visual materials so as to involve others and convince them of the validity of your ideas.

Fees

If you bring an architect in as a volunteer, patron or sponsor, you should involve him or her as soon as possible. If that is not possible, you might buy some consulting time using the architect on an as-needed basis and then bring the architect back on a contract if and when the project proceeds. Otherwise, while you are casually exploring ideas, you may inadvertently spend the fees for the architect too quickly.

The cost of services by architects can be negotiated on a project or hourly basis. Typically, architects use one of the following methods to charge for their services:

- percentage of construction cost—the larger the cost of construction, the lower the percentage charged. The fee may range from 7 percent to 20 percent

- lump sum—a method often used for specific requested tasks

- hourly rate plus expenses—the most frequently used method of billing—used to cover hourly personnel expenses plus other costs if the scope of the work is unclear.

Scope of Services

You need to decide up front how much involvement you are willing to pay for and expect from the architect. This decision can be made clear in your preliminary discussion with the architects you interview. Some professionals are more amenable than others to the client's participation in the design or to the provision of limited services. Be sure you find an architect who fits your group's needs and expectations.

Your local chapter of the AIA can supply you with a sample contract detailing the full scope of the services your architect might provide. Looking over a contract will give you a good idea of project phases, services and the respective responsibilities in an architect-owner agreement. Project phases may include, but are not limited to, the following:

1. **PREDESIGN SERVICES.** Existing facilities surveys, marketing studies, economic feasibility studies and project programming.

2. **SITE ANALYSIS SERVICES.** Document checking, owner-supplied data coordination, site utilization studies, environmental studies.

3. **SCHEMATIC DESIGN SERVICES.** Architectural, structural, mechanical design, etc., ideas and materials researched to reach basic conceptual options.

4. **DESIGN DEVELOPMENT SERVICES.** Same areas as (3) above but in greater detail, to refine the chosen design direction, including finishes.

5. **CONSTRUCTION DOCUMENTS SERVICES.** design documentation for construction, materials research/specification, special bidding documents/scheduling.

6. **BIDDING OR NEGOTIATIONS SERVICES.** bidding materials, negotiations and analysis of alternatives/substitutions, bid evaluation, construction contract negotiation.

7. **CONSTRUCTION CONTRACT ADMINISTRATION SERVICES.** Construction field observation, interpretation of specifications, city inspection coordination, schedule and workmanship monitoring, construction cost accounting, project closeout.

8. **POSTCONSTRUCTION SERVICES.** Maintenance and operational programming, start-up assistance, record drawings, warranty review.

Whittier Townhomes, Minneapolis. New construction of artist live/work spaces.

DESIGN ISSUES

The process of acquiring live/work space often begins as an economy move. However, it has an equally strong bearing on one's quality of life, which for the artist often means creativity.

Your working space requirements are an obvious factor in selecting a building that accommodates an appropriate design for your personal space. Design characteristics can always be enhanced by careful organization of activities within the space.

New construction provides an opportunity to design space that is tailored specifically to your needs. Accommodating toxic materials, special lighting, plumbing or storage needs may be planned from the outset. Design can also solve broader community goals. For example, Whittier Artists Studio Homes by the Whittier Alliance and Artspace Projects, Inc. in Minneapolis were designed as a buffer between business and residential uses.

LIGHT, SPACE AND ACCESS

Regardless of whether you use an architect, the threefold elements of light, space and access will be the most important influences on the design of your space (see box 9.1). When designing your space, keep the following in mind:

- building and zoning code requirements (see chapter 4) must be met to secure long-term access to the space

- existing sources of light for your work and your living space may be augmented by artificial or natural sources (for example, by skylights, clerestory or added windows)

- the effect of separating or overlapping activities because of working and living space needs or of your organization's program space requirements

- movement and circulation patterns and work flow to maximize the benefits of available space

South Prescott Village. Live/work spaces with abundant natural light.

- the degree of flexibility needed for walls and storage to accommodate mixed uses

- the influence of the size of the space on the size of the art work, on the ability to experiment, and on the ability to work on several pieces at once

- storage needs for large or hazardous materials and equipment, normal "dead" storage, closets and areas to store work

- needs for accessibility for equipment or handicap uses and the ability to bring your largest works in and out of your space with relative ease

- provision of common facilities for laundry, meeting, socializing or other amenities desired by you or your group

Most artists seek an open and flexible design plan, with utilities placed in their most cost-effective location. If the working area is a strong priority, the living space may be kept to a minimum. You may be comfortable with living and working spaces flowing together or you may

9.1 SOUTH PRESCOTT VILLAGE AND HENRY STREET STUDIOS
Oakland, California

Artist Bruce Beasley hired architect Thomas Dolan to create two new-construction live/work spaces for artists in Oakland, California: South Prescott Village and Henry Street Studios. Both complexes show Dolan's concern with the trinity of artists' needs: light, space and access.

At both South Prescott Village and Henry Street Studios, every unit has light on three sides. At no point in any studio is one more than 20 feet from a window or skylight. High ceilings and skylights provide light and air as well as a feeling of spaciousness. Each studio has large egress doors to allow moving large canvases or other artwork in and out. Walls separating units are double-sheetrocked on both sides, with an airspace or resilient channels and insulation between, to provide sound isolation. At both South Prescott Village and Henry Street Studios certain units contain two bedrooms and a bathroom on the ground floor, above which is a living/dining/kitchen area with a storage loft above the kitchen area. One wall of this living area is shared with the work space, which is up a short half-flight of stairs. Such units appeal to artists with families, to roommates, or to anyone who wants some separation from their work.

The design for South Prescott Village is a first attempt to answer the following questions: What is the ideal shape for a community of artists living and working in a single complex of studios? How can the best possible individual live/work studio spaces be combined with common areas that facilitate the informal interactions creating a viable, functioning community? A sense of community is designed into almost every aspect of South Prescott Village, starting with the common garden, courtyard and breezeways and encompassing the design of entryways—all of which open onto the common center courtyard. This facilitates informal day-to-day interaction between neighbors, encouraging artists to share ideas and approaches to their work. Dolan was influenced in his site design by the Islamic model of the pleasure garden in the midst of the desert. The interior at South Prescott provides a safe, green space for residents to relax and converse.

At Henry Street Studios, which contain two live/work units and three accessory work spaces, design considerations were to address the special housing needs of artists by providing affordable spaces with an emphasis on light, space and access; to promote community; to maximize the number of units within the eight-unit residential limit stipulated for the lots by the City of Oakland; and to design a safe and secure environment. The project's location in an inner-city neighborhood necessitated extra attention to security and safety issues. Lighting in the common areas is an important element; a three-part control system provides some lighting on a photocell (stays lit all night), some on a timer (stays lit during high-traffic evening hours), and a few lights controlled by motion detectors to deter unauthorized persons and to provide extra light for those entering late at night. Each building entry breezeway has a large security gate with a smaller "person door" controlled by an intercom/buzzer system. This same gate can open completely to provide access for large objects.

Other amenities were provided in anticipation of artists' rather specialized needs. Ceiling fans help deal with the difficulty of heating and cooling spaces with high ceilings; switched outlets in ceilings allow artists to install the kind of light fixtures that best meet their needs. Each unit has one 220-volt outlet, and each has a work sink for cleanup.

Dolan thinks that new construction is a viable—and sometimes preferable—option for developing live/work space. "A new building," he notes, "will be energy-efficient, weathertight, clean and earthquake-resistant, and its various systems will presumably need very little maintenance in the near- to mid-term. Then there's the joy of being able to start with a blank slate and design specifically for live/work: the freedom to do *exactly* what you want."

Data

South Prescott Village: Eight units with eight work spaces accessory to the main units totaling 22,000 square feet (10,000 sq. ft. in the West Building and 12,000 sq. ft. in the East Building). Common use areas include a common garden, courtyard, entry area with security intercom, mailbox area, breezeways and access to neighboring laundry facilities. There are no commercial spaces. Construction began in 1987.

Henry Street Studios: Building structure and type is wood frame, stud walls, platform construction, heavy timber trusses, roof members and mezzanine, concrete slab floors downstairs, painted plywood floors for second story, 2 x 6 tongue and groove flooring for mezzanine, cedar siding exterior, aluminum bronze anodized windows and skylights, asphalt composition roof, smooth wall sheetrock, full kitchens, metal exterior hollow-core entrance/exit doors or double French art-access doors. Two and one half stories (two stories plus a mezzanine). Construction began in May 1986.

Henry Street Studios, Oakland. Development includes live/work and studio-only spaces.

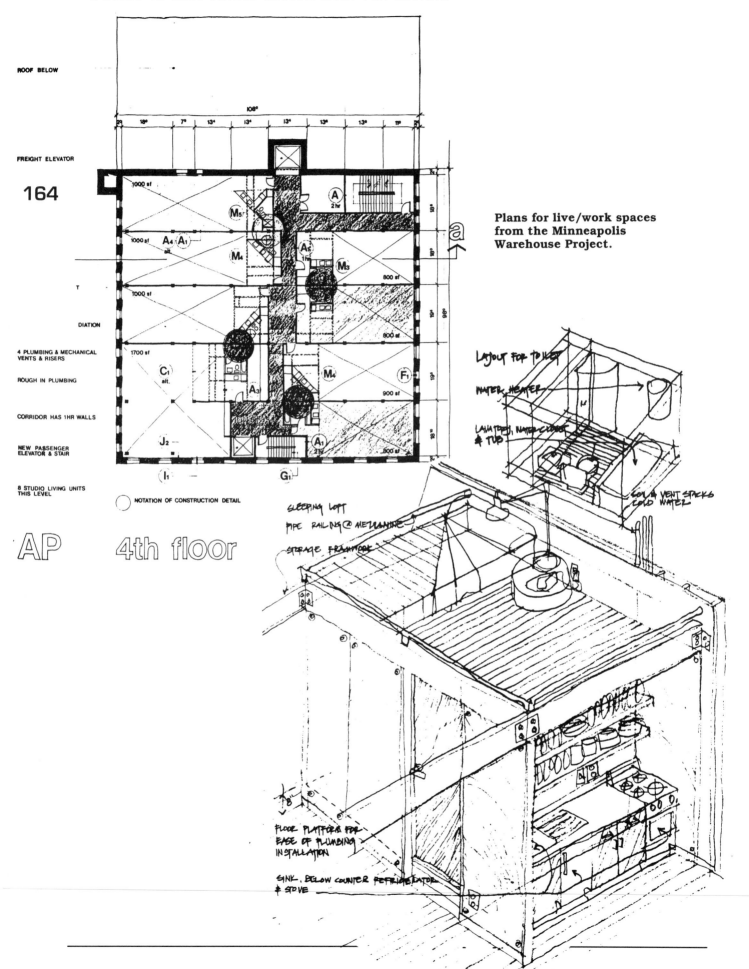

ROOF BELOW

FREIGHT ELEVATOR

164

1000 sf

M5'

A4 A1

M4

1000 sf

A2

M3

800 sf

T

1000 sf

DIATION

4 PLUMBING & MECHANICAL
VENTS & RISERS

800 sf

1700 sf

ROUGH IN PLUMBING

C1

M4

F1

CORRIDOR HAS 1HR WALLS

A3

900 sf

NEW PASSENGER
ELEVATOR & STAIR

J2

A1

8 STUDIO LIVING UNITS
THIS LEVEL

I1

G1

○ NOTATION OF CONSTRUCTION DETAIL

AP   4th floor

**Plans for live/work spaces
from the Minneapolis
Warehouse Project.**

LAYOUT FOR TOILET

WATER HEATER

LAVATORY, WATER CLOSET
& TUB

SOIL & VENT STACKS
COLD WATER

SLEEPING LOFT
PIPE RAILING @ MEZZANINE
STORAGE FRAMEWORK

FLOOR PLATFORM FOR
EASE OF PLUMBING
INSTALLATION

SINK, BELOW COUNTER REFRIGERATOR
& STOVE

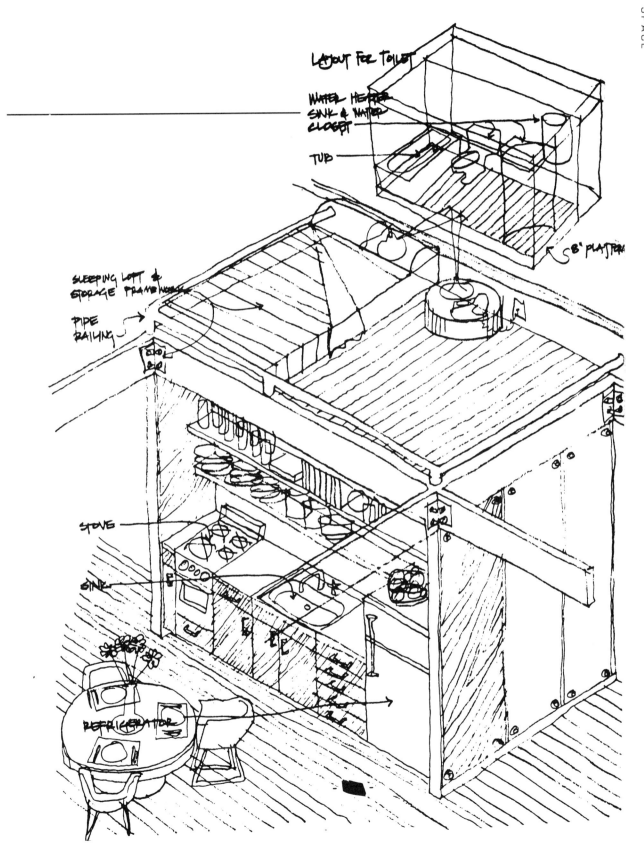

LAYOUT FOR TOILET

WATER HEATER
SINK & WATER
CLOSET

TUB

8" PLATFORM

SLEEPING LOFT &
STORAGE FRAMEWORK

PIPE
RAILING

STOVE

SINK

REFRIGERATOR

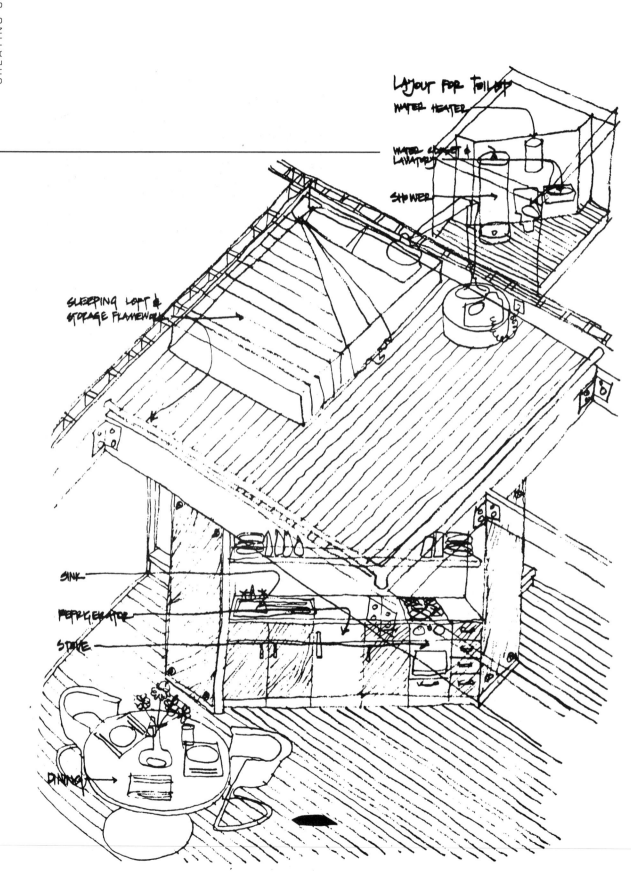

Layout for Toilet

Water Heater

Water Closet & Lavatory

Shower

Sleeping Loft & Storage Framework

Sink

Refrigerator

Stove

Dining

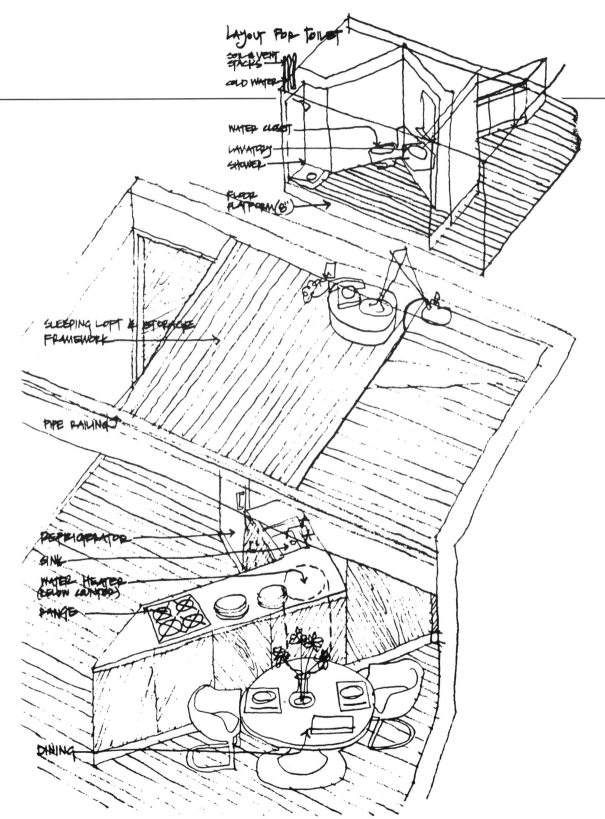

require some kind of separation of activities through storage partitions, screens or walls.

The conclusions of three independent studies conducted in Boston in 1977, Minneapolis in 1977, and San Francisco in 1984, reflected similar priorities for artists' spaces. The priorities included open interior space for maximum flexibility (see box 9.2); maximum natural light; ceilings 12 feet or higher preferred; floors that will not be damaged by the work; sprinklers or fireproof construction; access to a freight elevator; adequate heating; bathrooms and kitchens, with an additional sink for the work space; and adequate electrical service. Most respondents preferred designs for compact living space in order to maximize work areas. A high percentage preferred acquiring space in raw or unfinished space so that they could keep their costs low and build in desired features.

Design concepts for living and working in warehouses documented in the report *Minneapolis Warehouse Project: Artist Live/Work Space* (1979) involved the use of a space within a larger space. Construction methods ranged from a tent to full walls. The study noted that separate enclosures can be heated more effectively and avoid the necessity of heating or cooling the entire space for one particular activity. Consolidating bathroom, kitchen and sleeping facilities into stacked or modular units maximizes the available studio space.

COST-EFFECTIVE UTILITIES

The Minneapolis Warehouse Project also prepared a detailed design analysis of utility systems and their effectiveness for live/work space. The project's findings are as follows:

LIGHTING. The cheapest form of light is sunlight. Large windows or skylights, facing north (for diffused light) or south (for bright light), maximize natural light. Track lighting provides

flexibility and is easy to install, though it is usually expensive. A less costly alternative is adjustable ceiling sockets, which provide light that can be directed where needed. Fluorescent lighting is more efficient than incandescent lighting. Dimming switches can cut the costs of incandescent lights.

HEATING. Systems with steam or hot water, heated in a main boiler and distributed by radiators, offer the most economy, safety and control. To fire the boiler, natural gas is the most economical fuel source.

Warm air systems have the disadvantage of heating unevenly in large spaces, such as those found in warehouses. Individual unit heaters provide inadequate heat distribution, and those that are fired directly pose a hazard. Electric space heaters feature greater safety, but they should be used judiciously to keep energy consumption to a minimum.

COOLING AND VENTILATION. Air conditioning is too costly to be a real option for most warehouse dwellers. Less expensive means of cooling space include insulation, solar shielding (awnings or shades), natural ventilation and large low-speed fans.

Air shafts are expensive and can pose problems of code compliance. However, areas with windows on two sides and an open floor plan can take advantage of naturally occurring ventilation.

Wall insulation is more important for heating than for cooling. Roof insulation beyond the local energy code requirement can help make the top floor habitable during warm weather.

ALTERNATIVE ENERGY SAVINGS. At the time of its publication, the Minneapolis Warehouse Project found no cost-effective alternative energy systems. Existing systems in older buildings tended to be in poor repair and inadequate for live/work space. The most cost-effective method was to upgrade the system to make the space usable and to bring utility and maintenance costs under control. It was also assumed that whatever future fuels might be used would be delivered through existing fuel systems. After the "energy crisis" subsided, fears of increasing energy costs calmed, although the need for energy consciousness remains.

PARTICIPATORY DESIGN STRATEGIES

If you and your group expect to participate actively in the design process, the group must take responsibility for reaching consensus and providing clear direction to the architect. The group's leadership should provide methods of establishing group values and priorities, such as those referred to in chapter 2. Which is most important—low-cost rehab? creative design? dramatic spaces? simple efficiency? projection of an image?

An architect should be neutral and resourceful. The architect does not presume to make decisions for the group, but provides a context in which the group can make its own decisions. Alternatively, by minimizing the architect's involvement in the group's decision-making, the group would save professional fees—and also spare the architect from the frustration of dealing with ideas from too many people. The group would appoint a spokesperson to interact with the architect. That person, or a small committee, would be responsible for representing the desires of the larger group to the architect.

VISUALIZING DESIGN SOLUTIONS

Many in your group are probably visually

oriented, so you may want to incorporate visualization techniques, metaphors or drawing into the process. The design solution should reflect the group's agreed-upon "vision" of the project.

Visualization techniques range from loosely suggested ideas for group members to explore on their own time to structured sessions during which members are led through a series of imaging exercises. Effective imaging entails becoming relaxed, almost meditative. It engages parts of the mind that are rarely used in problem solving. Through guided imagery, participants can be taken on a journey to their "ideal" space—and then asked to draw or describe what they saw. By simply visualizing—or writing about, or drawing—an ideal day, living and/or working in the projected space, people may become aware of some values and expectations that may not have been consciously entertained. This technique is also useful in addressing problems of interconnected spaces and spatial organization.

Borrowing from the field of theater, you may want to create a storytelling session or "act out" your needs for space to bring out values for the group's shared vision. A writing technique called "mind mapping" or "clustering" can also increase awareness of previously unrecognized values. For example, you might simply write the word "studio" in the center of a blank page. Then, begin to develop some free associations, writing down the words you associate with "studio" and drawing a line from the word "studio" to the associated idea. When these associations, in turn, trigger other ideas, extend the line and write down the related idea. Once you have fully exhausted all your ideas, write one sentence that reflects the ideas you have just written.

These techniques are only a few of the ways to find a design solution that will include the activities, relationships and rituals that are an important part of your life. Draw upon your own creative strengths to think of other processes to use.

Kitchen on first floor.

9.2 WHITTIER STUDIO HOMES
Minneapolis, Minnesota

The developers of Whittier Studio Homes considered maximum flexibility of work space to be the highest priority design consideration, followed by size of private spaces and cost per square foot to the owners. The six town homes of new, wood-frame construction are located in Whittier, an inner-city neighborhood of Minneapolis, not far from downtown and the Minneapolis Institute of Arts and Minneapolis College of Art and Design. The projects serves as a "buffer zone" between commercial activities on nearby Nicollet Avenue and residential areas to the east.

An early collaboration between Artspace Projects, Inc. and the Whittier Alliance, a neighborhood organization and nonprofit developer, led the latter group to develop new live/work units for artists who already had been attracted to the neighborhood. The Whittier Alliance owned one of the lots and purchased the other lot and existing house that are now the site of the Studio Homes. The Alliance sought professional help in the architectural, legal and co-op management areas, and hired licensed contractors.

Artspace Projects, Inc. provided initial design advice on the project. Ultimately, the architect created simple, boxlike stacked spaces with prefabricated roofs and floor trusses, eliminating the need for load-bearing interior walls on each of the three levels. Because the project consisted largely of new construction, code compliance for renovation was not an issue. In addition to flexibility and cost, ceiling height, ease of access to the units, the size of public spaces, parking, security, light and space for large materials or equipment were also seen as important. The other factor involved in design considerations was the ability to use conventional (FHA) mortgage financing.

Using wood frame commercial-type shells and basic building materials made construction cost-efficient. The units were completed at a cost of $32 per square foot, compared to $44 per square foot for other recent "affordable" new construction in Minneapolis. With land costs, the total cost of the project was $350,000, or $45 per square foot. The base price of the units was $55,600. With additional closets, light fixtures etc., the custom-designed units ended up costing from $61,000 to $70,000.

Dance studio on second floor.

Artist-tenants were involved in planning the project from the beginning. Artspace Projects, Inc. was responsible for marketing the units in the early stages and held a series of informational meetings during the planning. Those who made a commitment to buy were able to design their own space, including location of bath, kitchen, stairs, interior walls, color and material selection. Each unit is 2-1/2 stories (on three levels), for a total of 1,800 square feet. Construction took place from October 1987 to April 1988. Six artists and four nonartist adults moved in soon thereafter.

The Alliance received an $80,000 grant from the Minneapolis Community Development Agency and the support of the U.S. Department of Housing and Urban Development (HUD), which sponsored the project as an official Joint Venture for Affordable Housing. The Minneapolis Community Development Agency, the local office of the U.S. Housing and Urban Development office, and local politicians supported this project because it was seen as a creative solution to bringing economic development to a troubled area; in addition, it provided much-needed housing to artists, whose housing and studio space needs had begun to receive attention in the local media.

The project's benefits were framed in terms of economic development, small business development/enhancement and a revitalizing project for a development district that creates a buffer between the business strip and other residences. Since the nonprofit developer is also the neighborhood organization and is a familiar and active presence in the Whittier neighborhood, relations with the residents of the community have been smooth, and the homes have been seen as a positive addition to the neighborhood.

Design studio on second floor.

172 _____

STRUCTURING YOUR DESIGN PLANNING PROCESS

Whether you use drawings, guided imagery or discussion, one effective way of helping a group to discover its concerns and values is through a facilitator and a recorder. A facilitator, in lieu of the architect, sets up procedures and moves the group through its agenda. He or she listens actively to the group's ideas, without expressing personal opinions on the issues. Instead, the facilitator reflects the group's ideas, restating what the group has discovered in its discussions. The facilitator may ask the group to create its own agenda, assign time limits, check for consensus or ask for clarification.

A recorder makes a visual record of the proceedings. Rather than "taking minutes" as a secretary would, the recorder writes out the group's ideas or creates simple drawings that act as metaphors on flip charts or large sheets of paper taped to the wall. Ideas are recorded as they are expressed, and group members can see what is being written out. The facilitator may also act as recorder during the meetings.

If the group is large, it may be useful to break up into smaller groups from time to time. Each smaller group brainstorms an issue and brings its ideas back to the larger group for further discussion.

Once the group has created a vision or metaphor for its shared space needs, the group's rep-

Lowertown Lofts, St. Paul. Sweat equity.

resentative to the architect communicates those ideas on the group's behalf.

ADJUSTING DESIGN PLANS

Along the way, you need to decide what level of finish you want from the contractors in the construction process. The architect specifies the level of finish to the contractors, with details about materials and hardware for the contractors to bid on. It is helpful to have decided, in advance of the bidding process, what elements can be eliminated if the bids come back too high.

To lower construction costs, the tenants of Lowertown Lofts in St. Paul, Minnesota agreed to finish the floors, paint the walls, and expand the storage and loft spaces themselves. The basic amenities in Lowertown consisted of a kitchen sink with a counter and storage, bathroom sink, ceramic tile floor, tub, and toilet. When high bids came in, several items were eliminated—tile around the tub, vanities, mirrors, toilet paper holders, extra lighting fixtures, refrigerators and stoves, and shared laundry appliances. They later found solutions to most of these features independently, and coin-operated laundry equipment provided the co-op with an additional source of income through a contract with the providers of the service.

REQUESTS FOR PROPOSALS AND DESIGN COMPETITIONS

If you are seeking an architect through an open selection process, you may consider either a Request for Proposal (RFP) process or a Design Competition. In either case, your project should be large enough to warrant the extra time and money such a process will require of you and the professionals whose services you are soliciting.

REQUEST FOR PROPOSAL PROCESS

Through the RFP process, a number of architectural firms are invited to make presentations about their services. Local AIA chapters can help you with this process.

It is important to do some basic planning before initiating an RFP to make sure that your group agrees on its expectations. Requests for Proposals should be clear about the extent and the nature of the work to be done. The following topics—a typical RFP format for hiring architects or consultants—should be discussed and the resulting information provided, in writing, to architects, stating your request for their proposals:

- definition and scope of the project
- anticipated project cost or cost limit
- credentials required
- value placed by the group on the firm's local or national base
- definition of consultant tasks
- contact name and address for accepting the proposals
- approximate interview schedule
- deadline for the proposal

The group should also discuss and agree upon the components to be requested in the firm's written proposal, such as the following:

- description of general background and strengths of the firm
- proposal on how they would perform consultant tasks
- experience on similar projects, local or national
- references from clients
- fees and payment schedule

After planning, preparing and distributing the RFP to architectural firms, the group should decide on the selection criteria it will use to

9.3 CONSULTANT EVALUATION FORM

W = Weighted Value of Criteria, based on values held by the group
R = Ranking Score, how well the proposal or firm meets the criteria
S = Total Score in Each Category

Description of Weighted values
5 = extremely important
4 = very important
3 = important
2 = less important
1 = not critical, but nice to have

Description of Ranking score
5 = Best meets criteria
4 = Meets criteria very well
3 = Meets criteria well
2 = Meets criteria but not as well
1 = Does not meet criteria

Selection Criteria	W x R = S	W x R = S	W x R = S
Firm names	Hott Arch.	Kool Arch.	ClassAct Archs.
1. Experience in live/work or similar facility projects	5 x 3 = 15	5 x 4 = 20	5 x 5 = 25
2. Quality of strategy	5 x 1 = 5	5 x 5 = 25	5 x 5 = 25
3. Experience with comparable-sized projects	4 x 3 = 12	4 x 4 = 16	4 x 5 = 20
4. Quality of clients' recommendations	4 x 4 = 16	4 x 4 = 16	4 x 5 = 20
5. Strong experience, local	4 x 5 = 20	4 x 4 = 16	4 x 4 = 16
6. Strong experience, national	3 x 5 = 15	3 x 4 = 12	3 x 4 = 12
7. Sensitivity to extra challenges in this project/participatory design	3 x 5 = 15	3 x 4 = 12	3 x 4 = 12
8. Personality traits: (communication skills, creative, enthusiastic, realistic, unites group)	2 x 5 = 10	2 x 2 = 4	2 x 4 = 8
9. Reasonable fees	1 x 5 = 5	1 x 3 = 3	1 x 2 = 2
10. Capacity to ensure work will be carried out: (number of principals, support staff or advisers available to project)	1 x 2 = 2	1 x 4 = 4	1 x 5 = 5
TOTAL SCORE (add each team's score from each category)	112	128	145

evaluate the proposals and the number of firms it will interview. Once proposals are received and reviewed, the firms to be interviewed may be selected by group vote. At that time, an interview schedule can be prepared for the group's selection committee and the architects.

Before starting any interviews, you may wish to create a "prompt sheet" that lists the questions you want to ask each candidate. One person may ask all the same questions of each candidate, or each of the selection committee members may ask a designated question of each candidate. The "prompt sheet" should contain space after each question for the selection committee members to make notes on the responses.

Plan a time to discuss the candidates' presentations, either between interviews or after all interviews are completed. If there is no immediate agreement among the group on which architect or consultant to select, you may want to distribute evaluation forms, such as the one pictured in box 9.3. (A blank form appears in appendix 9.1.) As the example in box 9.3 shows, by reflecting the group's priorities in "weighted" values, such a form can help the group separate issues when discussing proposals and candidates.

Once an overall score for each candidate has been determined by adding all scores in column "S," agreement on a candidate is usually easy to determine. If not, you may choose to reopen the selection process, to reinterview, or to continue discussing and reevaluating the candidates until the group reaches a majority vote on a candidate.

DESIGN COMPETITIONS

Design competitions provide a way of selecting an architectural firm based on a specific response to your project. A project with a "public purpose" may be able to raise money from local, state or national sources, such as the National Endowment for the Arts (NEA), for a Design Com-

petition. A nonprofit sponsor will be required for raising the money and overseeing the process.

It is also possible for the architectural firm you have chosen to sponsor an in-house competition to explore a variety of design ideas for your project. In-house competitions often best serve development schedules.

Generally, for a competition to be held, the project must involve some public sponsors, public money or both. Design competitions, historically, are successful means of spurring design excellence. They are most often used for important public buildings or arts facilities. The U.S. Capitol, the Centre National d'Art et de Culture Georges Pompidou, Toronto's City Hall, London Central Mosque and Cultural Centre, the Gateway Arch in St. Louis, and Fort Mason Center in San Francisco are just a few projects that resulted from design competitions.

Several Design Competitions have explored live/work space projects, among them A New American House, co-sponsored by the Minneapolis College of Art and Design and the National Endowment for the Arts, Design Arts Program in 1984; Boston's Artists Live/WorkSpace Project competition, sponsored by the Artists' Foundation and Vision, Inc. in 1987; and the Lowertown Lofts Design Charrette (see box 9.4), co-sponsored by the St. Paul Department of Planning and Economic Development, Artspace Projects, and the National Endowment for the Arts, Design Arts Program in 1984.

Types of Competitions

There are several types of competitions, some aimed at finding a project designer and including a commitment to build, others simply generating design ideas, with an award of some sort but no commitment to build. Competitions may also be "open" or "invited." In the latter case, invitations go only to specific firms or individuals.

9.4 LOWERTOWN LOFTS DESIGN CHARRETTE
St. Paul, Minnesota

Dialogue among architects, artists and the public was a key element in the Lowertown Lofts Design Charrette. For four days and nights during the summer of 1984, architectural teams worked in a public setting to design 30 studio/living units for artists in an older warehouse building located at 255 Kellogg in St. Paul, Minnesota.

The Lowertown area had been heavily populated by artists for several years, but many were living in old warehouses under substandard conditions and in violation of codes. In an effort to improve the situation for artists and to revitalize the area, St. Paul's Department of Planning and Economic Development decided to work with the St. Paul Art Collective, Artspace Projects, Inc. and Asset Development Services, a for-profit developer, to renovate three floors of warehouse space into creative and affordable artists' studio/living space.

Artists and design team discussing ideas.

The purpose of the Lowertown Lofts Design Charrette was to offer artists at 255 Kellogg—and in other warehouses—innovative and economical designs to use in planning loft space. The design charrette was part of the New Works/St. Paul performance and exhibition series, co-sponsored by the St. Paul Department of Planning and Economic Development with a grant from the National Endowment for the Arts, Design Arts Program. Artspace Projects, Inc. served as competition advisor and co-sponsor. Asset Development Services; Hammel, Green and Abrahamson Architects; and the St. Paul Art Collective were co-sponsors and advisory panel representatives.

Four architectural teams were chosen to participate in the competition based on submitted applications. The four-day design process was held at Union Depot Place, a recently renovated railroad station in St. Paul. Architects drew input from the public as well as from artists assigned as advisers.

The architects' task was to create innovative and space-efficient designs that address the special needs of living/working, storage and safety of professional artists. Each team designed two studio/living units, one 897-square-foot unit and one 1,306-square-foot unit, based on floor plans for the 255 Kellogg building. The teams designed the units for artists working in either two-dimensional or three-dimensional visual arts, or media arts. Each team was assigned one media for which they designed a unit and they could select another media for the second unit. Additionally, the teams designed a plan for an exhibition area in the central atrium.

Artists reviewing design proposals.

Daily briefings were held during the charrette so that questions from individual teams to the panel could be answered to whole group. Architectural tours were set up so that teams could visit artists' lofts in nearby buildings as well as view the vacant building for which they were designing units.

The completed designs were juried on the final day of the charrette. Design teams submitted elevation drawings plus two or more descriptive drawings for each studio/living unit and the gallery. Teams were encouraged to include a brief narrative about the concept. Each team was allowed 20 minutes to present its designs to the jury.

Jurors looked for designs that responded to the requirements with innovative solutions. The designs needed to adhere to code standards while minimizing costs of contracted labor. Designs also needed to be flexible enough to adapt to any artist's working and living needs. Although one team was singled out as presenting the best solution for the project, the overriding significance of the charrette was the generation of so many design possibilities by all the teams. The jurors described the results as a catalogue of ideas for the future.

The design considered best overall (and also best small-unit design) was praised for its warmth, sense of place and efficient use of space. Jurors described the design as eminently the most buildable, noting also the ability to manipulate the space while maintaining the overall integrity of the design.

Construction of Lowertown Lofts began in March 1985; artists moved in five months later. The collaboration between architects, artists and the public in designing studio/living space provided important momentum to the St. Paul Lowertown Lofts project and brought forth innovative and imaginative ideas. Beyond the St. Paul project, the charrette is a model for any city to use in developing space for artists. Co-operative ventures between architects, artists and urban planners to plan and design space for the arts helps nurture a city's arts community and contributes to the economic vitality of old warehouse districts.

OPEN COMPETITION. An open competition is the simplest to plan and the longest to execute. The sponsor must advertise widely in professional media and allow time—often a year—for all interested parties to respond. This type of competition is best for seeking a broad spectrum of ideas. A New American House competition was of this type.

PREQUALIFICATION COMPETITIONS. The prequalification competition is used when a sponsor wishes to invite only qualified participants, or a particular type of competitor, such as students. The first response by competitors is to show their credentials and portfolios, and usually to appear at a personal interview. Those applicants found eligible are then asked to enter the design phase of the competition.

INVITED COMPETITION. Invited competitions are best when a project's potential success seems to depend upon the previous experience of the designer. A professional advisor or advisory committee prepares a list of competitors, who are invited on the basis of research and professional recommendations. Hence, in invited competitions, the sponsor is giving up the innovative potential of an open competition for an established designer or design team.

STAGED COMPETITIONS. Competitions for extremely large projects are often held in stages. An open first stage, in which competitors submit conceptual designs, is narrowed down through a selection by judges. In the next stage competitors submit models, material specifications and cost estimates. In some instances, competitions have been set up to include teams of architects and builders.

ON-SITE CHARRETTE COMPETITIONS. A variation of the prequalification competition,

the on-site charrette competition entails selecting a roster of potential competitors on the basis of a review of their qualifications and experience. Competitors are then asked to convene at the project site for a specified time period to create their designs on site. This assures everyone equal advantage. The Lowertown Lofts Design Charrette (see box 9.4) was this type of competition.

Setting Up a Competition

To administer a design competition successfully, a qualified adviser willing to commit the necessary time, energy and expertise is needed. Advisers usually receive compensation for their services. The adviser should have some expertise in the field of architecture, design or urban planning and interest in your project.

Judges or jurors for the competition are most often selected from professional societies or among reputable design professionals, although client or public representatives are often included.

PROJECT DESCRIPTION. In any type of competition, competitors should be furnished with a program that gives as much information as possible about the desired project. The goals, rules, rewards, design problem to be solved, its size, site (if known), options, conditions and any special requirements of the project are all important elements in the program. Competitors should also receive clear information about the standards and criteria on which the designs will be judged.

AWARDS, RIGHTS AND RESPONSIBILITIES. Design competitions are a costly way for architects to get work if the prize money is only for the top competitors. Most firms entering such competitions are likely to be young and seeking visibility. In the Lowertown Lofts Design Charrette, one incentive for firms to enter was the offer of a fee equivalent to their daily rate for their

Designs proposed by charette participants.

Team A designed this unit for a photographer with
stepped-back walls, to provide more distance for
photographing images within a confined space.
The elevation illustrates planned storage areas.

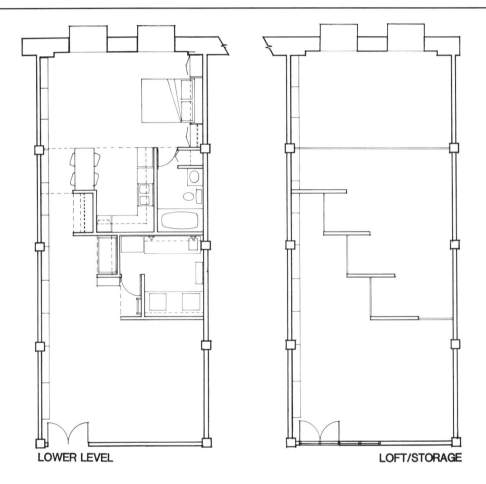

LOWER LEVEL

LOFT/STORAGE

UNIT B THE PHOTOGRAPHER

FIFTH FLOOR REAR

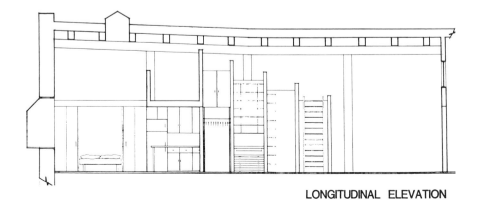

LONGITUDINAL ELEVATION

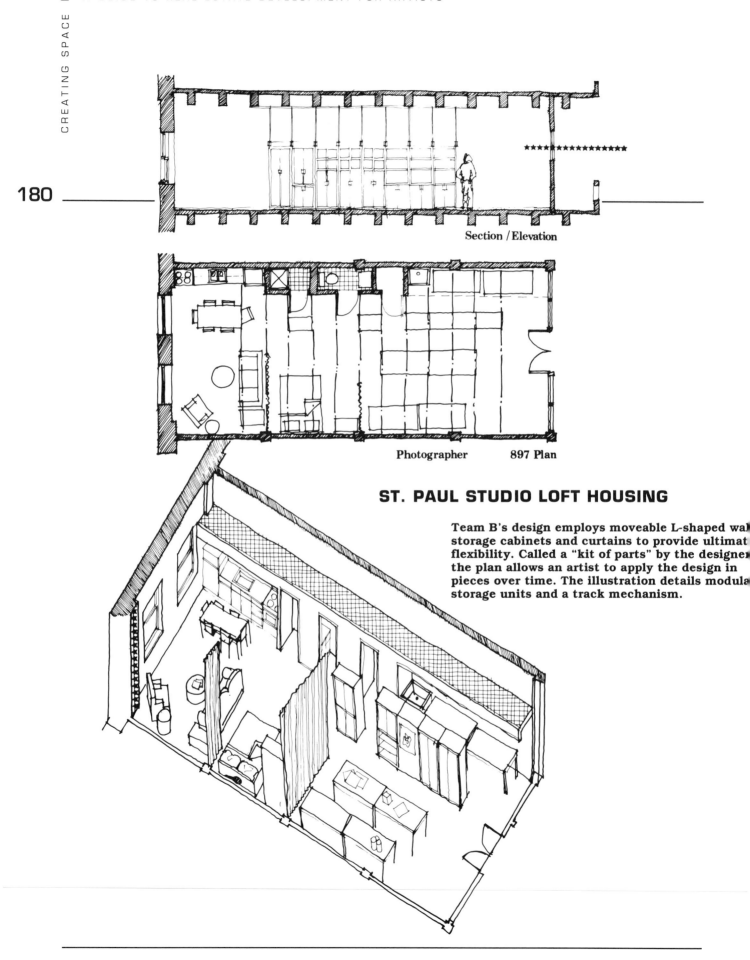

Section / Elevation

Photographer   897 Plan

ST. PAUL STUDIO LOFT HOUSING

Team B's design employs moveable L-shaped wall
storage cabinets and curtains to provide ultimate
flexibility. Called a "kit of parts" by the designer,
the plan allows an artist to apply the design in
pieces over time. The illustration details modular
storage units and a track mechanism.

Team C designed a "front porch" or "storefront" concept. The units are planned with living activity along the exterior wall space and studios surrounding the building's core. The studios have large garage-type doors opening onto the atrium, facilitating public interaction with artists.

ST. PAUL LOWERTOWN ARTIST LOFT HOUSING

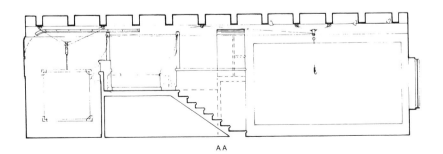

A A

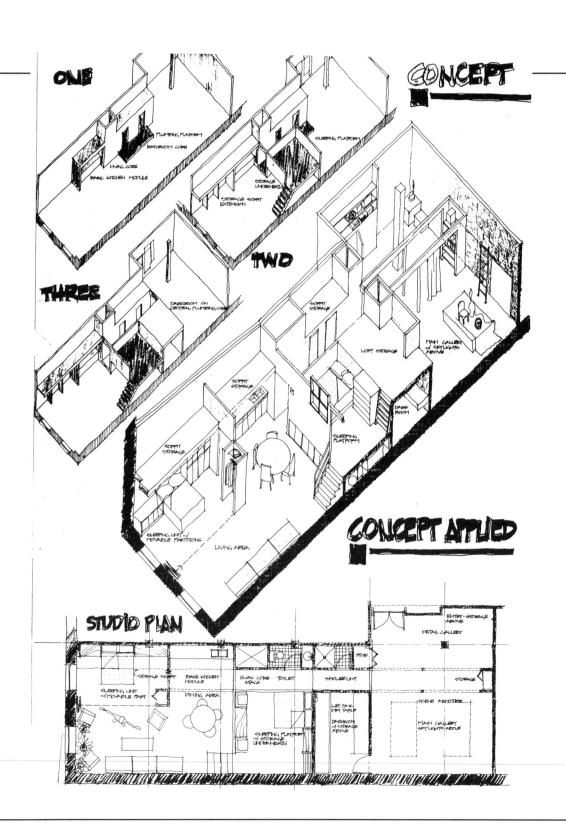

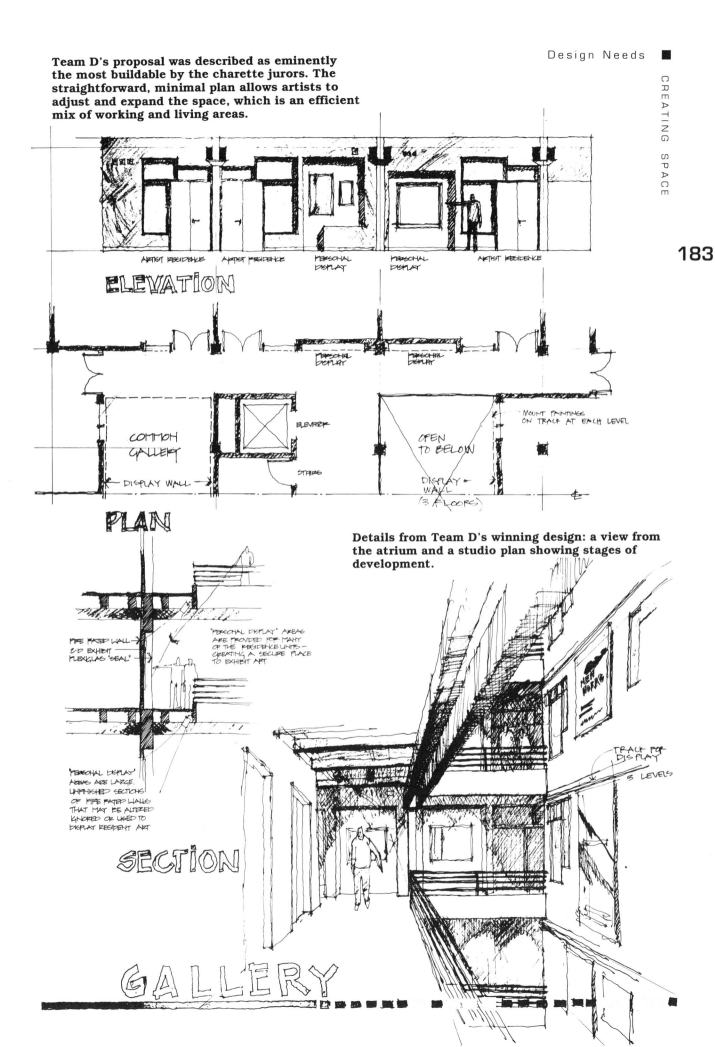

Team D's proposal was described as eminently the most buildable by the charette jurors. The straightforward, minimal plan allows artists to adjust and expand the space, which is an efficient mix of working and living areas.

ARTIST RESIDENCE   ARTIST RESIDENCE   PERSONAL DISPLAY   PERSONAL DISPLAY   ARTIST RESIDENCE

ELEVATION

PERSONAL DISPLAY   PERSONAL DISPLAY

COMMON GALLERY

DISPLAY WALL

ELEVATOR

STAIRS

OPEN TO BELOW

DISPLAY WALL (3 FLOORS)

MOUNT PAINTINGS ON TRACK AT EACH LEVEL

PLAN

Details from Team D's winning design: a view from the atrium and a studio plan showing stages of development.

FIRE RATED WALL 2-D EXHIBIT PLEXIGLAS "SEAL"

"PERSONAL DISPLAY" AREAS ARE PROVIDED FOR MANY OF THE RESIDENCE UNITS — CREATING A SECURE PLACE TO EXHIBIT ART

"PERSONAL DISPLAY" AREAS ARE LARGE, UNFINISHED SECTIONS OF FIRE RATED WALLS THAT MAY BE ALTERED, IGNORED OR USED TO DISPLAY RESIDENT ART

NEW WORKS

TRACK FOR DISPLAY 3 LEVELS

SECTION

GALLERY

184

on-site participation. An additional prize of $1,000 was available to the winning team.

Although the designs submitted in a competition remain the intellectual property of the designers, the materials submitted are usually the property of the sponsors. A prerequisite for the sponsor's use of the winning design is that the author be given contracts related to the design's use or its implementation. If the winning architect is not awarded the contract for construction drawings, the design may usually be used by the sponsor only upon payment of an appropriate fee. The sponsor may amend the design. However, if amendments are major, the sponsor should first consult with the winning designer.

National Endowment for the Arts Design Arts Program

The NEA has actively supported and encouraged public agencies and civic organizations that sponsor design competitions. The NEA Design Arts Program is committed to increasing public awareness and seeking new ideas and solutions to design problems, as well as discovering and encouraging talented designers.

The NEA publishes a comprehensive booklet entitled *Design Competition Manual*, which discusses the advantages of competitions, the types of competitions, the ways in which a design competition can be organized, and the major tasks in this type of undertaking. In addition to publications, the Design Arts Program provides access to technical assistance in organizing and managing design competitions.

The NEA is also an excellent resource for funding qualified projects—particularly those projects that benefit and involve your community or that have national impact (see box 9.5). Grant support to carry out a competition is available under the Design Advancement/Project Grant for Organizations category. Up to $50,000 in funding is available from the NEA, although funds must

be matched by other sources. Individuals cannot apply for funds in this category; they must be represented by an organization that meets NEA requirements. The granting criteria includes, but is not limited to, the following:

- quality of the project
- national or regional significance
- applicant's ability to describe the project and procedure clearly
- demonstrated ability to carry out the project
- ability to sustain the project without further funding from NEA
- presentation and quality of written and visual materials
- ability to meet relevant application requirements

9.5   DESIGN-RELATED PUBLICATIONS AND INFORMATION FROM THE NATIONAL ENDOWMENT FOR THE ARTS

The following publications of the National Endowment for the Arts (NEA) are available upon request:

- *Design Competition Manual*
- *Learning from Abroad, Handbook of Architectural Design Competitions*, edited by George G. Wynne
- *Urban Design Competitions: USA*, by Michael John Pittas and Janet Marie Smith
- *Handbook of Architectural Design Competitions*, by the American Institute of Architects

For further information about design competitions, write or call:

National Endowment for the Arts
Design Arts Program
1100 Pennsylvania Avenue, N.W.
Washington, D.C. 20506
(202) 682-5437

*"Loft building is a process, one which is constantly
changing and expanding . . . ."*
Jim Stratton
Pioneering in the Urban Wilderness

10
Planning and Implementation

Development is the marshaling of ideas, people and resources into a successful project. It can be creative problem-solving at its best. Regardless of size, every real estate development project requires similar tasks.

The development process has two primary components. The first, or planning phase, includes all of the items discussed in the preceding chapters. The second, or implementation phase, includes the acquisition of the property and the construction and management of the project.

Successful projects have (1) the right concept for the site, (2) support for the project concept either from market research or from the right combination of tenants and activities, (3) a suitable legal structure, (4) appropriate design, (5) affordable financing, (6) cost-efficient construction, and (7) sensitive ongoing management. The project solution that best meets the collective needs can be determined through planning and feasibility testing.

186

PLANNING PHASE

The best developers combine the skills of artist and businessperson. The developer—whether a team of several people or one person who emerges as director of the project—provides the vision that sets the stage for all the other players. The developer is often the only participant who perceives how the entire project will come together.

As in theater, development is a highly collaborative process, with roles representing dreamer/visionary, marketing ace, architectural wizard, creative attorney, conservative accountants and lenders, tenant motivator, resourceful contractor and efficient manager. All participants bring their talent and a commitment to work toward creating the project.

STAGES OF DEVELOPMENT

The development process is not linear. Several steps may be going on at once and, sometimes, steps occur out of order. Plans may be developing well until an obstacle forces a return to an earlier step or a total revision of the plan. Tasks in the development process include the following:

- defining the project concept
- testing the market through known or projected tenant needs
- inspecting buildings/sites and assessing suitability of location, needs met, and affordability
- evaluating zoning, site and design constraints
- preparing a preliminary project budget
- seeking, selecting and securing tenant commitments
- evaluating tenant resources
- preparing a statement on the source and use of funds/pro forma

- designing the project
- working with a lawyer to establish an organizational structure
- clarifying requirements of city agencies, lenders, tenants and others
- determining the project's feasibility
- obtaining permanent financing
- finding equity, gap and construction financing
- constructing/renovating the project
- managing the property

PACKAGING THE PROJECT

Packaging the project is the overall task of preparing a written plan or prospectus that summarizes the information gathered about the proposed project. Such information may range from intuitive observations and from what you have learned in talking to others experienced in similar projects to detailed research and planning on paper. The plan or prospectus is presented to a lender or investors to elicit their participation. Not all projects require a detailed prospectus. However, plans for several aspects of your project may be needed either to chart the course for implementation or to build a case for financial support. Moreover, testing feasibility on paper is a quick and cost-effective way to give your ideas a "reality test." (See chapter 6, on financing, for the components of the prospectus.)

The project concept describes the major direction and impetus for a project. It is the vision around which the participants rally their efforts. An operational plan describes how the project is to be organized, the actions to carry out the plans, and the expected timetable. Financial plans allow you to explore a variety of assumptions for hard and soft project costs, fixed and variable operating costs, and the impact of a variety of financing scenarios. To refine the project package, the plans and the design should be compared continually

Santa Fe Art Colony, Los Angeles. Live/work and studio units in a former commercial building. Developed by an artist and an arts patron, with funding from five private investors and a community redevelopment loan, to provide low-rent space for artists.

against the findings of market needs and overall financial feasibility. Planning prepares the way for the mid-course corrections that may be needed during project implementation.

PROJECT TASK SEQUENCING

The type and size of a project will determine the actual tasks and the amount of time needed between each task. A leasehold renovation project may be completed in as little as three months. An ownership project may take two or more years to bring to the occupancy stage.

To develop your project, begin planning the sequence of activities by listing your goals and objectives. Determine the dates by which you desire to achieve your goals. Next, decide the dates by which the objectives must be met to achieve your targeted goal dates. Make a list of the tasks that must be completed to meet your goals and objectives. Assign responsibility for completion of each objective and task. Evaluate whether you have sufficient expertise and resources to carry out the tasks in your project sequence in the time-frame that has been set. If not, extend your timetable to reflect more realistically your group's ability to meet the schedule. Adjust the timetable as new information changes your expectations.

See figure 10.1 for an overview of a possible project sequence for an ownership renovation project.

TIME FRAME	PROJECT STAGE	FUNDING NEED	POSSIBLE SOURCES OF FUNDING

Month 1	Concept/Planning
	Evaluate site/building
	Hold Predesign mtg
	  with inspections
	Conduct market study
	Prepare preliminary
	  pro forma
	Prepare option/purchase
	  agreement
		Predevelopment
		Funds
			Artists' own equity'
			Operating budget or
			planning grant/loan
			received by nonprofit
			sponsor in kind services
			or consultant fee at closing

Month 2	Prepare working agreement for development team Select architect Solicit/secure tenants Begin design process Revise pro forma	Predevelopment Funds	Same as month 1
Month 3	Plan ownership structure Meet with lenders Order appraisal Secure/involve tenants Complete design process Revise pro forma Submit plans to zoning/ planning	Predevelopment Funds	Same as month 1

Month 4	Plan operate/mgmt
	  structure
	Prepare legal documents/
	  leases
	Zoning/planning approval
	Seek contractor bids
	Finish pro forma
	Prepare lender package
		Predevelopment
		Funds
			Same as month 1

Month 5	Tenant prelease commitments Tenant income verify/ credit references Submit lender package Sign contract w/contractor	Predevelopment Funds	Same as month 1

TIME FRAME	PROJECT STAGE	FUNDING NEED	POSSIBLE SOURCES OF FUNDING
Month 6	Permanent financing approved Seek construction/ interim financing	Predevelopment Funds	Same as Month 1
Month 7	Construction loan approval Continue planning mgmt. Final commitment by tenants	Predevelopment Funds	Same as Month 1
Month 8	Close on property purchase File legal documents Building permit issued Construction loan funding Construction loan funded Construction/renovation begins	Acquisition & Development	Debt Financing
Month 9	Monitor construction Inspections approval	Development	Debt Financing
Month 10	Monitor construction Inspections approval Deposits by tenants	Development	Debt Financing
Month 11	Monitor construction Inspections approval Preliminary punch list Refine mgmt. plan/contracts	Development	Debt Financing
Month 12	Construction complete Move-in, final punch list Operations/management Celebrate!	Development	Debt Financing Resident payments

POINTERS FOR THE DEVELOPMENT PROCESS

GET ORGANIZED. Individuals and small organizations can be troublesome for city hall or a developer to deal with unless it is clear who is making the decisions or speaking on behalf of the group. Decide who will make decisions and specify the limits of their authority. Collaborations between arts organizations require decision-making standards and organizational rules to prevent misunderstandings caused by assumptions or "norms" from different environmental or organizational cultures.

PLAN. Think as far into the future as possible. Maintain a long-range perspective, think big and creatively to stretch beyond personal boundaries. Involve all the critical decision makers in the process. Those who are to implement the plan must be comfortable with the plan as it is being developed. Identify tasks, set decision points and make assignments for carrying out the tasks.

TAKE ONE STEP AT A TIME. The process often provides many decisions. Some choices create other choices, but not necessarily a clear path. When each task is taken on individually, the process can be manageable.

BE REALISTIC. Look honestly at the available resources for the project. Look at contingency and interim plans that will help you get where you want to go, even if not as quickly as you want. Arts organizations should assess the past, present and future health of the budget; the skills of the board and staff; the interest of volunteers; the effect of the project on programs; and the feasibility analysis of the project.

FOLLOW THROUGH. Do not make promises you cannot keep. Meet schedules to the best of your ability. Continue to involve people as appropriate to get the tasks accomplished.

ENJOY THE PROCESS. Inevitably there will be strained negotiations, delays and temporary obstacles (see figure 10.2). Retain your sense of humor; it not only provides a release of tensions but can lead to imaginative responses. Be especially sensitive to "people" issues. Seek "win-win" solutions to your negotiations. Periodically reward all the participants in your group, organization or partnership with some recognition and fun.

IMPLEMENTATION PHASE

The implementation phase consists of final negotiations, acquisition of the property, construction and ongoing management of the project. Once the lease or ownership agreements are in final form, financing is secure, and plans have been approved, the deal can be closed. It is the final decision point. The plan can then be implemented.

NEGOTIATIONS

"One for you, two for me. One for you, two for me.
One for you, two for me."
—*children's negotiation strategy*

A long time ago, when the only way to get anything was to trade or barter one thing for another, the fine art of negotiating was a common skill. Today many of us are uncomfortable with the process—even paying more in order to avoid haggling. The higher the stakes, however, the less one can afford this attitude.

DEALING WITH OBSTACLES IN DEVELOPING SPACE

**There are no failures,
only outcomes
that lead to a revision of your plans.**

EXCITING PROJECT VISION	OBSTACLES	RESPONSES	PROJECT SUCCESS

1. Collaboration requires "above and beyond" efforts by all parties

2. Important issues — difficult decisions; decision-making that is hidden rather than overt

3. New information; changed perspective; unforeseen barriers and obstacles; unmet expectations; "Murphy's Law"

4. Critics surface; uncertainties and anxieties arise; project suffers setback or loss of momentum

1. Tolerance for uncertainty and ambiguity; acknowledge extra efforts and commitment

2. Allow disagreement; generate creative solutions; build consensus openly; clarify roles in decision-making; final decisions made by small group of leaders

3. Question assumptions; change plans; redirect project; identify new opportunities; remember that success requires persistence and flexibility

4. Reconfirm shared vision; maintain enthusiasm; share dreams; listen to messages that indicate project is not feasible and reassess; celebrate milestones

---

Negotiating skills, whether for leasing, ownership or other situations, can be learned. You may act on your own behalf in negotiating with a building owner or employ someone to negotiate on your behalf. Either way, you have to know what you want, what you have to offer and what can be compromised so that the negotiator can deal effectively.

The range of assistance you require may vary from having an attorney review a final contract before signing to hiring someone as your chief negotiator. Most negotiations fall into a middle ground, in which you or your representatives work hand in hand over a period of weeks or months with a professional consultant.

The person who represents your group will probably be one of the following: (1) member (or members) of the group designated as a primary contact, (2) real estate broker, (3) real estate attorney, (4) development consultant, (5) representative of a nonprofit service or development organization or (6) city agency representative.

Basic Principles

Nearly everything is negotiable, and nearly everything has a price. A basic awareness of the principles at work will aid your negotiations.

ATTITUDE. Successful negotiations are built upon the "win-win" attitudes of the parties involved. A solid contract results when each party feels they have gained more than they have given up. Realize that each of you has something the other wants or needs and approach the person as an equal. Focus on the benefits the building owner will have with you as a buyer or tenant.

IT'S BUSINESS. Building owners are businesspeople. Most people have increased comfort with the familiar; therefore they will prefer being approached in a businesslike fashion.

FIRST IMPRESSIONS. At the first meeting, each party will be assessing the relative bargaining power and the fundamental needs of the other. Studies show that first impressions are long-lasting. Look and act the way you want to be perceived. Responsible. Knowledgeable. Friendly. Organized. Come prepared with facts and figures, and know where to find them easily.

WRITTEN AGREEMENTS. Negotiations form the basis of agreement between the parties. Oral agreements can be forgotten quickly or interpreted differently at a later time. Put *all* agreements in writing.

PROTECT YOUR INTERESTS. While negotiations are going on, contracts are communication tools. Once signed, however, they become legally binding. To protect your rights and interests, it is best to have your attorney review the written agreements, rather than rely on the building owner's agent or attorney for advice.

Strategy

Two of the most important negotiating tasks are (1) asking the right questions and (2) allowing both parties to benefit. If you approach negotiations as if they are a collaborative problem-solving session, you are more likely to emerge with a solution that works well for all parties. Especially if you are leasing, your relationship over time can be more efficient if it is built on respectful consideration for the people involved.

People tend to see things from their own base of perception. In a good negotiation process, both parties will educate each other about their interests and concerns, while generating alternatives and evaluating options. The final agreement must provide acceptable terms overall, regardless of the concessions made to reach it. Honoring each other's differences allows trust and confidence to be built into the final agreement, with the knowledge that as new issues arise they, too, can be resolved fairly.

Once each party's view of the issues is identified, a proposal for how a solution appears from each perspective can be presented, noting the areas of agreement. Alternatives continue to be proposed and discussed as the differences between parties are reduced and agreement is reached.

Another route to agreement is to list each party's needs and interests and then jointly create solutions to meet as many or all of the needs as possible. Prepare for the discussions by thinking through options that may serve both sides' needs. Be clear about your bottom line before going into the discussions.

Preparing for Negotiations

You can use much of the same information you assembled for a feasibility study or a lender's presentation package to establish your credibility and support your negotiating position. A building owner will want to know who you are, how responsible you are, whether you will be able to raise money and make payments, and, if your are leasing, how your tenancy will affect the market value of the property. Your general appearance and attitude, your degree of preparation, your name and reputation in the community, and the people you know in the community—all contribute to the building owner's picture of who you or your group are.

Financial stability can be demonstrated by a market study and a list detailing the potential tenants or buyers and projected income. Individuals or a developer partner may be asked to provide net worth, income and expense statements, and balance sheet information.

REVIEWING PRELIMINARY INVESTIGATIONS OF THE PROPERTY. You may want to have a brainstorming session with group members to define what is most important to you and what areas are most negotiable, as follows:

1. Determine the relevant facts and remaining questions:
   - value of the land and/or building
   - development trends in the area
   - size and structural quality of the building
   - appropriateness of the price
   - owner's motivations to sell

2. Know your position:
   - what can you afford
   - how well are your space and location needs met by the property
   - what conditions are important for you to achieve
   - what concerns are lower priorities—what can you allow the owner to "win" on

- what your initial offer will be and what your bottom line is—what you are willing to do to get the property
- what is your ability to make a commitment and the time needed to do so

SIZING UP THE SELLER. Credibility works both ways. To protect your own rights, make sure the person or persons you are negotiating with have the right or authority to sell, lease or donate the property. Make sure that all key parties to the negotiations are involved.

Ascertain the owner's position. The owner's circumstances shape the negotiation outcomes and may change how your desired results are structured. For example, if the owner has a special interest in your group's purpose, that interest may open the way for unique solutions.

One way to find out about the building owner's needs is to examine how the property is advertised. Unspecified options may satisfy both parties equally well. Negotiable items could include the total price, loan term, cost and number of monthly payments, proportion of monthly payments for principal and the interest rate. Is the seller most interested in ready cash? Steady income? Anxious to sell? A potential investor in your project? Willing to take a subordinated loan position?

If the seller is in need of money, conventional financing may be preferred to allow him or her to cash-out. However, a contract sale with a large down payment and a short term might also be acceptable. Older property owners or institutional owners may prefer a steady income. They might be willing to finance the entire loan with a full-term mortgage on a contract for deed or real estate contract. Arrangements that serve a primary need of the seller may include other variables that favor the buyer, such as a lower monthly payment and a lower interest rate.

194

A seller might prefer less money "up front," to reduce his or her tax liability. A large cash payment at the time of the sale can be eaten up by taxes. If the owner was selling in order to find other projects to invest in, the owner may be willing to become an equity partner in your project.

Negotiating Factors Affecting Price

Through your research, you will be able to get an idea of what the owner will be asking in the first round of negotiations and of the relative importance of factors other than money that may be motivating the seller. For a variety of reasons, some owners can be persuaded to donate the property as an outright gift or to sell well below market value. The owner may share a commitment to the arts or be concerned with upgrading the neighborhood and may welcome favorable publicity. Adjoining property owned may be expected to increase in value as a result of your activities. Various conditions in the building or the neighborhood may have made the property hard to sell. The owner may be anxious to get rid of it—perhaps to avoid tax delinquency or foreclosure. Additionally, the owner may realize tax benefits as a result of donating space to a nonprofit organization, as a property "write-down" or "in-kind" contribution.

Lease Negotiations

The owner may be willing to exchange reduced or "free" rent for the time your group spends renovating the space. You may be required to accept a longer lease term in exchange for improvements to be made by the owner. Sometimes an owner will agree to "buy back," at the end of the lease term, certain improvements a tenant intends to make. Your use of the space may require additional rent for increased insur-

ance or security costs incurred by the nature of your use.

If you are unable or unwilling to commit to a purchase, negotiating a lease with an option to buy will allow you a trial period. The lease will specify the length of time you have to exercise the option and enter into a purchase agreement. If agreeable, rent or improvements paid for by the tenant/buyer may be used as credit toward the purchase price. A variation of this is to negotiate a lease that gives you or your group the right of first refusal in the event the property is put up for sale during the course of the lease.

Anticipate concerns of the owner and how you would respond to them. Concerns usually revolve around noise levels; late hours; fear of the stereotypical artist's lifestyle; safety—for example, the use of flammable materials; and the production of dust, dirt and garbage.

Try to identify discussion points that show the advantages of your tenancy to the owner. Other people tend to feel good and work better in a building that is alive with the arts. Arts tenants may improve the dull or ordinary "image" of a building and also increase the building's desirability to new tenants. The arts provide an excellent interim use while attracting upscale tenants that will support the new uses intended. A building's traffic tends to be increased by arts activities that support other retail and restaurant activity. What is the unique contribution you would make?

Negotiating Neighborhood Support

Rich or poor, urban or rural, high tech or low, sophisticated or not, we all have territorial instincts and we raise defenses against "foreign" bodies invading our territory. The day someone sees you poking around that old abandoned building, the neighborhood will buzz with apprehension. Neighborhood opposition can be a

**Studios at 700, Minneapolis.
Open house.**

serious obstacle to the city approvals you need to complete your project.

Build community support and acceptance early in the process. Let people meet you to learn what you are planning to do and why. Explore ways to promote good feelings between your group and your new community that reflect the special nature of your group or the neighborhood. If you are working with a city agency, it may be able to identify key residents or neighborhood groups that you might contact.

Moving into a commercial building in a residential neighborhood may call for an old-fashioned block party or an outdoor picnic before construction even gets started. Finding a comfortable way to meet the neighbors will give you a feeling for neighborhood concerns and you may be able to anticipate problems that need early resolution. Residents may have concerns about traffic and parking problems. Incorporating a parking lot or relocating a driveway could offer a solution. Consider offering art classes to neigh-

borhood children, adults or senior citizens to promote acceptance and good feelings.

Moving into a warehouse district in the inner city may put you close to a commercial district. Your "neighbors" will be merchants in the area. Find out if some kind of association of business executives already exists in the locality. Again, you might host an event. Or, you might contact them and offer to address one of their meetings to explain how your group hopes to spruce up the building or to stimulate activity that will benefit area merchants.

In addition to bringing people and possibly new businesses to the area, there are economic incentives in keeping up or renovating the physical environment. More money comes to the city when property is maintained than when it is allowed to deteriorate. Renovation of older buildings renews appreciation of their quality, style and value, which in turn enhances property values and stimulates reinvestment in the neighborhood.

Negotiation is the backbone of the entire development process, since it is communication that involves all the players. Beyond a combination of vision, creativity, patience, timing, and perseverance in the face of setbacks, negotiation allows the planning to become implemented at acquisition.

ACQUISITION

Once negotiations indicate that you have found (1) the right building at the right price and location, (2) a seller receptive to doing business, (3) likely affordable financing, and (4) support from arts tenants or other community partners, your broker, attorney and lender can guide you through the acquisition process. The first step in acquisition is to make an offer for the property.

Letter of Intent

When you decide you are definitely interested in a property, you may wish to draw up a "letter of intent." This document is prepared when two or more parties want to express mutual interest and intent to buy, sell, lease or develop property without legal liability or obligation to do so. It outlines the conditions that would be acceptable to both parties.

The letter of intent is not a contract or an agreement to enter into a contract. However, it is expected that people will proceed promptly with

Lowertown Lofts, St. Paul.
Photographer in his live/work space.

the deal in good faith and as outlined in the letter. The letter may be prepared at any point in your negotiations before the preparation of a purchase agreement.

Option to Purchase

Similar to a letter of intent, the "option to purchase" outlines the intent to purchase with clearly defined contingencies. It provides time to assess the feasibility of the project before committing to a purchase agreement. An option is a right, for which consideration has been paid, to purchase or lease a property upon meeting specified terms by a specified date. For example, a developer may make the purchase contingent upon obtaining necessary variances, rezoning, affordable financing or other key concerns. If the project cannot be accomplished as planned, the developer would not be obligated to proceed with the purchase.

Purchase Agreement

A "real estate purchase agreement," "contract of sale" or "sales agreement" is typically a preprinted form used to clarify the terms of the sale. It is ordinarily presented to the seller with an earnest money cash deposit, generally 10 to 20 percent of the anticipated down payment. If the terms are acceptable, the seller signs and takes the deposit. If the terms are unacceptable, the seller responds by a counteroffer that specifies the conditions that would be acceptable. The buyer and seller continue to trade offers until they reach an acceptable agreement or break off negotiations.

Once the buyer has paid for the property, the seller is obligated to convey title to the buyer. The actions required to complete the transaction are specified within the contract terms, including the following:

- the parties to the transaction
- a legal description of the property
- the amount of earnest money being paid and accepted with the offer
- the size of the down payment (equity) to be paid at closing
- the financing terms for the remainder of the agreed-upon purchase price
- the proposed date and place of closing
- description of the deed that will be used
- list of any known encumbrances or title defects and the buyer's willingness to take title subject to these items
- any contingencies that were agreed to by seller and buyer (for example, the title search verifies satisfactorily clear title, proposed financing is secured at the rate designated in the agreement, repairs or inspections are made)
- warranties or guarantees made by buyer or seller
- list of personal property or fixtures that are part of the sale
- responsibility for costs of the transaction
- proration of property taxes and assessments
- other items required by state, lenders, or public agencies

Many sellers request the addition of a clause for the seller to accept the buyer's earnest money as their sole right to damages in the event of the buyer's default on the contract, including if the default is due to a contingency item that the agreement was "subject to." The purchase agreement becomes void and the earnest money can be returned if an item the agreement is "subject to" cannot be achieved.

The final event in the purchase transaction is the actual transfer of title, the transfer of ownership rights. This transfer occurs at the closing, which is described later.

198

**Project Artaud, San Francisco.
Performance space.**

Title

The title describes the ownership rights that are assigned to a parcel of land, including surface, air and subsurface rights. Rights to use property are described as either "freehold" or "leasehold" estates. Freehold estates give the owner legal title to the land and exclusive rights to its possession. Leasehold estates convey the right to use or improve the land for specified periods of time through the terms of a lease. The rights of taxation, eminent domain, escheat and police power are retained by the government. Therefore, title to private property is subject to public restrictions through planning, zoning, building, fire and health codes. The remaining "bundle of rights" is called "fee simple."

CLAIMS ON TITLE. Sometimes there are costs associated with a piece of property that have nothing to do with its physical condition. Rather, they represent the claims of various individuals or public agencies against a property's value. These claims become part of the negotiated purchase price. Because hidden costs can pose a hidden liability, the lender will typically require you to have a title search conducted as assurance that the title is "clean" and to protect your interest with title insurance.

Liens, back taxes, special assessments or debts owed to past contractors are types of claims that might be filed with the county. These claims will usually be paid out of the proceeds of any sale of the property before the seller is paid the balance. You need to decide on a method of settlement in your sales agreement to make sure you will not be held responsible for these past debts.

Easements are another type of claim that may affect how a property can be used. An easement is a right held by someone else to use your property without paying rent. For example, easements allow utility companies to lay pipelines. An adjacent property owner may also have an easement that allows a portion of your property to be used for his or her driveway.

TITLE INSURANCE. Title assurances are provided through the Torrens system of title registration, a personal warranty from the grantor, a lawyer's Title Opinion, an Abstractor's Certificate, and/or a title insurance policy.

Title insurance provides the safest assurance of title and should identify any liens or other defects in the seller's title through an investigation before the insurance policy is issued. Title insurance also provides protection from unknown claims against the property. For a one-time premium charge, this insurance guarantees that the purchaser (or mortgagee) will be indemnified (protected) from any insured loss in the event his title fails for any defect that accrued before the effective date of the policy.

Deeds

Titles are transferred through a written legal document called a deed. There are several types of deeds: general warranty deeds, special warranty deeds, trustee's deeds, court-ordered deeds, deeds of bargain and sale, and quitclaim deeds. The general warranty deed is the most widely used. It usually assures the highest possible warranties recognized by state laws. Essentially, it states that the grantor (the seller) will "warrant and defend" the title against all persons whomsoever. The quitclaim deed is valuable in clearing up any "clouds" on the title of a property. Basically, the grantor quitclaims to the grantee all of his right, title and interest to the property, without, however, a warranty that the grantor actually has rights to grant.

DELIVERY AND RECORDING OF DEEDS. A deed, which must be in writing, must be signed by the grantor using the exact same signature as on the title. The deed must also contain an adequate description of the property being conveyed (street names and numbers are not used because they change—rather, a metes and bounds system, government survey or recorded plat system is used. The deed must be properly delivered to the grantee (buyer) and show an intent to convey title.

The deed's proper "delivery" includes being recorded, and it also requires being signed in the presence of a notary public. Title passes to the buyer upon delivery, rather than upon the date the deed is signed.

Deeds may contain exceptions and/or reservations. Exceptions are existing deficiencies in the grantor's title. Reservations are property rights retained by the seller in the same deed in which he transfers the balance of his ownership interests in a given tract of real estate.

Promissory Notes and Mortgages

Both the promissory note and the mortgage document are contracts that are used in tandem for the provision of a mortgage loan. The promissory note, which includes details about the lender, the borrower, repayment terms, the debt amount and the interest rate, is the "promise to pay" the debt. The mortgage provides a description of the collateral (real or personal property) the lender can sell if the debt is not paid. Typically, these contracts or any other financing contracts would also be signed on the day of "closing."

The Closing

The "closing" is the final act in the transfer of ownership. It consists of the transfer of title along with a financial accounting statement and whatever assurances are necessary.

The length of time a closing takes is usually directly related to the number of financing sources and complexity of the project. A simple mortgage involving one equity payment and relatively few parties requires few documents. Large projects generate a tremendous amount of paper, with many legal documents required to give assurances to all parties involved.

A traditional closing requires the physical presence of all interested parties or their representatives. The documents required by the purchase agreement or contract of sale are all reviewed and, if acceptable, executed. A closing statement is put in final form, allocating closing costs between the parties. Ongoing expenses, including property taxes, insurance, service con-

10.1 STUDIOS AT 700
Minneapolis, Minnesota

Space before construction.

DEVELOPER AS GENERAL CONTRACTOR. Studios at 700 was developed by Artspace Projects, Inc., a nonprofit organization created to develop and secure long-term control of space, with the participation of artists interested in being tenants. Artspace Projects, Inc. also acted as architect and general contractor. The organization sent out a Request for Proposal (RFP) for contractors' bids and provided contractors with scale floor plans and detailed specifications. To maximize the square feet available to lease out, a variance in city codes was obtained to approve blocking access to one of four stair towers, which is now located in one unit.

The third and fourth floors of the building were developed in two stages: construction of the 22 units on the third floor was completed by January 1982, and the 15 units on the fourth floor were developed during the fall of 1982. The construction team for the third floor was a group of artists who did general construction work to support themselves. For the fourth floor, a full-time professional firm was contracted. With prior agreement, the second contractor hired a number of artists to do some of the work.

Renovating each floor was a straightforward procedure. Only minor demolition was needed. Walls meeting minimum fire code for separation between spaces and containing sound barriers were laid out on the columns. The walls met office-type code, 5/8" sheetrock with metal studs. The electrical system was also upgraded. The building owner paid for rehabilitation of common areas, including exit signs and hallway lights. Total cost of rehabilitation per square foot was approximately $4.30.

For the first development phase, Artspace held a demonstration on how to tape walls—that is, covering the seams where the panels of sheetrock meet. The artists either taped walls themselves or hired another artist to do it for them. On the fourth floor a contractor taped walls. Artists also provided "sweat equity" by painting and adding special features to their spaces.

MANAGEMENT. The 700 North Washington project is an unincorporated, unregistered artists/tenants affiliation. The contract agreement is based on a leased cooperative. The artists signed a five-year master lease as a tenants association, with a five-year option to continue. A coordinator is designated by the tenants association to receive rent checks from the tenants and to make the rent payment to the owner as well as to notify the owner when people move in and out. A small pool of money is collected monthly toward a vacancy fund, so the group can pay the rent if one or more tenants is late or can use the excess funds for purposes of their choice. Artists meet at least once a year, as required in their association agreement. Meeting

Artist in renovated studio space.

Printmaking studio.

topics include discussions about subletting, an issue that has created perhaps the most tension. Another thorny issue is who should have priority to assume a vacancy if there are somewhat equal positions on the waiting list.

FINANCING. Overall, the greatest problem in the development of 700 North Washington was coming up with money to renovate the floors. Artspace no longer had rehabilitation grant funds to invest in renovation of space and needed to find financing at low enough cost to make the studios affordable. The size of the studios, even at the extremely low cost per foot that had been negotiated, meant that rents were higher than many artists were prepared to pay. The response was the creation of the revolving loan fund.

Each artist contributed a $100 nonrefundable fee to ensure commitment to the master lease. In-kind contributions of materials were donated by various suppliers. The 22 units on the third floor required $86,000 for total development, $26,000 of which was provided by Artspace in the form of a revolving loan fund. The total cost per unit (CPU): $3,909. The 15 units on the fourth floor cost a total of $72,000 to develop ($8,000 in Artspace development dollars) for a CPU of $4,800.

The artists took out a total of 18 loans at 3 percent interest over a five-year period from the Artspace revolving loan fund. The total principal of the loans was $34,000. Funds for the revolving loan fund were obtained from City of Minneapolis Community Development Agency Block Grant Funds, the Dayton Hudson Foundation, Norwest Banks, and Horncrest Foundation as well as from some private individuals. Artspace has experienced no defaults on revolving loan fund repayments and the total loans have been paid off.

DATA. Each floor of the building contains 38,500 rentable square feet. Wide widths between "mushroom"-style concrete pillars made a fairly uniform layout of studios possible. The average studio size is 1,000 square feet, although there are a few large photo studios averaging 3,500 square feet. All studios have concrete floors, 12-foot ceilings and large, factory-height windows (20' W x 10' H) with operable center panels. Egress is excellent: three large freight elevators, one passenger elevator and four concrete stair towers serve each floor. There is a weather-protected, drive-in loading dock.

Studio tour.

tracts and mortgage insurance, are prorated. If all the documents are in order, the seller signs the deed and completes the transaction by handing it to the buyer.

CONSTRUCTION

If the transaction entails renovating or constructing a project, the closing may include the signing of a "buy-sell" agreement. A buy-sell agreement is a contract that sets out the rights and obligations between the developer (and equity partners), the construction lender, and the permanent (take-out) lender. The construction lender agrees to make a loan and to sell it to the permanent lender after satisfactory completion of the project. The permanent lender agrees to "buy" the construction loan from the construction lender.

The developer agrees to construct and manage the project, to permit liens to be placed on the property by the lenders, and to inject sufficient equity to cover the difference between the project cost and the long-term mortgage. Once the agreement is signed, construction can begin. Upon completion, occupancy will occur, the permanent lender will buy out the construction lender and the developer's property management team (or the self-management by the group) will take effect.

The Construction Process

New construction or renovation begins by gathering materials, labor and equipment at the building site. Most often, a contractor is hired to carry out the plans. Contractors are firms or individuals who renovate or construct a building, translating architectural plans for a fee based on a contractual agreement. General contractors undertake responsibility for ensuring coordination of all functions necessary to complete the project. Licensed general contractors must meet requirements for knowledge and experience in the construction business. Subcontractors typically specialize in construction tasks (for example, plumbing, electrical, painting) and may be hired by the owner/developer or the general contractor.

In large projects, using a general contractor allows you to hold another person or firm responsible for the efficient coordination of the subcontractors, project scheduling, payments to subcontractors, etc.

Artists have acted as "general contractors" in smaller renovation efforts, particularly if a single unit or small building is being rehabilitated. In these instances, artists may choose to forego hiring a general contractor to manage contracts (subcontractors) with each construction trade and supplier separately. You can save approximately 10 percent of the construction costs if you act as the general contractor. In small projects, acting as the general contractor allows you to stay in close touch with the construction details and saves the expense of a "middle man." If you have enough time to devote to the task, can be at the construction site daily, and have a good sense of the flow and priority of the tasks required, acting as the general contractor can be an effective move.

BID DOCUMENTS. A request for bids has three main parts, all of which are provided equally to each of the bidders. The "invitation to bid" is simply a cover page stating who the developer or group is and the address, phone number and representative to be called. The invitation also summarizes the work to be done, desired starting and/or completion date, its location, and the closing date of the call for bids. For some projects the anticipated or maximum budget is identified.

The "bid form" provides a format for their quoted price, a place to list subcontractors to be used, insurance or bonding requirements, and

South Prescott Village, Oakland. Construction.

date of bid opening. It may also provide a statement that, if the bid is accepted, the contractor agrees to enter into a contract. There is a place for the contractor's signature.

The "contract documents" include a specific description of the work to be done, the standards, and the fixtures or materials to be used. Drawings may be included, specifying the location of walls, fixtures, electrical, plumbing or other features. A second part states general conditions of how the contract will be administered (inspections, payments, time framework, cleanliness requirements, lien waivers).

In competitive bidding, the lowest-priced responsible contractor is often selected. The lowest price is best used as a tie breaker between two equally qualified contractors. If your project has specialized features or limited preliminary completed design work, you may prefer a negotiated contract with a predetermined contractor. To assist in comparing contractors, you may wish to adapt the form for comparing consultants shown in appendix 9.1.

SELECTING THE CONTRACTOR. Before considering the price bid of a contractor, you need to apply the following selection criteria:

1. **EXPERIENCE WITH SIMILAR TYPES OF CONSTRUCTION PROJECTS.** You should ask the contractor for a list of similar projects, their original estimates and the actual project costs. Interview the owner, architect and tenants for their response to the completed job.

2. **LOCAL EXPERIENCE.** Ask about familiarity with building codes, material purchasing practices and suppliers, and local labor practices. Make reference checks with building inspectors or trade unions.

3. **FINANCIAL CAPACITY.** Request a financial statement to check profitability and cash flow to handle day-to-day operations. Verify with the contractor's bank.

4. **SUBCONTRACTOR QUALITY.** Request a list of subcontractors proposed to work on your project. Interview subcontractors if you wish.

5. **PROJECT MANAGER.** Interview the project manager to determine his or her experience with similar projects, working style, and other projects the manager would be responsible for during the same construction period. Is this someone you will be comfortable working with?

204

TYPES OF CONTRACTS. Like architects' contract formats, there are three general categories of construction contracting:

- fixed price or lump-sum—the project is completed for a specified amount, usually through competitive bidding
- cost-plus-fixed-fee—actual costs are reimbursed, plus a predetermined fee; a desirable method when exact plans are incomplete
- guaranteed-maximum-price—developer pays only actual costs incurred up to a maximum price, the contractor sharing in any savings

Contracts include information about materials, labor and equipment necessary to complete the working drawings that are addenda to the contract. A fee is added for a contractor's overhead and profit. Contracts may be awarded on the basis of competitive bidding, negotiation with a preferred contractor, or through a joint venture on larger projects.

CONTRACT NEGOTIATIONS. Analyze the contract to ensure that all your expectations have been included. As in all other contracts, the written word is what has been agreed to, not the variety of ideas you may have discussed before signing the contract.

The project estimate, or bid, should define the various task components and clarify which will be undertaken by the contractor's crews and which will be subcontracted. The general contractor's hourly rate, as well as the rate of employees, should be written into the contract. If any work is to be done as sweat equity by the artists, for example, construction clean-up or painting, it can also be noted in the contract.

Changes, compromises and corrections of materials or methods are often required even in the best-laid plans. Once changes are negotiated between the contractor and the architect, the change order and price difference are brought to the owner/developer for approval. An architect may be asked to certify the payments to be made to the contractor, based on approval of completed construction phases.

You should consider hiring an attorney to spell out boundaries and protective measures in your contract. Include a Waiver of Mechanics Lien Rights to protect you from liens filed on your project if the general contractor has not passed on your payments to the subcontractors.

The larger your project, the more money at risk, and the more likely you will want to require a general contractor to get a construction bond from a surety company. A performance bond guarantees that the job will be completed, regardless of what happens to the general contractor. To protect the general contractor against nonperformance by subcontractors, subcontractor bonds are required. A payment bond ensures that suppliers will be paid. These and other bonds are selected based on the type of project and the degree of protection the owner/developer requires.

Project Management

The general contractor will determine what skills are required and when they are required, and will ensure they are on site at the most cost-efficient time. Because of problems with on-site storage, materials and equipment must be selected and delivered to the site as needed. On-site working needs—for example, safe work practices, tool storage, trash removal, clean-up areas, lunch and rest-room accommodations—are also identified, planned for and monitored by the general contractor. Procedures are established to fairly resolve disputes should they arise between workers and/or with management.

To ensure that the project is completed on time, that it meets design specifications, and that it falls within the budget, the general contractor monitors an action plan. The logical sequence of

Lowertown Lofts. Artist checking construction progress.

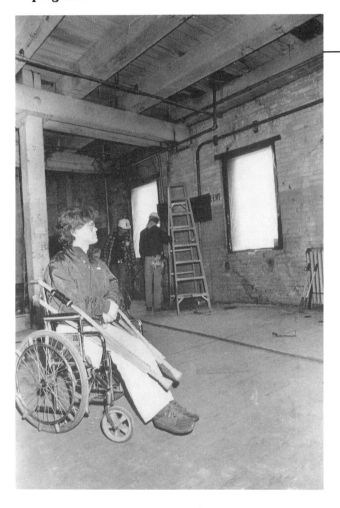

Never pay for work that has not been completed at agreed checkpoints. Withholding money is the best incentive for ensuring the job is properly finished. A typical schedule for payment dispersal follows:

- 10 percent up front
- 25 percent when structural work is completed
- 25 percent when mechanical work (electricity, plumbing, heat) is completed
- 25 percent when the finish work is completed
- 15 percent after the "punch list" of work that must be finished or redone, systems checks, and clean-up has been finished

Quality Control

If you are inexperienced in the processes of construction, your architect can monitor the quality of the workmanship. The architect should understand what constitutes a proper construction method or quality job and can be effective in seeking needed corrections in work that is under way. Later changes usually require a new contract and fee arrangement.

You and the architect should make a detailed list of any construction defects, called a "punch list," that require correction by the contractor before you provide a final payment.

If you are acting as an owner/developer, you are ultimately responsible to lenders and the building inspections department for the final result of the project. Most contractors will seek to satisfy the recommendation of a field inspector for the manner of handling any code-related task. Double-check requirements and timing for permits and inspections with your local building inspections department. Good communication between the contractors, the inspectors and yourself will ensure satisfactory completion of the construction tasks.

major phases of building activity are diagramed using the critical path method (CPM) or the program evaluation and review technique (PERT). Both provide a means of maximizing overall efficiency and of making accurate calculations of resources needed, working time between tasks, and comparisons between contract dates and major milestones.

Make a schedule of meetings with your contractor and architect. Ask questions about the materials being used or on order, the coordination of the subcontractors, expected job progress, and payment schedules. Changes in schedule, materials or construction techniques can be evaluated and revised action approved in a timely manner.

"I sometimes envy my friends who are lounging around on the weekends sipping coffee and perusing the Sunday paper. Of course we still do that too, but there's always some project to lure me from my easy chair. Some projects are fun, others are hard work, but they all seem to foster community and help people generate their own creative energy like nothing I've ever seen before. The important thing is not to get burned out on them."
Resident, Sun and Wind Cohousing project, Beder, Denmark
In Kathryn McCamant and Charles Durrett,
Cohousing: A Contemporary Approach to
Housing Ourselves

11
Operations:
A Self-Managed
Community

THE VALUE OF SELF-MANAGEMENT

Artists who share a self-managed work and living environment help to expand the meanings of "home" and "community." Unlike standard housing developed to ensure privacy, self-managed projects are the expression of a conscious choice to create a stake in one's environment, to care about the spaces and the people in one's immediate vicinity, to talk about common concerns, to deal with issues collectively, and to solve common problems. From this choice to create a community springs a sense of companionship and increased security from knowing and making friends with neighbors.

Condominiums, cooperatives, intentional communities, communes, co-housing and co-ownership structures lend themselves to self-managed live/work environments. Each allows for unique responses and solutions that support chosen ways of living and working together. For convenience, all the above forms will be referred to generically as cooperatives, although your group's chosen self-management organizational structure may vary.

Once empowered by sharing the tasks of the development process democratically, your group will likely prefer to maintain an active role in the management of its environment. The skills gained through participatory decision-making will translate directly to the needs for self-management, making the transition easier, and ensuring the ongoing success of your project.

Certain management requirements are likely regardless of the unique aspects of your project. Ongoing management operations include collecting monthly payments from each member or owner, finding new members for spaces when they become vacant or for sale, paying operating expenses and debt service, and keeping the property well maintained.

If your member organization is small, you may be able to divide these tasks among yourselves with few problems or hire one member of the group to perform key tasks. A slightly larger group might share responsibility for all nonfinancial tasks, but consider hiring a professional accountant for preparing tax returns and keeping the building's books.

Moderate-size to large organizations that choose not to have a professional management service need to set up formal mechanisms for managing the property. The members' preferences or the requirements of others may lead to contracting for various management services. Written agreements are used to detail the division of volunteer labor within the group and the process of hiring help for jobs that volunteers are unwilling or unable to do.

Certain forms of loans, such as FHA mortgages, may require that you employ a professional management service. Some condominium associations also require this. A professional management team usually receives a fee of from 3 to 5 percent of rents collected for managing the property.

FOUNDATION FOR SELF-MANAGEMENT

The successful management of finances, property and personnel allows a self-managed project to operate effectively. If, during the development phase, you have already organized as a cooperative or residents' association, with a board of directors, officers and committees, and if you have a newsletter or other means to facilitate communications, you have a solid foundation for efficient management to provide the following:

- lines of communication within the group
- a division of tasks
- a routine of set meeting times
- a system of committees to deal with important issues
- established goals and elected leadership to help you achieve those goals
- policies for dealing with potential problems

The strength of your cooperative organization is in its democratic processes. These processes set it apart from ordinary tenant-landlord relationships. The sense of community and group control is a key benefit. A participatory spirit incorporated into the conduct of your co-op will ensure a viable business enterprise. Management success will ultimately depend upon your group's ability to direct the affairs of the corporation and to carry out routine and preventive maintenance.

RESPONSIBILITY

In all cooperatives, the members are the owners and, through their board of directors, the highest authority. It is their responsibility to keep informed and vote intelligently. The membership elects the board of directors and delegates power to it. It is the board's responsibility to administer

**Lowertown Lofts, St. Paul.
Artists relaxing in studio space.**

to control their environment. Through democratic decision making, a foundation is built to create a special place for living and working that celebrates its own diversity. When efforts are made to make life together pleasant and successful, the benefits of community life become evident.

For a group of individuals, learning how to work together toward a common goal is seldom easy. Living in the same building together can heighten the stresses. Therefore, the group must learn to honor differences of opinion without losing sight of shared goals. Individuals must sometimes put ego aside for the common good.

Often a few members do most of the work, while others are reluctant to participate. Encouraging new people to volunteer helps them to get involved and perhaps to learn new skills. Those who do not volunteer may need to be drafted directly. Designated board liaisons can act as official communication links with other members to reduce the probability of misinformation or mistrust developing among those less directly involved. A shared task gives everyone something in common to talk about. Members of the group learn about one another through the process of working together.

All groups will experience changes in the level of members' participation. Some members may change the types of activities that interest them. Others may go through periods of personal changes, leaving little time to devote to group activities. Keeping the group informed, focused on a common goal, and ready to share tasks helps rejuvenate group energy and keeps participation broad.

the affairs of the organization, assisted by committees and often by hired staff, and report back to the membership. Committees act as assistants to the board, making recommendations on policy and carrying out specific tasks. Ultimately they are responsible to the membership.

WORKING TOGETHER TO BUILD COMMUNITY

Cooperative members benefit from participation in the entire planning and management process because the process provides the means

The First Annual Meeting

Many members are likely to have been active all along in planning your project. Nevertheless, your first meeting after the move-in phase of a project is an excellent time for a review of the basics of your organizational structure. Responsibilities of the board and committees can be reviewed and the overall project mission reaffirmed. The chain of command and necessary paper trail may be noted.

During the meeting it may be helpful to break into small groups for a discussion of issues so that everyone has an opportunity to speak or to ask questions. For example, small groups can discuss current needs, clarify what members want, and then report back to the reconvened group.

This meeting is also an occasion for recognizing those who worked hard to bring the vision to fruition and to celebrate what has been accomplished.

Initial Leadership Changes

Moving into the building signals a move into the next management phase. The procedures and schedule for electing new officers usually will have been established before your move into the building, and the election of your first board usually occurs at the first annual meeting. The leadership that brought you into the building may have acquired a good deal of expertise. However, they may also be tired. Hard-working committee members may also need a break. The move into the building is a good time for fresh energy. Perhaps new leadership has been groomed and is ready to take over. To maintain some continuity,

Lowertown Lofts.
Artists inspecting construction together.

210

staggered appointments are useful. Allow experienced people to serve as a transition team to advise less experienced or new board members.

PLANNING

Planning is the means through which the group creates its future together. The planning skills you have developed along the way will continue to be called upon in a self-managed property.

IDENTIFYING COMMITMENTS AND PRIORITIES

Create a visual master calendar for each year showing the meetings and commitments as set forth in your articles, bylaws and other documents. Add to it as the work of committees dictates. It will help everyone to be realistic about the amount of work that may be accomplished in a given period.

Identify the important issues that need the group's attention and rank the priority order in which they will be addressed. Assess the amount of attention each needs and establish dates for recommendations from assigned committees. Now that you have moved into the building, new issues may have arisen, and committees may have to be reconfigured to reflect them.

Each committee should brainstorm and decide upon the priorities among its monthly routines, annual routines, and other responsibilities as members perceive them. Committees should annually review and, if necessary, prepare new committee job descriptions detailing the purpose, specific duties and responsibilities, the role in educating members, and the role in planning, monitoring and reporting on the plan. Committee job descriptions should also define the nature of

members' authority, specify their regularly scheduled meeting dates, and include a list of committee members.

Committee task recommendations should be prepared as objective statements in a consolidated written plan, listing due dates, resources needed and people responsible for completion. You should evaluate annually whether goals are being met and revise the overall plan to keep moving toward a goal despite changes in conditions or a failure of some ideas.

EVALUATING PERFORMANCE AND BUILDING CONTINUITY

Organizational health will come by establishing continuity through written goals, policies, management structure, records and evaluation procedures. These elements allow an organization to learn from and build upon its experiences. Written records establish accountability and increase efficiency to ensure that the group does not lose the insights gained in completing a project nor lose track of important goals because of changes in committee membership.

Year-round evaluation practices enable the organization to respond continually to changes. Evaluation procedures track the processes that were used and the goals that were reached for each effort undertaken. The information is a valuable resource when a similar task is to be undertaken by a new group of volunteers. In this manner, the cooperative is not dependent on specific individuals and the expertise of the group is increased.

A report format can be developed to document the processes used on each task, to be filled out before attention is turned to the next task. The form should have a place to list the name of the program or task, the dates of initiation and completion, and the committee or people responsible. The format should meet the needs of your group and provide a quick and consistent means of gathering evaluative data from your committees or staff.

A list of questions can be developed that reflects the group's goals and needs for evaluative data. Questions may include the following: What was the goal and how well was it accomplished? How could the process used to accomplish the goal be improved? What were the major areas of difficulty and how were they overcome? What side benefits resulted from the project? How much time did the project take? How much money and what other resources did the project require? Should the project be done again and in what manner?

An annual evaluation of plans and operations can help to guide plans for the upcoming year. By confirming what has been done, how effective it was, how much was spent, and what can be done to sustain progress, the group gains important awareness of its current status. This annual evaluation may also be the appropriate time for evaluating the effectiveness of staff and volunteers, committee chairs, the board and its officers, and the group's relationships with outside service providers, neighborhood groups and city agencies.

To improve the skills of staff, board, committees or others, it is important to begin with formal job descriptions that set out clear job responsibilities for which staff can be made accountable. Once it has been determined that different tasks or skills are needed in a position, the person holding that position should be given an opportunity to meet the expectations of that position. Paid staff should be replaced if they are unable to meet the stated expectations of the group.

Create a process that is impersonal, yet one that allows differences to be heard. The emphasis should be on improving skills, creating more realistic plans, and adjusting budget projections. If program progress is not being furthered or if efficiency is being hampered, something should

be changed. The management structure must be flexible to respond to the changing needs of the group. Changes should come formally, officially, and with advance notice to ensure that all parties understand the basis for them.

POLICY SETTING TO EASE OPERATIONS

Policies are statements of intent. They provide a consistent basis for decision making to alleviate misunderstandings at the beginning. Once policies have been adopted, they save the group's time for more important things. In creating policies, the group learns how "to be" together. The number of policies a co-op develops is reflective of the time and energy members are willing to devote to creating them and the collective sense of how much control the co-op should exert over its members.

Policies often state desired types of behavior or establish limits, for example, on how late at night loud noise can be made. Behavioral policies are usually stated as "house rules." Management issues that reoccur will also benefit from policy guidelines and may include methods for handling different situations, maintenance, improvement standards and governing relationships.

COMPLAINTS AND HOUSE RULES

Many complaints can be avoided by compiling information about general agreements between residents in a set of "house rules" or operating policies. These rules of "etiquette" can guide disputes about noise levels, animal conduct, use of common space, and other issues of common courtesy.

An established procedure and chain of communication for complaints is usually incorpor-

Project Artaud, San Francisco. Artists' meeting.

ated into your occupancy agreements. A complaint usually is submitted to a designated person in writing, proposing a solution, and then is discussed at the next appropriate meeting.

Project Artaud, a live/work space project established in 1971 in San Francisco, has an arbitration committee with authority to "conduct fair and objective hearings of disagreements between members." Hearings are to result in a course of action to be followed by the involved parties, but are subordinate to rulings established by the board of directors or members' ballot.

House Rules at Project Artaud describe both informal and formal hearings. Failure to comply with a mandatory decision of the arbitration committee can result in eviction. Nonmandatory decisions are recommendations for a course of action between parties and are not binding. Appeals can be made to the board of directors or to the membership if requested.

LISTING CONCERNS

To establish policies, a committee may wish to begin by listing issues and concerns that face the group. Once all issues are listed for the group to see, they can be discussed and clarified. Policy statements can then be developed to state how the committee feels each issue should be addressed, as a "means" or an "end." The group ranks the relative importance of each issue by consensus or majority vote. By the end of the meeting, the committee will have decided what policies it wishes to recommend to the board and membership for approval.

REVIEWING POLICIES

When creating or changing policies, your group should refer to its mission and goals. A periodic evaluation by the board or a committee will determine the effectiveness of current policies in serving the group's goals and objectives. If a review indicates that certain policies are not serving their functions, appropriate changes or new policies can then be recommended to the membership for approval. The board should schedule time and resources to ensure that policy review is not neglected in the flurry of other business.

A policy can be reviewed with the following questions in mind: Does it aid in the achievement of goals and objectives? Does it facilitate decision making? Does it provide a fair and consistent basis for decision making? Is it being followed consistently?

Equally important, members must understand what the policies or standards are, how to implement them, and why they are important. Publicize policies and amendments so that the members are familiar with them and are able to understand the basis for decisions made by the board of directors. Publicity can take the form of announcements in the newsletter, special flyers, announcements at members' meetings, or postings on bulletin boards. A "Policy Book" that lists all policies and amendments by subject as they are adopted will provide an up-to-date reference.

OPERATING HANDBOOKS

Many essential documents should be organized for ready reference by the board of directors to aid its decision making. Ideally, the board handbook should contain agendas and minutes of board meetings; operating and capital budgets; financial statements; policies; articles; bylaws; occupancy agreements; master lease; partnership agreements or other important documents; organizational charts; job descriptions for board members, committees and staff; a list of committee members; membership phone directory; and a long-range plan, including goals and objectives.

To avoid having to answer the same questions repeatedly, your organization may want to create a member's handbook to give to each resident. The handbook could be prepared by the membership committee, the newsletter committee, the maintenance committee or an ad hoc committee drawing on members at large.

The members handbook typically covers a wide range of information. It is an opportunity to tell the history of the group as well as to present general policies and house rules. Copies of articles and bylaws may be included along with names and numbers of other residents, staff and committee members, and emergency phone numbers. Once prepared, such a handbook is typically presented at the time a member receives his or her signed occupancy agreement. A refundable deposit paid by each new member ensures that the handbook will remain with the unit and be passed from member to member.

MAINTENANCE

Whether you rely on paid staff, an outside management team, or almost totally on member volunteers, occupancy of your project will require the formation of a maintenance committee. The committee members do not perform the labor of maintenance, but rather study conditions and recommend policies and procedures for the following functions:

- maintaining a sound building structure, ensuring safety and security
- keeping mechanical systems and services in good functioning order
- providing good housekeeping and cleanliness in all common areas, recreation areas and around the exterior
- scheduling periodic capital improvements, such as exterior patching and painting, new roof, plumbing or electrical upgrades when needed

Mechanical systems such as heat, light, and water require some services even when they are operating smoothly. Who will be responsible for replacing furnace filters or common area light bulbs, or dealing with plumbing problems? The maintenance committee generally sets up a maintenance team, which consists of the maintenance committee, the property manager and the maintenance staff. Through planning and organizing a maintenance program, the team establishes what is to be done, when, how, and by whom.

The maintenance team will review activities every month to evaluate progress and determine how to improve existing procedures to get the desired results.

Making Work Assignments

Make a detailed work list (see box 11.1) for the common areas, exterior and mechanical systems, noting the job and frequency of performance.

11.1   WORK LIST

	Task:	Schedule:
Entrance Lobby Floors	Sweep, damp mop and/or vacuum	daily
Walls/Ceilings	Spot clean walls	weekly
	Wash walls	twice yearly
Light Fixtures (hallways, laundry, stairwells, storage room, garage, elevator)	Check all fixtures and replace bulbs	weekly

---

Once you have a comprehensive list, you can assign the work. At a general meeting the membership should discuss which tasks members are willing and able to do on a volunteer basis, and which ones will have to be done by hired employees. Wages, if approved, would come from the operating budget. Volunteer assistance for minor tasks allows funds to be put into the contingency fund to help pay for emergency repairs and capital improvements and keep overall costs lower to members.

A schedule or chart shows who is responsible for what. Make sure all tasks are covered by correlating the Assignment Chart (see box 11.2) with the Work List.

Establishing Maintenance Policies

To ensure the long-term maintenance and desirability of units to future members, the management committee may choose to define standards for care of individual units. Many co-ops hold annual unit inspections. Maintenance standards need not be strict or rigid, but those selected should be formally described in the house rules or operating policies section of the member's handbook. Information about how the general maintenance program works and procedures for inspections, repairs and emergencies might also be provided.

The maintenance committee can consider policies for the maintenance care of walls, windows, floor coverings, etc. For example, when and how often should common areas be cleaned or painted? Will it be a policy to have members clean common areas, or will staff be hired to perform that function? On what basis will private live/work areas be painted? Who will do the painting, and who will supply the paint? Who chooses the color, and who supplies the tools? If members are to do the painting, helpful information on materials and procedures may also be provided.

Policies may also set out approved and unapproved methods for hanging pictures or objects on walls; whether the member is responsible for taking down and putting up screens and storm windows; who is responsible for cleaning inaccessible exterior sides of windows; how heat should be conserved, for example, keeping windows closed. Other policy areas that the maintenance committee may address are the operation of ap-

11.2 ROUTINE MAINTENANCE ASSIGNMENT CHART

	Residents	Manager	Other Paid Help
clean lobby			
clean halls			
shovel walks			
maintain bulletin boards			
check lighting			
water grass			
cut grass			
clean laundry room			
painting			

pliances, electrical systems, heaters, and air conditioners.

Policies may be established to address health and safety hazards, including materials and procedures that are forbidden or the precautions to be followed. For example, members may be prohibited from storing gasoline, oil or large quantities of paint in their units. Basic safety rules for avoiding electrical or other hazards may also be provided. Common sense requests may be listed to ensure that members do not block fire exits or disconnect smoke detectors. The procedure in case of fire can be described and, in some cases, periodic fire drills may be warranted. The garbage pickup schedule can be noted along with special instructions for separation of particular items for recycling.

IMPROVEMENTS BY MEMBERS

Members may want to make major alterations to their units tailored to their unique space and storage needs. These might include replacing or refinishing flooring, adding lofts or mezzanines, adding electrical outlets or fixtures, installing or replacing plumbing fixtures, altering the number of rooms, or building in darkrooms, storage closets, wall units, etc. The cooperative must be consistent in handling approvals for changes and consider a number of factors when determining policies. Will the renovation increase or reduce the number of rooms? Is this desirable? Will the renovation plans violate any local or state building or safety codes? Will the renovations enhance the unit in terms of future marketability? Is the addition a generic improvement that most artists can use? Is it an improvement that will be unique to a media type or an individual need? Will the workmanship be of acceptable quality? Will the work be finished in a reasonable length of time? Will the cooperative pay for any materials? Who will "own" the improvements should the member leave? How will improvement costs be calculated as a transfer value when the member leaves the cooperative? Will a depreciation factor be applied?

Some protection against inferior workmanship might be insured by entering into a simple contract between the member and the board before the work is started. For example, the job should be done in a certain length of time and meet the standards of local building codes and of

216

the group. Group standards should be objectively defined and written as policy before any improvements are made by members. If the standards are not met, the member might be required to return the unit to its original state or to pay to bring the alterations up to stated standards. The Lowertown Lofts Cooperative in St. Paul keeps a design committee active to oversee unit improvements, exhibitions in common areas, and to track changes in share transfer values.

Each case may be decided individually, keeping a written record of the decisions made. The maintenance committee should try not to act like a landlord, yet it should keep the overall interests of the group in mind.

PAPERWORK SYSTEMS

All committees and any paid staff will generate a fair amount of paper. A cardboard box will quickly become an inefficient way to store important data about the members, the building, suppliers, programs, financial matters, and tool and supply inventories.

Create a filing system that ensures easy filing and retrieval of information by all users. Labeled notebooks can help keep many kinds of information in order, especially so that "only" copies of documents are not lost. Standard forms are excellent for keeping track of information in a consistent way and may be stored in labeled boxes or manila folders with appropriate headings. One set of all the important documents, minutes, policies, reports and records should be maintained for ready reference. A safe deposit box is the best place for original copies of the mortgage, deed, articles of incorporation and other important papers.

Photocopying machines will get a lot of use in most cooperatives, as will a typewriter or computer and a calculator. Include them in the capital costs for your project during the planning phase if possible. Used equipment may be a cost-effective choice. Consider policies for their use and service contracts as part of your planning.

Members' Records and Building Data

The following records should be kept for members: applications, signed occupancy agreements, condition of unit, improvements to unit, damages, and violations of policies. Files will be important for tracking building information, including the square footage of each space, warranties on equipment, "as-built" drawings, and records of additional improvements for planning renovations or repairing mechanical systems.

Lowertown Lofts. Resident artist/member of the management committee sweeping up.

Management of Keys

Controlling security through the management of keys will require a storage cabinet, with hooks and labels, that can be locked. A notebook or card file can be used to record lists of which doors have locks, who is entitled to a key for each lock, systems that are on master keys, and who has copies of those keys. Your file should include a place to record when the key was given out and returned. Areas of the building with limited access include those areas for the use of members only, such as laundry or storage rooms, and those limited to certain personnel, such as the co-op office or mechanical rooms.

Policies and procedures will need to be determined for the use of keys, when locks can be changed and by whom, and whether members can make duplicate keys. A related topic for policy development is how members are to be assisted if they inadvertently lock themselves out of their units. Who is to be called? Will there be a fee for the assistance?

PERSONNEL

Certainly the more tasks and responsibilities that can be done by group member volunteers, the more money the cooperative will save. Committees and individuals who volunteer their time are a tremendous resource. Jobs well done should be given formal recognition and expressed appreciation.

When a task requires more than a reasonable commitment of time and energy, the organization should consider paying someone to do it. Asking too much of a single member or an overworked committee can be exploitative. Other reasons for hiring staff or a property management company might be the need for particular skills or the need to have a task performed regularly at a certain time. If staff are hired, you will need to establish personnel policies and hiring procedures, set up lines of communication and supervision, and write a job description by which to monitor performance.

A large cooperative may wish to hire one or more part- or full-time employees to take on part of the workload. The group may hire a property manager, for example, who would report to the board of directors. The manager would hire and manage other needed service people on contract.

Whether paid or volunteer, personnel may be needed to act in the following capacities, among others:

- **MEMBER SELECTION COMMITTEE.** Establish and periodically review member selection criteria and selection process; accept and review applications; interview and select new members; in cooperation with the property manager, oversee moves into or out of units.

- **PROPERTY MANAGER.** Hire and supervise repair people for complex repairs; collect member carrying charges and other receivables; accept deliveries, answer phone inquiries; in cooperation with the membership committee, assist moves into or out of units; control keys.

- **BOOKKEEPER.** Prepare general ledger and trial balance; write checks (payables).

- **FINANCIAL MANAGER.** Manage accounting records, long-term financial planning; plan capital improvements; develop budgets; complete tax forms.

- **GENERAL HANDYMAN.** Handle basic repairs and routine maintenance; stock building with required supplies; maintain heating and electrical systems, periodically checking for bootlegged circuits.

- **JANITORIAL SERVICES.** Clean common areas, wash windows, take out garbage; provide for periodic heavy cleaning tasks, maintenance of outdoor areas.

218

HIRING MEMBERS

One option when hiring staff is to draw from the group membership, assuming the member has the desired skills and qualifications. Hiring from among the members would contribute to the overall purpose of the cooperative—to benefit its members. It could also ensure greater availability. For example, a member who worked on the maintenance staff would be readily on hand for emergencies.

On occasion, however, hiring members can backfire. It is more difficult to reprimand a neighbor and fellow member for a poor job than it would be to do this to an outsider. You can avoid most misunderstandings by preparing a written work order, describing the work to be done, the materials to be used, and the date the work is to be completed. Be sure the person being hired has the skills that are needed. If possible, have an outside staff member responsible for supervision of staff members hired from the building.

SUPERVISION

Whether members or strangers are employed, it is important to spell out duties in a job description. Also, employees should be made accountable to a specific person, whose name should be noted in the job description. It is impossible for a person to be accountable to a whole group of people. The supervisor, who should be responsible for reviewing the job periodically, is the liaison between the group and the employee.

Poor supervision, a lack of schedule, or unclear expectations with regard to quality can lead to slow work, poor workmanship, and costs that are out of control. Organizing the tasks, instructing the employee as necessary, and inspecting the quality of the work will best serve the overall needs of the cooperative.

SERVICE CONTRACTS

Some jobs needed on a regular basis will require skilled, professional maintenance services, for which service contracts are needed. The most common areas of service contracts are the following:

- fire equipment—regular inspection and servicing of all fire equipment including extinguishers, sprinklers, detector systems, etc.

- pest control—initial extermination, periodic visits to control the problem

- heavy cleaning—cleaning firms can be contracted for shampooing rugs, stripping and waxing floors in common areas, washing windows, etc.

- furnace—yearly cleaning and servicing of the furnace, burner and the supply of small parts

Other service contracts may cover the elevator; coin-operated laundry; snow removal; office equipment service, such as computers and copiers; mechanical systems (ventilators); water treatment equipment; pump service; and landscape service. Major repairs, improvements, or renovations may entail hiring members of the construction trades.

Even though the contractor performs the service, it is still your group's responsibility to see that the service is carried out and the terms of the contract are met. The property manager, supervisor, or member of the maintenance team should oversee or inspect important services.

For small jobs—under $500—most contractors prefer not to give quotes or bids. The contractor is required to visit the job site for which time the contractor will not get paid and for a job they may not even get. Contractors prefer simply to do the required task for time and materials. Sometimes they can give you a rough estimate over the phone, or at least provide their hourly rate and give a verbal description of how they would handle a task. It is best to give these small jobs to a contractor whose skill and honesty are respected by the co-op or recommended by others.

Jobs ranging from $500 to $2,000 should have a written description of the desired task and materials to be used, along with a simple contract. Two or three contractors should be asked to bid on the job.

For technical or expensive jobs ($2,000 or more), it may be a good idea to get bids by issuing a "request for bids" or "bid call." The maintenance committee collects all the facts relevant to the work to be done and confirms the co-op's ability to pay the anticipated cost using replacement reserves or alternative financing. A request for bid is prepared outlining the conditions of the work, schedule, provisions for inspection of work, etc. Contractors then submit their bids with enough information for the cooperative to make an informed decision about which contractor to hire. (See box 11.3)

All contractors should be asked to bid on the same specifications. If design or material changes are proposed by some contractors or other changes are approved by the committee in order to lower the costs, consider giving all contractors the changed information to ensure that you are comparing "apples to apples."

Members often have friends who want to bid on work. Anyone who knows a bidding party should excuse themselves from a vote on which contractor is to be hired, in keeping with conflict-of-interest policies.

FISCAL PLANNING

For the corporation to succeed, it must be established on sound financial principles, ensuring that the income at least equals the expense. Once mid-term and long-term objectives

---

11.3 FROM BIDS TO CONTRACTS

- Maintenance committee recommends work and procedure after consulting with finance committee
- Board of directors and general membership approves proposal and budget
- Maintenance committee prepares bid request, selects contractors to invite to participate in making a bid
- Call for bids issued
- Bids received and opened at designated place and time
- Board of directors approves awarding of contract
- Meeting(s) with contractor to confirm contract
- Work begins and is monitored by co-op representative
- A signed lien waiver is obtained before making a final payment

---

have been identified and given priority, planning decisions must be made about the best and least costly methods of achieving the goals. The heart of this process is fiscal planning.

The co-op corporation budget is prepared on an annual basis. Under some circumstances, the budget may need to be submitted to the mortgage insurer or a property owner in a leasehold co-op for review and approval 60 days before the end of the fiscal year. In all periods other than the first year of operation, budgets are prepared with only nine months of actual operating information on hand, requiring that operating costs be estimated for the remaining three months.

The budget will usually be reported on and reviewed at monthly meetings. Through committee requests, what everyone needs or wants becomes known. The group may wish to consider, beyond rent, other potential sources of income, including parking space rental, laundry and vending machines, rental of common space for events, and rooftop rental for billboards. Looking together at its resources and funds, the group can come up with a realistic set of priorities. Budget items costing more than $500 will usually be discussed and voted upon by the board of directors, unless there is an emergency or safety consequence. The membership may choose to vote on proposed expenses that exceed $2,000.

CLASSIFYING EXPENSES BY AREAS

Good planning will balance the group's interest in minimizing expenses with the need to plan for maintenance of the property. The group can set up policies with controls to ensure that authorized purchases are made. Members can be educated to conserve energy to lower utility costs. Typically, the expenses associated with operating your property will be in three major areas: current operations, long-term needs, and unexpected financial needs.

Current Operations

Planning for current operations should include provisions for payment of the following:

- debt service—prompt payment of mortgage interest, principal and mortgage insurance premium (if any) must be made to avoid substantial penalties or mortgage default

- utilities—those paid by the cooperative

- insurance—adequate coverage should be determined for workers' compensation (including members doing volunteer work), liability, property, director's and officer's liability, employee dishonesty, "rent" interruption (Insurance should be reviewed periodically to adjust coverage for inflation.)

- payroll, payroll taxes, fringe benefits— prompt and adequate compensation allows you to demand top performance from your employees

- service contracts—attorney, auditor, elevator, pest control, other maintenance and janitorial should be included

- administrative costs—manager, committee and co-op communications, office expenses, postage, copying should be included

- supplies—maintenance and janitorial

- taxes—real estate, personal property (if taxed), licensing fees

- insurance loss—when a loss is incurred, you are required to pay any deductible amount and the insurance company will pay the rest

Long-Term Needs

Provisions for replacement of plant and equipment, capital improvements and reserve requirements are long-term needs and may change with the needs of your group. They include the following:

- physical structure

- systems—plumbing, heating, electrical

- underground—utilities, sewage, water

- sidewalks and parking

- painting of common areas

- upgrade and improve grounds; seed or sod, shrubs, etc.

- recreational equipment

- increase parking facilities

- security fencing and/or lighting

- signs

Unexpected Financial Needs

Your organization needs to set aside a General Operating Reserve (GOR) to cover unexpected financial needs. To make provision for unexpected costs, it is recommended that you set aside additional rents on a monthly basis at a rate of 3 percent of budgeted carrying charges. Some costs you may not anticipate are:

- real estate tax increases in mid-fiscal year

- excessively hot or cold weather, which causes cooperative-paid utility bills to increase beyond budget projections

- unexpected large increases in water/sewer rates

- casualty losses not fully covered by insurance

- immediate energy-related capital costs that cannot wait, such as energy-saving measures or retrofitting of individual electric meters on master-metered projects

- breakdown of a major system

- legal costs

CLASSIFYING EXPENSES BY DEGREE OF CONTROL

Most cooperative members are unaware that the board of directors actually controls a relatively small percentage of the operating budget. The difficulties encountered in preparing the budget are best illustrated by looking at budget items in another way—dividing the budget into three categories of expenses: fixed, partially controllable, and controllable expenses:

Fixed Expenses

Fixed expenses are stipulated by contract or by law, and the board is obligated to meet them in the required time period. They include the following:

- real estate taxes
- special assessments
- permits, registration fees
- payroll taxes
- property and liability insurance
- workers' compensation
- mortgage interest and principal
- mortgage insurance premium
- General Operating Reserve

Partially Controllable Expenses

Although the board can determine the level of funding for the following expenses, it cannot eliminate the items:

- vacancy and collection loss
- management fee
- miscellaneous administration expenses
- legal expenses
- janitor and maintenance supplies
- audit expenses
- office expenses
- telephone
- payroll
- fuel
- electricity
- water and sewer
- trash collection

Emeryville Artists' Cooperative, Emeryville, CA. Old gas stove in live/work space.

Controllable Expenses

The board not only sets the level of funding for controllable expenses but may also eliminate specific items. Standard budget items are as follows:

- rehabilitation expenses
- employee health insurance
- employee apartment rent
- grounds maintenance
- petty cash
- painting and decorating
- association dues
- repairs
- vehicle expense
- painting reserve
- uniforms
- project equipment purchase
- miscellaneous insurance
- exterminating

Required Reserves

The maintenance committee will often be best suited to planning for the cooperative's reserve funds. The co-op may wish to set aside reserves in addition to those that are required. It costs more to repair than to maintain a building, so it makes sense to plan for the ongoing expenses.

The General Operating Reserve is generally used for anything that affects the operation of the cooperative. It is meant to be a source of help in case of short-term financial hardship. Generally, no more than 20 percent of the GOR should be used at any one time, although its use is at the discretion of the cooperative board. Any use of funds from GOR must be paid back in subsequent budget periods. The GOR should not take the place of long-range financial planning and sound management. Funding the reserve is made by collecting additional rent at 3 percent of monthly collections. The amount collected is reduced after the GOR reaches 25 percent of cooperative's annual operating expense. The purpose of the Reserve for Replacement (RR) is to ensure availability of funds to replace a variety of installed appliances or other items in a building that suffer from wear and tear. Funding the reserve is made by collecting additional rent at 2 percent or more of monthly collections.

Common items needing eventual replacement include refrigerators, stoves, water heaters, furnaces, clothes washers and dryers, etc. Less obvious items that may require replacement include cabinets and counter tops, floor tile, ceramic tile (bathroom), wood floor (refinishing), windows, wiring, plumbing, exterior surfaces (siding), roofs (shingles, etc.), parking lot or sidewalks (resurfacing).

The board of directors or management must establish long-term plans to care for, maintain, and replace some of the following items in a cooperative. Check with manufacturers as you prepare your replacement reserve. Depending on the quality of the product, estimated life expectancies are as follows, all in years:

- roofs   15-20
- furnaces   10-15
- stoves   10-15
- dryers   10-12
- reroofing   8-15
- refrigerators   8-12
- dishwashers   8-12
- water heaters   8-12
- carpeting   6-10
- washers   6-8
- floor tile   5-10
- garbage disposal   5-8

COLLECTING MONTHLY INCOME

At the heart of your budget and operations are the monthly association dues or carrying charges. For groups operating as some form of nonprofit organization, monies paid go directly back into the building budget for its operations or its reserves. If payments are not received on time, your expenses as a group will not be covered, and the group could lose its building.

To avoid confusion about when or where payments should be made, or who should collect them, this information can be included in the occupancy agreement or house rules provided to each resident.

Before the beginning of your occupancy, a group meeting can be held to discuss monthly payments. Seek agreement on a time of the month to pay and a person to receive it. This same officer

or committee can be responsible for keeping records or for delivering the monthly carrying charges to whomever is in charge of keeping income records. A separate person should be responsible for paying bills to provide for checks and balances.

Most groups collect an additional month's rent as a security deposit, and some collect monthly charges as much as two weeks early to ensure that there is time to deposit all checks. Some groups allow security deposits to be paid in partial payments. Policies for late payments usually require an escalating fee, although a $5 discount on rent paid early often has a more positive effect than imposing a $5 fine for late payment. In those situations, the discounted rate is really the amount of monthly charges that would need to be collected per unit to begin with. Require members to make all payments by check or money order to avoid accounting problems and arguments. Accepting cash payments creates a security problem for the collecting agent and the cooperative.

PREPARING TO FIND NEW MEMBERS

SETTING POLICY

Long before you need to use it, determine the policy that applies to the resale of a unit, particularly the equity and transfer value available to the vacating member. The value will be guided by the decisions made in establishing your cooperative, although refining the details can be one of the most stressful decisions a committee may have to make. The choice will be between benefiting the vacating member and ensuring that the entry costs remain low for prospective members. Both sides of the discussion have valid points. Each cooperative group must decide for

224

itself. Records will need to be maintained for each unit to retain the history of improvements, increases in share values, and accounting records for unit changeovers.

When a member decides to move, the maintenance committee will usually complete an inspection before the move to evaluate the condition of the unit and the value of any improvements made by the member. Information will be kept on a form in a file for that unit. If annual inspections or inspections after improvements have already been made, and records have been kept, the committee may inspect the unit after the member has moved out, but before the return of the security deposit. The departing member should be provided with an opportunity to make repairs

or clean the unit to avoid an assessment.

Inspecting the Space

The committee makes an appointment with the vacating member to inspect the space jointly. The inspection should determine whether the unit is ready to show to prospective members, whether any damage occurred during the move, and whether any parts need to be replaced or repairs need to be made. At issue will be the transfer value of the vacating member's share and the marketability of the unit to a new member. Policies will determine who is responsible for repainting and repairs. In some cases, it may be the vacating member, in others the co-op. It may

Torpedo Factory, Alexandria. Artist in studio.

also be possible to locate a new member who is willing to undertake the repairs. From the maintenance committee's perspective, it is important that whoever does repaint or repair the unit does so in a proper manner. Ongoing maintenance care will avoid the gradual deterioration of the unit and the accompanying erosion of the character of the building.

Showing the Unit

In lieu of arranging for a paid property manager to show the available space to prospective members and to receive phone inquiries about it, a membership committee may decide to have one its members take responsibility. One committee member with an answering machine may be designated as the primary representative, with other committee members taking responsibility for the other tasks.

SELECTING THE RIGHT MEMBERS

Policies, which may already be incorporated in your bylaws or house rules, will vary on the procedures for selecting new members. The selection criteria used when getting your project initiated may continue to be valid, with some alterations. When qualifying prospective members, you will probably need to be even more rigorous than the average landlord. And with good reason! You are selecting someone to join your community, to share in the tasks of management, and to bring his or her unique qualities to join in the group's vision.

It is critical to apply selection criteria to all candidates uniformly. Legally you cannot reject an applicant on the basis of race, color, religion, nationality or sex. Further, you cannot discriminate against families with children. In some

states it is also illegal to reject applicants because of their source of income, physical disabilities, or marital status. You may discriminate against nonartists if you have been established to serve artists. Applicants may also be turned down if they have no rental history, a poor rental history, no credit or bad credit, insufficient income, inaccurate or incomplete information on their application form, or their family size exceeds the number of persons legally allowed to share the number of bedrooms you have available. In projects using city financing to serve low- and moderate-income artists, applicants may be turned away if their income exceeds the limits established for your project.

Your application process may include a portfolio review, interview by a committee of members, and a processing fee to cover the costs of a credit check. The interview process is an excellent opportunity to provide information about the importance each member plays as part of the cooperative. Remember that questions during the interview should not touch on matters related to the candidate's protected-class status.

Because of the special needs met in an artist's live/work space project, there is likely to be a waiting list of potential members. Or a quick response may come via the artist "grapevine" when a unit becomes available.

On occasion, it will be necessary for the group to solicit potential members actively. Sources for low-cost advertising include bulletin boards, especially in art colleges and neighborhoods where artists already frequent. A flyer, with space information on it, may be posted, handed out, or mailed. You should contact other artist spaces in your community and put the word out with local arts organizations. Ads may be placed in local arts newsletters, or a sign may be placed on your building. If all else fails, you may want to try paid advertising in the local newspaper, which is most cost-effective if printed in the Sunday edition. (See box 11.4.)

11.4 TEN COMMON PROBLEMS FACED BY COOPERATIVES AND HOW TO HANDLE THEM

ANXIETY WHEN A UNIT BECOMES AVAILABLE AND A NEW MEMBER MUST BE SELECTED. A co-op is membership based and the most important decision a co-op can make is the selection of new members. Do not panic. It is better to use your vacancy fund to cover a vacant space for a month than to accept an inappropriate member. Build a waiting list for future vacancies.

The membership committee should be delegated full authority and the "sacred duty" of selecting new members without being overruled by the board. At least three members of the committee should commit to going through all of the interviews at any one time to provide a consistent review for all candidates. If a friend or relative is applying, the related member should not be involved in the selection decision due to a conflict of interest. Consider a policy to establish a preliminary provisional membership level for three months, and if the new member becomes active in the co-op at that time, they can then convert to a full membership.

A NEED TO TRAIN AND EDUCATE MEMBERS IN THE RIGHTS, RESPONSIBILITIES, OPTIONS AND OPERATIONS OF A COOPERATIVE. To ensure that members become effective participants in the co-op, establish an education committee to prepare a standard process for introducing new members to those things with which earlier members have become familiar. It is important to be clear about the history of the project, expectations and responsibilities. Create a "buddy system" so that a new member has one person they can always go to if they have a question. Rotate responsibility for hosting and chairing each month's meeting to build leadership skills.

If co-op leadership or management training was not provided to the initial members before moving in, seek local, regional or national sources to hire a training consultant for the full group. Information may include co-op laws, the role of board, committees, parliamentary procedures, legal documents, management tasks and contracts, co-op annual budget, cash flow reports, monthly financial reports, purchasing procedures, maintenance, resale policies, new member selection, volunteer opportunities and community relations.

FEELING OVERWHELMED BY ALL THERE IS TO BE RESPONSIBLE FOR. Planning and setting goals and policies are tools to keep the group from falling into crisis management patterns. Put tasks in priority order and schedule reasonable completion dates. As a creative group of people you will always have many more ideas than can be carried out. The committee process can enable the most important ideas to be implemented and other ideas to be scheduled at a later date.

CONFRONTING DELINQUENT MEMBERS FOR PAST DUE PAYMENTS. A co-op is a legal business entity and must operate like a business, even though it is one with "a heart." Begin by selecting members that are likely to be able to afford the unit they wish to rent and check their credit rating. Develop eviction policies that are clear and fair. Become familiar with local unlawful detainer processes and decide what conditions must be met to begin eviction proceedings. Discuss the options with the member and agree upon a course of action as soon as the payment is deemed late. If payment schedules are approved for monthly charges or the security deposit, always get a written, signed, dated and preferably notarized promissory note that details conditions for the approved payment plan. Remember that the other co-op members become liable for any expenses incurred on behalf of the delinquent member. It can be costly to other members to lose more than several months' rent plus incur the costs for filing an unlawful detainer. This aspect may not apply to all self-managed groups if legally established on an independent owner basis.

MISUNDERSTANDINGS AND FRUSTRATION CAUSED EITHER BY A LACK OF POLICY OR BY POLICIES THAT ARE UNCLEAR TO THOSE WHO NEED TO IMPLEMENT THEM. It takes time to develop policies, and experience can be the best teacher concerning the policies you will need to have. The key features of effective policy statements are that they have arisen from a need, they are in writing, and they are clear, objective and enforceable.

PARTICIPATION AT MEETINGS SLACKS OFF, LEAVING SOME BOARD AND COMMITTEE MEMBERS TO "BURN OUT" DUE TO TOO MUCH RESPONSIBILITY. Prepare good agendas, plan for meetings, avoid interpersonal conflicts, and have order at the meetings. Plan some fun. Voluntary participation can be made mandatory. Create an air of expectation that everyone will participate. All members can serve as directors of the board. It is better to trade off the inefficiencies of meetings where the whole membership is engaged in the decisions than it is to create an "us/them" relationship. Keep people motivated by making them feel that what they have done is worth while and that their contributions are considered valuable.

NEW MEMBERS ARE UNCERTAIN AS TO HOW TO GET INVOLVED AND ARE UNFAMILIAR WITH THEIR FELLOW CO-OP MEMBERS. Create a process for new members to meet other members informally and feel welcomed by the group. Build trust by answering questions warmly and openly. Ask about their interests and skills. Invite them to participate in a variety of volunteer tasks, although do not pressure at first. Give a brief sample of committee work, start by assigning a short, easy task or fun job. In addition to developing the business aspects of the co-op, it is important to develop its human and social aspects.

COMMUNICATION PROBLEMS CREATE TENSION OR CONFLICT. The diversity of a cooperative requires special attention to active listening and negotiation skills. It is helpful to be capable of listening to another's point of view without becoming defensive or responding with provoking replies. Clarify the problem or issue, evaluate possible solutions and decide together on the solution most acceptable to all parties. Focus on the areas of agreement instead of those of disagreement. Look at the issue from the angle of what is right rather than who is right. Plan the implementation of the solution and later evaluate whether the solution was satisfactory.

NO ONE IN THE CO-OP HAS ADEQUATE SKILLS TO HANDLE THE BUDGET AND THE ACCOUNTING FOR THE COOPERATIVE. The money must be handled in a scrupulous manner to ensure there are no questions in anyone's mind. It is better to pay for training or actual assistance from a professional accountant or property manager and to pay for an annual audit than to have anyone in the co-op question how the funds are being handled. A financial report should be presented monthly to the members.

VOLUNTEER TASKS NEED TO BE BALANCED WITH MANAGEMENT COMPANY TASKS. Create job descriptions for all tasks, whether performed by the management company or co-op members. Define the management or financial tasks for which to be contracted. Clarify supervision responsibilities between volunteer and paid leadership. Prepare an evaluation process and schedule for both paid and unpaid positions.

Coldside Building, Minneapolis. Live/work space.

Epilogue: Interdependence

Self-managed cooperatives are a means of responding to individual needs that are experienced in common. When living in otherwise nonresidential buildings or neighborhoods, artists tend to be even more dependent on one another to meet their shared needs. Although members of the group will differ widely in their motivation, energy, and contribution to the common good, working collaboratively provides the "human glue" for successful projects. As in all human experience, the benefits of symbiosis are sometimes hindered by parasitic elements. Once problems are identified, however, changes can be implemented, and the synergy of the group enhanced. (See box 11.4.)

In the diversity of their membership, cooperatives contain the seeds for their own regeneration, often with energy enough to carry over for needs outside their own. Within a self-managed community, artists can decide what needs to be done and control how those things will get done. In designing an environment where people work together, share ideas, and learn to respect one another, artists can enjoy the opportunity to create a sense of ownership in the future of the broader neighborhood. Artists can give new life to a building and a neighborhood, creating an identity that is unique.

We live in an age of shifting paradigms. The growing number of artist-run live/work projects parallels other changes on a global level. Hierarchical models of top-down decision making are giving way to the growing empowerment of grassroots, collaborative leadership. As we see our planet-wide interdependence increasing, ecologically and politically, we become more aware of the interdependence of our lives with others in our community. Rather than seeing "what we can get away with," we have a greater sense of responsibility for "doing the right thing."

A collaborative effort to develop and manage a multiunit live/work space project is a good place for you to begin the experience of building a sense of community, while meeting your basic needs and supporting your creative life work.

"Whatever you can do or dream you can do, begin it.
Boldness has genius and magic and power in it."
Goethe

APPLICATION FOR MEMBERSHIP

Greene Street Artists Corporation, a Pennsylvania Non-Profit Corporation
c/o PHPC, 1616 Walnut Street, Suite 2210, Philadelphia, Pa 19103 (215) 546-1146

PLEASE TYPE OR PRINT LEGIBLY

Personal Information:

Name (Applicant 1) _____

Name (Applicant 2) _____

Current address _____

City, State, Zip _____

Phone numbers: Day: _____ Evening: _____

Current monthly rent/mortgage payment $ _____

Current monthly utilities $ _____

How long at current address? _____

Current landlord's name and address _____

City, State, Zip _____

Phone number _____

If you have been at your current address less than one year,
please give your previous address _____

City, State, Zip _____

Previous monthly rent/mortgage payment $ _____

Previous monthly utilities $ _____

How long at previous address? _____

Previous landlord's name and address _____

City, State, Zip _____

Previous landlord's phone number _____

Others who will live with you:

	Name	**Relationship**	**Age**	**Sex**
1.				
2.				
3.				
4.				

Artistic Information:

Artistic Media: _____

_____

Please submit 10-15 slides or other evidence of your recent work. If slides, please indicate media, size and top side. Please also submit a resume describing your art education, professional training, exhibitions, performances and other career information. Include the names of three professional references. A selection committee of artists will go over the materials and interview applicants.

Financial Information:

Income:

Applicant 1:
Primary employer name and address _____

_____

_____

Job title _____

How long employed there? _____   Gross annual income $ _____

Secondary employer name and address _____

_____

_____

Job title _____

How long employed there? _____   Gross annual income $ _____

Applicant 2:
Primary employer name and address _____

_____

_____

Job title _____

How long employed there? _____   Gross annual income $ _____

Secondary employer name and address _____

_____

_____

Job title _____

How long employed there? _____   Gross annual income $ _____

Gross income from your art during the past two years (please explain):

_____

_____

_____

_____

Other income (child support, Social Security, dividends, etc.):

    Source _____

    Years received _____ Years will receive _____

    Gross amount $ _____

Assets (checking accounts, savings accounts, other securities):

1. Bank name and address _____

_____

Account number _____ Type _____

Account balance $ _____

2. Bank name and address _____

_____

Account number _____ Type _____

Account balance $ _____

3. Bank name and address _____

_____

Account number _____ Type _____

Account balance $ _____

Other assets (house, car, etc.):

Item _____ Value $ _____

Item _____ Value $ _____

Item _____ Value $ _____

Liabilities (student loans, car loans, mortgage loans, credit loans, ect.):

1. Creditor name and address _____

_____

Loan/Account number _____ Type _____

Payment amount $ _____   Period _____

Balance $ _____

2. Creditor name and address _____

_____

Loan/Account number _____   Type _____

Payment amount $ _____   Period _____

Balance $ _____

3. Creditor name and address _____

_____

Loan/Account number _____   Type _____

Payment amount $ _____   Period _____

Balance $ _____

4. Creditor name and address _____

_____

Loan/Account number _____   Type _____

Payment amount $ _____   Period _____

Balance $ _____

SOURCES OF TECHNICAL ASSISTANCE AND REFERRALS FOR ARTISTS' SPACE NEEDS

The following organizations provide referrals to other artists, technical information, or development expertise for artists' space needs.

UNITED STATES

National

American Council for the Arts
One East 53rd Street
New York, NY 10022
Marie Walsh Sharpe Foundation
Artist Hotline
(800) 285-2789

Artspace Development Network
c/o Artspace Projects, Inc.
400 First Avenue North, Suite 518
Minneapolis, MN 55401
(612) 339-4372

National Artists Equity
P.O. Box 28068, Central Station
Washington, DC 20038
(202) 628-9633
Catherine Auth, *Executive Director*

National Assembly of Local Arts Agencies (NALAA)
1420 "K" Street N.W., Suite 204
Washington, DC 20005
(202) 371-2830
Olive Mosier, *Vice President and Director of Member Services*

National Assembly of State Arts Agencies (NASAA)
1010 Vermont Avenue N.W., Suite 920
Washington, DC 20005
(202) 347-6352
Jonathan Katz, *Executive Director*

National Association of Artists Organizations
918 "F" Street N.W.
Washington, DC 20004
(202) 347-6350

Partners for Livable Places
1429 21st Street N.W.
Washington, DC 20036
(202) 887-5990
Robert NcNulty, *President*
Ben Silverstein, *Director of Information Resources and Clearinghouse Services*

Arizona

Artlink, Inc.
P.O. Box 3426
Phoenix, AZ 85030
(602) 256-7539
Beatrice Moore, *Director*

Tucson Arts Coalition
P.O. Box 43160
Tucson, Az 85733
(602) 623-2577
Roger Hecht, *Director*

Tucson Pima Arts Council
166 West Alameda
Tucson, AZ 85701
(602) 624-0595
Dian Magie, *Executive Director*

California

ArtHouse
1095 Market Street, Suite 820
San Francisco, CA 94103
(415) 431-0556
Jennifer Spangler, *Director*

Artist Equity Association, Inc.
Northern California Chapter
Carmel, CA 94102
Richard Mayer

Artspace Development Corporation
3004 16th Street, #102
San Francisco, CA 94103
(415) 621-8458 or 331-2076
Martha Senger, *Executive Director*

Bay Area Partnership
337 17th Street
Oakland, CA 94704
(415) 763-8447
Steve Costa, *President*

California Lawyers for the Arts
Fort Mason Center, Building C
San Francisco, CA 94123
(415) 775-7200
Alma Robinson, *Executive Director*

Emeryville Artists Cooperative
1420 45th Street
Emeryville, CA 94608
(415) 655-2880

Innovative Housing, Inc.
Co-Housing Program
325 Doherty Drive
Larkspur, CA 94612
(415) 763-8447
Ann Howell, *Executive Director*

Project Artaud
499 Alabama Street
San Francisco, CA 94110
(415) 621-8430

Santa Barbara Arts Services
629 State Street, Suite 203
Santa Barbara, CA 93101
(805) 962-9163
Gary Sampson, *Co-Director*

Colorado

Business of Art Center
513 Manitou Avenue
Manitou Springs, CO 80829
(719) 685-1861
Deborah Thornton,
Executive Director

Colorado Lawyers for the Arts
P.O. Box 300428
938 Bannock, #227
Denver, CO 80201
(303) 892-7122
Lola Farber, *Executive Director*

Connecticut

Arts Council of Greater New Haven
70 Audubon Street
New Haven, CT 06511
(203) 772-2788
Frances Clark, *Executive Director*

Florida

Bakehouse Art Complex
561 N.W. 32nd
Miami, FL 33127
(305) 576-2828
Helene Pancost

South Florida Art Center
924 Lincoln Road
Miami Beach, FL 33139
(305) 674-8278
Ellie Schneiderman

Georgia

Georgia Volunteer Lawyers for the Arts, Inc.
32 Peachtree N.W.
Atlanta, GA 30303
(404) 577-7378
Lita Menkin

Nexus Contemporary Art Center
535 Means Street N.W.
Atlanta, GA 30318
(404) 688-1970
Louise Shaw, *Executive Director*

Illinois

Chicago Artists Coalition
5 West Grand
Chicago, IL 60610
(312) 670-2060
Arlene Rakoncay,
Executive Director

Chicago Department of Cultural Affairs
174 West Randolph, 3rd Floor
Chicago, IL 60601
(312) 744-1375/1373
Jim Law, *Director of Planning*
Juana Guzman, *Cultural Development Coordinator*

Lawyers for the Creative Arts
213 West Institute Place, Suite 411
Chicago, IL 60602
(312) 944-2787
Daniel Mayer, *Executive Director*

Near NorthWest Arts Council
1579 North Milwaukee
Chicago, IL 60622
(312) 278-7677
Laura Weathered, *Executive Director*

Pilsen East Artists' Complex
1831 South Halstead
Chicago, IL 60608
(312) 923-1804
Lynn Thomsen, *Manager*

Indiana

3001 Building
3001 North Jersey Street
Indianapolis, IN 46205

(317) 923-1804
Lynn Thomsen, *Manager*

Louisiana

Arts Council of New Orleans
821 Gravier, Suite 600
New Orleans, LA 70112
(504) 523-1465
Shirley Trusty Corey,
Executive Director

Maryland

Artist Housing Cooperative
1442 East Baltimore Street
Baltimore, MD 21231
(301) 675-9807
Katherine Rutter

Mayor's Advisory Committee on Art and Culture (MACAC)
Baltimore Arts Tower
21 South Eutaw Street
Baltimore, MD 21201
(301) 396-4575
Claire List, *Director*

Massachusetts

The Artists' Foundation, Inc.
8 Park Plaza
Boston, MA 02116
(617) 227-2787
Barbara Baker, *Executive Director*

ArtistSpace, Inc.
7 Cazenove Street
Boston, MA 02116
(617) 482-5484
Jero Nesson, *Director*

Brickbottom Artists Building
One Fitchburg Street, Box C-125
Somerville, MA 02143
(617) 628-1018
Obie Simonis

Fort Point Arts Community, Inc. of South Boston
249 A Street
Boston, MA 02210
(617) 423-4299 space listings, book orders
(617) 423-1573 office
Barbara Kaplan, *Executive Director*

HOME, Inc.
731 Harrison Avenue
Boston, MA 02118
(617) 266-1386
Alan Michel, *Director*

Volunteer Lawyers for the Arts of Massachusetts
c/o 8 Park Plaza
Boston, MA 02116
(617) 227-2787
Laurie Morin, *Co-Director*
Carolyn Rosenthal, *Co-Director*

Minnesota

Artspace Projects, Inc.
400 First Avenue North, Suite 518
Minneapolis, MN 55401
(612) 339-4372
Kelley Lindquist, *Executive Director*

Lowertown Lofts Artists' Cooperative
255 East Kellogg
St. Paul, MN 55101
(612) 224-6711
Marla Gamble

Studios at 700
700 North Washington
Minneapolis, MN 55401
(612) 333-7913
Marilyn Summers Cool

The Northern Warehouse Artists' Cooperative
308 Prince Street
St. Paul, MN 55101
(612) 224-0048
Carol Tombers

Whittier Studio Homes
12-18 East 27th Street and
2640-2642 First Avenue South
Minneapolis, MN 55404
(612) 871-7756
Lisa Kugler

Missouri

Arts St. Louis
515 North 6th Street, 1st Floor
St. Louis, MO 63101
(314) 241-4810
Nina Guirl, *Director*

Artspace (201 Wyandotte and Delaware Lofts)
218 Delaware
Kansas City, MO 64105
(816) 471-6789
Mel Mallin, *Developer*

Nebraska

Alternative Worksite/Bemis Foundation
614 South Eleventh Street
Omaha, NE 68102
(402) 341-7130
Ree Schonlau, *Executive Director*

New York

Artists Community Federal Credit Union
5 Beekman Street, #600
New York, NY 10038
(212) 285-0595
Sandra De Sando, *Manager*

Exploring the Metropolis, Inc.
10 Gracie Square
New York, NY 10028
(212) 650-0211
Eugunie Cowan, *Director*

Institute for Contemporary Art
c/o P.S. One
46-01 21st Street
Long Island City, NY 11101
(718) 784-2084

or c/o The Clocktower, Floor 13
108 Leonard Street
New York, NY 10013
(212) 233-1096
Alanna Heiss, *Executive Director*

New York City Department of Cultural Affairs—Real Estate Office
2 Columbus Circle
New York, NY 10019
(212) 974-1150
Luis Cancel,
Commissioner
Janet Heit, *Artist Certification*
Patrick O'Leary,
Director of Real Estate

New York City Loft Board
116 Nassau
New York, NY
(212) 566-1438
Lee Fawkes, *Commissioner*

New York Foundation for the Arts
5 Beekman Street, #600
New York, NY 10038
(212) 233-3900
Ted Berger, *Executive Director*

The Urban Homesteading Assistance Board
40 Prince Street, 2nd Floor
New York, NY 10012
(212) 226-4119
Andy Reicher, *Executive Director*

Volunteer Lawyers for the Arts
1 East 53rd Street
New York, NY 10022
(212) 319-2787

236

North Carolina

Artspace
P.O. Box 27331
Raleigh, NC 27611
(919) 821-2787
Rock Kershow, *Executive Director*

Ohio

St. Vincent's Quadrangle
c/o 1404 East 9th Street
Cleveland, OH 44114
(216) 241-4355
William Gould

Pennsylvania

Artspace Collaborative
251 South 18th Street
Philadelphia, PA 19103
(215) 545-3385
Ann Hoskins-Brown,
Program Coordinator

**Philadelphia Historic
Preservation Corp.**
1616 Walnut Street, Suite 2210
Philadelphia, PA 19103
(215) 546-146
David LaFontaine,
Director, Artists Housing Program

**Philadelphia Volunteer
Lawyers for the Arts**
251 South 18th Street
Philadelphia, PA 19103
(215) 545-3385
Dorothy Manou, *Executive Director*

Texas

**Austin Volunteer Accountants
and Lawyers for the Arts**
P.O. Box 2577
Austin, TX 78768
(512) 476-7573
Kathy Keegan-Davis,
Executive Director

D-Art
2917 Swiss Avenue
Dallas, TX 75204
(214) 821-2522
Katherine Wagner, *Director*

**Texas Volunteer Lawyers &
Accountants for the Arts**
1540 Sul Ross
Houston, TX 77006
(713) 526-4876
Sara Rhody, *Executive Director*

Utah

Artspace, Inc.
325 West Pierpont
Salt Lake City, UT 84101
(801) 531-9378
Stephen Goldsmith,
Executive Director

Virginia

Torpedo Factory Art Center
105 North Union Street
Alexandria, VA 22314
(703) 838-4199
Steven Majors, *Executive Director*

Washington

Allied Arts of Seattle
107 South Main
Seattle, WA 98104
(206) 624-0432
Jay Lazerwitz, *Artist Housing
Committee*

Seattle Arts Commission
305 Harrison Street
Seattle, WA 98109
(206) 684-7171
Jack Duggan,
Public Information Officer

Washington D.C.

A. Salon, Ltd.
Jackson School Art Center
R Street and Avon Place N.W.
Washington, DC 20007
(202) 337-4888
George Koch

District Curators
Arts Space Clearinghouse
P.O. Box 14197
Washington, DC 20044
(202) 783-0360
Bill Worrell, Director

Consultants

Carmi Bee, FAIA
RKT & B Architects
30 West 22nd Street
New York, NY 10010
architect

Tom Dolan
Pinetree Studios
434 Avon Street
Oakland, CA 94618
(415) 652-5036
architect

Dan Gonzalez
1015 Trestle Glen
Oakland, CA 94610
(415) 465-4509
architect/development consultant

Cheryl Kartes
Kartes & Associates
2519 California Street N.E.
Minneapolis, MN 55418
(612) 788-2107
arts/space consultant

Rebecca Lee
34 Orchard Street
Cambridge, MA 02140
(617) 547-7306
attorney/real estate consultant

Karen McGraw, AIA
McGraw, Marburger & Associates
4315 Avenue "C"
Austin, TX 78751
(512) 452-4139
founder, Artspace—Austin

Jim Minden, NAE
3614 S.W. Canby
Portland, OR 97219
(503) 244-67770
arts/space consultant

Enid Rieser
5515 South Dorchester
Chicago, IL 60637
(312) 324-7090
arts/space consultant

CANADA

National

**Cooperative Housing
Federation of Canada**
275 Bank Street, Suite 202
Ottawa, ON K2P 2L6

Alberta

Syntax Arts Society
1111 Memorial Drive N.W.
Calgary, AB T2N 3E4

**Southern Alberta Cooperative
Housing Association**
B50-4221 Sarcee Road S.W.
Calgary, AB T3E 6V6

British Columbia

**ACE (Artists for Creative
Environment)**
152 West Hastings, 3rd Floor
Vancouver, BC V6B 1G8
(604) 688-3558 or 327-2561
David MacDonald

Vancouver Arts Commission
1050-700 West Georgia Street
P.O. Box 10018
Vancouver, BC V7Y 1A1

**Vancouver Island Cooperative
Housing Association**
514-620 View Street
Victoria, BC V8W 1J6

Labrador

**Co-operative Housing
Association of Newfoundland
and Labrador**
P.O. Box 453
Mount Pearl, NF A1N 2C4

Manitoba

ARTSPACE
405-100 Arthur Street
Winnipeg, MB R3B 1H3

**Housing Cooperative Council
of Manitoba**
107-167 Lombard Avenue
Winnipeg, MB R3B 0T6

Nova Scotia

**Cooperative Housing Federa-
tion of Nova Scotia**
6074 Lady Hammond Road
Halifax, NS B4K 2R7

Ontario

**Cooperative Housing Associa-
tion of Ontario**
2 Berkeley Street
Toronto, ON M5A 2W3

**Cultural Facilities Policy
Working Group (CFPWG)**
City Hall
Toronto, ON M5H 2N2

Toronto Artscape, Inc.
141 Bathurst Street
Toronto, ON M5V 2R2
(416) 392-1038
Billie Bridgeman, *Executive Director*

Québec

**Commission d'initiatives et de
developpement Culturels (CIDEC)**
425 Place Jacques-Cartier,
bureau 300
Montréal, PQ H2Y 3B1

**Fédération régionale des
Coopératives d'habitation de
Québec**
1080, de la Chevrotiére
Ville de Québec, PQ G1R 3J4

EUROPE

Finland

Suomen Taiteiljaseuva
(Finnish Artists Union)
Ainoukatu 3
00100 Helsinki
(0) 495-169

France

**Ministere de la Culture et de
la Communication**
Service d'information des artistes,
createurs et interpretes (SICI)
3 rue de Valois
75001 Paris
(1) 4015-8012
Genevieve Ravaux

Germany

Kunsterhaus Bethanien GMBH
Mariannenplatz 2
1B36 Berlin
(030) 614-9021

German Academic Exchange Service
Steinplatz 2
Postfach 12640
1B12 Berlin

Israel

Israel Painters & Sculptors Association
9 Alharizi Street
Tel Aviv

Ireland

The Arts Council
70 Merrion Square
Dublin 2
(01) 764-685

The Netherlands

BBK
(Dutch Artists Union)
Koggestraat 7
Amsterdam
(020) 235-456

Raad voor de Kunst
(Dutch Arts Council)
RJ Schimmelpennincklaan 3
2517 JN, Den Haag
(070) 46-96-19

Stichting Woon- en Werkruimten voor Kunstenaars
(Foundation for Living and Workspaces for Artists)
Afdeling Kunstzaken
Sint Agnietenstraat 2
Amsterdam
552-3386/3387
Jos Riymers, *Secretariaat*

Norway

Norwegian Artists Council
P.O. Box 8396
Hammersborg
0129 Oslo 1
(02) 204-333

United Kingdom

ACME Housing Association Ltd.
15 Robinson Road, Bethnal Green
London, England E3 9LX
(081) 981-6811/6821
David Panton, Jon Harvey

Arts Council of Great Britain
14 Great Peter Street
London, England SW1P 3NQ
(071) 333-0100
Sandy Naime, *Visual Arts Director*

British American Arts Association
116 Commercial Street
London, England E1 6NF
(071) 247-5385
Dani Salvadori

SPACE
8 Hoxton Street
London, England N1 6NG
(071) 613-1925
Jim Madge

WASPS (Workshops & Artists Studio Provision Scotland)
26 King Street
Glasgow, Scotland G1 5QP
(041) 552-0564
Linda Galbraith, *Director*

AUSTRALIA

Visual Arts Board
Australia Council
Northside Gardens
168 Walker Street
North Sydney, NSW 2060
(02) 922-2122

Date of Visit: _____

Building Name: _____

Address: _____

Contact: _____   Phone: _____

Building Orientation: N   S   E   W   NE   NW   SE   SW

Dimensions:	Height	Width	Depth	Total Sq. Ft.
lst floor				
2nd floor				
3rd floor				
4th floor				
5th floor				
Basement				
Other:				

Total Square Footage of Building: _____

Total Land Area: _____

Acquisition Price: _____   Cost Per Square Foot: _____

Rent Per Square Foot: _____

Building Age: _____

Historical Significance:
Eligible for Tax Benefits
- ❑ Historical Preservation Site
- ❑ National Register Site
- ❑ Historic District
- ❑ National Register Preservation District

Property Identification Number:
Zoning Code and Use:
Neighborhood: ❑ Residential ❑ Commercial
 ❑ Manufacturing/Industrial ❑ Combination
Building Type: ❑ Warehouse ❑ Commercial ❑ Storefront ❑ Other

Previous Use:
Neighbors: ❑ Business ❑ Residence ❑ Occupied ❑ Vacant

Notes on CurrentUses:

Neighborhood Amenities:
On Street Parking ❑ Yes ❑ No
Off Street Tenant Parking: ❑ Yes Number of Spaces: _____
Parking Restrictions:
Nearest Parking Lot: Parking Fee: _____
Nearest Public Transportation Stops:
Streets and Sidewalks: ❑ Good ❑ Poor ❑ Cracks ❑ Crumbling ❑ Potholes
StreetLights: ❑ Well-lit ❑ Adequate ❑ Poor
Garbage Collection: ❑ Regular ❑ None Fee: _____

Nearby Shops, Laundry, Hardware Stores, Etc. _____

_____

Nearby Groceries and Restaurants: _____

_____

General Impressions:

Exterior Conditions:
(Circle or check all that apply)

Foundation:	*Type:*	Concrete	*Condition:*	Good
		Block		Cracking
		Stone		Settling
		Other		Spalling
				Seepage

General Impressions:

Walls:	*Type:*	Concrete	*Condition:*	Good
		Stone		Cracking
		Block		Paint/Finish
		Brick		Missing material
		Other		Out-of-plumb

General Condition Notes:

Entrances:	*Type:*	Concrete	*Condition:*	Good
		Stone		Cracking
		Block		Missing material
		Brick		
		Wood		
		Steel/Metal	**Weather Lock:**	
		Glass	*Operation:*	Dimensions:
				Paint/Finish:
				Definition:

General Condition Notes:

Loading Dock:	*Type:*	Metal	*Condition:*	Good
		Concrete		Cracking
		Hinged		Spalling
		Wood		Settling
	Access:		*Height:*	
			Width:	

Loading Doorway:

	Type:	Overhead	*Condition:*	Operation
		Sliding		Paint/Finish

General Condition Notes:

Windows: Floors with windows: 1   2   3   4   5   other

                      Oriented: N   S   E   W   NE   NW   SE   SW

            Type: Wood   *Condition:*   Good
                           Metal   Paint/Finish
                                                               Glazing
                                                               Rotting
                                                               Operation
                                                               Boarded windows

            Size: *Glass:*   Broken/cracked
                                                               Missing panes
                                                               Single pane
                                                               Double pane

General Condition Notes:

Fire Escape/Outdoor Exit Stairs:

            Type: Wood   *Condition:*   Good
                           Metal   Paint/Finish
                           Concrete   Allowed by City Code

General Condition Notes:

Courtyards, Backyard, Alleys:

            Oriented: N   S   E   W
            Dimensions:

            Type: Dirt   *Condition:*   Good
                           Concrete   Cracking
                           Brick   Settling
                           Asphalt   Runoff
                           Other

General Condition Notes:

Roof: Access: Ladder   Stairs   Trap Door

            Type: Built Up   *Condition:*   New
                           Tile   Old
                           Shingle   Holes/Leaks
                           Metal   Cracks/Bubbles
                           Other   Insulation

            Parapet:

General Condition Notes:

Drainage:	*Type:*	Gutters Downspout Other	*Condition:*	Good Paint/Finish Leaking Missing Material
Facia, Eaves:	*Type:*	Wood Metal Brick Stone	*Condition:*	Good Paint/Finish Rotting Level/Plumb
Decorative Detains:	*Type:*	Stone Wood Brick Significant	*Condition:*	Good Paint/Finish Weathering Staining
Electrical Service:	*Type:*	Overhead Underground	*Condition:*	Good Fraying Location

General Impression/Repairs Needed:

Interior Conditions:

Floors:	*Type:*	Wood Concrete Linoleum/Tile Other	*Condition:*	Good Sagging/Warping Surface
		Live Weight Load: _____ lbs. per sq. ft		

General Condition Notes:

Basement:	*Type:*	Finished Unfinished	*Condition:*	Good Dry
	Beams:	Wooden Steel Concrete		Damp Water Marked Seepage
	Floors:	Dirt Wood Linoleum/Tile Concrete		Missing material Settling
Heating:	*Type:*	Steam Hot Water Forced Air Unit Ventilating Oil/Gas Gravity Electricity Coal	*Condition:*	Good Seepage Missing Material Age Operation Cleaning Corrosion
Air Conditioning:	*Type:*	Throughout Roof Units Window Units None	*Condition:*	Good Seepage Missing Material Age Operation Cleaning Corrosion

Plumbing: *Type:* Galvanized *Condition:* Good
Iron Missing
Copper Seepage/Stainig
Plastic Corrosion
Venting

Number, Condition and Location of:

_____ Toilets _____, _____

_____ Wash Basins _____, _____

_____ Showers/Bath Tubs _____, _____

_____ Slop Sinks _____, _____

_____ Floor Drains _____, _____

Hot Water Heater: Capacity: _____ Gallons
Adequate
Inadequate
Inoperable

General Condition Notes:

Walls: *Type:* Plaster *Condition:* Good
Concrete Block Paint/Finish
Sheet Rock/Drywall Settling
Brick Cracking
Other Insulation

General Condition Notes:

Columns/Structural System: Yes _____ No _____

Distance between Columns:_____

Type: Wood *Condition:* Good
Metal Meet Fire Code
Concrete/Masonry Bending/Bowing
Bearing Wall Crack/Check
Shear Failure

Ceilings: *Type:* Wood *Condition:* Good
Plaster Paint/Finish
Sheet Rock/Drywall Settling
Metal Cracking
Other Fire Barrier Requirement met?

General Condition Notes:

Stairs: *Type:* Wood *Condition:* Good
Concrete Open
Metal Enclosed
Stone Paint/Finish
Carpet Settling

*Height:*_____ *Width:* _____

General Condition Notes:

Corridors: *Type:* Brick *Condition:* Good
Plaster Paint/Finish
Sheet Rock/Drywall Settling
Concrete Block Cracking
Other

*Height:*_____ *Width:*_____

Fire Doors: Yes _____ No _____

Elevators:

Type: Passenger *Condition:* Good
Freight Enclosed
Manual Partially Enclosed
Automatic Vacant Shaft
Handicap Accessible

Dimensions: _____ Capacity: _____ lbs._____

Electrical:

Service to Building: _____ Phase: _____ Wire _____ Amps _____ Volts _____

To Floor/Unit: _____ Phase: _____ Wire _____ Amps _____ Volts _____

Power Panel: _____ Fuse Box _____ Circuit Breaker _____

Location of Main and Sub Power Panels:

Number and Location of Outlets:

Additional Service Required: Yes _____ No _____
Overhead Lighting Wall Lighting
Wall Outlets Floor Outlets
Separate Meters Other

Type of Wiring: *Condition:*
Knob and Tube/ Good
Cloth Wrapped Frayed
Non-Metallic Sheathed Missing Material

Conduit/E.M.T.
Flexible Conduit
Plastic Sheathed

Emergency Systems:

Sprinklers: Wet _____ Dry _____ Operable _____ None _____

Fire Alarm: In Building Only _____ Wired to Fire Department _____

Extinguishers: _____ # UL Rated _____

Emergency Lighting: _____ Halls _____ Exits

Security: _____ Entrances Secured _____ Floors Secured
_____ Elevators Secured

Windows: _____ Locks _____ Gates _____ Bars _____
_____ Electronic Alarm System _____ Other

Repairs Needed/General Impressions:

Property Address:_____

Purchase Price: $_____   Down Payment: $ _____   Amount to Finance: $ _____

Land Value: $_____   Personal Property Value: $ _____   Building Value: $_____

SOURCES OF FUNDS

Financing Source:

_____   Amt. $_____   Rate _____ % Term _____   Principal + Interest $_____/yr.

_____   Amt. $_____   Rate _____ % Term _____   Principal + Interest $_____/yr.

_____   Amt. $_____   Rate _____ % Term _____   Principal + Interest $_____/yr.

Total Available for Development $ _____
(compare this with Estimated Total Start-Up Costs, below)

Total Annual Principal & Interest / Debt Service (DS): $ _____

÷ 12 = Total Monthly Principal & Interest / DebtService (DS): $ _____

USES OF FUNDS

SOFT COSTS

"Soft" costs include design and legal fees, insurance and taxes
during construction, and construction financing. Generally
20 - 35 percent of project costs.

1. Appraisal $ _____

2. Design fees $ _____
   architects
   engineers
   environmental study

3. Legal/Accounting Fees $ _____
   pro forma/prospectus
   entity documents
   closing documents

4. Title Search/Insurance $ _____

5. Permits and Fees $ _____
   financing fees (points, etc.)
   real estate commission
   construction/SAC/WAC

6. Syndication costs $ _____
   printing
   marketing/sales

7. Closing costs $ _____

8. Taxes $ _____

9. Insurance $ _____

10. Construction loan $ _____

11. Management training/coop structure $ _____

12. Other consultants $ _____

13. Unit Marketing $ _____

14. Contingency fund $ _____
    (15 percent or more of subtotal)

15. Other $ _____

Total Soft Costs: $ _____

HARD COSTS:

"Hard" costs include bricks and mortar expenses to acquire, build or renovate a building and may include equipment to run a facility. These costs are typically 65 - 85 percent of the total project costs.

1. Site acquisition $ _____
       land
       existing buildings

2. Personal property $ _____
       equipment
       fixtures
       other building contents

3. Construction/Renovation costs $ _____
       demolition/site preparation
       utility extensions
       materials/labor

4. Site construction
       parking /landscaping $ _____

5. Other $ _____

                     Total Hard Costs: $ _____

MONTHLY OPERATING COSTS;

1. Taxes $ _____
2. Insurance $ _____
3. Gas/Electric/Water/Waste/Phone $ _____
4. Repairs/Maintenance/Supplies/Services $ _____
5. Capital Improvements/Replacement Reserves $ _____
6. Legal/Accounting/Advertising $ _____
7. Management Salaries/Taxes $ _____
8. Contingency (@5-10%) $ _____
9. Vacancy & Credit Losses (@5-15%) $ _____
10. Other $ _____

                Monthly Operating Costs $ _____

COMPARING COSTS FOR TESTING FEASIBILITY

Soft Costs: $ _____
+ plus Hard Costs: $ _____
= equals Estimated Total Start-Up Costs: $ _____

Total Start-Up Costs: $ _____
÷ divided by Building's Gross Square Footage: _____ sq. ft.
= equals Development Cost per Square Foot: $ _____ / sq. ft.

Building's Useable/Rentable Square Footage: _____ sq. ft.
÷ divided by Estimated Monthly Income: $ _____
= equals Monthly Rent per Square Foot: $ _____ / sq. ft.

Estimated Monthly Income: $ _____
— minus Monthly Operating Costs: $ _____
= equals Funds Available for Monthly Debt Service: $ _____

Note: If Debt Service is higher than the amount available to pay Debt Service, you need lower cost financing, lower project costs, less debt or more monthly income.

APPENDIX 6.2   EQUITY FINANCING SOURCE ESTIMATES

Estiimate current assets, potential funding and financing from public and private sources, for use in pro forma. Sources must equal or exceed the projected expenses.

1. **Group assets available for capital construction** $ _____

2. **Private Investment** $ _____

    Bank or Credit Union Loans $ _____

    Private or Special Low Interest Loans $ _____

    Developer's Contributions $ _____

    Property Write-Down by Property Owner $ _____

    Equity Syndication $ _____

    Other $ _____

3. **Private Contributions and Grants** $ _____

    Individual Contributions $ _____

    Corporate Grants and Business Contributions $ _____

    Foundation Grants and Program Related Investments $ _____

    Donated services, materials etc. $ _____

    Fundraising Events $ _____

    Matching Gifts $ _____

    Other $ _____

4. **City or County Funding Sources** $ _____

    General Obligation Bonds $ _____

    Industrial Revenue Bonds $ _____

    Community Development Block Grants $ _____

    Rehabilitation Loan Programs $ _____

    Eminent Domain/Property Write-Down $ _____

    Loan Guarantee $ _____

5. **State Government Funding Sources** $ _____

    State Housing Finance Agency $ _____

    Special Programs $ _____

    State Arts Board $ _____

    State Historical Society $ _____

6. **Federal Government Funding Sources** $ _____

    Department of Housing and Urban Development (HUD) $ _____

    National Endowment for the Arts

        (planning/design competition) $ _____

    Department of Commerce $ _____

    Department of Energy $ _____

    Other Programs $ _____

Property Address:_____

Purchase Price: $_____   Down Payment: $ _____   Amount to Finance: $ _____

Financing: Amt. $_____   Rate _____ % Term _____   Principal + Interest $ _____/yr.

Financing: Amt. $_____   Rate _____ % Term _____   Principal + Interest $ _____/yr.

Financing: Amt. $_____   Rate _____ % Term _____   Principal + Interest $ _____/yr.

Total Annual Principal +Interest/Debt Service (DS): $ _____/yr.

Appraised Values:

Land Value: $_____   Personal Property Value: $ _____   Building Value: $_____

Annual Rental Income: $ _____   — Vacancy @ 15% $ _____   = Gross Operating Income (GOI) $ _____

Annual Operating Epenses

    Real estate taxes $ _____
    Insurance $ _____
    Utilities $ _____
    Supplies $ _____
    Repairs/Services $ _____
    Management $ _____
    Advertising/Accounting $ _____
    Miscellaneous/Other $ _____

Total Operating Expenses $ _____

1. Cash Flow Benefit   *Tax Benefits*
    Gross Operating Income (GOI) $ _____
    — minus Operating Expenses $ _____
    = equals Net Operating Income (NOI) $ _____
    — minus Annual Debt Service (DS) $ _____
    = equals Cash Flow Before Tax (CFBTx) $ _____ $ _____

2. Principal Reduction Benefit
    Annual Debt Service (DS) $ _____
    — minus Interest Paid $ _____
    = equals Principal Reduction (P/R) $ _____ $ _____

3. Tax Benefits
    Net Operating Income (NOI) $ _____
    — minus Interest paid $ _____
    — minus Depreciation* $ _____
    — minus ITC or other Credit** $ _____
    = equals Taxable Income $ _____ $ _____
    x multiplied by tax bracket***   X _____% = $ _____
    = equals tax paid or saved: $ _____

4. Appreciating Benefit (estimate)**** $ _____ $ _____

Calculating Return on Investment (ROI)
CFBTX + P/R + Tax Saved + Appreciation ÷ Total Investment = _____%

NOTES: This form is a variation of an investment analysis form used by real estate agents and investors and is much like the Annual Property Operating Data Form (APOD). It is used to make an initial assessment of the investment potential in a property. Artists can use this format for a preliminary budget to compare properties that are available. Operating information from the current property owner can be requested to fill out the form. Calculating the four tax benefits for investing in real estate can provide informatin about the potential to interest an investor in your project. More complete project budgeting can be done with the pro forma and the cash flow projection form (Appendix 6-4).

*__Depreciation__. The IRS allows for a deduction in taxable income through real estate due to depreciation. A building may depreciate in value due to: **1.** functional obsolescence (new designs make old buildings obsolete); **2.** physical deterioration through wear and tear; and **3.** economic obsolescence through market need changes. Land is not considered to lose value due to depreciation. Personal property and buildings are depreciated according to different charts provided by the IRS and can be determined by your accountant. Bookkeeping records keep tract of the deduction allowable for each year, subject to changes by the IRS.

Land Value: $_____   Personal Property Value: $ _____   Building Value: $_____

**Low-Income Housing Credit, Historic Rehab or Investment Tax Credit.

*****Tax Bracket.** Currently 15% or 28%

******Appreciation Benefit.** Estimate the amount of appreciation that is reason ably given current market conditions, generally not exceeding the Consumer Price Index (CPI) or inflation rate.

Property Address:_____

Purchase Price: $_____ Down Payment: $ _____ Amount to Finance: $ _____

Financing Source:

_____ Amt. $_____ Rate _____ % Term _____ Principal + Interest $ _____/yr.

_____ Amt. $_____ Rate _____ % Term _____ Principal + Interest $ _____/yr.

_____ Amt. $_____ Rate _____ % Term _____ Principal + Interest $ _____/yr.

Total Annual Principal +Interest/Debt Service (DS): $ _____

Land Value: $_____ Personal Property Value: $ _____ Building Value: $_____

	Year	Year	Year	Year	Year
TAXABLE INCOME					
Annual Scheduled Rental Income: $					
Vacancy/Credit Losses @ _____% $					
= Gross Operating Income (GOI) $					
GOI					
— minus Operating Expenses $					
= Net Operating Expenses (NOI) $					
NOI					
— minus Non-Operating Expenses $					
— minus Interest, 1st Mortgage $					
— minus Interest, 2nd Mortgage $					
— minus Depreciation, Bldg $					
— minus Depreciation, Pers Property $					
= Real Estate Taxable Income* $					
CASH FLOWS:					
Net Operating Income (NOI) $					
— minus Annual Debt Service $					
— minus Funded Reserves $					
— minus Capital Additions $					
— minus Investment Tax Credit (ITC)					
or Rehab Credit $					
= Cash Flow Before Tax $					
Cash Flow Before Tax $					
— minus Tax Liability on Real Estate** $					
= Cash Flow After Taxes $					

> *Note*: Real Estate Taxable Income* $_____ (usually a negative number) = equals tax paid or saved. This number (at*) is then multiplied by tax bracket (usually 28%) to equal Tax Liability on Real Estate (at**). Since the number at* is usually a negative number, it is added rather than subtracted at**.

ANALYSIS AT TIME OF SALE

ADJUSTED BASIS		CALCULATION OF GAIN		SALE PROCEEDS	
Original Basis	$ _____	Sale Price	$ _____	Sale Price	$ _____
+ Capital Improvements	$ _____	— Adjusted Basis	$ _____	— Cost of Sale	$ _____
— Depreciation	$ _____	= Gain on Sale	$ _____	— Mortgage Balance	$ _____
— partial Pntshp Sales	$ _____	x Tax Rate (28%)	$ _____*	= Proceeds BeforeTaxes	$ _____
— Unused Tax Savings	$ _____			— Tax Liability on Sale	$ _____
— Cost of Sale	$ _____			= Proceeds After Taxes	$ _____
= Adjusted Basis	$ _____				

This document states the scope of business for the cooperative. To incorporate the cooperative, you must file this document with the state office of Secretary of State. Check with an attorney, the Secretary of State or managers of other live/work space projects to obtain information about the specific requirements of your state. The following is a sample document.

Articles of Incorporation

We, the undersigned, do hereby voluntarily associate ourselves as individuals for the purpose of organizing and incorporating a cooperative association under (your state statutes) and to that end, we hereby adopt and sign the following Articles of Incorporation:

Article I

The name of the association is ———— Cooperative.

Article II

The primary purposes for which the association is formed and the nature of its business are as follows:

a)   To provide housing and work space on a not-for-profit cooperative basis for its members, who must be persons who are artists and their families, irrespective of race, creed, national origin, or sex, and who are of low or moderate income at the time they become members;

b)   To construct, operate, manage, maintain, improve, and to buy, own, sell, convey, assign, mortgage, or lease any real estate and any personal property necessary or incident to the provision of such housing;

c)   To borrow money and issue evidence of indebtedness in furtherance of any or all of the objects of its business; to secure the same by mortgage, pledge, or other lien;

d)   To enter into any kind of activity and to perform and carry out contracts of any kind necessary to, or in conjunction with, or incidental to, the accomplishment of the not-for profit purposes of the cooperative association;

e)   To make patronage refunds to members as provided in the bylaws and/or occupancy agreements; and

f)   To conduct its affairs as a limited equity cooperative within the meaning of (your state statutes).

Article III

The principal place of business of the association shall be _____ (list complete mailing address).

Article IV

The period of its duration shall be perpetual.

Article V

(A statement of whether the association is organized with or without shares, and the number of shares or memberships subscribed for; or, whether the property rights of members shall be equal or unequal, and if unequal, the rule by which their rights shall be determined. If organized with shares, a statement of the amount of authorized capital, the number of types of shares and the par value thereof ,which may be placed at any figure, and the rights, preferences, and restrictions of each type of share.)

There shall be one class of capital stock of the association which shall be the common shares of the association. The total authorized shares of the association shall consist of (determine number) voting common shares. The par value of a share of common stock shall be (set $ amount). No dividends shall be paid on the common stock of the association.

Only common stockholders shall have voting power, and individuals owning common stock shall be restricted to one (1) vote in the affairs of the association. Voting by proxy shall not be permitted. Voting by mail shall be permitted in accordance with the procedures set forth in the Bylaws.

Shareholders shall have no rights of cumulative voting. Shareholders shall not be entitled as a matter of right, preemptive or otherwise, to subscribe or apply for, or purchase, or receive any part of any unissued shares or other securities of the association.

No share shall be issued for less than its par value or until such payment has been made to the association. No shareholder shall be personally liable for any debt or obligation of the association except to the extent of the unpaid portion of the subscription price of his/her stock.

The association shall have a prior lien with the right of enforcement of ordinary liens upon all outstanding shares for any indebtedness of the shareholder to the association.

Article VI

(The value of shares which must be owned in order to qualify for membership and how the value accumulates equity for transfer purposes.)

No transfer, assignment or pledge of shares of or membership in the association shall be made except with the prior written approval of the Board of Directors of the association.

The sale price of occupancy entitling cooperative shares of the association, within the meaning of (your state statutes) shall not exceed a transfer value which is the sum of the following:

(These features vary for different types of cooperatives and from state to state; those presented here are shown only as an example.)

a)   The consideration paid for the shares by the first member to occupy the live/work unit, as shown in the records of the association.

b)   The fair market value, as shown in the records of the association, of any improvements to the real property that were installed at the sole expense of the member (including labor furnished by the member) with the prior approval of the Board of Directors;

c) (i) accumulated interest, or (ii) an inflation allowance not to exceed the greater of (A) a 10 percent annual noncompounded increase on the consideration paid for the shares by the first member to occupy the unit, or (B) the amount that would have been paid on that consideration if interest had been paid on it at the rate of the percentage increase in the revised Consumer Price Index for All Urban Consumers for (your metropolitan area) prepared by the United States Department of Labor; provided that the amount determined pursuant to this clause may not exceed $500 for each year or fraction of a year the shares were owned; plus

d) Real property capital contributions shown in the records of the association to have been paid by the previous holders of the shares of the same shares that had entitled occupancy to the unit involved. These contributions include contributions to a corporate reserve account, the use of which is restricted to real property improvements or acquisitions, and the amount of principle amortized by the association over the term of its real property-related indebtedness.

Article VII

The names and mailing addresses of the first Board of Directors, who shall hold office until the first annual meeting of the shareholders or until their successors are elected and qualified, are as follows: (list all here).

Article VIII

(Operations to benefit members.)

The association shall be operated for the mutual benefit of its shareholders. The association shall retain from receipts any amounts necessary to pay expenses, including adequate reserves for repair and replacement, doubtful accounts, and other reserves required or permitted by law. Any net income in excess of additions to reserves shall be distributed on the basis of patronage.

The total distribution out of capital to a shareholder shall not exceed the transfer value determined in accordance with Article VI above.

Article IX

(Conflict of Interest Policy)

Any shareholder, director or officer of this association may be party to, or have a direct or indirect, financial or other interest in, any contract or transaction of this association, provided that the fact of that interest shall be disclosed in the minutes of the association; and any such shareholder or director may be counted in determining the existence of a quorum at any meeting of members or of the Board of Directors where such a contract or transaction may be authorized.

Article X

(Powers of the Directors)

The Board of Directors shall have the right to prescribe bylaws which shall be binding on the association and its members and may be amended as provided therein.

The management of this association shall be vested in a Board of Directors, who shall be elected by and from the members at the annual meeting. The Board shall not be less than three in number; and the qualifications, compensation, terms of office, manner of election, time and place of meeting, powers and duties of directors, shall be such as prescribed in the Bylaws of this association.

The Board of Directors shall have and may exercise all powers of the association, except those powers which are by law, by these Articles of Incorporation, or by the Bylaws conferred upon or reserved for the shareholders.

Article XI

(Amendments and dissolution, the method by which any surplus, upon dissolution of the association, shall be distributed.)

These Articles of Incorporation may be amended by a majority vote of the stockholders in the manner provided by law.

This association may be dissolved in the manner provided by law. Upon liquidation of the association, any assets remaining after retirement of corporate debts and distribution to shareholders or members will be conveyed to a charitable organization 501(c)(3) or public agency.

We the Incorporators, have signed these Articles of Incorporation this _____ day of _____ (month/year).

(Signature lines for at least three persons, and Notary's verification added here.)

Bylaws describe how your cooperative or nonprofit corporation will handle its business. It is a flexible document that may be changed by the members, as provided in the bylaws. Bylaws are not filed with any local or state authority. As a framework, bylaws may be written to define the agreements made within your group, whether detailed or simplified.

Article I: Name and Location

The name of this association is _____ Cooperative. Its principal office *location* is (list full mailing address).

Article II: Purpose

The *purpose* of this association is to provide its members with housing and work space on a not-for-profit association basis.

Article III: Property Description

The property shall be defined as *(give full legal description and other pertinent information)*.

Article IV: Membership

Section 1 *Members*
a. *Definition of Voting Members*

b. *Nonvoting members (if any)*
The members shall consist of the first Board of Directors and subscribers or purchasers as approved by the Directors and who have paid for and received shares of common stock of the association (sometimes called "shareholders"). The status of a Director on the first Board of Directors as a temporary member shall terminate at the first annual meeting of members unless such Director has become a shareholder.

c. *Eligibility*
All persons approved by the Board of Directors shall be eligible for membership, provided that s/he executes a Subscription Agreement and Occupancy Agreement in the usual form employed by the association for a specific live/work unit in the project. Priority will be given to artists, as defined by the Board of Directors. Selection criteria will be established by the Board of Directors. *(Note: You may also choose to define here an "eligible artist"; materials to submit [slides, resume, etc.]; selection criteria; composition of the selection committee [current members or outside art community representation]; and selection procedures. Detailed selection procedures may be defined in your Operating Policies and may be left broadly stated in the Bylaws.*

d. *Application for Membership*
Application for membership shall be made in a manner prescribed by the Board of Directors. The Board may require payment of a nominal application fee which is nonrefundable All applications shall be acted upon promptly by the Board of Directors or a committee or person designated by them.

e. *Waiting List*
The association may maintain one or more waiting lists for persons who shall have applied

to the association for membership. The association may establish procedures for the selection of persons from a list to whom an offer to sell shares in the association may be made.

f. *Subscription Funds*
All subscription funds (except funds required for credit reports) received from applicants shall be deposited promptly without deduction in a special account of the association as trustee for the subscribers; which monies shall not be association funds, but shall be held solely for the benefit of the subscribers until transferred to the regular account of the association as provided. Special account(s) may be established with any insured bank; and may be interest bearing to the benefit of the association. Such funds may be disbursed upon certification by the President and Secretary that: *(define conditions).* If these conditions have been met, the subscription escrow account may be transferred to the association and the association shall issue stock certificates to all regular members.

Article V: Meetings of Members

Section 1 *Place of Meetings*
Meetings of the membership shall be held at the principal place of business of the association, or at another suitable place reasonably convenient to the membership, as may be designated by the Board of Directors.

Section 2 *Meetings*
a. *Annual Meetings*
The first annual meeting of the association shall be held on _____(date) _____, at an hour to be designated by the Board of Directors. Thereafter, the annual meetings of the association shall be held on the first Xxxxday of (month) each succeeding year at an hour and location as designated by the Board of Directors. At annual meetings, there shall be elected by ballot the members of the Board of Directors, in accordance with these bylaws. The members may also transact other business of the association as may properly come before them.

The order of business at all annual meetings shall be as follows: *(define)*

- Call to order and role call
- Proof of notice of meeting, or waiver of notice
- Approval of minutes of preceding meeting
- Reports of officers
- Reports of committees
- Election of inspectors of election, or waiver of inspectors
- Election of Directors and committee chairs
- Unfinished business
- New business

b. *Quarterly Meetings*
(Define who calls such meetings, the type of business to be transacted, the regular order of business to be transacted, the proposed schedule for meetings, and the manner in which notice will be provided.)

c. *Special Meetings*
(Define who calls special meetings, conditions for meetings to be called [e.g., a petition

signed by (the number) of members, or a resolution by the Directors], and the manner in which notice will be provided.)

Section 3 *Notice of Meetings*
The Secretary shall post, deliver or mail a notice of each annual, quarterly, or special meeting, stating the purpose, time and place of the meeting. *(You may also wish to define the minimum and maximum amount of notice required for each type of meeting, e.g., at least 5 days but not more than 20 days prior to a quarterly meeting.)*

Section 4 *Quorum at Membership Meetings and Adjourned Meetings*
a. The presence of at least 51 percent of the shareholders, may be counted toward a quorum for the transaction of business. If other business is raised and the number in attendance drops below a quorum and the question of a quorum is raised, no business may thereafter be transacted.

b. When a meeting of members cannot be organized or completed because a quorum has not attended or remained, the members who are present may adjourn the meeting to a date not less than _____ from the time the original meeting was called, at which subsequent time the quorum requirement will be _____ percent.

Section 5 *Voting; Voting Methods*
Each owner of common stock in the association shall have only one vote in the affairs of the association. Co-owners of a share shall together have one vote, which shall not be split. The vote of the majority present shall decide any question brought before a meeting, unless otherwise required by statute.

Robert's Rules of Order shall govern as to procedure at meetings on other matters not covered in these Bylaws.

No member shall be eligible to vote or stand for election to the Board when shown to be more than 30 days delinquent in payments due the association or otherwise in material default under his or her Occupancy Agreement.

(Note: In this section define the conditions and procedures for voting by mail and/or voting by proxy, if either is to be allowed.)

Article VI: Board of Directors

Section 1 *Number and Qualification*
The affairs of the association shall be governed by a Board of Directors of at least __(#) but no more than __(#) persons, all of whom shall be members of the association in good standing. There may not be more than one occupant of a studio or live/work space serving on the Board at any occasion.

Section 2 *Election, Compensation and Term of Office*
(Define the conditions and procedures for the election of Directors.)
Directors shall be elected for two year terms at the annual meeting. To alternate the initial terms from the first election, half of the Directors receiving the highest number of votes at the initial election shall serve for two years and the remaining Directors shall serve for one year. No member shall serve as a Director for more than two successive terms. No compen-

sation, including abatement of rent or fees, shall be paid to Directors for their services in any capacity unless a resolution authorizing such compensation has been adopted by the Board prior to services undertaken.

Section 3 *Removal from Office*
(Define the conditions and procedures for removal of a Director.)
At any annual, quarterly, or special meeting of the members duly called, any Director may be removed with or without cause by the affirmative vote of the majority of the regular membership and a successor then elected. Any Director whose removal has been proposed by the members shall be given an opportunity to be heard prior to a vote on that proposal. Any Director more than 30 days delinquent in payment of their carrying charges shall be automatically terminated and the remaining Directors shall appoint a successor.

Section 4 *Vacancies on the Board*
Vacancies caused on the Board for any reason shall be filled by vote of the majority of the remaining Directors, even though they constitute less than a quorum; and each person so elected shall be a Director until a successor is elected by the members at the next annual meeting.

Section 5 *Meetings of the Board*
a. *Organizational Meeting:* The first meeting of the Directors following an election of Directors shall be held within 10 days of election *(define time, place, notice requirements or if to be fixed by the Directors).*

b. *Regular Meetings: (Identify the minimum number of meetings, time, place, and notice requirements. You may also define Special Meetings, Emergency Action without Meetings, provisions for Open attendance , Waiver of Notice and Quorum requirements for Directors Meetings.)*

Section 6 *Rights and Duties of the Board*
The Board of Directors shall have all the powers and duties necessary for the administration of the affairs of the association, and may do all things except those prohibited by law or are directed to be done by the members. The powers of the Board shall include, but not be limited to the following:

a. To cause the Property and any other property, real or personal, of the association to be maintained and kept in good repair;

b. To retain or employ a manager, other employees, or independent contractors as necessary, and to prescribe their duties;

c. To promulgate reasonable and appropriate House Rules, to amend them from time to time, and to cause notice of such rules to be given to the members;

d. To adopt and amend from time to time monthly carrying charges, based upon an annual operating budget formally adopted by the Board, and to make emergency or special assessments, if necessary, as further described below, and to authorize patronage refunds;

e. To enforce the provisions of the Articles of Incorporation, these Bylaws, Occupancy Agreements, and House Rules and Policies; including the undertaking of legal proceedings for enforcement of Occupancy Agreements;

f. To terminate membership and occupancy rights for cause, as provided in these Bylaws;

g. To approve or disapprove the transfer of shares of common stock;

h. To apply reserves to defray operating costs, capital or replacement expenses, or for other purposes for which such reserves are established and maintained;

i. To cause to be kept detailed and accurate records of the acts and proceedings of the association and books of account showing all income and expenditures of the association, including a monthly financial statement;

j. To procure and maintain adequate property, hazard, liability, and other insurance on the Property, and any other real or personal property owned by the association or as related to activities of the association;

k. To procure adequate fidelity bonds on behalf of officers and employees handling or responsible for corporate or trust funds;

l. To meet with representatives of the owners and occupants of the adjoining commercial space in the building, and to exercise such rights and duties as are prescribed in the Declaration of Easements for the building. (When cooperative shares a building with other ownership entities, such as through a condominium agreement.)

Article VII: Rights and Duties of the Officers

(You may choose to provide greater detail and clarification of the members' expectations of each officer and the role of the executive committee. You may also wish to define procedures for the election and removal of officers or the appointment of assistant officers.)

Section 1 *President*
The President shall be the chief executive officer of the association. He or she shall preside at all meetings of the members and of the Board of Directors and shall have all of the general powers and duties which are usually vested in the office of president of a corporation, including but not limited to the power to appoint committees from among the membership to assist in the conduct of the affairs of the association.

Section 2 *Vice President/Treasurer*
The Vice President and Treasurer positions will be combined and that officer shall take the place of the President and perform the President's duties whenever s/he is absent or unable to act. The Vice President/Treasurer shall have responsibility for association funds, securities, and accurate accounts of all receipts and disbursements in books belonging to the association. He or she shall be responsible for the deposit of all monies in the name and to the credit of the association in the depositories designated by the Board of Directors.

Section 3 *Secretary*
The Secretary shall have responsibility for keeping the minutes of all meetings of the Board

of Directors and the members. He or she shall have charge of the membership transfer books, other documents, and perform all the duties incident to the office of Secretary. The Secretary shall also cause to be prepared a report summarizing the previous year's activities for presentation at the annual meeting of the members.

Article VIII: Committees

Section 1 *Standing Committees*
There shall be (#) permanent standing committees, namely: (list). The Board may establish other temporary committees as it deems necessary. *(Define role of committee chairs, how appointed or elected and term to serve. Officers may be nominated for a specific office on the Board and a specific committee chair position if desired by the group.)*

Section 2 *Appointment of Committee Members*
With the advice of the Board, the President shall appoint not less than two members for each standing committee from the membership. Members in good standing shall serve for one year, unless otherwise designated by the President or removed with or without cause.

Section 3 *Certain Committee Duties*
(List each committee separately, its purpose, specific responsibilities, degree of authority, and reporting schedule. Standing committees may include:

1. Management [common area services and operations] ;

2. Membership/Communications [identify, evaluate and recommend potential members; provide education; mediate disputes; general communications];

3. Design [Improvements and Exhibitions].)

Article IX: Finance and Operations

Section 1 *Capital Stock*
a. *Conditions.* No stock shall be issued except in connection with the execution of an Occupancy Agreement. Ownership of stock entitles the holder to occupy the unit to which it is appurtenant, subject to the Occupancy Agreement.

b. *Form and Share Register.* Share certificates shall be in the form adopted by the Board and shall be signed by an Officer. All certificates representing shares of stock shall bear a legend noting the restrictions on transfer and other limitations as contained in the Articles and Bylaws of the association.

Certificates shall be numbered in the order issued, and there shall be recorded the name of the person and the date of the issue. Each certificate exchanged shall be cancelled and retained in the records of the association. A new share certificate may be executed by the Board after the making of an affidavit by the person claiming the certificate to be lost or destroyed.

c. *Transfers.* Transfers of shares shall be made upon the books of the association in person or by power of attorney, executed and filed with the Secretary on the surrender of the certificate for a share. No transfer shall be valid until approved by the Board and entered in the stock ledger by an entry stating from whom and to whom transferred *(or as required by law)*. The Board may fix a reasonable fee for expenses and attorney's fees.

In any transaction involving the issuance, transfer, or reissuance of common stock or the assignment of rights to the unit, the total consideration exchanged shall not exceed the sum of the Transfer Value plus the Allowable Transfer Fees.

d. *Transfer Value.* Transfer Value means the maximum consideration which may be paid for stock and the rights to a unit and its Occupancy Agreement. The Transfer Value of units may be determined by the Board, provided the Transfer Value never exceeds the amount permitted in the Articles of Incorporation. Allowable transfer fees which may be charged by a party to the transaction are limited to the cost of investigating the transferee and other amounts authorized by the Board bearing a reasonable relationship to costs and expenses paid in connection with permitted transactions as per *(your state statute)*.

Transfer Value shall not include payments made by a transferee for personal property, equipment, fixtures, or similar items which may be sold by the transferor as an ancillary transaction.

(Note regarding Transfer Values and Fixture Fees: Typically, the value of structural or other permanent improvements to a live/work space within a cooperative can be included in the Transfer Value. A fixture fee then becomes the sale price of improvements made to a unit of a nonpermanent nature. Fixture fees are a private negotiable transaction which does not guarantee future reimbursements by subsequent parties, and the fee becomes whatever the market will bear. When utilized to gain preferred placement, fixture fees become a form of extortion. The Lowertown Lofts prepared a Transfer Value Worksheet to assist calculations and clarify their operating policies on Transfer Values and Fixture Fees for their members.)

e. *Lien and Foreclosure.* The association shall have a lien on outstanding stock in order to secure payment of sums due by the holder. In the event a member shall be thirty (30) days in default of payment of any assessment or carrying charge, the Treasurer shall give written notice of the default. Said notice shall specify all existing defaults and give notice that unless defaults are remedied within thirty (30) days, the member's stock will be sold and the member's interest in the stock and the Occupancy Agreement terminate. The association or its assignee may bid at the private sale of the stock to acquire the stock for the amounts owed to the association, as specified in the notice to the member. Provisions of the Uniform Commercial Code shall govern the foreclosure of the lien upon the stock.

Section 2 *Membership Transfers*
a. *Removal From Membership*
Causes for termination of the rights of a member are defined in the Occupancy Agreement. The member shall upon notice promptly vacate the unit and deliver his/her stock certificate and Occupancy Agreement. If not delivered within 10 days, the certificate shall be deemed cancelled and may be reissued to a new purchaser. The association, at its election, shall either (1) repurchase stock at its transfer value or original price, whichever is less, or (2) proceed to effect a sale to an acceptable purchaser. The member shall receive the transfer amount, less amounts due, estimated cost of repairs, and legal or other expenses incurred due to the default and resale of the stock.

b. *Withdrawal From Membership/ Option of Association to Purchase*

A member desiring to withdraw shall notify the association in writing not less than sixty (60) days in advance. The association shall have exclusive option, but not obligation, for thirty (30) days to purchase the member's stock. The price shall be reduced by amounts due or the estimated cost of repairs as are deemed necessary. Purchase of the stock will immediately terminate the member's rights to the unit and occupancy agreement, and the member shall vacate not later than the date specified or acceptable to the association.

c. *Death of a Member*

If a share passes by will or intestate distribution, that legatee may become a member, subject to approval by the Board, if the party assumes in writing the terms of the occupancy agreement within sixty (60) days after the death and after paying all amounts due to the association. If a member dies and obligations are not so assumed, the association shall have an option to purchase the shares, with written notice of the death equivalent to timely notice of an intention to withdraw.

d. *Association Does Not Exercise Option*

If the association waives its option to purchase shares from the withdrawing member or legal representative of a deceased member, the member or representative may propose to sell the stock to any person approved by the association. The member shall provide a copy of the agreement defining the price, terms, conditions, and information about the purchaser as the Board may require, together with fees to cover the association's expenses of investigating the transferee. Within thirty (30) days, the Board shall act upon the proposal. If approved, the Board shall give written notice to both parties, defining any conditions fixed by the Board. If the Board fails to act within thirty (30) days, the transfer shall be deemed approved.

e. *Member Remains Liable Until Transfer*

With any transfer of stock, the member or representative shall remain liable for obligations until a transfer has been approved and completed.

Section 3 *Occupancy Agreements*
a. *Form of Occupancy Agreements*
The Board shall adopt a form for leasing of all units to members.

b. *Amendments*
Any change in the form of Occupancy Agreement must be approved by not less than two-thirds (or ____percent) of the members.

c. *Assignment*
No person shall occupy a unit without first complying with the requirements of the Bylaws and Occupancy Agreement respecting transfer of common stock, Occupancy Agreement and approval by the board.

d. *Lost Occupancy Agreement*
A new Occupancy Agreement may be executed by the Board after the making of an affidavit by the person claiming the agreement to be lost or destroyed.

Section 4 *Patronage Refunds*
a. *Refund*

At the close of each fiscal year, the association shall refund its net income, in excess of reserves, in proportion to each member's actual contribution during such year. *(Reserve accounts may be described here, or in other policy documents.)*

b. *Consent*
Every member consents to report to the I.R.S. any patronage dividends and any distribution of income derived by the association from business done or sources other than patronage as provided in Section(s) 1385(a), 1388(a), 1388(c)(1), 1382(c)(2)(A), or 1388 (c)(1) of the I.R.S. code.

Notice of this provision shall be provided to each prospective member.

Section 5 *Fiscal Management*
a. The *Fiscal Year* will be fixed from time to time by the Board of Directors.

b. *Monthly Carrying Charges; Assessments* shall be fixed by the Board of Directors, payable by the members on the first day of each month; and may levy special assessments *(define conditions and procedures)*. Carrying charges will be sufficient to cover all debt, maintenance, repair, and other proper expenses. Notice of budget decisions and respective carrying charges shall be given to all members, not less than thirty (30) days preceding the commencement of each fiscal year. The Board may re-determine charges or make any special assessment known at any duly called regular or special meeting. Collection of delinquent charges and assessments may be enforced by action at law, foreclosure of the lien, or any other means. The association shall be entitled to recover interest and all costs incident to collection of delinquent charges.

c. *Contribution to Capital*
Carrying charges shall be credited upon the books of the association as paid-in surplus, not as income, and deemed a contribution by members to the associations capital.

d. *Books and Accounts; Reports*
Books and accounts shall be kept under the direction of the Treasurer in accordance with accepted accounting principles. Members shall be furnished monthly and annual financial statements and all records shall be available for inspection.

e. *Execution of Corporate Documents*
The Board shall authorize the President or the Vice President/Treasurer and one other Director (any 2) to execute all notes, contracts, Occupancy Agreements, checks, or other documents on behalf of the association.

Section 6 *Other Provisions*
(Define the corporation's agreements or procedures regarding the following if appropriate to your needs: (1) Right to Borrow, (2) Investments in Other Cooperatives, (3) Subsidiary Corporations, (4) Partnerships.)

Article XI: Amendments

These Bylaws may be amended by the affirmative vote of not less than a majority of the members of record at any annual or special meeting. Amendments may be proposed by the Board of Directors or by petition signed by at least twenty (20%) percent of the members. A description of any proposed amendment shall accompany the notice of any regular or special meeting at which such proposed amendment is to be considered.

Article XII: Dissolution

In the event of dissolution, the membership shall name a nonprofit 501(c)(3) organization to receive any surplus after all obligations have been paid and all stock redeemed at par.

Other Articles

You may add articles reflecting any other special agreements of your cooperative. Some artist cooperatives detail agreements related to health hazard provisions and responsibilities. Other features may include definitions and interpretations of terms used in the Bylaws; whether and in what manner the association will provide indemnification insurance for its directors, officers, manager, employees or agents; and whether there will be a corporate seal.

The undersigned hereby certifies that the foregoing Bylaws were adopted for the _____ Cooperative, a (state) cooperative association, by its Board of Directors, as provided in a Resolution approved at a meeting held on (date).

_____

Secretary, Board of Directors

CONSULTANT EVALUATION FORM

W = Weighted Value of Criteria, based on values held by the group
R = Ranking Score, how well the proposal or firm meets the criteria
S = Total Score in Each Category

Description of Weighted values
5 = extremely important
4 = very important
3 = important
2 = less important
1 = not critical, but nice to have

Description of Ranking score
5 = Best meets criteria
4 = Meets criteria very well
3 = Meets criteria well
2 = Meets criteria but not as well
1 = Does not meet criteria

Selection Criteria	W x R = S	W x R = S	W x R = S
Firm names	X_____	Y_____	Z_____
1. _____	5 x ___ = ___	5 x ___ = ___	5 x ___ = ___
2. _____	5 x ___ = ___	5 x ___ = ___	5 x ___ = ___
3. _____	4 x ___ = ___	4 x ___ = ___	4 x ___ = ___
4. _____	4 x ___ = ___	4 x ___ = ___	4 x ___ = ___
5. _____	4 x ___ = ___	4 x ___ = ___	4 x ___ = ___
6. _____	3 x ___ = ___	3 x ___ = ___	3 x ___ = ___
7. _____	3 x ___ = ___	3 x ___ = ___	3 x ___ = ___
8. _____	2 x ___ = ___	2 x ___ = ___	2 x ___ = ___
9. _____	1 x ___ = ___	1 x ___ = ___	1 x ___ = ___
10. _____	1 x ___ = ___	1 x ___ = ___	1 x ___ = ___

TOTAL SCORE   _____   _____   _____
(add each team's score from each category)

The following tasks are typical of a project in which a group of artists or a small artist-run organization is leasing a commercial space and renovating it to fill studio, presentation and living needs.

— Identify core group of artists with shared goals for space

— Meet with artists to obtain agreement on roles and responsibilities for tasks; agreement on whether a neutral facilitator should be hired to guide group efforts; agreement on the level of financial commitment by each artist towards exploratory planning expenses

— Identify appropriate building; if uncertain of ownership and if building not listed with an agent, contact City Assessor or Tax Information Office

— Check allowable building uses at city zoning office

— Check anticipated development plans for the area with city planning office

— Meet with artists to plan space design and allocation; estimate costs per square foot on monthly basis for each space including proportionate share of any common areas created by hallways

— Prepare memo detailing preliminary plans and costs; seek preliminary written financial commitment to loan if certain conditions are met

— Meet with artists to establish preferred organizational structure for leasing; reach agreement on who signs the lease—one? some? all?

— Consult with an attorney for further information on organizational structures, especially if group is large or all artists are willing to share responsibility for the lease

— Meet with artists to clarify which issues are critical to secure in the lease and which issues are optional; reach agreement about whether to hire an attorney to negotiate on behalf of the group

— Negotiate lease with building owner; clarify all understandings in a written draft of lease

— Review proposed lease with an attorney, especially if one was not hired to negotiate the lease

— Review all lease provisions and recommendations of attorney with prospective artist-tenants

— Set up meetings to market space to additional artist-tenants if necessary; it is best if all artists are committed before the signing of lease

— Prepare preliminary floor plan; contract with architect (in most cases)

— Review floor plan with all prospective tenants for corrections/approval

— Request (by designer) City Building Code Field Inspection and review of preliminary floor plan; send letter to Field Inspector stating all understandings and variance approvals

— Make final decisions on floor plans with architect and artists, including preliminary cost estimates and written specifications as required by City Building Inspections Office; identify which tasks will be undertaken by artist-tenants

— Identify contractors to hire as required by city; clarify your needs and any expectations for demolition or clean-up work to be provided by artists to lower overall costs

— Review floor plans and city approvals with building owner; negotiate agreement on any improvements required to be made by building owner and include written agreement of allocated tasks in lease

— Obtain plan approval from City Building Inspections Office; on small projects you can pay for the building permit the same day unless you have the city's agreement that the building permit will be taken out by a general contractor you intend to hire

— Prepare several sets of stamped and approved plans and specifications for distribution to contractors you wish to bid on your project; provide clear written description of any information required to be submitted with the bid

— Review bids from contractors, make selection and notify all contractors of choice

— Revise cost information for artist-tenants; secure financial contributions from artists or seek financing from lender(s), patrons and others, providing a summary of project information as needed

— Decide on the final tenant organizational structure with attorney and artists

— Decide on the final probable schedule for receipt of construction funds, construction activity and postconstruction tasks by artists, including preferred move-in date

— Decide on final lease provisions with building owner; establish anticipated date for lease signing and construction start

— Confirm final selection of tenants, commitment of artist funds and allocation of spaces

— Review lease for the last time with attorney and artists

— Confirm receipt of construction funds from all sources

— Sign lease, which is signed by all required parties

— When construction begins, monitor work of contractors and construction budget

— Refine tenant self-management structure through additional planning

— Complete construction cleanup and finish tasks through artists' "sweat equity," after which artists move in and celebrate!

The following tasks are typical of a project in a group of artists or an artist-run organization is buying a commercial space and renovating it to fill studio, presentation and living needs.

— Identify core group of artists with shared goals for space

— Meet with artists to obtain agreement on roles and responsibilities for tasks; agreement on whether a neutral facilitator should be hired to guide group efforts; agreement on the level of financial commitment by each artist towards exploratory planning expenses and final costs

— Identify appropriate building and evaluate closely for structural integrity

— Check allowable building uses at city zoning office

— Check anticipated development plans for the area with city planning office

— Meet with artists to plan space design and allocation; estimate costs per square foot on monthly basis for each space including proportionate share of any common areas created by hallways

— Prepare memo detailing preliminary plans and costs; seek preliminary written financial commitment to loan; determine what lending conditions are to be met

— Meet with artists to establish preferred organizational structure for ownership and proportionate share of financial investment

— Consult with an attorney for further information on organizational structures appropriate to the ownership opportunity

— Meet with artists to clarify which issues are critical to secure in the purchase agreement and which issues are optional; reach agreement about whether to hire an attorney to negotiate on behalf of the group

— Conduct purchase negotiations with building owner; clarify all understandings in a written draft of the purchase agreement; deposit "option" money with the building owner's real estate broker

— Review proposed purchase agreement with an attorney and all probable "buyers"

— Set up meetings to market space to additional artist-tenants if necessary; it is best if all artists are committed before the final signing of purchase agreement

— Prepare preliminary floor plan; contract with architect in most cases

— Review floor plan with all prospective tenants for corrections/approval

— Request (by designer) City Building Code Field Inspection and review of preliminary floor plan; send letter to Field Inspector stating all understandings and variance approvals

— Make final decisions on floor plans with architect and artists, including preliminary cost estimates and written specifications as required by City Building Inspections Office; identify which tasks will be undertaken by artist/tenants

— Identify contractors to hire as required by city; clarify your needs and any expectations for demolition or cleanup work to be provided by artists to lower overall costs

— Review floor plans and city approvals with building owner; negotiate agreement on any improvements required to be made by building owner and include written agreement of allocated tasks in lease

— Obtain plan approval from City Building Inspections Office

— Prepare several sets of stamped and approved plans and specifications for distribution to contractors you wish to bid on your project; provide clear written description of any information required to be submitted with the bid

— Review bids from contractors, make selection and notify all contractors of choice; negotiate contract with contractor

— Revise cost information for artist-tenants; secure financial contributions from artist-owners

— Seek financing from lender(s), patrons and others, providing a summary of project information including preliminary design and cost estimates, market study, preliminary tenant profile, equity contribution of artist-owners and other partners

— Make final decisions on tenant organizational structure and any leasing terms with attorney and artists

— Make final decisions on probable schedule for receipt of construction funds, construction activity, postconstruction tasks by artists, preferred move-in date

— Make final decisions on all purchase agreement provisions with building owner; establish anticipated date for "closing" and construction start

— Confirm final selection of tenants, commitment of artist funds and allocation of spaces

— Confirm receipt of construction funds from all sources

— Schedule the "closing" and ensure that all necessary documents have been prepared as requested by lenders and attorneys

— Sign all closing documents, which are signed by all required parties

— Acquire building permit; as construction begins, monitor work of contractors and construction budget

— Complete construction cleanup and finishing tasks through artist "sweat equity," after which artists move in and celebrate

1. All shareholders and tenants agree to abide by all documents related to the co-op, including the Master Lease, Articles of Incorporation, the Bylaws, the Occupancy Agreement and these Rules and Regulations, as amended from time to time by the co-op.

2. All shareholders and tenants shall comply with all applicable laws, ordinances and regulations and shall save the association and other tenants harmless from all fines, penalties, costs and prosecutions for any violations thereof.

Maintenance

3. No garbage cans, trash barrels or other obstructing personal property shall be placed in common areas. Laundry areas should be left clean and neat when you are through.

4. All refuse shall be properly disposed of in suitable plastic garbage bags and placed in provided cans or dumpsters.

5. Hallways, sidewalks, stairways and other portions of the common areas shall not be obstructed for any other purposes than ingress and egress from the unit.

6. Each shareholder shall keep his or her unit in a good state of cleanliness. No refuse or private property shall be placed in the common areas without the permission of the Board of Directors.

7. The water closets and other water apparatus shall not be used for any other purpose than that for which they were constructed, and no sweepings, rubbish, rags, paper, ashes or other substances shall be thrown therein. Any damage to the property of others, including the common area resulting from the misuse of such facilities, of any nature whatever, shall be paid by the tenant of the unit.

8. No shareholder or tenant shall interfere in any manner with any portion of the heating or lighting apparatus in, or about, the property.

9. Tenants shall close all windows when necessary to avoid possible damage from storm, rain or freezing.

Use

10. No noxious or offensive activity shall be carried on in any unit, or in the common areas, either willfully or negligently, which may become an annoyance or nuisance to other occupants. No occupant shall make or permit any disturbing noises to be made on the property. Nor shall occupants do or permit anything to be done by other persons that will interfere with the rights, comforts and conveniences of the other occupants.

11. No member shall play or allow to be played any musical instrument, radio, television, phonograph, power tools or any machine or device that can be heard outside of the unit between the hours of 10:00 p.m. and 8:00 a.m. (12:00 p.m. on weekends).

12. No radio, television or other antennae shall be installed by the occupant anywhere on the property, except as approved by the Board of Directors.

13. All radio, television or other electrical equipment of any kind or nature installed or used in the unit shall fully comply with all rules, regulations and requirements or recommendations of the Board of Fire Underwriters and other public authorities having jurisdiction. Each tenant shall be liable for any injury or damage caused by any radio, television or other electrical equipment in the tenant's apartment.

14. Nothing shall be done or kept anywhere on the property which will increase the rate of insurance for the property or the contents thereof. No occupant shall permit anything to be done, or to be kept in the apartment or limited common areas which will result in the cancellation of, or increase in the cost of, insurance on the property or contents thereof, or which would be in violation of any law.

15. No "For Sale," "For Rent" or "For Lease" signs or other window displays or advertisement shall be placed on any part of the property accept as approved by the Board of Directors.

16. Occupants shall not place identification or other signs in any place in the building, unless approved by the Board of Directors.

17. The agents of the co-op and any contractor or worker authorized by the co-op or its agent, bearing proper identification, may enter any apartment at any reasonable hour of the day, after notification to the shareholder (except in case of emergency), for the purpose of correcting any condition which presents a danger of loss or damage to the property or injury or death to any person.

18. Pets shall be permitted only upon the written approval of the Board of Directors with respect to each unit and each pet, and then only upon such conditions as the Board of Directors may establish in each instance and from time to time.

Procedures

19. Agent of the Co-op:

   - Whom do people pay rent to?
   - Who accepts maintenance complaints?
   - Who makes payments for the co-op?
   - Who receives and serves termination notices?
   - Who inspects apartments on move out?
   - Who has extra keys if someone gets locked out?
   - Rules for replacement of lost keys?
   - Rules for accepting deliveries?
   - Rules for allowing salespeople in building?
   - How are fires handled and reported?
   - Types and amounts of reserve accounts?

20. Responsibilities of Tenants

- Participation required on committees?
- Assignment of common area maintenance tasks?
- Time commitment expected each month?
- Who monitors the work?
- Required minimum of participation hours set by board.
- Definition of a tenant in good standing?
- Policy on children's behavior/participation?

21. Moving In and Moving Out

- When is rent due?
- To whom are checks made out?
- To whom is rent paid?
- Penalties for late rents?
- What notice of intent to vacate is required?
- Who is the notice given to?
- Who does the move out inspections?
- Who are keys returned to?
- Who returns deposit?

22. Insurance and Wills

- Renter's insurance is required for personal liability and property losses
- A will is recommended for all nonrelated co-tenants of an apartment to ensure that upon death of the shareholder the equity and membership share may pass to the co-tenant directly, and not to the shareholder's immediate heirs

23. Design Review and Fixture Fee Policy

- Determine value of "sweat equity" portion of transfer value
- Maintain records of each tenant's hours and material costs for work common to all tenants
- Toss out the high and low numbers for each and average the remainder for each size of unit
- Determine depreciation schedule
- Determine policy for further improvements by tenants

SELECTION PROCEDURES

1. Application shall be in the form and manner prescribed by the Board of Directors.

2. Vacancies shall be advertised publicly if there is no waiting list of qualified applicants. Spaces will also be listed with Artspace Projects Inc., or other suitable art service organizations.

3. All applications received by the corporation shall be kept in separate files, and maintained for one year by the Secretary (after which they may be deemed cancelled or renewable).

4. No applications shall be accorded preferential weight for vacancies based upon time or order of receipt.

5. All applications shall contain an agreement, signed by the applicant, that should the applicant be chosen as a "finalist" for consideration of a vacant unit, the applicant will promptly forward a nonrefundable check or money order payable to Lowertown Lofts Co-op in an amount to be determined by the Board of Directors and specified in the application form as payment for credit reference reports.

6. The Board of Directors will have the right to verify incomes of "finalists" to determine if they have acceptable credit, and to reject otherwise acceptable candidates if the filling of a vacancy would result in less than 51 percent of the corporation's members being at or below 80 percent of the median income adjusted for household size as determined by the U.S. Department of Housing and Urban Development for that calendar year.

7. The Board of Directors or their duly appointed representatives shall select four (4) applications found most suitable for membership from all valid applications as "finalists."

8. "Finalist" applicants shall be further screened in such manner prescribed by the Board of Directors, including personal interviews at the sole discretion of the membership.

9. Determination of the successful applicant for membership in the corporation from the "finalist" applicants shall be by a majority vote of the Board of Directors, (or their designees).

MEMBERSHIP SELECTION CRITERIA

Eligibility

1. Any natural person approved by the Board of Directors shall be eligible for membership.

2. Membership in the corporation is open to all persons regardless of race, religion, creed, political belief, sex preference, or status as a parent.

3. The determination of any further eligibility shall rest with the discretion of the Board of Directors, and may include the following;

a. Artistic Commitment (4 points)

- Previous studio work
- Education
- Exhibition/performance
- Sales/teaching

b. Financial Capability (3 points)

- Low/moderate income qualification
- Credit history
- Cash flow/35 percent of income ceiling

c. Commitment to Lowertown (2 points)

- Current working/living resident
- SPAC, or other Lowertown arts group membership
- Housing project involvement
- Commitment to co-op membership (long term).

d. Need For Space (1 point)

- Threat of displacement
- Excess rent, above 50 percent of income
- Unsafe conditions (overcrowding)

Selection Policy

Between financially capable applicants equal in need, and otherwise eligible for occupancy, preference will be given to serious artists who have shown a commitment to the Lowertown Art Community through involvement in the Lowertown Lofts Housing Project. Units may be assigned based on media requirements of tenants. An annual Selection Committee Meeting will be held to plan solicitation of the active waiting list.

SUBSCRIPTIONS

1. Selected applicants will be required to execute a Subscription Agreement for a share of stock in the Co-op association which shall call for the payment of the subscription price of a share, which must be paid in full upon execution of the Subscription Agreement.

2. Execution of the Subscription Agreement and payment of the subscription price shall entitle the applicant to a membership certificate. A membership certificate is the same as a certificate of common shares in the Association.

3. Upon issuance of a membership certificate, the new member will be required to execute an Occupancy Agreement.

List of Abbreviations and Acronyms

AHOP	Artist Home Ownership Program	**GOR**	General operating reserve
AIA	American Institute of Architects	**HUD**	Housing and Urban Development
AIR	Artist-in-Residence	**HVAC**	Heating, ventilating and air conditioning
APOD	Annual Property Operating Data		
ARM	Adjustable rate mortgage	**IRR**	Internal Rate of Return
ATA	Artists Tenants Association	**ITCs**	Investment Tax Credits
BMIR	Below market interest rate	**LISC**	Local Initiatives Support Corporation
C.A.	Commercial and Artcraft District	**MDL**	Multiple Dwelling Law
CDBG	Community Development Block Grant	**MGIC**	Mortgage Guaranty Insurance Corporation
DCR	Debt coverage ratio		
DS	Debt service	**MLS**	Multiple Listing Service
C of O	Certificate of Occupancy	**M&O**	Management and operating cost
CFATx	Cash flow after tax	**NEA**	National Endowment for the Arts
CFBTx	Cash flow before tax	**NEF**	National Equity Fund
CFRATx	Cash flow rate after tax	**NOI**	Net operating income
CRA	Community Reinvestment Act	**PRI**	Program-Related Investment
DC	Direct current	**REIT**	Real Estate Investment Trust
DS	Debt service	**RFP**	Request for Proposal
FHA	Federal Housing Administration	**SAC**	Sewer Access Charge
FHLMC	Federal Home Loan Mortgage Corporation	**S&L**	Savings and loan
FNMA	Federal National Mortgage Association	**SoHo**	Area south of Houston St. in New York City
FPAC	Fort Point Arts Community		
GFI	Ground Fault Interrupter	**SOMAA**	Area south of Market St. in San Francisco
GNMA	Government National Mortgage Association		
		UDAG	Urban Development Action Grants
GOI	Gross operating income	**VA**	Veterans Administration

Glossary of Real Estate, Development, and Financial Terms

A

ABSOLUTE NET LEASE: A lease that requires the tenant to be responsible for taxes, insurance, operating expenses and structural repairs to the property, in addition to a base rent.

ABSTRACT: Historical summary of all recorded documents affecting the title of a property.

ACCELERATED DEPRECIATION: A method of reducing the taxable value of a property at allowances that are greater in early years and then decline according to a formula specified by law.

ACCELERATION CLAUSE: A clause in a deed of trust or mortgage that allows a lender to demand immediate repayment of a loan upon default, sale or demolition.

ACKNOWLEDGMENT: A formal declaration in front of an authorized officer or notary public by a person that he or she is signing a document as a voluntary act.

ACTUAL CASH VALUE: Dollar value of a property arrived at by taking the cost of restoring the property to its condition immediately preceding a loss (e.g., fire damage), and subtracting the accumulated value of depreciation (physical wear and tear on the property).

ADJUSTABLE RATE MORTGAGE: A loan in which the interest rate can be changed over the life of the loan according to agreed-upon criteria.

ADJUSTED BASIS: The original price of a property plus capital improvements and minus depreciation.

ADJUSTED GROSS INCOME: Base income, less allowable adjustments and plus capital gains, for tax-benefit analysis.

ADJUSTED MARKET PRICE: The value of a comparable property after adjustments have been made for differences between it and the subject property.

ADJUSTED SALES PRICE: The sales price of a property less commissions, fix-up and closing costs.

AD VALOREM: A tax charged in proportion to value.

AGENCY: The business of one (the principal) delegated to another (the agent).

AIR RIGHT: Right to occupy air space above surface of land or improvement.

ALIENATION CLAUSE: A clause that allows the lender to demand payment in full if property is sold.

AMORTIZATION: Periodic payments of a constant amount on a mortgage loan or other debt that includes both interest and partial repayment of principal to reduce the unpaid loan balance.

ANNUAL PERCENTAGE RATE (APR): The relationship of the total finance charge to the amount of a loan (interest, loan fees and discount points) expressed as a percentage.

APPRAISAL: An estimate of the real or fair market value of a property prepared by an appraiser. Different types include competitive market analysis, cost approach, gross rent multiplier, income approach, market approach and square foot method.

ARBITRATION: A method for settling disputes that avoids lawsuits or court action.

ARTICLES OF INCORPORATION: The legal documents filed with a state government defining the purpose and operations of a corporation, under provisions of state law.

ASSESSED VALUATION: The value assigned to a property by a governmental agency for real estate tax purposes.

ASSESSMENT: The imposition of a tax, charge or levy by a governmental unit.

ASSETS: Refers to property owned by a person or other legal entity that has an exchange value or is readily convertible into cash, e.g., savings and checking accounts, stocks and bonds, or real estate.

ASSIGN: To transfer to another one's rights or interest in property, real or personal, under a contract.

ASSIGNEE: One to whom property or rights to property have been transferred by an assignor.

ASSIGNMENT OF RENTS CLAUSE: A clause in a mortgage or deed that provides the right of a lender to collect rents generated by a property should the borrower cease to repay the loan.

ASSUME LOAN: Buyer obligates himself or herself to repay seller's existing loan as a condition of the sale.

ATTORNEY IN FACT: One who is legally appointed by another to execute legal documents on behalf of the grantor of the power.

B

BALLOON LOAN: Loan in which final payment is the amount of the outstanding balance on the debt. The final lump sum payment is called a balloon payment.

BARGAIN SALE: The sale of a property to a nonprofit organization for less than its fair market value.

BASIS: Original price paid for property; used in calculating income taxes.

BEFORE-TAX INCOME: Gross income minus all expenses except income taxes.

BILL OF SALE: A written agreement by which one person transfers his or her personal property to another.

BINDER: A contract used to secure a real estate transaction until a purchase agreement can be signed.

BLANKET MORTGAGE: Secured by more than one real property.

BLIGHTED AREA: Term used in urban planning to describe areas that, by reason of identified adverse conditions, qualify the area for urban renewal assistance.

BLIND POOL: Properties to be acquired by several investors not specified to the investors.

BMIR: An FHA abbreviation for Below Market Interest Rate mortgage insurance programs in which a low interest rate makes it possible for low- to moderate-income families to secure housing.

BONDING: Bonding ensures that the contractor, if unable to finish the building, has access to funds to satisfy the obligations of the contract or loan.

BORROWER: One who receives funds with the expressed intention of repaying the loan in full.

BORROWER'S POINTS: Fees paid by a borrower to obtain a loan, charged in one-percent units of a loan.

BREAKEVEN POINT RATIO (BEP): The sum of total expenses and debt service is divided by the gross rent to indicate to an owner/developer how much vacancy a property can tolerate yet generate sufficient cash to cover expenses if vacancies were to increase significantly. Lenders prefer BEP ratios of 65-85 percent.

BROKER: One who brings parties together and assists in negotiating contracts between them for a commission or fee. The real estate broker usually brings together the buyer, the seller and the mortgage lender.

BUDGET: A document prepared annually to project income and expenses for the coming year. Projections, based on previous experience or plans, are the basis for the calculation of the monthly charges for each unit of a multiunit development project.

BUDGET MORTGAGE: The lender collects payments that include principal, interest, taxes and insurance (often called PITI) and then pays the taxes and insur-

ance when due from the escrow account to protect the value of the property.

BUILDING CODE: A set of laws specifying the minimum standards (materials, size, exits, etc.) for constructing a building.

BUILDING PERMIT: Authorization by a city for construction, renovation or demolition of a building to take place, consistent with the city's building, zoning, or other requirements.

BUILT-UP ROOF: Roofing material comprising layers of asphalt felt laminated with coal tar, pitch, or asphalt and topped with gravel or crushed slag for use on flat or low-pitched roofs.

BULK: The relation of a building on a lot to its size. Regulations for bulk include lot coverage, setback requirements and height limits for buildings.

BUYER'S MARKET: A condition in which there are few buyers and many sellers.

BYLAWS: Written regulations that set forth the structure and governance of an organization, secondary to its Articles of Incorporation.

C

CAPITAL GAIN: Gain (profit) on sale of a property that has appreciated in value.

CAPITALIZATION RATE: Rate of return on net operating income considered acceptable for an investor and used to determine estimated market value.

CAPITALIZE: To convert future income to current asset value.

CASH FLOW (PRETAX): (1) The income remaining each year after paying operating expenses and mortgage payments. (2) A compilation of reports and documents prepared for the purpose of informing the owners about the continuing financial status of a development.

CASH FLOW RATE AFTER TAX (CFRATx): The pretax cash flow less income taxes (affected by the amount of depreciation, equity build-up and the owner's tax bracket) incorporates tax benefits into the cash flow analysis.

CASH-ON-CASH: A decision-making tool for developers to measure the income stream to be received from a project; cash flow (net operating income less debt service) is divided by cash required to purchase (equity).

CASH-OUT: A condition of a sale that requires the seller to be fully bought out of his or her interest in a property either at the time of sale or a predetermined future date.

CASUALTY INSURANCE: Insurance designed to protect from loss or liability resulting from accidents.

CAVEAT EMPTOR ("Let the buyer beware"): The principle that the seller cannot be held liable for the quality of what is sold unless it is guaranteed in writing.

CERTIFICATE OF OCCUPANCY (C of O): A document issued by a municipality which authorizes the use of a certain space or building for specified activities by a certain number of people. Also called an Occupancy Placard.

CERTIFICATE OF REASONABLE VALUE (CRV): Informs an applicant for a Veterans Administration (VA) loan of the appraised value of the property and the maximum VA guaranteed loan a private lender may make.

CERTIFICATE OF TITLE: Proves ownership of property and contains the legal description of buildings and land.

CERTIFICATION: The process of determining the eligibility of an applicant for housing prior to occupancy, usually applying regulations that govern income and family composition.

CHAIN OF TITLE: Successive conveyances of property ownership transactions that connect the present owner to the original source of the title.

CHARACTERISTICS OF LAND: Fixity, immobility, indestructibility, modification, scarcity, situs and nonhomogeneity are characteristics that make land different from other commodities.

CHARACTERISTICS OF VALUE: Demand, scarcity, transferability and utility are the characteristics that a property, a good or a service must possess to have value in the marketplace.

CHATTEL: An article of personal property.

CHATTEL MORTGAGE: A pledge of personal property to secure a note or mortgage.

CLEAR TITLE: Title that is not encumbered with defects.

CLOSING: The act of finalizing a mortgage transaction or transfer of title to property when documents are signed and delivered to entitled person(s).

CLOSING COSTS: Various fees and expenses in the transaction of selling or buying real estate, changing title, and procuring and processing a mortgage which are not covered by financing.

CLOUD ON TITLE: Any claim, lien or encumbrance that impairs the owner's title to the property.

CODE ENFORCEMENT: The inspection, notification, issuance of citations or court action to require property owners to maintain or improve their property according to minimum standards set by the government.

CODES (Building, Health, Housing, Electrical, Plumbing, Fire, etc.): Laws governing the construction and operation of public and private facilities, codes are intended to safeguard life and promote health and safety through the establishment of minimum standards for construction and operating conditions.

COLLATERAL: The specific real property which the borrower pledges as security for a loan, such as stocks, bonds, evidence of deposit, and other marketable properties.

COLLECTION LOSS: The monetary loss to a development resulting from noncollection of money from residents of occupied units or from units where a cooperative member is responsible, although not actually in occupancy.

COMMERCIAL POLICY: Insurance contract used in the insuring of business risks.

COMMITMENT: A binding agreement indicating the terms and conditions on which FHA will insure a lender against default on a mortgage used as the basis for final arrangements for closing the loan.

COMMON AREAS: Those areas of a cooperative or condominium whose use is shared by all occupants, such as halls, lobby, elevator, recreation areas, grounds.

COMMUNITY PROPERTY: Co-ownership of property by a husband and wife, who are treated as equal partners with each owning a one-half interest.

COMPARABLES: Properties with similar physical amenities or features that are compared to estimate the value of a property to be placed on the market.

COMPETENT PARTIES: Persons considered legally capable of entering into a binding contract, including persons of legal age (18-21 years) and of sound mind.

COMPETITIVE MARKET ANALYSIS: A method of valuing property that looks not only at recent property sales but also at property now on the market plus property that was listed but did not sell.

COMPREHENSIVE PLAN: Master long-term plan for physical growth of a community.

CONDEMNATION: A municipal proceeding which denies the current use of a property, either because it presents a danger to public safety, or because it is needed for some public use.

CONDEMNATION CLAUSE: A clause in a mortgage note requiring that any money received for property taken by eminent domain must be used to reduce the balance of the note.

CONDITIONAL SALE CONTRACT: A contract for the sale of property to be delivered to the buyer, with the seller to retain the title until the conditions of the contract have been fulfilled. Such a contract is also known as a contract for deed.

CONDITIONAL USE: A principal or accessory use of a property that is specifically authorized by a municipal zoning agency after the proposed use has been determined to be compatible with surrounding property uses.

CONDOMINIUM: A form of ownership that combines individual ownership of a dwelling unit with joint ownership of those common areas or facilities that are shared by occupants of two or more dwelling units.

CONSIDERATION: Something of value given in exchange to enter into a contract.

CONSTRUCTION COST: The cost of building, including both labor and material expenses, but not land.

CONSTRUCTION LOAN: Short-term or interim loan enabling a developer to pay the contractor's bills during the construction period, later replaced by long-term permanent financing.

CONTINGENCY FEE: A fee paid to an attorney or technical consultant depending on whether the client receives the claim, grant or award with which the consultant assisted.

CONTINGENT INTEREST: Lender's equity-sharing provision calling for a percentage of profits exceeding a base amount.

CONTRACT: A legally enforceable agreement that creates, modifies or ends a legal relationship.

CONTRACT FOR DEED: Method of selling and financing property whereby the buyer obtains possession but the seller retains title until the loan is paid. Also called an installment or conditional sales contract.

CONVENTIONAL LOAN: A mortgage loan obtained from a private lender (e.g., bank or savings and loan association) that is not insured by FHA or guaranteed by VA and generally has a fixed market interest rate.

COOPERATIVE: An ownership structure in which the occupants of a building own a membership or

share in a corporation or association which owns or leases the property.

CORNICE: A prominent horizontal architectural feature overhanging an exterior wall at or near the top of a building, may also be the overhang of a pitched roof at the eaves.

CORPORATION: A business that is chartered by the government and controlled by a board of directors and that distributes economic or other benefits to owner/shareholders, who are liable only for the amount of their investment.

CORRELATION PROCESS: An appraisal step wherein the appraiser assigns more weight to a more similar property and less to other comparables used to assess the value of the subject property. Also, the process of selecting a single estimated value based on comparing the Cost, Market, and Income approaches to valuation.

COST APPROACH: An appraisal process based on land value plus current construction costs minus depreciation.

COST CERTIFICATION: A requirement under some federal programs that the mortgagor and related contractors or suppliers certify the actual costs incurred upon completion of a project.

COUNTEROFFER: An amended offer made in response to an offer.

COVENANT: A written agreement or promise, especially clauses promising performance or nonperformance of certain acts, found in leases, deeds and mortgages; e.g., the covenant to pay taxes or insurance, or those listed below.

COVENANT AGAINST ENCUMBRANCES: Grantor warrants that the title is not encumbered other than as stated in the deed.

COVENANT OF FURTHER ASSURANCE: Grantor agrees to acquire and deliver to the grantee any subsequent documents necessary to fulfill promises regarding the grantee's title.

COVENANT OF QUIET ENJOYMENT: Grantor/lessor warrants right of possession and use of property to the grantee/lessee without undue disturbance by others.

COVENANT OF SEIZIN: Grantor guarantees that he or she is the owner of a property and has the right to convey it.

CPI ESCALATOR: A process through which a tenant's base rent is increased by the percentage increase in the consumer price index (CPI) or a proportion of that increase from a fixed point in time, usually referred to as the base year. For example, a tenant's rent may be increased by 25 percent of the increase in the CPI over the base year. If the CPI increases at an annual rate of 8 percent, then the tenant pays a 2 percent increase in rent; if the base rent is $500/month, the rent goes up $10/month after the first year and compounds thereafter. Also known as a "cost of living" adjustment. You may negotiate a "cap" on the amount of the increase per year, e.g., "the CPI or 10 percent, whichever is lower."

CREDIT: The ability to borrow due to the trust of the lender that the loan will be repaid.

CREDIT UNION: A cooperative finance company whose shareholders are also its depositors and borrowers; specializing in consumer loans, it is also a potential source of mortgage loans.

CRITICAL PATH METHOD: A development management tool for scheduling and monitoring construction activity. It is a step-by-step breakdown of a job into its components and the plotting of sequential relationships and lead time required for all operations.

D

DEBT COVERAGE RATIO (DCR): The ratio of Net Operating Income (NOI) to the debt service (D/S). It provides a measure of the lender's income cushion on a loan. The higher the DCR, the more favorable it is for the lender, with lenders preferring higher cushions on riskier projects. The DCR range is usually 1.1 to 1.4, with lenders preferring 1.25 and up.

DEBT FINANCING: Money loaned on a long-term basis as distinguished from equity financing.

DEBT SERVICE (D/S): The borrower's payments on a mortgage to satisfy principal and interest on the loan indebtedness. The lender will require the loan to be structured to provide adequate net operating income (NOI) to cover the loan payments (D/S) plus other expenses.

DEDUCTIBLE: Predetermined amount of money agreed to in an insurance contract that is subtracted from an insurance award due to a loss or liability.

DEED: A document that signifies ownership duly executed and delivered, conveying the title to real property from one party to another. The deed may contain a transfer, a bargain or a contract. There are two general types of deed: see QUITCLAIM DEED and WARRANTY DEED.

DEED OF TRUST: A document that conveys title to a neutral third party as security for a debt until paid or defaulted, used instead of mortgage in some states. The power of sale clause gives authority to the third party to sell the secured property if the borrower defaults without having to go through a court-ordered foreclosure proceeding.

DEED RESTRICTIONS: Statements in a deed limiting or restricting the future use of the land.

DEFAULT: Declaration of failure to perform a legal duty; failure to fulfill an agreement or contract; or failure to meet an obligation; the legal result of delinquent actions.

DELINQUENT: To neglect the terms of an agreement; failure to pay agreed-upon rent or other monthly housing charges in a timely manner; or failure to pay various contractors, suppliers or a mortgage holder as agreed.

DENSITY: A zoning restriction on the number of square feet of residential or nonresidential space that may be built within a specified zoning district.

DEPRECIATION: Presumed reduction in property value through ordinary wear and tear, loss of functional or economic value, etc., represented by a federal tax deduction from net income to arrive at taxable income.

DETERIORATION: The decline in the perceived physical, economic or social quality of buildings and areas.

DEVELOPER: A person or company that organizes, invests in and brings into being the construction or renovation of real estate development projects.

DEVELOPMENT LOAN: Short-term loan used to acquire land and install basic utilities prior to construction loan.

DEVELOPMENT PROCESS: Process through which investment projects are conceived, initiated, designed, analyzed, financed, constructed and managed.

DISBURSEMENT STAGE: The time in the construction process when the borrower begins to receive installments of the construction loan proceeds.

DISCOUNT POINTS: Charges made by lenders to adjust the effective yield of interest on a loan without raising the interest rate, used primarily during periods of tight money.

DIVIDEND: A return of profits made by a cooperative or other corporation to its member shareholders.

DOWN PAYMENT: A portion of the sales price paid by a buyer at the time of closing, which may augment the earnest money paid in a contract for deed or complete payment if less than a 100 percent mortgage loan is secured. The down payment is the buyer's initial equity investment.

DOWNSIDE RISK: The likelihood that an investor will lose money in an investment.

DOWNSPOUT: A pipe used to carry rainwater from the gutter to the ground or to a drain.

DRAW: A construction lending procedure which allows the developer to receive the loan proceeds at predefined stages of construction; e.g., foundation, plumbing, interior walls.

DUAL AGENCY (Divided Agency): Representation of two or more parties in a transaction by the same agent, resulting in a conflict of interest. Both buyer and seller must be informed before negotiations and either may decline to participate or seek other representation.

DUCTS: Rectangular or round metal pipes for distributing air for heating and air conditioning.

DUE-ON-SALE: Gives lender right to call entire loan balance due if property is sold or otherwise conveyed to allow the lender to reloan the money at current rates or increase the rate if it is assumed.

DWELLING UNIT: A legal description of a room or rooms intended for living accommodations for an individual or family. The presence of a food preparation area may be considered evidence of a dwelling unit and require additional residential codes to be complied with by an inspections department unless it can be shown to have a valid business use.

E

EARNEST MONEY DEPOSIT: Advance payment of part of the purchase price that accompanies an offer to purchase as evidence of good faith. It is refundable if the offer is not accepted or if the seller does not meet stated terms or conditions by a certain date. It is forfeited if the buyer does not complete the purchase as stated by the terms or conditions in the accepted offer.

EARTHQUAKE CODE: An ordinance regulating design, materials and construction of buildings in communities threatened by the potential public safety hazards resulting from earthquakes.

EASEMENT: The privilege one party has to use land belonging to another for a special purpose not inconsistent with the owner's use of the land and usually agreed to in writing; e.g., to provide for pipelines, pole lines or roads.

EAVES: The overhanging lower edge of a roof which may be covered by a sheathing called a soffit. The entire projection is called a cornice.

ECONOMIC OBSOLESCENCE: A loss of value due to external forces or events affecting buildings, land or both; e.g., disinvestment in surrounding properties, air or noise pollution.

EFFECTIVE YIELD: A calculation of a lender's or investor's return which considers price paid, interest rate and the time held.

EGRESS: The path of exit, including any combination of doors, stairwells and passageways.

ELEVATION: An architectural drawing of the face of all or part of a building "head-on," without allowances for the effect of the laws of perspective.

ELIGIBILITY: The qualification standards or requirements a person must meet to qualify for various governmental programs.

EMINENT DOMAIN: The right of the government to take private property for public use upon paying the property owners the fair market value of the property.

ENCROACHMENT: An unlawful extension of one's building or other improvement upon the land of another.

ENCUMBRANCE: Any limitation to a clear title, such as a lease, easement or lien.

ENERGY CODE: An ordinance regulating design, materials and construction of buildings to conserve the energy used in heating or cooling buildings.

EQUAL CREDIT OPPORTUNITY ACT: Legislation that prohibits discrimination against applicants for credit on the basis of race, color, religion, national origin, sex, marital status, age, income from public assistance programs, or exercised rights under the Consumer Protection Act.

EQUITY: The market value of real property less the total amount of all mortgages or liens against the property. It reflects the proportionate dollar amount of the owner's interest in a property.

EQUITY BUILD-UP: The increase of one's equity in a property due to mortgage balance reduction (principal pay-down) and price appreciation.

EQUITY FINANCING: Investment by owners or limited partners in anticipation of a return.

EQUITY OF REDEMPTION: After default, the right of a borrower to repay the balance due on a delinquent mortgage loan before foreclosure.

EQUITY SYNDICATION: A financing method that sells the anticipated cash flow and tax shelter from income-producing (rental) properties to investors who provide capital needed for a project.

ESCALATOR CLAUSE: Provisions in a lease for adjustments in rent due to changes in property taxes, utility charges or other operating expenses. See also CPI ESCALATOR.

ESCROW: Placing property or cash into a neutral party's account.

ESCROW ACCOUNT: An account into which the lender places monthly tax and insurance payments collected as part of a budget mortgage. Also called a Reserve Account.

ESTATE: The extent of one's rights in land or one's personal property.

ESTATE AT WILL: A lease that can be terminated at any time by the lessor or lessee.

ESTATE FOR YEARS: Any lease with a specific starting and ending time; it does not automatically renew.

ESTATE IN SEVERALTY: Owned by one person, sole (or "severed") ownership.

ESTOPPEL CERTIFICATE: A document in which a borrower verifies the amount he or she still owes and the interest rate; used when the mortgage holder sells the mortgage to another investor.

EXCLUSIVE AGENCY LISTING: A listing wherein the owner reserves the right to sell his or her property without paying a commission, but guarantees not to list with any other broker during the listing period.

EXCLUSIVE RIGHT TO SELL: A listing that entitles the broker to collect a commission no matter who sells the property during the listing period.

EXPRESSED CONTRACT: A contract made based on written or orally declared intentions.

EXTENDED COVERAGE: Insurance protection added to a basic fire policy for additional perils, including windstorm, hail, explosion, riot, civic commotion, aircraft, vehicles and smoke.

F

FAIR HOUSING LAWS: Federal laws designed to make housing available on equal terms to all applicants without regard to race, color, sex, national origin or religion.

FANNIE MAE: A real estate industry expression for the Federal National Mortgage Association (FNMA).

FASCIA: A flat board located on the outer edge of a cornice.

FEASIBILITY: An analysis of a proposed project's economic factors to assist determination that a project can be completed successfully within its economic limitations. Factors assessed include the cost of the land and construction, the mortgage loan limits, the income needed to amortize the debt service and the number of prospective tenants and their ability to pay.

FEDERAL HOME LOAN MORTGAGE CORPORATION (FHLMC): Provides a secondary mortgage market for savings and loan associations.

FEDERAL HOUSING ADMINISTRATION (FHA): Insures mortgages and provides subsidies to make financing available to buyers, owners and sponsors of housing developments.

FEDERAL NATIONAL MORTGAGE ASSOCIATION (FNMA): Provides a secondary market for home mortgages. Also acts as agent for GNMA in some localities.

FEE SIMPLE: The most complete ownership interest that may be held in real property.

FIDELITY BOND: An insurance bond purchased to protect against loss of money due to misappropriation by persons handling funds. Such bonds are often purchased by cooperatives and management agents for those employees and/or officers with access to funds.

FIDUCIARY: A person in a position of trust and responsibility for another, such as a broker for a client.

FINANCIAL LIABILITY: One's exposure to risk; the amount of money one can lose.

FINANCING: The process of raising the money necessary to carry out a project through arranging for loans or alternative funding.

FINDER'S FEE: A fee paid to a banker or broker to locate debt or equity financing.

FIRE CODE: An ordinance administered by a municipal fire department to promote fire protection and safety measures for building construction and tenants.

FIRE DISTRICTS: Areas within cities that require more stringent fire ratings on construction materials or fire protection systems due to the age or proximity of the structures. Such areas may also require higher insurance premiums.

FIRST MORTGAGE: A mortgage that holds priority for being paid in the event of a foreclosure on the property pledged as security.

FIXED EXPENSES: Costs that remain relatively unchanged in the month-to-month operation of a building.

FIXTURES: Objects or materials so attached as to become part of the real estate.

FLASHING: Sheet metal used on roof valleys and wall connections to prevent water seepage.

FLOOR AREA RATIO (FAR): A means of determining the total floor area permitted to be built on a given lot, often governed by bulk regulations, which do not permit some combinations.

FOOTING: The foundation of a building that rests on the soil, usually comprising masonry, stone or concrete.

FORECLOSE: To terminate a mortgagee's claim to property after she or he defaults.

FORECLOSURE: The procedure by which a person's property can be sold to satisfy an unpaid debt.

FRAUD: Act intended to deceive.

FREDDIE MAC: Real estate industry expression for the Federal Home Loan Mortgage Corporation.

FRONT MONEY: Equity capital used for expenses to initiate a development project.

G

GAIN ON THE SALE: The difference between the amount realized and the basis; actual profit.

GAP FINANCING: Additional loan(s) or grants required to make up the difference between the amount of mortgage funds available and the total projected costs; also, the difference between the construction loan and the permanent loan which may be the result of an unmet contingency.

GENERAL OPERATING RESERVE: A reserve for the purpose of providing funds in emergencies or crises.

GENERAL PARTNERSHIP: Ownership by two or more partners, each having a voice in its management and unlimited liability for its debts.

GINNIE MAE: A real estate expression for the Government National Mortgage Association.

GOVERNMENT NATIONAL MORTGAGE ASSOCIATION (GNMA): An agency that purchases insured and conventional mortgages unattractive to private secondary markets (especially below market interest rate mortgages) to encourage housing production.

GOVERNMENT RIGHTS IN LAND: Types include eminent domain (q.v.), escheat (the reversion of a person's property to the state when he/she dies and leaves no will or heirs), police power, property taxes.

GRADE: The finished surface of the ground, either paved or unpaved.

GRADUATED PAYMENT MORTGAGE: Fixed interest rate loan in which monthly payment starts low and then increases.

GRANT: Sums of money given to nonprofit organizations and others for specific requested purposes.

GRANTEE: The person named in a deed who acquires ownership.

GRANTOR: The person named in a deed who conveys ownership.

GRANTOR-GRANTEE INDEXES: An alphabetical directory for locating recorded documents.

GROSS INCOME: Total project income before expenses are deducted.

GROSS LEASE: The tenant pays his/her own expenses, such as heat and utilities, in addition to the rent.

GROSS RENT MULTIPLIER: A rule-of-thumb number which, when multiplied by property's rental income, produces an estimate of value.

GROUND LEASE: The lease of land alone.

GUTTER: A channel located on the fascia to collect water from the roof.

H

HIGHEST AND BEST USE: The use of a building or land that will result in the highest profit.

HOLDOVER TENANT: A tenant who stays beyond his/her lease period who may be evicted or given a new lease.

HOME OCCUPATION: An occupation carried on within a residence in a residential zone which is incidental to the use of the building as a dwelling.

HOMEOWNER'S POLICY: Package insurance contract covering the most common property and casualty risks for dwelling units.

HOMESTEAD EXEMPTION: A reduction allowance for property taxes on residences in some states.

HOMESTEAD PROTECTION: State laws in some states that protect against the forced sale of a home.

HOUSING FINANCE AGENCY: A public agency in some states which is empowered to raise money and make direct loans to sponsors of low- and moderate-income housing under favorable terms.

HUD: The federal Department of Housing and Urban Development, which has administrative responsibility for a wide range of assistance for housing and economic development of communities in partnership with local municipalities.

HVAC: Heating, ventilating and air conditioning systems.

I

ILLIQUIDITY: The potential that an asset, such as property, may be difficult to sell on short notice.

IMPLIED CONTRACT: A contract created by the actions of the parties involved.

IMPROVEMENT DISTRICT: An area that receives benefit of a special public improvement and that is paid for by taxing properties within the designated area.

IMPROVEMENTS: Any permanently attached development of land, such as buildings, roads, fences and pipelines, etc.

INCENTIVE ZONING: A zoning concept which enables a developer to build a larger building than the existing zoning would permit in exchange for providing a prescribed amenity.

INCOME APPROACH: A method of determining property value based on the investment income a property can produce.

INCOME LIMITS: Requirements for admission or continued occupancy in housing developments involving federal subsidies or below market interest rate financing; either set by HUD/FHA or a local authority.

INDICATED VALUE: Worth of a subject property as compared with recent sales of similar properties.

IN LIEU PAYMENTS: Payments instead of taxes. See Tax Abatement.

INSTALLMENT CONTRACT: A method of selling and financing property whereby the seller retains title but the buyer takes possession while making his or her payments.

INSTALLMENT SALE: The selling of an appreciated property on terms rather than for cash so as to defer payment of income taxes on the gain.

INSTITUTIONAL LENDER: A lender that invests its own funds in mortgages and retains a majority of such loans in its portfolio, including mutual savings banks, life insurance companies, commercial banks and savings and loan associations.

INSURANCE: A contract whereby one party undertakes to compensate the other in the event of loss on a specific property by reason of specific perils or liabilities for an agreed payment.

INTEREST: The price of borrowing money, expressed in a percentage and paid over and above the actual loan.

INTERIM LOAN: A construction loan.

INTERNAL RATE OF RETURN (IRR): Used by some developers/investors to determine a composite rate of return that represents the cash flow rate after tax and incorporates the effects of the time value of money (net present value).

INVESTMENT STRATEGY: A plan that balances returns available with risks that must be taken to enhance the investor's overall welfare.

IRB: Industrial Revenue Bonds, which may be a source of financing from a city agency.

J

JOINT TENANCY: A co-ownership form that features the right of survivorship. All joint tenants own one interest together and enjoy the same undivided possession of the whole property. Each joint tenant must acquire his/her ownership interest at the same moment from the same deed or will.

JOINT VENTURE: The organization of two or more persons or firms to carry out a project.

JOINT AND SEVERALLY LIABLE: Obligations are enforceable on the group and upon each signer individually.

JUNIOR MORTGAGE: Any mortgage that has subordinate priority to the first mortgage.

L

LAND USE: The type of activities (commercial, residential, etc.) on an area of land.

LATE CHARGE: Penalty covering any monthly payment not made by a specific date of the month in which payment is due.

LEASE: Agreement conveying right to use property for a specific period in exchange for rental payments.

LEASEHOLD ESTATES: A right to possession but not ownership.

LEASING CO-OP: A form of cooperative which leases but does not buy a property, yet manages and makes all decisions pertaining to the property. Also a form of ownership in which all equity and tax benefits go to limited partners but the co-op retains decision-making power over the property.

LESSEE: The tenant.

LESSOR: The landlord.

LETTER OF INTENT: A document that expresses mutual intent but without liability or obligation.

LEVEL ANNUITY PLAN: An amortization schedule for paying off a mortgage which maintains, at a constant level, payments that include principal, interest and mortgage insurance premiums.

LEVERAGE: The use of borrowed funds to acquire income-producing property with expectation of a higher rate of return on the equity investment; trading on equity.

LIABILITY INSURANCE: Coverage that provides protection in the event a person carelessly causes bodily injury or property damage to others.

LIEN: A claim that one person has upon the property of another to secure payment of a debt.

LIMITED COMMON ELEMENTS: Walls and ceilings between condominium units, the use of which is limited to abutting owners.

LIMITED DIVIDEND CORPORATION: A housing corporation that is restricted as to rents, capital structure, rate of return and methods of operation; and that requires housing to be made available for moderate-income families in exchange for property tax benefits.

LIMITED PARTNER: A partner who provides capital, has limited liability, has a limited or no management role and receives a direct pass-through of profits and losses for tax purposes.

LIMITED PARTNERSHIP: A combination of general partners who operate the partnership with unlimited personal financial liability and limited partners who provide most of the capital.

LIQUIDATED DAMAGES: Amount of money specified in a contract as compensation to be paid if a contract is breached.

LISTING AGREEMENT: An employment contract between a property owner and broker.

LIVE/WORK SPACE (also called studio/living and work/live space): The use of one space for both living and working. One or more rooms in an apartment may be set aside for working; however, the term generally refers to an artist's adaptation of space in commercial or industrial buildings for both living and working.

LOAN: The "renting" of money by a lender to a borrower to be repaid with or without interest.

LOAN FEE: Charge made for negotiating a loan in addition to interest, similar to a finder's fee or commitment fee.

LOAN SERVICING: The task of collecting monthly payments, handling insurance and tax escrows, delinquencies, early payoffs and mortgage releases.

LOAN-VALUE RATIO: The relationship between the amount a lender will loan and the appraised value of the property, usually expressed as a percentage.

LOT COVERAGE: The percentage of a lot which is or can be covered by buildings.

M

MAINTENANCE COSTS: The cost to a condominium owner for upkeep of the property; it includes day-to-day cleaning, preventive and emergency repair, salaries and benefits of employees, service contracts, materials and equipment.

MAKER: The person who signs a promissory note.

MANAGEMENT AGREEMENT: A contractual agreement between the owner(s) of a development and a firm or entity (management agent) outlining responsibilities and performance expectations.

MANAGEMENT COOPERATIVE: A form of cooperative housing development in which a central body owns and operates the project for the occupant members on a nonprofit basis. It is generally distinguished from a sales or ownership cooperative under which units are built through a cooperative body and sold to individual buyers.

MANAGEMENT PLAN: A plan of operation for a building facility that encompasses its use, administration and financing provided by a management agent to the owner(s) of a development.

MARKET APPROACH: A method of valuing a property based on the prices of recent sales of similar properties.

MARKET RATE INTEREST: This refers to the interest rate a bank or other lender usually charges for lending money.

MARKET STUDY: Projection of future demand for a specific type of project.

MARKET VALUE: The price a willing buyer and a willing seller would agree upon, with reasonable exposure of the property to the marketplace, full information as to the potential uses of the property, and no undue compulsion to act.

MARKETABLE TITLE: Title clear from reasonable doubt about who the owner is.

MASTER DEED: A document to convert land into a condominium subdivision.

MASTER PLAN: A comprehensive guide for the physical growth of a community.

MATURITY: The length of time during which the loan is repaid.

MAXIMUM MORTGAGE AMOUNT: The largest real estate loans that can be insured under specific government programs.

MECHANIC'S LIEN: A claim placed on land and buildings by mechanics or other persons who have performed work or furnished materials for which they have not been paid.

MEETING OF THE MINDS, MUTUAL AGREEMENT: A meeting of the minds is an agreement to the provisions of a contract by all parties involved.

MEMBER: A resident of a cooperative who has executed a subscription or occupancy agreement and purchased a membership in the cooperative.

MEMBERSHIP SHARE: A portion of a co-op corporation owned by an occupant and required for voting as a member of the co-op. Active shares are usually limited to the number of units in the project. All occupants of one unit generally own only one share together. Documentation may be in the form of a membership certificate or a stock certificate.

MILL RATE: Property tax rate that is expressed in tenths of a cent per dollar of assessed valuation.

MIXED-USE BUILDING: Nonhomogeneous uses within a building including commercial, retail and/or residential mix.

MODIFIED PAR VALUE RESALE: The sale of memberships for an increase in value according to a prearranged formula and schedule that allows for inflation. Usually the shares are sold back to the cooperative, which resells them to new members.

MONTHLY HOUSING CHARGES: The amount determined by a board of directors of a cooperative to be sufficient to meet the financial and operating costs proportioned to the various unit sizes within the development; also called "carrying charges."

MORTGAGE: A pledge of property as collateral to secure the repayment of a loan.

MORTGAGE BANKER: Person or firm that makes loans and then sells them to investors.

MORTGAGE BROKER: Person who brings borrowers and lenders together.

MORTGAGE COMMITMENT: Legal contract between borrower and lender to advance a mortgage loan when borrower meets certain conditions.

MORTGAGE COMPANY: A business firm that specializes in making real estate loans and selling them to investors.

MORTGAGE CONSTANT: A measure of the relative annual debt service (D/S = principal and interest) divided by the original loan amount. Fixed-rate mortgages have constant monthly payments over the term of the loan. Adjustable rate mortgages have constant monthly payments over particular time periods. As the loan is paid, larger amounts of each payment become principal reduction. The constant is the portion of the loan that is paid in debt service each year of the loan. Using mortgage tables, the constant can be calculated by multiplying the debt service by 12 and dividing that number by the loan amount.

MORTGAGE DISCOUNT POINTS: An amount that is paid over and above the price of real estate to receive a low interest government-backed mortgage.

MORTGAGE INSURANCE: An insurance policy issued by a private mortgage company or by the FHA to insure the lender against loss if the buyer defaults on the loan.

MORTGAGE POOL: A common fund of mortgage loans in which one can invest.

MORTGAGEE: The lending institution or individual that lends money to buy, build or rehabilitate a building or property.

MORTGAGOR: The individual or group that pledges property to borrow money.

MORTGAGOR-MORTGAGEE INDEXES: Alphabetical lists used to locate mortgages in public records.

MOTION: A formal proposal put to a vote under the provisions of parliamentary procedure in a meeting of an assembly, such as a cooperative's board of directors (see RESOLUTION).

MULTIFAMILY DEVELOPMENTS: Housing developments for four or more families without limit on the number.

MULTIPLE LISTING SERVICE (MLS): An organization that enables brokers to exchange information on listings.

MUNICIPAL BOND PROGRAMS: A source of home loans that is financed by the sale of municipal bonds.

MUTUAL AGREEMENT, MUTUAL CONSENT: There must be an agreement to the provisions of the contract by all parties involved.

MUTUAL HOUSING ASSOCIATION: A nonprofit organization that creates an ongoing program to develop independent cooperatives or housing owned by the MHA, and provides management support, training and auxiliary services helpful to cooperatives.

MUTUAL RESCISSION: Voluntary cancellation of a contract by all parties involved.

N

NEGATIVE CASH FLOW: A condition where expenses exceed income on an investment.

NEGOTIABLE NOTE: A note that may be transferred from one person to another in the course of business and that entitles the last holder to collect the sums due.

NET LEASE: The tenant pays taxes on the property leased in addition to rent and tenant expenses.

NET LISTING: A listing wherein the commission is the difference between the selling price and a minimum price set by the seller.

NET OPERATING INCOME (NOI): Gross income less operating expenses, vacancy and collection losses.

NET PRESENT VALUE: The value of a stream of payments discounted back to a present value.

NET RENTABLE AREA: The amount of space available for rent, measured in square feet, generally excluding the elevator core, stairs, lobby, corridors and toilets, unless provided for the exclusive use of one tenant.

NET SPENDABLE: The income remaining after collecting rents and paying operating expenses and debt service; same as cash flow.

NET WORTH: The equity of the owners, that is, the net assets determined by subtracting all liabilities from the value of the assets.

NONASSUMPTION CLAUSE: A clause that gives the lender the right to call the entire loan balance due if property is sold or conveyed. Also called an alienation clause or due-on-sale clause.

NONCONFORMING USE: An improvement that is inconsistent with current zoning regulations.

NONPROFIT CORPORATION: A corporation organized for charitable, educational or civic purposes. Any money or profits above operating expenses are usually used for facilities and services, low-income housing, etc., to further the corporation's purposes, not to benefit its shareholders financially.

NONPROFIT SPONSOR: A group, organized for reasons other than making profit, who will undertake a housing project. The sponsor may develop housing units on a nonprofit basis to create individual, cooperative or condominium ownership. The FHA can insure mortgage loans up to 100 percent for such sponsors.

NONRECOURSE: Financing in which the loan is secured by property only, not assets of the borrower; exculpatory.

NOTARY PUBLIC: A person authorized by the state to administer oaths, attest and certify documents, and take acknowledgments.

NOTE: A written promise to repay a debt.

O

OBLIGEE: The person to whom a debt or obligation is owed.

OBLIGOR: The person responsible for paying a debt or obligation.

OCCUPANCY AGREEMENT: An agreement, similar to a lease, which allows occupancy of a specific unit in a cooperative development by a member of the cooperative.

OFFEREE: The party who receives an offer.

OFFEROR: The party who makes an offer.

OFF-SITE MANAGEMENT: Property management functions that can be performed away from the premises being managed; for example, accounting for collected rents, paying bills or addressing legal matters.

ON-SITE MANAGEMENT: Property management functions that must be performed on the premises being managed; for example, showing space to prospective tenants, handling tenant complaints, supervising maintenance and repair.

OPEN-END MORTGAGE: Mortgage, or deed of trust, written to permit additional advances on the original loan.

OPERATING COST: The expenses of operating a development; including maintenance, mortgage payments, insurance, utilities and the loss of revenues from vacant units.

OPERATING EXPENSE RATIO: Total operating expenses divided by effective gross income.

OPERATING PASS-THROUGH: A lease provision that calls for the tenant to pay his/her proportionate share of the increase of operating expenses and/or real estate taxes over a stated base year. Also called pass-through escalation.

OPTION: An agreement to buy or lease property within a certain time at a predetermined price.

ORIGINATION FEE: A charge for making a loan.

OVERALL RATE: A mortgage-equity factor used to appraise income-producing property to determine property value for investments.

OWNERSHIP: The right to possess, use and transfer property.

P

PACKAGE MORTGAGE: A mortgage or deed of trust secured by real and personal property, such as stoves, refrigerators, washing machines and garbage disposal units.

PARAPET: An exterior wall that extends above the roof line.

PARKING REQUIREMENTS: Zoning regulations regarding the number of automobile spaces required per housing unit and the spaces businesses or arts organizations must provide for their patrons.

PARTIALLY AMORTIZED LOAN: A loan that begins with amortized payments but ends with a balloon payment.

PARTICIPATION LOAN: The lender charges interest and takes a cut of profits.

PARTITION: To divide jointly held property into distinct portions so that each co-owner may own sole title to his/her proportionate share.

PARTNERSHIP: A form of co-ownership for business purposes. Tax liabilities and profits flow through and are divided among the individual partners.

PARTY/PARTIES: A legal term referring to a person or group involved in a legal proceeding.

PARTY WALL: A wall built along a lot line in which adjoining owners have a mutual interest.

PATRONAGE REFUND: Money that may be authorized to be given to the members of a cooperative at the end of the fiscal year because of excesses in income collections or savings in anticipated expenses.

PERIODIC ESTATE: A tenancy with continuing automatic renewal until cancelled, such as a month-to-month rental.

PERMANENT FINANCING OR PERMANENT LOAN: Long-term mortgage as opposed to interim or construction loan.

PERSONAL PROPERTY: Estate or property consisting of things temporary or movable—chattels.

PIER AND POST: A foundation system in which a post rests upon a concrete or masonry pad (pier), which in turn rests on soil.

PILES: A foundation system of long wood or concrete columns driven into the ground.

PITCH: The angle of the slope of a roof.

PITI PAYMENT: A loan payment that combines principal, interest, taxes and insurance.

PLAN: Architect's drawing of a space, structure or object as seen from above.

PLAT: A map showing dimensions of a piece of real estate based upon the legal description.

PLUMB: Vertical alignment of a building or aspect of a building.

POINTS: One point equals one percent of the loan amount. Both the purchaser and the seller may pay one or more points as a service charge for closing the deal.

POLICE POWER: The right of government to enact laws and enforce them for the order, safety, health, morals and general welfare of the public.

POSITIVE CASH FLOW: A condition where cash received exceeds cash paid out.

POSSESSION DATE: The day on which the buyer or lessee can move in.

POWER OF ATTORNEY: A written agreement whereby one person, the principal, authorizes another, the attorney in fact, to act for him or her or to carry out the powers expressly granted.

POWER OF SALE: The power of sale allows a mortgagee to conduct a foreclosure sale without first going to court.

PREMIUM: The premium is the cost of insurance for a specified policy period determined by multiplying the coverage's ratio by the amount of coverage desired.

PREPAYMENT PENALTY: A penalty for satisfying a debt before it actually becomes due.

PRINCIPAL: (1) A loan consists of two parts: principal and interest. The principal is the repayment of the loan itself. See AMORTIZATION. (2) A person who takes the lead or authorizes another to act for him/her.

PRO-FORMA STATEMENT: Projection of anticipated annual income, expenses and cash flow.

PROJECT COST: The total cost of carrying out a building project, whether new construction or rehabilitation. It may include purchase of property, construction cost, interest on loans, professional fees and administrative expenses.

PROMISSORY NOTE: Written promise to repay a debt, transferable by endorsement.

PROPERTY IDENTIFICATION NUMBER: A number assigned to each parcel of land by the assessor, not to be confused with a subdivider's lot number.

PROPRIETARY LEASE: A lease issued by a cooperative corporation to its shareholders.

PRORATING: The proportionate division of ongoing expenses between the buyer and the seller, or within a cooperative.

PROSPECTUS: A disclosure statement that describes an investment opportunity, including a pro forma.

PROXY (PROXY VOTE): The authorization of one person to act on behalf of another, usually in writing. For parliamentary purposes, the votes cast for himself/herself and for the proxy are counted. The proxy is free to act and is not bound by any direction of the person authorizing the proxy.

PUBLIC AUCTION: The usual method for the sale of foreclosed property.

PUBLIC LIABILITY: The financial responsibility one has toward others as a result of one's actions or failure to take action.

PUBLIC RECORDER'S OFFICE: A government office where documents are entered in the public records.

PURCHASE AGREEMENT: A contract for the purchase and sale of real estate; also called an earnest money contract.

PURCHASE MONEY MORTGAGE: The seller extends the credit and retains a security interest in the property in exchange for a mortgage from the buyer.

Q

QUIET ENJOYMENT: The right to use property without undue disturbance from others.

QUITCLAIM DEED: Legal instrument containing no covenants, warranties, or implication of the grantor's ownership, used to convey whatever title the grantor has.

QUORUM: The minimum number of officers and/or members of a corporation who must be present for the valid transaction of business as set in the bylaws.

R

RATE OF RETURN: Annual net operating income related to the capital invested, the appraised value, other investment options, or the net yield during the investment period, expressed as a percentage.

REAL-COST INFLATION: Higher prices due to the greater effort needed to produce the same product today versus several years ago.

REAL ESTATE: Land and physical improvements as well as the rights to own or use them; also called real property.

REAL ESTATE INVESTMENT TRUST (REIT): A method of pooling investor money using the trust form of ownership and featuring single taxation of profits.

RECAPTURE: Depreciation in excess of straight-line rates is subject to recapture at ordinary income rates when property is sold.

RECONCILIATION: The appraiser weighs the cost, market and income approaches to determine the final indicated value.

RECORDING ACTS: Laws that require the placing of documents in the public records to protect the new owner's claim to the land.

REDLINING: The practice of refusing to make loans in certain neighborhoods.

REFINANCE: A new or second mortgage is used to repay the first mortgage and/or to pay for any repairs, etc. The purpose of refinancing is to get a more favorable loan (in terms of lower interest rates, lower monthly payments, longer maturity, or federal insurance) than the original mortgage loan or to utilize equity through appreciation as security for renovation loans.

REGULATION Z: A federal law requiring lenders to show borrowers how much they are paying for credit. Truth-in-lending legislation.

REGULATORY AGREEMENT: A contractual agreement between the agency insuring the mortgage, the mortgagor and the mortgagee, providing for mutual obligations and responsibilities.

REHABILITATION: Substantial upgrading or improvement of property.

RELEASE OF MORTGAGE: Withdrawal of the lender's interest in the property when the loan has been repaid.

RELOCATION ASSISTANCE: Services and assistance provided by a public agency to compensate displaced people for the inconvenience and expense of moving caused by governmental action.

RENTAL ATTAINMENT PROVISION: A mortgage commitment clause requiring a minimum occupancy level before the full amount of a mortgage is paid.

RENT CONTROL: Government-imposed restrictions on the amount of rent a property owner can charge to keep rents from rising faster or higher than a particular level.

RENT STRIKE: Tenants withhold their rents from a landlord in order to make him/her take a particular action.

REPLACEMENT COST: The current cost of constructing a building with the same usefulness as the building being appraised.

REPRODUCTION COST: Current cost of constructing an exact replica of the building being appraised.

RESERVE: Money set aside for specific purposes by the owners of a development. Cooperatives may choose to establish a General Operating Reserve, Replacement Reserve, an Equipment Reserve, Painting Reserve, etc.

RESIDENT MANAGER: Refers to the individual who is employed by the owner(s) or management agent to perform an on-site management function. The Resident Manager may or may not reside on-site and may or may not be employed full time on-site.

RESOLUTION: A formal statement of a decision or expression of opinion put before or adopted by an assembly, such as a cooperative's board of directors.

RIGHT OF FIRST REFUSAL: A lease clause that provides the lessee the opportunity to purchase a property before it can be offered to anyone else.

RIGHT OF REDEMPTION: The right of the owner to reclaim title to his/her property if the owner pays the debt to the mortgagee within a stipulated period of time after foreclosure.

RIGHT OF SURVIVORSHIP: A feature of joint tenancy and tenancy by entireties whereby the surviving joint tenant(s) automatically succeed to the ownership rights of the deceased joint tenant.

RISER: The vertical distance in a staircase between the treads.

RISK: Chance or probability of loss.

ROOMS: Under FHA underwriting regulations, a room count is one of the bases for determining maximum mortgage and average costs. This has inhibited financing options for living/working spaces that are only one to three rooms but otherwise of large square footage.

S

SALE AND LEASEBACK: Financing arrangements in which owner-occupant sells property and leases it back from buyer to remain a tenant.

SALES AGREEMENT: An agreement by which the seller passes title to property in exchange for an agreed-upon price to the buyer.

SATISFACTION: Settlement of a claim or demand; payment.

SCALE: The proportion of the size of a drawing of a structure to its size in reality. A scale of 1/4" = 1' means every 1/4" of the drawn structure is equal to one foot length.

SCATTERED SITE COOPERATIVE: A form of co-op corporation in which several semi-autonomous groups operate as co-ops within a larger co-op of which all occupants of all buildings are members.

SCHEDULED GROSS (PROJECTED GROSS): The estimated rent that a fully occupied property can be expected to produce on an annual basis.

SECOND MORTGAGE: One which ranks immediately behind the first mortgage in priority.

SECONDARY MORTGAGE MARKET: A channel for loan money that saves investors from the work of making and servicing loans and provides lending institutions with a way to sell loans they originate, sometimes at a higher rate.

SECTION: A drawing of a structure as it would appear if it were seen through a certain plane, usually vertical.

SECURITY: Something given, deposited or pledged to make secure the fulfillment of an obligation or the payment of a debt.

SEED MONEY: Monies needed to defray initial expenses in organizing a project and formulating a proposal, including such items as the cost of an option, preliminary architectural drawings and legal expenses; also called Front Money.

SELLER'S MARKET: A market with few sellers and many buyers.

SELLER'S POINTS: Loan discount points paid by a seller so that a buyer can obtain a loan.

SENIOR MORTGAGE: The mortgage against a property that holds first priority in the event of foreclosure.

SERVICING: The collection of payments of interest and principal and escrow or trust fund items such as fire insurance and taxes on a note by the borrower in accordance with the terms of the note. Servicing by the lender also consists of procedures covering accounting, insurance, tax records, loan payment follow-up, delinquent loan follow-up and loan analysis.

SETBACK: The minimum distance from a lot line which, by law, regulation or restriction in the deed, must be left open to provide front, side and back yards; the linear distance between the lot line and the buildings or building line.

SETTLEMENT: Compensation for a loss.

SEVERALTY OWNERSHIP: Owned by one person; sole ownership.

SHERIFF'S DEED: A deed issued as a result of a court-ordered foreclosure sale.

SOFFIT: The underside of a cornice.

SOLE OWNERSHIP: Owned by one person; in severalty.

SOUNDPROOFING SYSTEM: Walls and floors specifically constructed or covered to prevent sound from escaping or transferring.

SPECIAL ASSESSMENT: A special charge against real estate for street, sewer or other public improvements from which the property benefits.

SPECIAL WARRANTY DEED: Contains only the covenant against encumbrances.

SPECULATION: The practice of buying properties for a low price and selling them unchanged or with little rehabilitative work for a much greater price.

SQUARE-FOOT COST: The result, in dollars, of dividing the cost of the improvements by the number of square feet of floor space.

STANDBY COMMITMENT: Long-term commitment accepted by interim lender.

STANDBY FEE: One or two percent good faith fee submitted along with loan application.

STATUTE OF FRAUDS: A law requiring that certain types of contracts be written in order to be enforceable in a court of law, for example, leases of one year or longer.

STATUTORY REDEMPTION: Right of borrower after foreclosure sale to redeem property by paying the defaulted loan.

STEP-UP RENTAL: A lease that provides for agreed-upon rent increases.

STRAIGHT-LINE DEPRECIATION: Depreciation in equal amounts each year over the life of the asset.

SUBJECT TO EXISTING LOAN: A buyer of already mortgaged property makes payments but does not take personal responsibility for the loan; the seller remains personally liable to the lender.

SUBLEASE: A lease provided by a lessee.

SUBLESSEE: One who rents from a lessee.

SUBLESSOR: A lessee who in turn leases to another, or sublessee.

SUBORDINATION: The acceptance by a lender of a loan position lower than one the lender would be entitled to.

SUBSCRIPTION AGREEMENT: An agreement to purchase a membership in a cooperative in return for consideration and promises of residency if qualified and approved.

SUBSIDY: Financial assistance given by a government entity to a person, group or enterprise, such as rent supplement or interest rate reduction.

SURETY: One legally liable on default of another.

SWEAT EQUITY: Repairs and improvements by an owner or members of a co-op or tenant association where compensation is represented by increased equity with little capital investment.

SYNDICATION: A group of persons or businesses that combine to undertake an investment.

T

TAKE-OUT LOAN: Permanent loan which replaces a construction loan.

"TAKING BACK PAPER": A seller allows a purchaser to substitute a promissory note for cash.

TAX ABATEMENT: Reducing or exempting a building from property taxation.

TAX BASIS: The price paid for a property plus the value of improvements and some expenses.

TAX DEED: A deed for property that has been sold because of nonpayment of taxes.

TAX LIEN: A claim by the government against property to insure the payment of taxes.

TAX SHELTER: Income tax savings which real estate investment produces for owner.

TEMPERED GLASS: Glass that is heat-treated to become much stronger than ordinary glass.

TENANCY BY THE ENTIRETY: A form of joint ownership reserved for married persons; provides right of survivorship and may otherwise be terminated only by joint action of husband and wife.

TENANT: One who possesses and uses a property; lessee.

TENANTS IN COMMON: Shared ownership of a single property among two or more persons; interests need not be equal and no right of survivorship exists.

TERM: The time period within which an agreed upon action, such as repayment of a loan, must take place.

TERM LOAN: Loan requiring interest-only payments until maturity, at which time a balloon is due.

TERMINATION OF MEMBERSHIP: Action by a resident/member or by the board of directors to invalidate a membership, as provided in the bylaws of a cooperative.

TIED WALLS: The attachment of a masonry wall to the interior structure of a building to resist separation of the wall from the structure due to earthquakes or horizontal stresses.

TIGHT MONEY: When lenders are unable to accommodate requests for loans due to limited funds.

TITLE: A document to constitute proof of ownership.

TITLE INSURANCE: Insurance that provides property owners protection against unforeseen legal defects which may jeopardize ownership rights.

TITLE REPORT: A statement of the current condition of title to a parcel of land.

TITLE SEARCH: Inspection of documents on public file to determine whether a property is free from encumbrances.

TORRENS SYSTEM: A simplified method of registering land titles in some states.

TRADE FIXTURE: Business or trade-related items attached to a rental building by a tenant, usually with the right to remove them at the end of a lease.

TRANSFER OF MEMBERSHIP: Action by a member of a cooperative to transfer his/her rights and obligations to another person who is qualified and acceptable to the cooperative.

TRANSFER VALUE: The worth of a membership or stock in a housing co-op; also called resale value.

TREAD: The horizontal surfaces of a staircase.

TRUST: A transfer of property from one person for the benefit of another.

TRUST DEED: A document conveying property from an owner to a trustee as security for a debt. Used in many states rather than mortgages to secure loans on real property; also called Deed of Trust.

TRUSTEE: A person who is appointed to administer a property held in trust.

TRUTH IN LENDING: A federal law requiring disclosure of the true annual cost of credit.

TURNOVER: The in-and-out flow of tenants in a building.

U

UNDERWRITING: The task of a lender or insurer to assess risks of lending or insurability by using a technical set of criteria, such as minimum income of applicant and review of appraised value of the property.

UNDIVIDED INTEREST: The right to use the entire property when owned by two or more persons.

UNENCUMBERED PROPERTY: Property that is free and clear of any assessments, liens, leases, easements, encroachments or encumbrances of any kind.

URBAN RENEWAL: A coordinated effort, with the aid of public funds, to eliminate or prevent slum and blighting conditions in areas designated by a local community.

USE PERMIT: Authorization of a new use or a change in use for an existing structure or property issued by a building inspections department.

USURY: Charging a rate of interest higher than permitted by law.

V

VACANCY FACTOR: A measurement of vacant rental units as a percentage of the total units available for rent. An estimated factor is deducted from gross income on financial projections.

VACANCY LOSS: The monetary loss to a development resulting from empty or vacant units that are not occupied or producing income.

VACANCY RATE: The percentage of unoccupied dwelling units within an area. A very low vacancy rate (below 4 percent) indicates that available space is scarce.

VA-GUARANTEED LOAN: Veterans loan secured by the property and guaranteed by the Veterans Administration up to a stated percentage of the property's value.

VALID CONTRACT: A contract that meets all requirements of law, is enforceable in a court of law and is binding upon its parties.

VALUABLE CONSIDERATION: Money, property, services or anything worth money.

VALUATION: The act of establishing the value of real property (see APPRAISAL).

VARIABLE PAYMENT MORTGAGE: A loan whose monthly payment varies; for example, the graduated payments mortgage has low payments in its early stages then increases.

VARIABLE RATE MORTGAGE: A loan with interest rate that varies with changes in the prevailing interest rates.

VARIANCE: A permit granted to vary slightly from strict compliance with zoning requirements.

VENDEE: The buyer.

VENDOR: The seller.

VOIDABLE CONTRACT: A contract that binds one party but gives the other the right to withdraw.

W

WAIVER: The surrender of claims, rights, privileges etc.

WARRANTY: Guarantee or assurance that something is true.

WARRANTY DEED: The seller conveys all claim, right and clear title, subject only to written provisions of the deed. It usually contains the covenants of seizin, quiet enjoyment, encumbrances, further assurance and warranty forever.

WARRANTY FOREVER: The grantor's guarantee to bear the expense of defending the grantee's title.

WASTE: Abuse or willful damage to property.

WIRE GLASS: Wire mesh or parallel wires embedded within glass as reinforcement.

WITHOUT RECOURSE: When the maker of a note does not guarantee its payment to future holders.

WORKING CAPITAL: Funds needed to begin a project—to buy the land, get a construction loan or begin development of a property.

WORK LETTER: A building standard installation. The owner defines the quantity and quality of walls, doors, ceilings, lights, paintings, and floor covering to be constructed in the tenant's space; all items are defined in the work letter as an attached exhibit to the lease.

WRAPAROUND MORTGAGE: A mortgage that retains any existing mortgages as part of the financing and that is subordinate to them.

Z

ZONING: Public regulations on the specific use of land in a given district.

Suggested Reading

The business section of your library can be a helpful resource for numerous books about real estate law, development and construction information. For books on safety and health issues in various arts, see box 4.5 for a list of books available from the Center for Safety in the Arts. Some of the following resources related to arts policy, cultural districts and artist live/work space issues may also be available at your library.

BOOKS

Biberman, Nancy, and Roger K. Evans. *Artists' Housing Manual: A Guide To Living in New York City.* New York: Volunteer Lawyers for the Arts, 1987.

Brown, Catherine R., William B. Fleissig, and William R. Morrish. *Building for the Arts: A Guidebook for the Planning and Design of Cultural Facilities.* Santa Fe: Western States Arts Foundation, 1984.

Educational Facilities Laboratories and the National Endowment for the Arts. *The Arts in Found Places.* New York: Educational Facilities Laboratories, 1976.

Green, Kevin W., ed. *The City as a Stage: Strategies for the Arts in Urban Economics.* Washington, DC: Partners for Livable Places, 1983.

Kreisberg, Luisa. *Local Government and the Arts.* New York: American Council for the Arts, 1980.

Lipske, Mike. *Artists' Housing: Creating Live/Work Space That Lasts.* New York: Publishing Center for Cultural Resources, 1988.

Mayer, R., ed. *Live/Work Space: Changing Public Policy.* San Francisco: Artists Equity Association, Northern California Chapter, 1980.

McCamant, Kathryn, and Charles Durrett. *Cohousing: A Contemporary Approach To Housing Ourselves.* Berkeley: Habitat Press, 1988.

Nesson, Jero. *Artists in Space: A Handbook for Developing Artists' Studio Space.* Boston: Fort Point Arts Community, Inc., 1987.

Porter, Robert, ed. *The Arts and City Planning.* New York: American Council for the Arts, 1980.

Snedcof, Harold. *Cultural Facilities in Mixed-Use Development.* Washington, DC: The Urban Land Institute, 1985.

Stratton, Jim. *Pioneering in the Urban Wilderness.* New York: Urizen Books, 1977.

Uhl-Nordlinger, Carol, ed. *Design Arts 2: The Places and Spaces for the Arts.* New York: The Municipal Art Society of New York, 1981.

Urban Innovations Group. *The Arts in the Economic Life of the City.* New York: American Council for the Arts, 1979.

STUDIES

Artists Equity Association, Inc. *Live/Work Space: Changing Public Policy.* San Francisco: 1981.

Arts, Tourism, and Cultural Resources Committee of the National Conference of State Legislatures. *Art Spaces and Economics.* Denver, January 1984.

Bee, Carmi. *Artists' Housing: A Survey of Live/Work Space.* Washington, DC: 1983.

City of St. Paul, Department of Planning and Economic Development. *Arts Development Program 1986-87 Workplan.* St. Paul: 1986. Also, updated version, 1990.

Cucitis, Peggy. *Economic Impact of the Arts in Colorado.* Denver: University of Colorado, 1983.

Cultural Assistance Center, Inc. and the Port Authority of New York and New Jersey. *The Arts as an Industry: Their Economic Importance to the New York-New Jersey Metropolitan Region.* New York: Cultural Assistance Center, Inc. (American Council for the Arts), 1983.

Fuller, John W. *Economic Impact of the Arts in Iowa.* Iowa City: University of Iowa, Oakdale Campus, December 1982.

Governor's Commission on Economic Vitality in the Arts. Preliminary Report. St. Paul: February 1984.

Kahn, Vivian, and Larry J. Mortimer. *Seattle Artists' Housing Handbook.* Seattle: City of Seattle Department of Community Development and Arts Commission, 1980.

Kartes, Cheryl. *Arts Enterprise Zones.* Minneapolis: Artspace Projects, Inc., 1984.

Kibbe, Barbara. *Live/Work: The San Francisco Experience.* San Francisco: San Francisco Arts Commission, 1985.

Macris, Natalie B. *Artists' Live/Work Space in San Francisco: Strategies for Preservation and Development.* San Francisco, CA: San Francisco Arts Commission, 1985.

Minneapolis Arts Commission. *Minneapolis Warehouse Project: Artist Living/ Working Space in Renovated Warehouses,* Minneapolis: Minneapolis Arts Commission, 1978.

Minnesota State Arts Board. *Activities of the Minnesota State Arts Board,* Fiscal year 1985. St. Paul: 1985.

National Endowment for the Arts. *Economic Impact of Arts and Cultural Institutions.* New York: Publishing Center for Cultural Resources, January 1981.

New England Foundation for the Arts. *The Arts and the New England Economy.* Cambridge, MA: New England Foundation for the Arts, 1981.

Partners for Livable Places. *Economics of Amenities News.* Washington, DC: Partners for Livable Places (newsletter).

Rieser, Enid. *The Chicago ArtSpace Study.* Chicago: Chicago Department of Cultural Affairs, 1986.

Spencer, June, and Mary Berryman Agard. *Local Government and the Arts.* Madison: Opinion Research Associates, Inc., 1985.

The Artists Foundation, Inc. *Artists' Space: A Study of the Development of Artists' Living and Working Space in Boston.* Boston: 1981.

U.S. Conference of Mayors. *The Taxpayers' Revolt and the Arts: A U.S. Conference of Mayors' Position Paper.* Washington, D.C.: 1978.

Volunteer Lawyers for the Arts. *Housing for Artists: The New York Experience.* New York: 1976.

ARTICLES

"American Artists on the Rise." *Place*, November 1983. p. 15.

Anderson, Karen. "Unlikely Partnership Eases Artists' Housing Needs." *The Christian Science Monitor*, 4 November 1985, p. 87.

"Artless Economics." *Economist*, vol. 296 (21 September 1985).

"Arts Groups Confront Growing Space Crisis." *Arts Management*, No. 154 (January-February 1988), p. 3.

"Arts Spending: Fast and Luce." *Economist*, vol. 301 (22 November 1986), p. 61.

Berlowe, Burt. "Armageddon in New Bohemia." *Twin Cities' Reader*, 23 April 1980, pp. 6-7.

Budhos, Marina. "Real Estate and the Arts." *California Federation of the Arts Newsletter*, Fall 1985.

Burgard, Ralph. "What Makes a Cultural Policy?" *Place*, January 1984, pp. 8-9.

Cahan, Richard and Catherine. "Chicago's Urbane Pioneers: Living It Up in Lofts." *Historic Preservation*, April 1985, pp. 52-57.

Cuthbert, Neal. "Stay Hungry." *Artpaper*, Minneapolis.

Lehmann, Phyllis and Kenneth Fain. "Staying Aloft." *National Endowment for the Arts*, No. 23 (May/June 1979), pp. 1-9.

Leinberger, Christopher B. and Charles Lockwood. "How Business Is Reshaping America." *The Atlantic Monthly*, October 1986, pp. 43-52.

Martin, Mary Abbe. "The NoLo Syndrome." *Twin Cities*, December 1979.

Nodus, D. "Loft Living Isn't Always the Answer." *CAC Newsletter*, October 1979, pp. 2-3.

Sanderson, Linda. "Warehouse Living." *Express*, vol. 4, No. 18 (26 February 1982), pp. 1-6.

"The Real Estate of the Arts." *The Minneapolis Tribune*, 29 July 1978, p. 6A.

Winegar, Karin. "Developers Encroaching on Artists' Warehouse Quarters." *Minneapolis Star*, 4 December 1978, p. 1A.

About NADN

The National Artspace Development Network (NADN) serves as a link between individuals and organizations seeking affordable space where artists can create, rehearse and present their work. The desire of many artists to live where they work throws a twist into the real estate development process, enough of a twist that dozens of city agencies and arts organizations around the country have struggled with solutions to artists' space needs. The goal of NADN is to share solutions and avoid duplication of effort.

In the early 1980s, several organizations in different parts of the country realized that they were all independently doing similar work. Their response was to establish a computer network to increase communication and information sharing. Apple Computer Corporation donated computers, software, training and electronic bulletin board access to Artspace Projects, Inc. in the Twin Cities, The Bay Area Partnership in Oakland, the Foundation for the Community of Artists in New York City, Innovative Housing in Marin County, California, and National Artists Equity in Washington, D.C.

Each of these organizations contributed to the development of program concepts, and in 1986 the National Artspace Development Network was established as a conduit for communication and cooperation between organizations involved in arts space issues. Initial projects included

- the writing of this book
- the creation of software applications for a space referral system and a space needs database
- on-line communications through the bulletin board
- regional workshops
- gathering information about successful projects

- plans for expansion to a national service program.

By 1989, NADN began to expand by moving its base of operations to the Bay Area, hiring Robin Orden as its part-time director, and established a board of directors and an advisory board. An effort to acquire separate nonprofit status was explored and later dropped, due to difficulties in raising support for NADN activities. As 1991 began, so did efforts to reorganize the Network.

Today the National Artspace Development Network has returned to its roots, drawing upon the strengths of key participating organizations to provide access to a variety of programs. In the best tradition of not duplicating efforts, the Network is healthiest when it is truly a collaboration of several organizations.

Artspace Projects, Inc. has reassumed a leadership role, especially in providing technical assistance and referrals through their toll-free information line (800-229-5715). The American Council for the Arts (ACA) has a toll-free hotline (800-232-2789) for information about space, funding, insurance and other artist needs. National Artists Equity (NAE) monitors public policy issues and lobbies Congress. NAE is also developing a traveling workshop series to inform artists about real estate and other business skills. Artspace, Inc. of Salt Lake City monitors the Handsnet electronic bulletin board for information to share with other participants through the NADN AppleLink, and is exploring the expansion of the NADN network in cooperation with Arts Wire.

As participation in NADN grows, so can its programs and services. Potential programs, such as a national artists' space conference, can be realized if artists and arts organizations support them. This is your invitation to help in creating a vision of what is possible and in determining the best means of achieving that vision.

About ACA

Founded in 1960, the American Council for the Arts (ACA) is a national organization whose purpose is to define issues and promote public policies that advance the contributions of the arts and the artist to American life. To accomplish its mission, ACA conducts research, sponsors conferences and public forums, publishes books, reports, and periodicals, advocates before Congress for legislation that benefits the arts, and maintains a 15,000-volume specialized library. ACA is one of the nation's primary sources of legislative news affecting all of the arts and serves as a leading advisor to arts administrators, individual artists, educators, elected officials, arts patrons and the general public.

Board of Directors